THE INSIDE PASSAGE

(North)

Area of detail

Wrangell

Ernest
Sound

Meyers Chuck

Ketchikan

Revillagigedo Channel

UNITED STATES
CANADA

Port Simpson/Lax Kw' Alaams

Metlakatla

Prince Rupert

Grenville Channel

Lowe Inlet

Hecate Strait

Butedale

Princess Royal
Channel

PASSAGE
TO
JUNEAU

A Sea and Its Meanings

JONATHAN RABAN

PICADOR

First published 1999 by Alfred A. Knopf, Inc., New York

First published in Great Britain 1999 by Picador
an imprint of Macmillan Publishers Ltd
25 Eccleston Place, London SW1W 9NF
Basingstoke and Oxford
Associated companies throughout the world
www.macmillan.co.uk

ISBN 0 330 34628 8

3 5 7 9 8 6 4 2

A CIP catalogue record for this book is available from
the British Library.

Printed and bound in Great Britain by
Mackays of Chatham plc, Chatham, Kent

For Julia

Je sens vibrer en moi toutes les passions
    D'un vaisseau qui souffre;
Le bon vent, la tempête et ses convulsions

    Sur l'immense gouffre
Me bercent. D'autres fois, calme plat, grand miroir
    De mon désespoir!
    — Charles Baudelaire, *Les Fleurs du Mal*

'That's a funny piece of water,' said Captain Hamilton
    — Joseph Conrad, *The Shadow Line*

PASSAGE TO JUNEAU

I. FITTING OUT

He was walking the dock; a big lummox, yellow hair tied back in a ponytail with a red bandanna, bedroll strapped to his shoulders. His plaid jacket looked like a fruitful research area for some unfastidious entomologist. I took him for a displaced farm boy, a Scandinavian type from Wisconsin or Minnesota, adrift in the new world of the Pacific Northwest. He held a scrap of paper, folded into a wedge the size of a postage stamp to keep its message safe inside. For what was evidently the hundredth time, he fingered it carefully apart and stared at the two words inscribed there in wonky, ballpoint capitals.

'*Pacific Venturer?*' he asked. The late March sun (this was Seattle's first high-pressure, blue-sky day after weeks of low overcast) glittered in the pale stubble on his cheeks. 'That's the boat I'm looking for. *Pacific Venturer.*' He spoke the name syllable by syllable, and I could see him in first grade – a large, vacant, uncoordinated child, already far behind the rest of the class. 'You seen that boat, man?'

Three, maybe four hundred boats were moored hull to hull at Fishermen's Terminal. They formed a wintry thicket, over fifty acres of water, of masts, spars, trolling poles, whip-antennas, radar scanners, deck-hoists, and davits. Looking at the names around us, I read *Vigorous, Tradition, Paragon, Sea Lassie, Peregrine, Resolute, Star of Heaven, Cheryl G., Cheerful, Immigrant* (a green cloverleaf blazoned on its wheelhouse), *Paramount*, *Memories*. I saw a *Pacific Breeze*, but no *Pacific Venturer*.

'What is it – a purse-seiner?'

He took it as a trick question, staring at me as if I were an unfriendly examiner. He had Barbie-doll blue eyes. 'I dunno. *Salmon boat*.' He consulted the piece of paper in his hand. 'Yup. That's a salmon boat – I heard.'

He stank of the road – of hitchhiking on interstates, diving in Dumpsters, spending nights in cardboard boxes under highway bridges, gargling with Thunderbird.

'I been here since seven.'

It was two in the afternoon. Purposeful men were pushing past us, dressed in the local uniform of hooded smocks and black peaked caps, arms full of gear, impatient with the two rubbernecks in their path.

'You better ask one of these guys.'

'I asked already.'

He shambled off – 'Be seeing you, man' – up the next finger pier, and I could see his lips moving as he spelled out the words on the sterns of *Oceania*, *Prosperity*, *Stella Marie*, *Enterprise*, *Quandary*, lost among these resonant abstractions and women's names. The working men were giving him a wide berth. On his behalf, I kept an eye out for the *Venturer*; but if it had ever existed at all, it was probably now steaming for Ketchikan and points north.

The boats were fitting out, at the last minute, as usual, for their spring migration to the Alaskan fishing grounds. The resinous, linseed-oily smell of varnish and wet paint hung thickly in the still air of the terminal, and there was the continuous happy racket of electric saws and sanders, hammers, drills, and roaring blowtorches. Diesel engines were being hastily disembowelled, their black innards laid out, part by part, on afterdecks, while their bloody-knuckled owners muttered to themselves as they puzzled over camshafts and clearances. Pick-up trucks, laden to the gunwales, were drawn up alongside those boats that were now most nearly ready to leave, and wholesale boxes of Dinty Moore stew and Campbell's soup and plastic-wrapped bales of toilet tissue were being swung aboard on hoists. On the broad plaza of the net-mending area, a man and a woman were 'hanging web': threading white cigar-shaped floats at two-foot intervals along the top of their quarter-mile gill net. The jade-green gossamer nylon mesh shimmered at their feet like a river.

In Seattle, the city of virtual reality, it was always a pleasure to come to this last bastion of old-fashioned work, with its nets, crab pots, paintbrushes, and carpentering; to its outdoor faces, seamed with experience; and to its long-established family air, generation following generation into the same industry. Grandparents, now too shaky on their pins to make the trip, were still important figures at fitting-out time. They drove trucks, varnished brightwork, repaired nets, tested circuits; unlike nearly all of their contemporaries, their skills had not dated. And beyond the grandparents there stretched the ghostly presences of European fishing communities on the fjords, bays, and sounds of Norway, Sweden, Denmark, Scotland, Ireland, from where most of the families had come. These, too, were com-memorated in boat names: *Cape Clear, Stavanger, Solvorn, Lokken, Tyyne, Thor, Saint Patrick, Uffda, American Viking*. A clever parodist, tired of the prevailing Scandinavian homesickness, had christened his gill-netter *Edsel Fjord*.

Centuries of seagoing converged on Fishermen's Terminal. Though its corrugated steel buildings, painted in pastel blue and beige, were new, the place felt older than the city in which it stood. Like the fishermen, it went a long way back. Its boats, built for the Pacific, were the direct descendants of the trawlers, smacks, and lug-gers of the North Sea and the Baltic. The high flared bow and steep sheer that had worked well in the Maelstrom waters off the Lofoten Islands were here recreated for service off the Aleutians. The trollers, with their upswept fifty-foot poles of raw fir, were old acquaintances, for I'd seen their ancient Dutch and Danish cousins. At Fishermen's Terminal the past – and sometimes the far distant past – was alive and usable, as it was almost nowhere else in the future-fixated United States. For someone my age, there was comfort in that. Most days, I found an excuse to drop by. I liked the boats, their redolent names, their house-proud captains, and the amiable, understated gossip of the sea.

Now, with the sun come back from exile, and the voyage north and the fishing season stretching clear ahead, everyone radiated the nervous elation – half high hopes and half cold feet – that marks the start of a big adventure. The weeks to come were full of flawless promise. The reality of the season would take hold soon enough: unforecast gales and groundings, engine failures, fish gone AWOL, lost sleep, lost tempers, and all the rest. In a little while the fleet would be scattered over 1,000 miles and more of water, from Dixon Entrance to the Bering Sea. Then each boat would become a stranger to the others; members of the same family, aboard rival vessels, would treat one another as spies. But in the communal ceremony of fitting out, tools and expertise were passing freely from boat to boat, as the moment neared when the last line is cast off, the goodbyes are waved, the screw makes the water boil under the stern, and the passage to Alaska is under way.

I wanted as much of the mood as I could borrow for my own use. For this year I was going too – not to fish, but to follow the fisher-men's route; to go to sea in my own boat for the going's sake. I hoped to lay some ghosts to rest and come to terms, somehow, with the peculiar attraction that draws people to put themselves afloat on the deep, dark, indifferent, cold, and frightening sea. 'Meditation and water are wedded for ever', wrote Melville. So, for the term of a fishing season, I meant to meditate on the sea, at sea.

In the United States, wherever young men hang out together, on college campuses as in homeless shelters, this story went the rounds: if you could get to Seattle and talk your way aboard a fishing boat bound for Alaska, you could make $1,000 a day. Or more. Someone always knew someone who'd taken home $100,000, sometimes $200,000, for just two months' work.

You could turn your life around on money like that – buy a house, start a business, become captain of your own gold-spinning boat. In the land of self-reinvention, the Alaskan fishery was said to be a magical place where poor men were transformed, at a stroke, into rich ones. Eight weeks was all it took to make a hellacious sum of money.

The young men flocked to Seattle in the spring to make their fortunes. They walked the docks, trying to ingratiate themselves with any captain who would speak to them. They were a pest, this seasonal ragtag band of college kids, druggies, winos, fugitives, unemployed computer programmers, checkout clerks, waiters, pizza-delivery drivers. The sea experience of many of these hopeful applicants amounted to no more than the occasional trip as a passenger on a ferry.

Yet the most persistent 'greenies' did eventually manage to get taken on, for a half share (5 per cent) or a full one (10 per cent) of net profits at the end of the voyage. Of these, a tiny handful finished up with a wad of money within crying distance of the fairy-tale numbers. There were just enough jobs for deckhands, and just enough money, to keep the supply of young men copiously flowing.

The money talked loudest, but the sea talked too, with its antique promise of escape and adventure. Many greenies came from flat inland towns, and the only waves they knew rippled through the fields of standing wheat. But they'd read C. S. Forester, and they pined, in happy ignorance, for the yo-ho-ho of life at sea. In Des Moines, it's easy to dream fondly of the heaving deck, the gouts of freezing spray, the struggle with the net in fifty knots of wind, because nothing like that ever happens in Iowa.

More than that, going fishing in Alaska was the last true Western adventure. At the end of the twentieth century, the Alaskan fishery presented itself as a romantic anomaly – an armed, masculine world of unbridled free enterprise, where a rolling stone, a latterday Huck Finn, on the run from the Widow Douglases of civilization, could still walk tall. For the boys (and some girls) at the back of the class, with no diplomas to their names, the fishery was their last shot at the exemplary American life of travel, excitement, and riches.

Alaska liked to advertise itself as 'The Last Frontier', a slogan tinged with self-cancelling whimsy since it appeared on vehicle registration plates, courtesy of the state licensing department. If the phrase could now be held to mean anything at all, it belonged to the sea, not the land; and the sea around Alaska was a real wilderness, as wild and lonely as any territory in the American past.

The Gulf of Alaska is a weather-kitchen. Pacific depressions, drifting over the ocean from the far south-west, hit the gulf, stall there, and intensify. As the atmospheric pressure at the centre of the system sinks, the winds spinning around the hub speed up, to fifty, sixty, eighty knots. The waves build into untidy heaps; the sea goes streaky-white. Made steeper and impeded by the powerful tidal currents that pour out of the narrow passages between islands, the wave-trains turn near the coast into a short, precipitous, hollow sea of rearing fifty-foot crests and ship-swallowing holes in the water. These storms are a regular assignment for Alaska fishermen; for the greenie, they offer a crash course in retching misery and terror, keenly sharpened by the knowledge that every year boats go down in seas like this, all hands lost, due, in the standard phrase, 'to stress of weather'.

It was a last frontier in another sense, too. The great bonanza fisheries, from the Dogger Bank to the Grand Banks of Newfoundland, were dead or dying, wrecked by overfishing, pollution, and disease. The local inshore fishery of the Pacific Northwest, on the Oregon and Washington coasts, had been exploited to exhaustion. In some areas, the chinook salmon – which used to pack the rivers and inlets wall to wall – had been nominated as an endangered species. At Fishermen's Terminal, dozens of little gill-netters, too small to make the Alaskan trip, lay abandoned, rotting at their moorings, with faded for sale notices in their wheelhouse windows. Their owners were on food-stamps now, the boats – and the once-valuable licences that went with them – going at yard-sale prices. Yet the Alaskan fishery went on. It was now more closely regulated than it had ever been, with a maze of small print governing season openings, boat lengths, net materials, and mesh sizes, an increasingly bridled free-for-all. But by comparison with what was happening elsewhere, the fishing in Alaska was still the Big Rock Candy Mountain of far-Western fantasy, like the Comstock Lode, or the miles of virgin forest ripe for the chainsaw.

Greenhorns walking the dock, hoping for a piece of this action, would find a frontier that was all but closed. True, you could make $1,000 a day long-lining for halibut. But the halibut season had been squeezed down to a few days, and the captains of the halibut schooners were able to pick and choose from a throng of experienced hands. No chance for the greenie there. Most gill-netters, and trollers, too, were family boats, husband-and-wife or father-and-son concerns with no room aboard for a stranger. A big crabber . . . maybe. A purse-seiner would be the greenie's best bet; though the boats themselves were small (fifty-eight feet the maximum length permitted in Alaska), the encircling net was manoeuvred in the water by a big, slab-sided aluminium skiff with a 350-horse inboard motor. Crewing the parent boat and its skiff required at least four people, and sometimes six or seven; so purse-seiners sometimes took on an extra hand from outside the circle of family and friends.

As the saying went, 10 per cent of the fishermen catch 90 per cent of the fish, and the crack purse-seiners in the fleet were known to everyone. When they hired extra hands, they chose people they knew. There remained the 'shit-boat': a floating catastrophe, its captain on the sauce, its hydraulic power-gear on the fritz, its nets riddled with holes, its bronze seacocks crumbling away with electrolysis and turning into waterspouts. Shit-boats took on greenies.

On the dock, I was summoned by the captain of the *Glenda Faye*, a 58-foot purse-seiner. 'You want to see a living miracle?' He had a paintbrush in one hand, a bottle of phosphoric acid in the other.

'Watch this—'

He brushed a swath of acid across a nasty-looking fish tray that had taken on the appearance of an old brown badly oxidized oil painting. As the brush touched the surface, the rust dissolved and the original white metal showed through. 'Magic! I never used this stuff before—'

'You could serve it up with a dash of soda and a slice of lemon.'

'They do that – in Cana-nada.'

The *Glenda Faye* looked like a crack boat: built of steel and massively deep-draughted, the hull freshly painted in maroon with black trim. It carried more electronic gear than most, the wheelhouse roof fairly bristling with antennas. Through the galley window I could see mugs and dishes newly washed and neatly stacked to dry, spotless teak cabinetry, the wink of polished brass. A tidy ship.

Last year's season had been good, the captain said. In one day, they'd netted $5,000 worth of 'pinks'. That was their red-letter day, but they'd come close to matching this haul several times as the boat worked round the inlets north of Dixon Entrance. He and his cousin ran the boat together. Each season they took on a crew of two or three. 'College kids. Hard workers. No drugs, no smokes.' Always family, or family friends. Last year, at settlement time, when the cost of fuel and grub had been deducted from the gross, each kid pocketed nearly $11,000 for his two months' work – big money for a student's vacation job, but a far cry from the legends of instant wealth that kept the greenhorns coming to Seattle.

'Did you talk to the blond guy with the bedroll who was here a bit ago?'

'*Which* guy? There's a hundred like that.'

'Would you ever take on someone like him – a stranger, walking the dock, looking for a boat?'

He laid a lick of magic acid on another fish tray. 'Most of those guys? I wouldn't use 'em for bait.' Swivelling on his haunches to take a closer look at me, he guffawed at what he saw. 'Hey, mister, you ain't looking to be taken on? Oh, boy!'

Happy to contribute to the mirth of his afternoon, I shrugged and went off to do my shopping.

Foraging for marine ironmongery in the strip-lit gloaming of Seattle Ship Supply, one could read the character of the fishery from the goods on display. A drum of three-ply rope, considerably thicker than my arm. A pile of elephantine lyre-shaped galvanized shackles. You'd have to be in weight training to pick one off the floor. Everything – fenders, wrenches, blocks, turnbuckles, chain – looked designed for use by hulking giants, and made the fishermen who roamed the store seem puny beside their massive hardware. The stuff spoke grimly of the punishment inflicted on boats by the Alaskan winds and seas – the huge destructive tonnage of the breaking wave, the turmoil and violence of the fishermen's workplace.

I collected a handful of baby shackles, some clevis pins, a bottle of lamp oil, and ten feet of quarter-inch shock-cord. At the checkout, the man behind me, who was toting a coil of rope and a five-gallon can of paint, looked over the contents of my basket and said, 'Going yachting, huh?' Then, thinking of all the damnfool pleasure boats that were the bane of his profession, he said gloomily, 'Well, it's the season for it, I guess' – the only person in my hearing to greet fair weather as seriously bad news.

Beyond the net-mending area lay the terminal's focal point – the Fishermen's Memorial. High on his plinth stood a bronze fisherman, in the classical heroic mode, his hair shaped by the wind into the laurel bays of a Roman conqueror. He was hauling in a giant halibut on a longline. Around the circular base of the plinth there swam – or scuttled, or clung on with sculpted suckers – all the major species of the fishery: bronze salmon, cod, herring, squid, crab, snapper, hake, prawn, octopus, dogfish, clam, flounder. On the low wall nearby were inscribed, in die-cast metal lettering, the names of those lost at sea. In six years of living in Seattle, I'd watched the list grow steadily by a column and a half – seventy people, mostly men and boys. Cut flowers, in jam jars and plastic vases, were set out on the ground before the wall, with handwritten messages, their ink blurred by rain. *I miss you, Daddy. Matt – I love you always. Ben – in sad remembrance – Mom and Dad. Kirk – we miss you so much! We will love you for ever. Terri and the boys. Happy Birthday, Daddy! Love, Jeffrey.*

Winter was the memorial's busiest season, when the big crab boats were raiding the gulf and the Bering Sea. Top-heavy with stacked pots and deck-cranes, the crabbers were the most prone to capsize. In Arctic weather, when spray froze instantly on everything it touched, and the sea stuck to the boats in great dollops, like leaden glue, the crews would be on twenty-four-hour duty, smashing ice out of the rigging with baseball bats. Every so often, one of these overburdened 125-foot vessels would ease into a normal roll, then go on rolling, until it rolled right over. It happened in a couple of seconds – no time to radio for help or clamber into survival suits. *Steer into the roll!* was the injunction passed down in maritime folklore, though Coast Guard post-mortems deplored this practice and advised captains to keep the rudder amidships. In other words, *Do nothing!* A terrible precept when the world is turning turtle and the frigid water yawns.

The bodies of these crews were rarely found, and the boats themselves sometimes sank without trace. Missing, presumed lost, the usual epitaph, was cruel in the room it left for loopholes and crazy flashes of hope. Long-drowned fishermen were sometimes spotted in the crowds at sports stadiums and on TV. Once in a blue moon, dreams of miraculous resurrection were given credence, when a dead man was arrested for a traffic violation and found to be alive and well, living a new life in Anchorage or Santa Fe.

That afternoon, the memorial was awash in flowers. The centrepiece was a life-size anchor made of white chrysanthemums and roses. It was ironic that the most intractable, weighty, and shin-bruising piece of hardware in the entire stock of the marine supply store should be the chief symbol of Christian hope; yet as St Paul, himself a shipwreck victim, wrote to the Hebrews, 'Hope we have as an anchor of the soul, both sure and stedfast, and which entereth into that within the veil.' So the floral anchor stood at once for the fisherman and his dangerous trade, and for his expectation of the life of the world to come.

A crowd was beginning to gather as I arrived. From every finger pier, men were leaving their boats and converging on the memorial in twos and threes. At just before three o'clock, the dead man's family arrived, conspicuous in Sunday suits and ties, their faces still raw with shock. They were led to the memorial by a man, clearly a minister, in buttoned dark blazer and white rollneck sweater – a combination meant to put one in mind of the priest's costume of cassock and dog collar, though in a studiedly informal, democratic, unpriestly sort of way. He stood by the anchor of hope, gravely smiling, chatting with the family, a fresh-faced, young-old hand at death and grief.

As he brought us to order, I realized that the crowd had swollen, suddenly, to more than three hundred people, pressed in a broad crescent around the parents of the dead man. Some took off their caps and stood, heads bowed, as if in church; others sucked reflectively on cigarettes throughout the proceedings. The terminal fell silent, except for the complaining gulls and the bronchial rattle of generators aboard the emptied boats. When the minister spoke, he barely had to raise his voice to be heard from the back of the crowd.

Lester, he said, had been a rich man – not in the goods of this world, but in the multitude of relationships he had forged, both here and in Alaska. The number of us gathered here today to remember Lester stood as a testament to . . . The words, if trite, were proper and comforting. The minister made a decent, priestly job of cloaking the meaningless shipyard explosion, in which the man had died, in a language of moth-eaten dignity.

A letter from a friend in Kodiak was read aloud. An uncle delivered a halting reminiscence. 'Farewell, Lester – and smooth sailing . . .' he said, and broke down.

The minister took over again. We mumbled an Our Father and recited the doxology. The entire service lasted twelve or thirteen minutes; no longer than a coffee break, yet long enough to show the parents that their son had belonged to a real village, and that the village cared.

The surrounding city was a honeycomb of *soi-disant* 'communities' that were empty fictions: the 'arts community', the 'public-radio community', the 'retail community'. Fishermen's Terminal was perhaps the last place in Seattle where that poor overextended word still had meaning. The fishing community really was a tight, intimate, memorious society, cruel and kind in equal parts. It gave its members ribald nicknames – Pus-gut Chadwick, Three-Finger Bob, Truthful Tom. It rejoiced in cutting people down to size. It nourished old slights and grudges over the decades, and was divided by resentful factions – seiners versus gill-netters, Sons of Norway versus The Rest. But when a boat went down, or a fisherman went into the cancer hospital, or a child died, the community closed around the survivors. His seagoing – incommunicable to outsiders – set the fisherman far apart from his suburban neighbours; only here at the terminal could the full dimensions of his life be comprehended, and given their true weight when his name was added to the list on the wall.

On the last 'Amen' the crowd dissolved as fast as it had formed. Droop-shouldered still, in deference to the occasion, the men trooped back to their boats. From the piers came the first ding of a hammer, the shrill churring of a sander, and, in death's warning afternoon shadow, the cheerful business of fitting out again got under way.

I walked back to my boat, which lay moored at a small boatyard on the Ship Canal, a quarter-mile east of Fishermen's Terminal. Built in Sweden in 1972 as a smart cruising ketch, expensively outfitted in varnished mahogany and teak, it had deteriorated in the six years of my ownership into a comfortably down-at-heel floating cottage, cluttered with books and pictures, box files, two manual typewriters, furry animals (my daughter's contribution), wine, photographic stuff, curling manuscripts, dead ballpoint pens, and all the rest of the impedimenta of a singularly untidy writer's life. Its dark ultramarine hull was coated in a layer of black dust, thanks to the shipyard next door; the foredeck was a spaghetti of uncoiled ropes. I had no taste for nautical spit and polish. The boat was a working vessel – my narrative vehicle.

Though I lived in a house overlooking the canal, and could see from the upstairs deck whether or not the boat still floated, I usually spent several weeks each year, and sometimes months, aboard the ketch. When a concentrated bout of reading was called for, or a wrong chapter needed righting, or when my Furies dogged me to distraction, I'd take off for the nearby scribble of islands and let go the anchor. With the floor sashaying underfoot, the chain grumbling on the sea bottom, and the view from the boat's windows revolving slowly on the tide, I found the equilibrium that I was prone to lose on the unstable land. On winter mornings, the mud foreshore hoar with frost, forlorn gulls circling under a misty sky, I'd fire up the heater, light the lamps, and work with an intense single-mindedness that evaded me at home. The creaks and groans, the smells of paraffin and diesel, were conducive to thinking and remembering. Afloat, the boat was an unplace – a bubble world, off at a useful tangent to the insistent here-and-now of the American shoreline. Cramped, dark, and coffin-like, it was my Yaddo, my asylum, my ark.

It was *it*, not *she*. Its first purchaser had given the boat a woman's name, sign-painted, with curlicues, across the stern. But the name meant so little to me that it would take me a moment – a catch of breath – to recall it. It was just the name of somebody else's wife or girlfriend, and anyway, the couple had probably split up now. Whenever possible, I preferred to identify the boat by its Washington State registration number, Whiskey November Eleven Ninety-six Romeo Bravo – a suitably complex mouthful for a complex lozenge of space that held three rooms, a shower–toilet, a honeycomb of concealed lockers, an engine compartment, a centre cockpit, a wrap-around deck, two masts, and a suit of sails. As Whiskey November et cet., it had a rational particularity that went nicely with its intended function.

That afternoon, the hatches were open, and an electrician was inside. The boat had once been owned by a San Diego electronics engineer who had installed a circuitry of marvellous, and perverse, sophistication: a maze of cables and crimped, multicoloured wires more appropriate to a mainframe computer than to a 35-foot sailboat. The current was never permitted to flow straight from A to B; it was diverted, at every possible opportunity, through a succession of shunts, bypasses, inner-ties, voltage regulators, resistors, fuses. My electrical control panel, admired by everyone, had a complement of forty-three switches that would have looked reassuring on the bridge of an ocean-going tug or a medium-sized coaster. Several electricians had been baffled by the labyrinthine ingenuities of the system; but after three years I found someone who looked at it, exclaimed over it, and basked in his intellectual mastery of it. He was now building in a series of emergency shortcuts, adding a few dozen more wires to the maze for simplicity's sake.

With the floorboards up, he was crouched in the bilges, holding a pair of pliers in his teeth. Six feet plus of swarthy, cadaverous skin and bones, he had the raccoon's knack of being able to insinuate himself into impossibly tight spaces. He had now reduced himself to a helmet of straggly black hair and a toilet-brush beard encircling the teeth that held the pliers. His right arm, severed at the shoulder, had been lost, or so I'd heard on the dock, to a runaway anchor chain in the Alaskan fishery, and his left hand was constantly being assisted by his mouth, his knees, or his feet.

John Munroe was agile, fast, and a perfectionist. He labelled every wire and installation in his beautiful copperplate handwriting. He was tolerant of my mechanical illiteracy, and would explain things over and over in a machine-gun tenor, until I believed that I had caught the essential drift of the boat's myriad rivulets of electricity, as they coursed, trickled, and, sometimes, went as dry as a prairie creek in summer.

What I now wanted him to explain was his past in the gold-rush fishery. What led him to Alaska in his greenhorn days?

'Herring.' His voice came, on echo, from deep in the bilges. 'In 1979, they were paying three thousand a ton for herring. Just poking around with a gill net, you could bring in maybe a hundred tons. Guys were making these *gobs* of money.'

After five years at college in San Luis Obispo, studying to be an aeronautical engineer, Munroe was employed as a jobbing electrician at a winery in Napa County. Nine-to-five suburban California was 'boring, dull, and hopeless'. He was a receptive listener to the stories of high adventure and easy money that were circulating on the docks of San Francisco, his hometown. And he had the sea in his blood. His father was a naval architect; John had grown up with boats, big and small. Laying circuits in the winery, he nursed a consoling, fugitive daydream of sailing alone to the South Pacific. *With the Gauguin maids, / In the banyan shades . . .* He'd put away $10,000 against this imagined other life of blue-water solitude and palm-fringed dalliances; a decent start, but it would be years before he could quit his job and cast off for Oceania.

'But if I could get up to Alaska, and parlay that into, like, a hundred grand, I'd be fat.'

An elderly San Francisco fisherman – nicknamed Joe Shaft, supposedly for sexual rather than financial wolfishness – offered to sell Munroe a wooden gill-netter, *Vagabond,* only six years old and in fine nick, for $40,000. Ten thousand down, with the balance due at the end of the season. 'If we were going fishing in Alaska, we could be trusted. The money was as good as in the bag.'

Two college friends, Curt and Joe, were as bored and footloose as Munroe himself. The three formed a partnership around the purchase of *Vagabond* and its attendant gear. 'It was a chance to get out of this insane thing – dicking around in second-rate jobs with no futures.' They trucked the boat to Seattle and shipped it on a barge to Alaska while, back in San Francisco, they provisioned for the summer. In the parking lot of a Berkeley co-op, they loaded a '53 Chevrolet with tofu paste, brewer's yeast, lecithin powder, lentil loaf, sacks of flour and garbanzo beans. 'We were manic vegetarians. That's how long we'd been living in California. *Way* too long.'

The Chevy sagged on its axles as they made the 2,500-mile drive to Anchorage, then flew on, with their supplies, to Togiak, on Bristol Bay.

Bristol Bay is the bottom right-hand corner of the Bering Sea, in the crook formed between the mainland and the long skinny arm of the Aleutian chain as it reaches out across the ocean to Russia. Its eastern shoreline is perforated with estuarine inlets on which squat dozens of roadless fishing communities like Togiak: hamlets in winter, roistering towns in the summer, when fishermen, buyers, and cannery workers keep the bars hopping, and the sky is loud with the continual arrivals and departures of float-plane taxis.

The barge Munroe and his friends awaited was twelve days overdue; caught in a prolonged storm in the Gulf of Alaska, it had shed much of its cargo, including several fishing boats, in the heavy seas. Unable to find out whether their boat had gone to the bottom, the three Vagabonders slept rough, and uneasily. Meanwhile, the price of herring was in free fall. From $3,000 a ton the year before, it slid below $1,000 and now was dropping quickly through the hundreds.

When the barge at last came alongside the dock, *Vagabond* was found to be safe and was promptly craned into the inlet. Supplies were hastily stowed aboard, and with only a few days left to the short herring season, Munroe and his crew headed out into a blustery north-west wind, with a heavy swell running, and began to fish.

New to the water, they followed the gulls. Their buoyed net ran out off the drum at the stern, and was set across the grain of the tide, its line of white corks glinting on the surface like a quarter-mile string of pearls. The herring, swimming north, came in a thin, straggling procession. 'There just wasn't the biomass there. It was the worst season anyone could remember.' Again and again, the men wound the net in on the drum and found only a measly handful of fish to pick out of the mesh. *Vagabond* took to tailing other boats at a careful distance. Rival theories flourished as the net came up and was found, yet again, to be nearly empty of fish. They ran close inshore and made a set within yards of a headland, where the tide boiled fast just off the rocks. They motored for miles offshore, in case the herring had grown allergic to the sight of land on the beam. They tried the flood, they tried the ebb, they tried the turn. No dice. Or, at least, shamingly few dice. Working night and day without sleep, they did eventually manage to fill the hold with six and a half tons of fish, harvested from the net in dribs and drabs.

The price of herring had now fallen to $200 a ton, and $1,300 split three ways fell so short of the Vagabonders' expectations as to be a joke. But it was the only $1,300 that they had. Somewhere off Cape

Constantine, they began the homeward run to Togiak and the cannery. Then the weather broke.

'It wasn't just a storm. It was this *huge* storm.' The boat climbed toppling seas. The wind blew the gulls away and shrilled in the rigging. They didn't stand a chance of rounding Right Hand Point and making Togiak Bay; instead, they ran before the wind and, grateful and chastened, took shelter in Kulukak Bay, where they dropped anchor below a rocky bluff with an abandoned native village on its summit.

The wind went on blowing. The ice in the fish-hold was melting fast, and the herring were starting to smell. An undiagnosed leak at the back of the cookstove was steadily dripping diesel fuel into the sack of beans stowed below.

After three stormbound days, they shovelled their stinking cargo overboard, but the odour of bad fish haunted the little saloon. The beans – their staple diet – tasted gaggingly of diesel. To cheer themselves up, the crew baked a pumpkin pie. As Munroe removed it from the oven, the boat rolled and the pie exploded over the furniture.

'Pumpkin pie everywhere! It was dripping out of the VHF, it was all over the floor. We sat around eating lecithin powder. That was, like, the nadir.'

When, finally, the weather cleared and the sea quieted, *Vagabond* put into Togiak, where the vegetarians abandoned their principles and hogged down plates of steak and French fries. The style and pace of Alaskan life were beginning to get to them. 'It was wild. The shit was really flying. Incredible mass destruction. Rammings. Sinkings. Shootings. A midair collision, right over town . . . Dead guys. A lot of dead guys. People you knew – friends – they'd drown, or get shot, or disappear. But it wasn't dull, like California.'

It was the first week in June. Herring finished, the salmon were about to begin. But a commercial licence for salmon fishing in Alaska cost outsiders $60,000. Since state residents and natives were granted special terms, the trick was to find a licence-holder to install on your boat for a share of the catch. In the Red Dog bar, Munroe met a man whose Aleut girlfriend had inherited a licence.

For the next six weeks, *Vagabond* went gill-netting for salmon. The inexperienced fishermen caught fewer fish than most, and the buyers' price was down to 75¢ a pound. With a haul of 55,000 pounds of salmon, and the money split fifty-fifty with the licence-holder and her boyfriend, Munroe and his partners came out with less than $7,000 apiece. It was bad maths, and a difficult letter had to be penned to the trusting Joe Shaft.

Munroe, alone among his partners, was seriously hooked on Alaska. 'It was wide open . . . no Fish and Game . . . it was nuts. You really feel free on Bristol Bay, because it's so dangerous, because of all that stress.' He was excited by the fierce weather and the 'weird' changing colours of the sea. 'I'd be out there, and I'd think, I don't want to be anywhere but here.'

He settled into Naknek, whose rows of canneries fronted the river. 'Dead little town. Great place. Four hundred people in winter, twelve thousand in summer.' He spent the winter tinkering with other people's boats. 'Nobody knows how to do anything in Alaska. That was my big discovery. They know how to fish, but they can't read a circuit or fix an engine. I kept busy.'

The following season, the fishery was suddenly in sync with the folk legend. Prices went up. Runs improved. Salmon ('pinks') fetched $2.40 a pound, and *Vagabond* landed more than fifty tons – enough for Munroe to settle with Joe Shaft, buy out his partners, and, as an Alaskan resident, get a commercial licence in his own name. 'I made scads of money.'

For the next ten years, he roller-coasted as the market surged and plunged. By the late 1980s, 'the fishing sucked'. The binge-and-bust cycle, which had kept him on an adrenalin high through his first few seasons, yielded its own brand of monotony and depression. When Munroe put to sea on Bristol Bay now, he set his net over a graveyard of drowned friends. In 1991, he sold *Vagabond* and came back to what Alaskans insist on calling 'the Lower 48' – states below the 49th in latitude, excitement, bodily risk, per capita income, and blood-alcohol level.

'My girlfriend goes on at me for driving too fast. But I lived in

Alaska. You can't get killed in Seattle – it's a statistical impossibility. People here die of cancer and old age. So I put my foot down and go like hell.'

His life had revolved in a perfect circle. Nearly twenty years on, he was back to being a jobbing electrician, working out of a villainous blue van with *Ocean Currents* painted on the side. He charged $35 an hour for squashing himself into other people's malodorous bilges, daydreaming still of the South Pacific. By now he had saved the money. Next summer, he and his girlfriend would take off for Tahiti, Samoa, the Great Barrier Reef . . . All they needed was a boat.

'I'm looking. I want a steel hull. Forty to fifty feet. Probably a ketch. But it has to be steel. If you hear of anything . . .'

His head, as it showed above the floorboards, was a boy's head ravaged by age and weather; a disquieting memento mori. The Bristol Bay years had given him a gunpowder complexion, stretching the skin over his cheekbones until the skull showed through. His eyes were deeply recessed in their sockets. The mouth behind his beard was drawn. Yet the face was young, more that of the Californian dropout than the man in his forties who was its present tenant.

'Your arm,' I said, 'you lost it in Alaska?'

'No. That was in my wild days. When I was in college, jumping freight trains.'

When I first saw the boat, the nautical stuff above-decks was less interesting to me than the dozen yards of teak bookshelving, with fiddles, that lined the walls of the three cabins. I endured the yacht broker's routine hearty patter about downhauls and Cunninghams, staysail halyards and self-tailing winches, because this boat could house a library. In the six years since, I had allowed the shelves to fill of their own accord as I poked around the southern end of the Inside Passage in Washington and British Columbia, and made some cautious excursions into the open ocean off the west coast of Vancouver Island. The collection started with George Vancouver's account of his surveying expedition of 1791–5, in the four-volume, blue-cloth-and-gilt Hakluyt Society edition. Among other early arrivals were Claude Lévi-Strauss's *The Way of the Masks*; several college textbooks on physical oceanography; *The Odyssey*, in Robert Fitzgerald's verse translation; the life (long and intimidatingly productive) of Lord Kelvin, the Victorian inventor of the tide-prediction machine and the piano-wire deep-sea sounding apparatus; W. H. Auden's *The Enchaféd Flood*; *Fishing with John* by Edith Iglauer; *Between Pacific Tides* by Ed Ricketts, the original of Doc in Steinbeck's *Cannery Row*; *Heavy-Weather Seamanship* by Adlard Coles; and James Gleick's *Chaos*, with its pictures of Lorenz attractors and Mandelbrot sets.

The books kept coming. They reflected a promiscuous addiction, to the sea in general and to the one on my doorstep in particular. I dipped and skimmed, jumping from the physics of turbulence to the cultural anthropology of the Northwest Indians, to voyages and memoirs, to books on marine invertebrates, to the literature of the sea from Homer to Conrad, trying to wrest from each new book some insight into my own compulsion. I looked the sea up in Freud and, more usefully, in the Book of Revelation. In *Dombey and Son*, Dickens (a fellow addict, whose idea of a holiday was to park himself on a windy shore and watch the waves) has a child, dying in a Brighton boarding house within earshot of the surf, beg of his older sister: 'I want to know what it says. The sea, Floy, what is it that it keeps on saying?' My question exactly.

I am afraid of the sea. I fear the brushfire crackle of the breaking wave as it topples into foam; the inward suck of the tidal whirlpool; the loom of a big ocean swell, sinister and dark, in windless calm; the rip, the eddy, the race; the sheer abyssal depth of the water, as one floats like a trustful beetle on the surface tension. Rationalism deserts me at sea. I've seen the scowl of enmity and contempt on the face of a wave that broke from the pack and swerved to strike at my boat. I have twice promised God that I would never again put out to sea, if only He would, just this once, let me reach harbour. I'm not a natural sailor, but a timid, weedy, cerebral type, never more out of my element than when I'm at sea.

Yet for the last fifteen years, every spare day that I could tease from the calendar has been spent afloat, in a state of undiminished fascination with the sea, its movements and meanings. When other people count sheep, or reach for the Halcion bottle, I make imaginary voyages – where the sea is always lightly brushed by a wind of no more than fifteen knots, the visibility always good, and the boat never more than an hour from the nearest safe anchorage.

When I moved from London to Seattle in 1990, the sea was part of the reason. The Inside Passage to Alaska, with its outer fringes and entailments, is an extraordinarily complicated sea route, in more ways than one. In continuous use for several thousand years, it is now a buoyed and lighted marine freeway, 1,000 miles long, and in places choked with traffic, as fishing boats, tows, barges, yachts, and cruise ships follow its serpentine course between Puget Sound and the Alaskan Panhandle. Parts of it are open ocean, parts no wider than a modest river. Some bits, like the Strait of Georgia, are small, shallow, muddy seas in their own right; others are sunken chasms, 1,500 feet deep. Where the tide is squeezed between rocks and islands, it boils and tumbles through these passes in a fire-hose stream. Water wasn't meant to travel at sixteen knots: it turns into a liquid chaos of violent overfalls, breaking white; whirlpool-strings; grotesque mushroom-boils. It seethes and growls. On an island in midstream, you can feel the rock underfoot shuddering, as if at any minute the sea might dislodge it and bowl the island, end over end, down the chute.

Its aboriginal past – still tantalizingly close to hand – puts the Inside Passage on terms of close kinship with the ancient sea of the Phoenicians and the Greeks. A nineteenth-century Kwakiutl or Tsimshian Indian would have found it easy to adapt to Homer's sea, with its reigning winds and creaturely powers. He simply used other names for them. For homicidal tricksters like Zeus and Poseidon he had had such counterparts as Raven, Killer Whale, Halibut. He could identify keenly with Ulysses in the Straits of Messina – though he might have found Charybdis a little tame after the canoe-guzzling whirlpools of his home waters.

High mountains and impenetrable forests crowded in on the coastal Indians and kept them within yards of the sea. The water was safer, more easily travelled, more productive, than the surrounding land. The Indians lived in an exclusively maritime culture, centred on the lavishly painted cedar canoe. Babies were rocked in miniature canoe-cradles; the dead were despatched in canoe-coffins. In their masks, rattles, boxes, woven blankets, and decorated hats, they created a marvellous, stylized, highly articulate maritime art.

The shelf at the front of the forecabin, where I slept, became the Art section of the boat's library: the driest place to store $75 and $125 books (made browser-proof with cellophane wrapping) on the art of the Salish, Kwakiutl, Haida, Tsimshian, and Tlingit Indians. The designs represented creatures of the sea and coast – some familiar, like whales, bears, frogs, halibut, sea lions, cormorants, octopuses; some unknown to natural history, fantastic sea-dwelling composites like the Tsimshians' Nagunakas, who reached up from the bottom of the sea to grab a canoeful of fishermen, then held them prisoner for four years in his octopus's garden.

The more I looked at these pictures, the more I saw that Northwest Indian art was maritime in much more than its subject matter. Its whole formal conception and composition were rooted in the Indians' experience of water (a fact that seems to have generally eluded its curators). The rage for symmetry, for images paired with their doubles, was gained, surely, from a daily acquaintance with mirror-reflections: the canoe and its inverted twin, on a sheltered inlet in the stillness of dusk and dawn. The typical 'ovoid' shape – the basic unit of composition, used by all the tribes along the Inside Passage – was exactly that of the tiny capillary wave raised by a cat's-paw of wind, as it catches the light and makes a frame for the sun. The most arresting formal feature of coastal Indian art, its habit of dismembering creatures and scattering their parts into different quarters of a large design, perfectly mimicked the way in which a slight ripple will smash a reflection into an abstract of fragmentary images. No maritime art I knew went half as far as this in transforming events in the water itself into constituent elements of design.

The Indians spoke most directly through the paintbrush and the chisel. Plenty of examples of their art were collected by the early explorers, between 1778 and 1800, before the artists had had a chance to be influenced by their invaders. But their stories were nearly all transcribed much later, toward the end of the nineteenth century and after, when colonization, Christianity, and tourism – a mighty influence on native art – had so eroded the culture that little was left except rags and tatters. The translations of local languages into German and English were crude; the eager-to-please Indian tellers were already familiar with imported Bible stories and European folktales; and when the collectors were faced with strange disjunctions, they provided transitions and linkages that gave these narratives the smooth shape of something by Aesop or the Brothers Grimm.

Even so, such collectors as Aurel Krause, John Swanton, and Franz Boas put together an enormous native literature of the Inside Passage. Their books filled several feet of shelving with stories full of strange transactions between humans and clams, bears, devilfish, and the other creatures with whom the Indians shared the water.

The saloon of my boat was dominated by the eighteenth-century white explorers – intruders from the Age of Reason, for whom measurement, with quadrants, chronometers, and magnetic compasses, was a form of taking possession. They squared up the Inside Passage with a graph-paper grid of longitudes and latitudes derived from the Royal Observatory at Greenwich and the equator. As part of the century's great communal project of Linnaean taxonomy, they went fossicking for specimens of plants, birds, mammals. They covered their emerging charts of the sea with names: naming it after themselves, their ships, their patrons, their national historic dates and occasions. The animist sea of the Indians was reinvented by the Europeans in the image of their own age. Besides Vancouver, I had on board Captain Cook, Peter Puget (Vancouver's lieutenant), Archibald Menzies (Vancouver's official naturalist), and, from Spain, Alessandro Malaspina and Alcalá Galiano, together with the journal of the Spanish expedition artist, Tomás de Suria. Each had his own voice and, looking at the same stretch of water, saw it in strikingly different terms from the others. To travel with these men, in their tight kneeboots and frogged waistcoats, was to be in on a continuous, sometimes quarrelsome, seminar about the character and significance of the new sea.

By accident, in an unrelated attempt to brighten the saloon, I'd hung prints from the same period as these explorers. A 1792 plate of assorted New World birds, evidently drawn from their pinned-out corpses, went up first, on the forward bulkhead. A cartoon of George III – poor, mad, kindly Farmer George – was Velcro-taped aft, alongside the VHF radio. A pair of hummingbirds (1789) perched above the barograph. The prints had come in a job lot, and it took me a while to notice how aptly they chimed with the swelling library: by losing the American colonies, the King had put a high premium on British acquisition of the as-yet-undiscovered coast of North America; while the bird prints neatly embodied the imperatives – *shoot! classify! name! describe!* – of eighteenth-century discovery.

When Captain Cook put into Nootka Sound, on the west side of Vancouver Island, the Indians offered him sea otter pelts in exchange for iron tools. In his journal he remarked:

> *Sea otters, which live mostly in the water, are found here. The fur of these animals . . . is certainly softer and finer than that of any others we know of, and therefore the discovery of this part of the continent of North America, where so valuable an article of commerce may be met with, cannot be a matter of indifference.*

Cook's ship, *Resolution*, had barely left Nootka for the north when the fur traders arrived. Like the fishermen prowling Seattle's docks in recent decades, these freelance captains were out to make a killing. Buying sea otter skins to sell on the Chinese market, they plagued the coast until the Indians had hunted the animal to extinction. The captains themselves survived, on the charts, as Meares Passage, the Kendrick Islands, Dixon Entrance, Barkley Sound, Gray's Harbor.

Their books were harder to locate than the long reaches of otterless water on which they'd left their names: I was still on the lookout for a copy of John Meares's *Voyages in the Years 1788–1789, from China to the Northwest Coast of America* (London, 1790), and George Dixon's *A Voyage Round the World* (London, 1789).

Then came the first, lonely white settlers. Often living many miles from their nearest English-speaking neighbours, they were dependent on the Indians for company and conversation; and keeping a journal, or writing a book, was a means of keeping at bay the psychological perils of the night. I particularly liked James Gilchrist Swan, who, in 1849, left his wife and children in Boston to join the California Gold Rush, then slipped north by ship from San Francisco to make a new life for himself on the Washington coast. Travelling with the Indians in their canoes, he learned their language and picked up much of their maritime lore. Though overfond of giving his native companions jocose titles such as 'The Duke of York', Swan on the whole was a modest, tender-hearted man; a good listener, a bit of a fusspot, a keen amateur ethnologist. He loved to be out on the water. He made sails for the Indians' canoes and decorated them with designs admired up and down the Strait of Juan de Fuca. He was also a walking drugstore, and dosed the Indians with pills and patent medicines.

He was forty-two when he published *The Northwest Coast: Or, Three Years' Residence in Washington Territory* in 1857. Eleven years later, the Smithsonian Institution brought out *The Indians of Cape Flattery*. Both books were full of the small voyages he'd made with the Indians, and conveyed – as no anthropologist has done since – the zigzag, stop-go pace of these journeys, the methods of aboriginal seamanship and navigation, the delicate skill of managing a dugout canoe in fast tides and heavy weather.

Combing through Swan's private diaries in the University of Washington library, in search of more canoe trips, I found myself becoming too intimate a witness to his miserable decline. In Port Townsend, at the top of Puget Sound, Swan became a justice of the peace, a correspondent for the eastern papers, and a morose whiskey-drunk. By the 1870s, his handwriting would go to pieces on him in the evenings, a jagged line of sepia ink betraying where his hand had skidded out of control on the page. Two shaky words – 'Fat Billy', every letter laboriously constructed, each looking like the outline of a collapsing shed – would pass for a day's entry, and some pages were still crinkled with 120-year-old spills of booze.

Yet the Indians with whom he had lived still visited, and took him on excursions in their canoes. Then he'd perk up, and his handwriting recover. Sitting in the stern sheets, or, camped out on Padilla Bay, wolfing down crabs and flounder caught by 'Patrick Henry' and 'The Duke of York', Judge Swan would almost succeed in persuading himself that he was back in happier days. Returned – too soon – to his Port Townsend house, he would sit in his usual pew at Sunday church, where mothers of teenage daughters saw him as a dangerous old goat.

Missionaries arrived with the settlers – men like the Dickensianly named Myron Eells, a Congregational minister whose physical deficiencies show up startlingly in his photograph. His eyes are magnified by a pair of thick-lensed, too-small, wire-framed glasses; his lips are thin and bloodless-looking; his beard, straining for luxuriance, achieves at best a tangled fluffiness. Eells's parishioners were the Skokomish Indians on the southern crook of the Hood Canal, a side channel to Puget Sound. His task was to save them from their savage superstitions, and to police their consumption of alcohol. If his own account is to be believed, he once joined them (reluctantly, for Myron was no sailor) on a long canoe ride to a potlatch at Dungeness, on the Strait of Juan de Fuca, because they'd begged him to rescue them from the temptations of the bottle. Yet even as he set about on a root-and-branch destruction of the foundations of Indian culture, he meticulously documented what remained of the Skokomish customs when he arrived on the reservation in 1874. He collected and labelled a vast collection of artefacts, and wrote a thorough, if colourless, monograph entitled *The Indians of Puget Sound*.

By contrast with James Swan, I found Myron Eells tough going as a travelling companion. A strain of self-preening piety in his writing put my back up, and there was something too obviously anal about his collecting habit. But his book was useful, chiefly for that uncomfortable canoe voyage – on which the Indians drew his ire for getting down in the bottom of the boat, muttering un-Christian incantations, whenever they neared a tide-race.

En route through British Columbia, I hoped to supplement Eells by finding a copy of Thomas Crosby's much jollier-sounding *Up and Down the Northwest Coast by Canoe and Mission Ship*. The missionaries, bent on stamping out one set of beliefs in order to impose another, must've tangled directly with stubborn fears and ideas of the water; and no one, Indian or white, is more prone to superstition than when at sea. I was also tracking two Catholic missionaries, Father Brabant and Father Blanchet.

It was bad luck for the anthropologists, and their comparatively recent discipline, that the missionaries got to the Inside Passage first. By the time Boas and his colleagues reached the coast, there was no way of telling whether an Indian story about a great flood and the tribe's rescue from it was generations old or just a garbled version of Genesis viii, or perhaps a bit of both. Had the Indians always believed in a creator – a sky god, the Great Spirit, the Transformer – or was this a recent idea, picked up at Shaker Sunday school, and merged with older native beliefs and stories? Did the totem pole, the most arresting symbol of Northwest Indian culture, date from time immemorial, or was it a product of fur-trade wealth and fur-trade leisure? In an unchronicled society, without writing, things that happened yesterday bleed into ancient history; and after a hundred years of rubbing up against explorers, traders, missionaries, and colonial administrators, the tribe members had ceased to be reliable authorities on their own traditions.

Of all the tribal groups in North America, the Indians of the Inside Passage had left the richest body of ceremonial and domestic art, and the most voluminous oral literature. Their culture was the most nearly intact because it had been invaded late in the era of New World discovery. Yet even when, say, Franz Boas arrived on the coast, the day-to-day reality of aboriginal life had faded into blurred snapshots and conjecture. Much later, Claude Lévi-Strauss would write of the Inside Passage that it was a 'stage . . . along whose entire stretch the actors of a play for which we do not have a script have left their footprints'.

The recency of that loss, and the vast quantity of those footprints (visible on almost every mile of shoreline), made the Northwest coast a magnet for theorists, speculators, freelance intellectuals. On the boat I had the stimulating and disputatious company of Boas, Lévi-Strauss, Edward Sapir, Edmund Leach; also Wayne Suttles, a social anthropologist local to the area, a sceptical empiricist whose essays applied small bright pins to the gas-filled balloons of received ideas about the Indians and their cosmology.

The anthropologists, too, lived in the saloon. The aft cabin, a useful wedge of space behind the cockpit and the engine, and usually my daughter's playroom, had been converted for this trip into the Travel section. I'd kept Julia's Dr Seuss books, *The Enormous Crocodile*, *Clifford the Big Red Dog*, *Sleepy Bear*, along with the Crayolas and Play-doh, because I couldn't stand to send them into even temporary exile. (Besides, her animal stories chimed interestingly with Sapir's in his *Nootka Texts*.) But the cabin was largely taken over now with a black vinyl artist's portfolio of charts; with tide tables, pilot books, and tourist guides with titles like *Gunkholing in the Gulf Islands* and *Live the Magic of the North Mile by Mile*.

After the Indians, the explorers, the fur traders, the settlers, the missionaries, and the anthropologists, tourists came to the Inside Passage, and witnessed the sea in their own terms. In 1879 John Muir, the Scottish-born naturalist, explored the northern reaches and in his own brand of lyrical, solemn, ringing prose conquered them for the high Romantic Sublime. The modern tourist brochure, with its majestic peaks and pristine fjords, harks straight back to Muir:

> *Sunshine streamed through the luminous fringes of the clouds and fell on the green waters of the fjord, the glittering bergs, the crystal bluffs of the vast glacier, the intensely white, far-spreading fields of ice, and the ineffably chaste and spiritual heights of*

the Fairweather Range, which were now hidden, now partly revealed, the whole making a picture of icy wildness unspeakably pure and sublime.

This rendering of the land and sea as a transfiguring religious experience did for south-east Alaska what Wordsworth's poems had done for the English Lakes: it called forth, from the Lower 48 and beyond, boatloads of would-be worshippers armed with cameras and sketchbooks, eager to take home some epiphanic fragment of the wilderness.

As Wordsworth's Lake District was populated with figures of antique rustic wisdom – toothless shepherds, leech-gatherers, idiot boys – Muir's Inside Passage was full of noble red men in canoes, invariably described as 'venerable', 'serene', or possessed of 'grave dignity'. When these Indians talked, via interpreters, they speechified, in ornate Victorian English, with sonorous periods and overextended similes drawn from the natural world. The John Muir Indian was a lineal descendant of the Fenimore Cooper Indian.

I am an old man, but I am glad to listen to those strange things you tell, and they may well be true, for what is more wonderful than the flight of birds in the air? I remember the first white man I ever saw. Since that long ago time I have seen many, but never until now have I ever truly known and felt a white man's heart. . . . It has always seemed to me while trying to speak to traders and those seeking gold-mines that it was like speaking to a person across a broad stream that was running fast over stones and making so loud a noise that scarce a single word could be heard. But now, for the first time, the Indian and the white man are on the same side of the river, eye to eye, heart to heart. . . .

It was John Muir Indians whom Edward S. Curtis, the Seattle-based photographer, pictured in the five volumes he devoted to the Inside Passage in his epic series, *The North American Indian*. His posed sepia studies, with every trace of the modern artfully banished from the frame, exult in the romance of the primitive. Most of Curtis's photos were taken between 1900 and 1916; he travelled, by railroad and steamship, through a world dominated by the mission school, the cannery, the timber mill, the Model-T, the phonograph; though you'd never guess that from his pictures, which show the Indians living in a state of primeval dignity and simplicity, their misty landscapes miraculously untouched by the logging crew and their traction engines.

Muir and Curtis between them manufactured the essential images needed by the twentieth-century tourist industry. By the time I arrived in the Northwest, fleets of white cruise ships were on regular patrol up and down the Inside Passage, and the sea had become a medium through which passengers could scan what Muir called 'the glorious pages of Nature's Bible'. As a copywriter for a cruise line put it:

> *You cruise this enchanted waterway, and each vista surpasses the one before. Your ship threads her sure course past forests, islands and inlets, surrounded by silence. You glimpse a deep fjord penetrating the wilderness. To the east the sun glints on snowcapped peaks. An incredible voyage.*
>
> *Watch, awestruck, as a pinnacle of ice cracks off the glacial cliff and crashes into the sea. . . . Harbor seals sun on an iceberg. Mountain goats are spied, high on the cliffs. You might see a humpback whale breaching, a school of leaping orcas. Maybe a black bear scavenging along the shore. . . .*

To the irritation of all the tugboat captains, gill-netters, and trollers who worked these constricted channels, the nature-loving cruise ships were joined by nature-loving kayaks, motor cruisers, and sailboats like mine – 'yachts and crap', in the gloomily derisive phrase of the captain of a log-tow on which I once spent a slow-moving week.

We all carried Muir, of course, along with a rack of yachtsman's guides – books with a distinctive late Romantic rhetoric of their own.

The guides competed with one another to describe anchorages so remote, so eccentric, their entrances so tide-encumbered and rock-strewn, that anyone brave enough to reach them was guaranteed absolute solitude. They harped, in beguiling technical detail, on close encounters with tide races and whirlpools. They made much of the few stretches of open ocean, their thirty-foot swells, sudden gales, treacherous tidal sets, and proven shipwrecking abilities. Dangers and difficulties were talked up as part of the voyage's allure. The writers referred to their reader as 'the mariner', as in 'The mariner will be well-advised to consult Egg Island lighthouse station on VHF Ch. 9 . . .' Their Inside Passage, especially in its outer reaches, was a solitary, self-reliant adventure in a watery wilderness untouched by spoiling human hands.

When the boat was under way, my still very incomplete library took on a shuffling, drunken life of its own. The books slammed and swayed on the shelves, bulged against the restraining belts of shock-cord, and sometimes liberated themselves and took flight through the boat like so many heavyweight pigeons. After a rough passage, I'd find Edmund Leach, Evelyn Waugh, George Vancouver, *Kwakiutl Art*, Anthony Trollope, *The 12-Volt Bible*, Homer, and *Oceanography and Seamanship* in an unlikely tangle on the saloon floor, their pages gaping, their jackets half off; Hannah Arendt in the sink with Myron Eells. I liked these chance couplings and collisions, and hoped that on the long trip north the entire library would be shaken, pitched, and rolled into a happy, interdisciplinary ragout.

Narcissus stares into the pool, and there discovers a face whose expression of wonder and yearning is a miraculously perfect match to his own; a smart move by Nemesis, to send Narcissus to the fountain. The refractive property of water ensures that when we look in deep, we see shallow. When we gaze down, searching for some shadowy profundity below the surface, what usually comes back to us is merely *us*.

Once, people looked at the sea with a religious abhorrence. It was chaos, the flux, the vast desert of waters; the inchoate abyss from which God had raised man and his fragile, precious civilization. As the creation story begins:

> *The earth was without form, and void; and darkness was upon the face of the deep. And the Spirit of God moved upon the face of the waters. . . .*

W. H. Auden wrote that in the Bible the sea 'is so little of a friendly symbol that the first thing which the author of the Book of Revelation notices in his vision of the new heaven and earth at the end of time is that *"there was no more sea"*'.

Later, in the Renaissance, the sea was seen as pure inviting space, a tabula rasa on which to inscribe new routes of trade, exploration, and imperial conquest. Cartographers decorated it with spouting whales, ruled compass courses, ships bustling importantly under sail, navigational instruments – quadrants, dividers, hourglasses. Like a full-dress portrait by Titian or Veronese, the map-makers' sea reflected back the glory of the merchant prince, his fleet of ships and hired adventurers. On this sea made for exploitation, set an argosy afloat and it would return, low in the water, with a cargo of gold.

Later still, under the influence of German Romantic philosophy and English Romantic poetry, the sea came to be regarded as the quintessence of the Sublime in nature: violent, beautiful, coldly indifferent to mankind. 'The eternal sea', or 'the immortal sea', apostrophized by Byron – 'Roll on, thou deep and dark blue Ocean – roll!' – and by Tennyson – 'Break, break, break, on thy cold gray stones, O Sea!' – was a morbid deity. In Melville's *Moby-Dick*, when the water at last closes over the smashed remains of *Pequod*, 'the great shroud of the sea rolled on as it rolled five thousand years ago'. In a secular, industrial age, we found in the sea a symbol of our own need for something that would mightily transcend us.

That mirror image had its day, and still survives, though it is being displaced by a counter-reflection. By the 1960s, people were looking at the sea in a mood of chastened self-recrimination, seeing in it their own greed, improvidence, and wastefulness. They had treated the sea as a toilet. Now full of polycyclic aromatic hydrocarbons and polychlorinated biphenyls, fouled with oil from grounded tankers, fished out, its clams poisonous, its Dover sole riddled with liver cancers, its species dying out in catastrophic numbers, the polluted ocean held up a looking-glass to the heedless, stupid face of humankind.

Slivery, partial images like these danced continually on the surface of the water, changing places, dissolving into each other, reigning for a moment, then suddenly losing their sharpness. I thought it might be possible to think of a sea as the sum of all the reflections it had held during its history. You'd never know the half of them, of course; but in the clashes and contradictions of image against image you might at least catch something of the provocative power of the sea, which has meant so much, so variously, to us.

To put oneself afloat on a sea route as old and heavily travelled as the Inside Passage was to join the epic cavalcade of all those, present and past, who'd found some kind of meaning in these waters. In an average day's sailing, one might have to alter course to give way to a Holland-America Line cruise ship; a squad of family gill-netters; an NOAA research vessel full of scientists doing fieldwork; the garbage scow, piled high with crushed cars, fridges, filing cabinets, on its regular fortnightly run between Juneau and Seattle. I always suffer from mild delusions when I'm alone for long at sea, and it would be no great surprise to find myself hauling the wheel to starboard to get clear of a survey-pinnace, under a yellowed lugsail, from the Vancouver expedition, or, skirting a fog-cliff, a red-and-black-painted Haida canoe, laden with Chilkat blankets, going south to trade.

In their versions of the sea, none of the people aboard these craft would agree on very much. The vacationing realtor from Omaha and Lieutenant Peter Puget could well find more to talk about than the ocean physicist, developing a theoretical model of how heat is exchanged between a breaking wave and the atmosphere, and his contemporary, the captain of the garbage scow. Each ship might as well be sailing a separate ocean. My conceit was that I could listen and talk about the sea to all these people, and somehow mediate between their rival images.

I had a boat, most of a spring and summer, a cargo of books, and the kind of dream of self-enrichment that spurs everyone who sails north from Seattle. Forget the herring and the salmon: I meant to go fishing for reflections, and come back with a glittering haul. Other people's reflections, as I thought then. I wasn't prepared for the catch I eventually made.

I topped up the gimballed brass lamps with oil and made a new shock-cord harness for the barograph, whose inked needle was making a steady horizontal line along the 1,025-millibar mark. Blue-sky-and-zephyr pressure. An Alaska-bound fish-processing ship, heading west down the Ship Canal, sent a breaking wake through the moorings. The books shuffled softly on their shelves, the boat creaked against its fenders, and impish scraps of lamplight skedaddled back and forth around the saloon. That evening, at home, it was my turn to cook, and I had only a few minutes left. John Munroe had gone off, an hour before, to check out a steel ketch I'd seen rigged as a troller at Fishermen's Terminal.

For my trip, I'd bought three ring-bound sketchbooks to keep notes in, plus two ruled logs in which to record meteorological and marine details of the voyage. I wrote 'Passage to Juneau 1' on the cover of a Grumbacher sketchbook, and copied onto the first page a passage from the last chapter of *The Way of the Masks*.

The myths thus put two codes in a relationship of correspondence: incest and the rejection of or dissatisfaction with procreation, kinds of antisocial behaviour, have their equivalent in the natural order where extreme modalities of turbulence and immobility can also be observed.

Lévi-Strauss's French prose is notoriously difficult to translate, and this particular translation made him sound even more impenetrable and cranky than usual. But the essence of his argument rang clearly through the mechanical translatorese. Writing of the many stories about whirlpools and their way of sucking human beings into the maelstrom, Lévi-Strauss recognized that this kind of turbulence was intimately linked to turmoil in society and the family.

The water on which the Northwest Indians lived their daily lives was full of danger and disorder; seething white through rocky passes, liable to turn steep and violent at the first hint of a contrary wind, plagued with fierce and deceptive currents. The whirlpool – capable of ingesting a whole cedar tree, then spitting it out again like a cherry pit – was the central symbol of the sea at large, and all its terrors.

Upwellings, swirls, overfalls . . . one moment of inattention would lead to capsize. Living like this provided the Indians with a natural model for social conduct. The tribe was a fragile canoe, and one had to be on perpetual guard against anything that might upset it. Disruptive human behaviour, such as sleeping with your sister or killing your brother, was like fooling with a whirlpool; it jeopardized tribal stability. The ship-of-state metaphor, usually rather a fancy notion, applied with peculiar literalness to the culture of the Northwest Indians, for whom the imperilled canoe was both a daily fact and, in their myths and stories, a figurative means of defining their society. The great protective web of customs, rules, and rituals that the coastal Indians spun around themselves was a navigational system, designed to keep the canoe of the family and village from drifting over the lip of the maelstrom.

I made some notes along these lines, blew out the oil lamps, locked the boat, and walked up to the house to cook dinner for my wife and daughter.

II. DEEP WATER

On April Fools' Day, I sat with my daughter at the top of the stairs and heard myself talking in a voice I despised.

'It's OK, Julia. I'll come home again to see you in twenty-one days. In a floatplane. I'll bring a special present for you.'

That overstressed singsong, those audible hyphens between syllables . . . The lines sounded to me like 'Twinkle, Twinkle, Little Star', tapped out, uncertainly, on a toy xylophone.

'Twenty-one days!'

'Jaybird, that's not long—'

Plink-plonk. Plonk, plonk. Plink.

Travelling always entails infidelity. You do your best to mask the feeling of sly triumph that comes with turning your back on home and all it stands for; but disappearing into the crowd in the departure lounge, or stowing your bags in the car at dawn, you know you're a rat. I was an experienced deserter, but never until now had I been squarely faced with my treachery.

The colours in Julia's face had run together. Lower lip thrust forward, eyes brimming, she stared down into the carpeted green depths of the stairwell; she seemed suffused with her own powerlessness. She didn't have a vote on this, and at three and a half, she had no idea of how to gain suffrage.

Then, suddenly, she found a voice – a tone-perfect echo of my own. Matching my singsong delivery, cadence for cadence, she said: 'I don't mind, I won't miss you. I love Mommy more than you.'

'Julia—'

She was constantly quizzing us about the limits and dimensions of the place she called 'our world'. 'Are there real bears in our world?' 'Is New York City in our world?' Now, through her eyes, I saw our world coming adrift from its regular orbit – a small planet, unbalanced by my departure, wobbling off into the dangerous blue.

She squirmed behind me on the top stair and pressed her face into the small of my back. 'I kiss you,' she said, measuring each word, 'because I love you. But I won't mind when you're not here. I'll be glad.'

She was talking like a grown-up, her words at war with her face. I'd always known that it would come, of course, but never thought it could come so early – this milestone moment when parent and child first find themselves speaking to each other through protective masks.

'Julia, I have to go. It's my work – it's what I do so we all can live here in this house. I'll be thinking of you every day, and I'll be home soon. I promise.'

She gazed back, bleakly sceptical, knowing otherwise.

'Will you be home on my birthday?'

From behind us, in the kitchen, Jean called: 'Julia! It's time to eat your cereal!'

'My birthday is November twenty-six.'

For her sake, I had arranged a going-away party down at the boat; two of Julia's friends and their parents were meeting us at noon for soda pop, champagne, cheese, and brownies. Before we left for the dock, I gave her a stuffed animal – a grey kitten she immediately named Juliette.

'I'll always look after her. I won't lose her. Ever.' She had the righteous glow that comes with possession of the moral high ground.

We piled into the car. The ridge of high pressure had collapsed the day before, and a front was moving in from the ocean. Under a spongy sky, a thin precipitation, more mist than rain, furred the outlines of Phinney Ridge and Queen Anne Hill. The windshield wipers squeaked noisily against the glass, while Julia kept up a low monologue of confidences addressed to her kitten, and her mother and I talked household bills. Julia said, 'Mommy, what's "inconsiderate"?'

At the boat, Julia's glum mood was instantly erased by the sight of her friends. She became the proud curator of a cabinet of wonders. 'We've got a toilet on our boat,' she announced, and led Zoe and Natalie downstairs to admire the yawning porcelain bowl, the fine pump handle, and the screw-top inlet valve that took two hands to turn it. Under her instruction, the children flushed the head a dozen times – rapt hydrophiles, engrossed by the swirl and gurgle of water in the bowl. Then they set up camp on the double bed in the forecabin, smearing the sheets with chocolate brownies, and leaving behind them a faint musk, like the smell of bruised apples, that lingered in the cabin for days afterwards.

Shoehorned into the saloon because of the weather, the adults sat elbow to elbow around the table, nipped warily at the Veuve Cliquot, and made station-platform small talk. Only Natalie's father, David Shields, kept out of the conversation, head swivelling on his shoulders; a spotted owl on watch for mice. I saw his eyes blink from the barograph to the clock, to the cartoon of George III, to the VHF radio, to the titles of the books on the shelves. He spotted one of his own, *Remote*, lower shelf, port side, and gave it a slight, involuntary nod. He stared past me at a framed photograph of Julia in forsythia raingear, and at the fire extinguisher bolted to the bulkhead above it. Then he said, in a rush, 'Your house is all clutter, but this has such . . . clarity. There's a use for everything, and all the books look chosen. It's, like, the perfect space – just the right size and shape for reading and writing. It's so habitable. You must be able to have thoughts here – waterthoughts – that you could never have on land.'

Pleased, I said, 'It's the only place I can be tidy in.'

'It's amazing!' David said, clearly thinking of the turmoil of my study, its snowdrifts of books and papers, its perpetual air of having just been inexpertly burgled. People looked inside and wanted to dial 911. 'And all this beautiful wood, it's how I imagine the office of an Oxford don . . . '

I thought of Shields's office. He worked in a concrete bunker beneath his house, by anglepoise lamplight. A long wall was lined with black filing cabinets, each one labelled with a theme related to his books. I thought his office forbiddingly severe, a likely sanctum for a puritanical chief inspector. His computer was always turned off when I visited, his notebook closed. I like to spy on other people at work; Shields, a spy himself, took careful security precautions. His office gave nothing away. I was interested that he should warm so to my boat. Perhaps it was because it gave everything away with its candid exhibition of the people I loved, the books I liked, the bits of equipment, like the course-protractor and the pair of brass dividers that went with my odd, late-flowering passion for being afloat.

The children tumbled, roaring, from the forecabin. 'We goed to Alaska! We goed to Alaska!' Julia said.

With difficulty – a lost shoe, a missing pacifier, a hunt among the bedclothes for abandoned stuffed animals – we shifted the farewell party onto the dock, where the precipitation had hardened into drizzle. I got the engine going, unwrapped the ropes from their cleats, kissed Jean and Julia goodbye, and eased the boat astern. From the cockpit, I reached down into the saloon for my camera, to snap this knot of people waving in the rain.

'Bye, Daddy!' Julia, aloft on her mother's shoulders, had much the loudest voice of all the callers on shore. I found her in the viewfinder and zoomed in: a happy face, eyes and mouth wide, both arms up in the air, like a football fan cheering a last-minute goal. As I pressed the shutter, I heard her shout, 'Byeeee!'

Many weeks later, in Juneau, I had the film processed, and was thrown by the print of this shot. Though it's in crisp focus and Julia fills the frame, her hands are clasped around her mother's head, and her mouth is closed in a dubious Giaconda smile.

More heartsore than elated, I motored down the Ship Canal. The canal was maritime Seattle's Main Street, a long, wide boulevard of ships and sheds, dry docks, cranes, riggers, marine railways, and fish-packing outfits. The uniform wash-grey was punctuated by splashes of surreal light from arc lamps and welders' blowtorches. In the watery nooks and crannies between the big yards, white-bearded pirates, all known as 'Captain' and suffering from emphysema, ran eccentric trading enterprises from lopsided floating shacks. You wanted a diesel manifold, a power winch, an old radar, a forty-eight-inch left-handed propeller, you had to go see Captain Mac, or Captain Don, or Captain Sorenson. The captains each had a stake in the junk that came off the ships that put in here for refit or to be broken up for scrap. The ships themselves had the names of ports as far apart as Anchorage, Vladivostok, Panama City, Lima, and Manila painted on their rusty flanks.

Seeing the city from the Ship Canal, you'd think Seattle's only business was to go to sea. On the north shore, Ballard, the Scandinavian fishermen's suburb, came crowding to the water's edge. The flags of Norway, Sweden, and Denmark flew over Market Street, and the Olsons and Johnsons could buy lutefisk at the neighbourhood deli. For months on end, Ballard was a place of absentee fathers. In house after house, there was the picture of Dad's boat on the wall; the weekly phone call, patched through by radio; the eking out and scraping by until settlement day and the father's return.

Small wonder, then, that the boats at Fishermen's Terminal had homesick names. The man who named his boat after his wife could take her name, at least, to sea, where it would daily be on many people's lips. So the growly male voice, calling over the VHF, 'Gilda? Gilda? This is Bettijean, Bettijean,' was making a necessary assertion of the survival of the intimate world of the family in the face of the rising wind and climbing sea.

I was in good company: ships and boats are instruments of separation. The wharves along the Ship Canal were dotted with solitary figures. Russian and Filipino seamen – stranded here a long, long way from home – stood smoking, killing time, watching the west-going current slide past as sluggishly as hours.

At Ballard Locks, the boat had to drop twenty-plus feet to reach the tidewater of Puget Sound. As it sank in the dripping echo chamber of the small lock, I chatted with the attendant overhead.

'Out for the afternoon?'

'No, I'm off to Alaska.'

'All on your own? Getting away from the wife, huh?'

'No, I'm on a job.'

'Delivery job? I could do with a job like that. Except I'd have a divorce on my hands.'

'I know the feeling. There was a touch of frost in the air at home this morning.'

'Yeah. Breakfast in the Ice Age . . .' He laughed – that complicit, American, male laugh, in which every man supposedly is married to the same motherly scold. But I wasn't a member of the boys' club.

The lock gates wheezed open, admitting the sudden salt smell of the sea.

'Have fun, Cap! Get laid in Ketchikan for me, will you?'

For him, as for so many men of his place and generation, Alaska was the land of lost youth, where you had money to burn and wild oats to sow. As the years passed by, the remembered money multiplied at a giddy annual percentage rate, and the oats of yore grew ever wilder. When I told men over fifty that I was going to Alaska, I might have said that all my hair was growing back, and that I was looking forward once more to my twenty-second birthday.

Beyond the locks, the sky was beginning to brighten. A small sun showed dimly through the cloud, like a tarnished dime, and the water ahead was silvered with light. A fitful southerly breeze was wrinkling the sea into wavelets that peaked but did not break. At the fairway buoy, I killed the engine and unrolled the headsail, letting the boat drift north on the wind at a speed that could have been comfortably outstripped by a very old lady on a bicycle.

The interest here lay not on the surface of the water but in what was happening underneath. The depth sounder, bouncing ultrasonic impulses off the seafloor, was the thing to watch. At the fairway buoy, it showed 46 feet. Then it began to spool through the numbers – 71 feet, 98 feet, 103 feet, 127 feet, 165 feet . . . With every boat-length travelled through the water, the bottom fell away, a ragged under-water cliff. Close to 200 feet, the depth sounder lost contact with the ground and, pleading helplessness, gibbered random numbers at me until I switched it off. The chart took over now: half a mile from shore, I floated over the fifty-fathom contour; another half-mile, and the hundred-fathom line was crossed. Six hundred feet.

A hundred fathoms is the conventional mark of the edge of a con-tinental shelf, where ships equipped with hundred-fathom leadlines 'came into soundings'. Sailing east into the Atlantic from New York, one would have to traverse more than a hundred miles of ocean to reach that depth; sailing west from Land's End, in Cornwall, about two hundred miles. And still the bottom kept on falling. After ghost-ing along under sail for less than half an hour, I was in 150 fathoms, and the sea still deepening. Like a bug planting its feet on the skin of the water, the boat was precariously aloft above a drowned rift valley.

The lie of the surrounding land gave no inkling of the sea's pro-fundity. Suburban hills, low and rolling, sloped gently to the water's edge. The woods had been cut down to make way for looping crescents of identical $500,000 homes, pastel-painted ranch-style bun-galows, built of cinderblock and Sheetrock, clad in colour-coordinated vinyl. Through binoculars, I could see their barbecue grills and picture windows; striped sun-loungers on decks; buzz-cut lawns terminating in a meagre strip of rocky beach. With a little imagination, I could see further: past the picture window to the Sears, Roebuck telescope on a tripod; nautical lamps, port and starboard of the open hearth with its electric logs; a faux-brass sign proclaiming the kitchen 'Galley' or 'Slave Quarters'; the Navajo rug, the Pilchuck glass, the open copy of the *Discovery Channel* magazine, the love seat, the ceramic tub of dried bulrushes, the snoozing, short-haired dog.

These impeccable lives were being conducted right on the lip of the abyss. Past the lawn statue of Cupid there yawned a world of frigid darkness, inhabited by slimy creatures with tentacles and fleshy suckers, of the kind that surface in exceptionally bad dreams. Did people know? Or was this a secret that realtors assiduously kept from their clients, like news of a projected neighbourhood methadone clinic?

At nine hundred feet below the sea, the pressure is thirty times the weight of the earth's atmosphere – enough to rupture every organ in a drowned man's body and, probably, to collapse his ribcage and spill his guts. It's dark down there, though not so dark that one wouldn't see (through the window of a bathysphere) the shadows of things, darker than dark, moving, with purposeful curiosity, close to one's face. Five-hundred-pound halibut, big as doors, slither languidly through the murk. The soft black silt, stirred by rapid tidal currents, moves in swirls and billows, like tumbled clouds.

The giant octopus searches the silt for prey with arms fifteen feet long. It has huge bedroom eyes, the great domed brainpan of a comic-book Martian, and a pert little parrot beak with a poisonous bite; an unfussy carnivore, it would polish off a human cadaver in no time at all. When Jacques Cousteau wanted to film the *Dofleini*, he based his ship in Seattle. Diving very close to shore, in five to ten fathoms, he met up with some small specimens – babies of ten to thirteen feet in diameter – and was moved by their grace, docility, and intelligence. Much bigger, older, craftier ones live in the deeps of Puget Sound, where they share their habitat with the even bigger cephalopod, the Pacific giant squid. *Moroteuthis robusta* has ten hooked tentacles, which it flings out, at dazzling speed, like a rodeo cowboy roping a calf.

If I lived in that Richmond Beach bungalow, I'd keep a close eye on the dog.

Every so often a bloated, decomposing tentacle would wash ashore. To the Indians who lived here, these occasional body parts were tangible evidence of a watery underworld where gigantic creatures reigned – and, if offended, would reach up to take their revenge. Should you happen, on a morning walk, to stumble on a fly-ridden chunk of *Dofleini*, you might willingly suspend your disbelief when you heard the Tlingit story, collected by John Swanton in Wrangell, Alaska, in 1904, about an octopus that destroyed a whole fishing village.

At their summer fish camp, the villagers were drying a great haul of red salmon on wooden frames. The colour of the salmon was reflected on the water, making it glow red. This bloody tinge drew the attention of a giant octopus, or 'devilfish', who lived in the deep. Rising to the surface, 'looking very white' (as a dead tentacle does, though a live octopus does not), it extended a single mammoth tentacle, encircled the fish camp, and swept it into the sea, gorging itself on the people and smashing their canoes. When two men and a small boy returned from hunting in the woods, they saw the canoes floating in pieces on the water, and found that the remains of the houses and fish frames were thickly coated in 'devilfish slime'.

So the commuter, after a hard day on the Microsoft campus in Redmond, might return to Richmond Beach. The story, after all, concerns the two men and the boy (the only specific characters in the piece) more than the victims: it speaks to everyone's fear of what might happen at home when you're away at work. Devilfish slime comes in a multitude of guises.

The water's spooky depth, so very close to land, and its justified reputation as the lair of many large, powerful, and repulsive beings, were all the more sinister because it looked so innocent on the surface. It was sheltered (Puget Sound is never wider than four miles). Gales were rare. The sound, the most canoe-kindly of all the waters along the Inside Passage, could be safely paddled at any time of year; its salmon runs and shellfish beaches made for a life of easy pickings. No tribe in North America was able to feed itself so extravagantly, and with as little effort, as did the southern Coastal Salish on Puget Sound.

Yet this tame-seeming, food-rich sea was full of menace. Dreadful, capricious creatures were known to haunt its lower depths, and Indians were treated daily to manifestations of submarine power – a reminder, if one was needed, that humans were, by comparison, foolish and puny.

The previous September, I had been standing at the wheel when a killer whale breached about seventy-five yards from the boat. The sea was smooth as a pool of molasses. Twists of smoke rose from its surface in the chilly early morning air. My propeller left a thick braid of wake that trailed from the stern for a quarter-mile, where it faded into mist. I had just put two eggs on to boil downstairs when the whale rocketed out of the water on the port beam – ten tons of patterned black and white, its dimpled skin like heavyweight PVC – and crashed back, raising a shock wave that rolled the boat half over.

The event had the sudden violence of a car bomb going off in a quiet city street. It changed the world. Within moments, there seemed to have been an abrupt ten-degree drop in temperature. The adrenalin of the explosion was fizzing in my nervous system; and when I tried to write, the ballpoint slewed out of control on the slick surface of the page. Minutes later, when the water had glazed over the turmoil, the ensuing calm was strangely calmer, the windless quiet more intense, the air charged and sulphurous with the memory of the whale's passage.

It's one thing to see an orca breach from a crowded, camera-ready excursion boat; quite another out of nowhere, when you're alone. To the solitary Indian fisherman, tending his halibut line of twisted cedar bark, the appearance of the whale was a warning visitation from the powers below, where Komogwa (his Kwakiutl name), the Wealthy One, Master of the Seas, ruled from his underwater treasure palace of beaten copper. Komogwa – represented in carvings as a fat man with see-all protruding eyes – could show himself in the form of a loon, a seal, an octopus, a spiny-finned bullhead; in whirlpools, and in the movement of the tides. But it was in the massive bulk and gleaming musculature of the killer whale that one came closest to meeting him in person – and, in that eruption of alien, careless power, came face to face with the brutal splendour of the sea itself.

There was High Gothic humour in this conception of Komogwa as a bloated plutocrat, avatar of malevolence and greed, lord of oceanic disorder and chaos. A canoe is lost to a tide race: put it down to Komogwa. A canoe is swamped by a surfacing whale: Komogwa's doing. A cargo of valuable blankets topples overboard: gone to Komogwa's treasure chest. At winter dances, the insatiable Komogwa was a favourite character. The dancer who took his part wore a mask painted in green for the colour of the sea, black for the hidden depths in which he dwelled. Many of these Komogwa masks represent his bulging cheeks as the suckered tentacles of *Dofleini*, the slimy grasper whose eight-armed embrace awaited the unfortunate visitor to Komogwa's underwater estate.

At four o'clock, lights were coming on in the windows of the houses along the shore and the sea was turning to ink. It was a little disappointing to still be in the Seattle suburbs at the end of the day; I'd hoped to get farther. Still, as the boat rounded the line of oil tanks on Edwards Point, I had a hundred and five fathoms under the keel, and at that depth anyone should feel a good long way from home. I put into the marina at Edmonds, only a twenty-five-minute cab ride back to the house. I reminded myself severely that, having made my departure, I must stay departed. I lit the lamps, put a fresh cassette in the tape recorder, propped the mike on the saloon table, and read the story of Eeyore's birthday from *Winnie the Pooh*.

'Eeyore, the old grey Donkey, stood by the side of the stream, and looked at himself in the water. "Pathetic," he said. "That's what it is. Pathetic.". . .'

Guessing at the postage, I mailed the tape to Julia, along with a postcard of a leaping killer whale.

On 29 April 1792, in thick and rainy weather, with wind gusting from the south-east and visibility down to less than three miles, HMS *Discovery*, closely followed by her ungainly tender, *Chatham*, rounded Cape Flattery, skirted the craggy rockpile of Tatoosh Island, and entered the Strait of Juan de Fuca. It was a happy day on an unhappy ship.

The men were thirteen months away from home. The expedition had set sail from Falmouth in Cornwall on 1 April 1791 – a date unfondly remembered in too many shipboard jokes. *Discovery* and *Chatham* had tacked down the width of the Atlantic, put in at Cape Town, sailed across the Indian Ocean to south-west Australia and Tasmania, crossed the Tasman Sea to New Zealand, then made their way north to Tahiti and Hawaii. On 16 March 1792 they left Niihau, the westernmost of the Hawaiian Islands, on passage for the north-west coast of America. On 17 April, in latitude 39°20′ N, they noted signs of impending land – pieces of driftwood, floating grass and seaweed, shags, puffins, and a faint, brownish discoloration of the sea. Visibility was poor, and Captain Vancouver ordered the leadsman to take up his position on *Discovery*'s port bow. The ships came into soundings, abruptly, at fifty-three fathoms, with the tallow on the base of the lead showing a soft brown sandy bottom. Minutes later, land was sighted – a ragged line of surf, breaking on an indefinite shore. Night was falling, so the ships turned west, back into deep water, under shortened sail. Next morning, Vancouver was reasonably certain that a distant headland away in the north-east was Cape Mendocino, two hundred miles north of the Spanish garrison of San Francisco.

It took twelve long days for the two ships to make their way up the coast, dogged by north-westerlies alternating with light airs, and by rain and fog that made it hard to pick out landforms, even though they were sailing as close inshore as they dared, trying to keep in view of the surfline. They were, frustratingly, committed to mapping this section of the American coast, about which the published charts were in hopeless disagreement. But the real interest of the officers lay in the waters ahead, in that 'expansive Mediterranean ocean', as Vancouver called the rumoured sea that would eventually be named the Inside Passage.

The long dull haul northward from Mendocino to Cape Flattery was made more trying by the corrosive atmosphere on *Discovery*'s quarterdeck. Vancouver was governing his little society of ninety-nine men (forty-five more aboard *Chatham*) by force of his naval rank alone, and by punishments that his rank entitled him to inflict on subordinates. His by-the-book efficiency, along with his punctilious skill as a navigator and chartmaker, earned him a continuing, if lukewarm, respect from commissioned officers who long since had lost any real sympathy or affection for the man. But the 'young gentlemen' – of whom there were fifteen on *Discovery*, variously enrolled as midshipmen, able seamen, and master's mates – loathed him. These well-connected patrician adolescents regarded their captain with a mixture of raw fear and snobbish disdain.

At thirty-four, Vancouver wasn't a naturally commanding figure. He was a short man, glandularly fat, whose weight was increasing noticeably during the voyage. He had lost most of his hair. He had protuberant, thyroidal eyes. He sweated a lot. In gentle weather, Vancouver's rattling graveyard cough made itself heard from bow to stern. His explosions of temper were frequent, and famous: puce-faced and bawling, he seemed possessed and transformed by some inner demon. In a period when symptoms of extreme psychological disturbance usually could pass as acceptable eccentricity, several gentlemen aboard *Discovery* diagnosed Vancouver as suffering from fits of temporary insanity.

Vancouver's lieutenants on *Discovery* – Zachary Mudge, Joseph Whidbey, Joseph Baker, and Peter Puget – were regular naval types, for whom the successful completion of the voyage would bring promotion to commands of their own. Along with the ship's naturalist and surgeon, Archibald Menzies, they found themselves in the delicate and uncomfortable position of having to mediate between the young aristos of the midships and their prematurely aged, bald, fat, apoplectic captain.

Discovery was a few inches short of one hundred feet long. Cramped and smelly at the best of times, it was far too small to contain the bitter class war that now smouldered aft of the mainmast. The quarterdeck – an area reserved for gentlemen of all ranks – was roughly twenty-eight by thirty feet; it was also the ship's farmyard. One could hardly take a step without tripping over a piglet or a chicken, or colliding with a bony goat. This cluttered and constricted space had been made even smaller by the addition, on the orders of Sir Joseph Banks, President of the Royal Society, of Mr Menzies's 'garden' – a glass greenhouse, eight by twelve feet, in which newly discovered plants could be returned, alive, to England. Vancouver considered the garden a lubberly profanation, and abused it, profanely, at every possible opportunity. By this point, Menzies could raise the issue of the garden with his captain only by sealed letter, even though he regularly visited Vancouver's cabin to dose him with medicines for his puzzling illness.

With five commissioned officers, a dozen or so animals, and the greenhouse, the quarterdeck was already overloaded. But *Discovery* had taken on an unprecedented number of young gentlemen, aged from sixteen to twenty-two. All fifteen had 'pull'; a family connection with an ear at the Admiralty. Voyages such as this promised to be novel and adventurous versions of the Grand Tour, and these boys would see Natural Man in his wild habitat, the scenery of the Sublime, the grandeur of Ocean in all its moods . . . *Discovery* would be a finishing school on an epic and glorious scale, an education in leadership, navigation, geography, nature, and anthropology.

Lord Bute sent his son the Honourable Charles Stuart; Lord Camelford, cousin to the Prime Minister, sent his son the Honourable Thomas Pitt. Marquess Townshend engineered a place for his young friend Thomas Manby. The Earl of Hardwicke did the same for Spelman Swaine. Sir Alan Gardner got two of his nephews, Robert Barrie and Henry Humphrys, aboard. And so it went. *Discovery* was swollen with the languid young scions of the Upper Ten.

Poor Vancouver. Of Dutch extraction, from King's Lynn in Norfolk, where his father was a prominent local Tory and assistant collector of customs, Captain Van, as he was called, though never to his face, was miserably incapable of serving as mentor to the immature finery of fashionable England.

As the ship inched past Tatoosh Island, its crew felt the inevitable current of excitement at having at last arrived at the object of a year-long voyage – an excitement greatly heightened by the prospect of escape, however temporary, from the personal and social tensions of the quarterdeck. From now on, there'd be shore parties, to set up the astronomical observatory, to meet and barter with the natives, and to brew spruce beer. There'd be survey parties in the small boats, to explore the coast and its waters in fine detail. Whole days might be spent without once having to meet the bugged-out eyes of Captain Van.

Clawing their way forward against the wind and the ebb stream, *Discovery* and *Chatham* made short tacks along the southern shore of the strait. They passed an Indian village (now Neah Bay): a jumble of wooden huts set back from the water behind a line of low dunes, with canoes drawn up on a crescent of sandy beach. Vancouver considered this for an overnight anchorage, but decided against it. At seven o'clock, three miles farther on, he found a nook tucked between two cliffs of dripping pines, and the ships dropped their anchors in twenty-three fathoms, on a bottom of black sand and mud.

From the forecastle came the thin, wheezy notes of 'Spanish Ladies' played on a fife. Grog was issued, and the men went to their messes for an unenviable supper of ship's biscuit and burgoo.

A glass of Fetzer Chardonnay and the blue plate special – ling cod with asparagus and baby red potatoes – were placed before me at Anthony's, the Edmonds marina restaurant, where I had a window table and a fine view of the matt-black hump of Whidbey Island, looming over the fork between Puget and Possession Sounds. In the dark space between Edmonds and Kingston, on the Kitsap Peninsula, a commuter ferry hung suspended like a Japanese lantern. Tumbled clouds occupied most of the sky, though in a rift over Admiralty Inlet a single fuzzy star shone wanly.

I had discovered this labyrinth of islands and inlets by a stroke of idle luck. In 1989, a chance conversation with a businessman in rural Alabama led me to post myself to Seattle for six weeks, because it sounded like an interesting city in which to set a chapter of the book I was writing. Facing a lonely Thanksgiving Day in a rented room on Second Avenue, I took the ferry from Seattle to Victoria, BC. It was a blustery morning, the empty streets streaming like rivers, stoplights tossing on their overhead wires. Elliott Bay was close-ribbed with white-caps. A perfect day for seagoing, if you were boarding a vessel as big as *Vancouver Island Princess*, a waddling tub of a ship, built in Glasgow in 1955 and a salt-caked veteran of heavy weather.

As soon as we were clear of the city, I clambered up the outside companionway to the wheelhouse to bother the captain. But it was like the meeting of Bouvard and Pécuchet. No sooner had we exchanged names than we were reaching into our wallets for snapshots of our respective sailboats. The mate, evidently used to his boss's strange addiction, took over the brass wheel and nursed the ferry through the chop, while the captain began to dig through the shallow drawers of the chart table, pulling out a dozen charts on which to show me the delights of his home waters.

There – he rapped the paper with a meaty forefinger – the tide ran at sixteen knots at springs. *There* he'd ridden on the lip of a whirlpool three metres deep. *Here* was a favourite winter anchorage. *There* were miles of estuarine shallows, where the sea kicked up in south-easterly winds, and where he once nearly lost his boat. I had never seen charts on which land and sea were so intricately tangled, in a looping scribble of blue and beige.

The captain took his annual vacation every February, he said, because it was the best month for reliable winds. He sailed alone. His wife, who no more shared his taste for this stuff than did the mate of the *Princess*, flew off for a Hawaiian holiday while he went gunkholing around the islands.

He'd just broached the interesting topic of inflow and outflow winds when he spotted a pod of orcas cavorting in the murk, a mile or so off the port bow. After instructing the mate to alter course, he announced the whales over the ferry's PA system. The rush of passengers to the windows gave the ship a sudden ten-degree list as we stumbled through the sea to take a closer look.

A few minutes later, we passed a sailboat wallowing in confused seas off Marrowstone Island. It was on a close reach, under a double-reefed mainsail and a meagre triangle of jib, spray pluming from its bow as it shouldered its way through the breakers. The captain gazed on it fondly through binoculars. 'They've got three knots of tide under them through there, maybe a tad more. See how short and steep that sea is?'

The face of the mate, above the wheel, was a study in deep habit-uated indifference. 'I've always wanted to go to London,' he said.

The captain, his binoculars still trained on the sailboat, said: 'Someone isn't happy on that boat.'

'My dad's family comes from somewhere over there,' the mate said.

In a whining falsetto, the captain said, 'If we ever get out of this alive, I'm never, ever coming out with you again.' It sounded like a verbatim quote from the captain's own domestic life.

Past the lighthouse on Point Wilson, to the west of the ferry's course, the water seethed like a pan of boiling milk. High conical waves smashed into one another ceaselessly, raising a thick penumbra of spray overhead.

'That's a serious race,' I said.

'Oh, we've got a lot worse than that over on the Canadian side. There's a race off Trial Island, another off Race Rocks . . . there've been big ships lost in both of those.'

'You ever see the race off Portland Bill in England?' I said.

'I never did. That's one I'd like to see, though – I read about it.'

'You don't need to. Your sea's got everything.'

And it was true. I loved the sense of being so close to the city, yet so far out on this magnificently eventful sea, with its wild creatures and mazy channels. I thought, if I lived in Seattle, I'd keep a boat of my own, and sail it to where the tide ran at sixteen knots at springs, and where there were whirlpools ten feet deep. I'd live on a sane frontier between nature and civilization, with one foot in the water, the other in a metropolis of restaurants and bookstores. I'd read and write in the mornings, and run away to sea in the afternoons.

Within a few days of my Thanksgiving ride, I was busy turning *I would* into *I will*.

At dawn the next morning, every cloud was gone. The air seemed thin and rarefied. A range of serrated mountains far to the east stood out black against a rose-pink sky. A faint breeze from the west barely ruffled the water. *Discovery* and *Chatham* drifted slowly around, on grumbling anchor cables, to face the young flood tide.

They were soon under way, ghosting down the Strait of Juan de Fuca under full sail, with tide and wind working in consort. To starboard, the low forested hills were rinsed and brilliantly green. The hills rose steadily into snow-capped mountains some twenty miles away, with glittering ice fields and jagged pinnacles of black rock. 'Sterile,' wrote Vancouver, describing their appearance in his log.

But the captain was relaxed and smiling. He presided over this unfolding new world as if he had conjured it from inside his hat. Usually secretive about even his most trifling plans, thinking it best to keep them shrouded in the mystery of command, he now chatted freely with his officers, inviting their opinions and making himself genially open to suggestion. Many people on board would remember this sunlit day as the happiest of the entire voyage. In his secret journal, Midshipman Thomas Manby wrote:

> *Never was contrast greater, in this days sailing than with that we had long been accustomed to. It had more the aspect of enchantment than reality, with silent admiration each discerned the beauties of Nature, and nought was heard on board but expressions of delight murmured from every tongue. Imperceptibly our Bark skimmed over the glassy surface of the deep, about three Miles an hour, a gentle Breeze swelled the lofty Canvass whilst all was calm below.*

Sailing close inshore, the ships slid past pretty falls of timber, speckled forest glades, and a grassy clearing where a family of long-shadowed deer gazed back, unafraid, into the lenses of the officers' telescopes. Encouraged by the captain, Midshipmen Sykes and Humphrys brought up their sketchbooks from below to record the passing Arcadian scene.

Joseph Baker, on the port side of the quarterdeck, spotted a smooth-sided white peak that rose well clear of the line of mountains on the eastern horizon. Vancouver ceremoniously announced that he would give it the name of Mount Baker, in honour of his third lieutenant.

Close to ten o'clock, ship's time, the moon rose in the north-east, where it hung in the blue like a smudge of pale ash. To Vancouver, and to the ship's master, Mr Whidbey, the two real navigators on *Discovery*, the moon's arrival was the high spot of this perfect morning. With the sea as flat as a lake, and the sun and moon simultaneously visible in the clear sky, they could find their true longitude and check the mounting error in the ship's chronometers.

In 1792, more than thirty years after John Harrison unveiled his marine chronometer, longitude was still a much more troubling problem than most popular books on the subject (like Dava Sobel's *Longitude*) have generally conveyed. The new chronometers worked well on short voyages of three or four weeks; but on longer ones they fell so far out of sync with Greenwich Mean Time as to be useless, unless they were continually corrected by some other means of ascertaining time.

One of Vancouver's commissions on the voyage south from Falmouth to Cape Town had been to experiment with a new method of determining longitude that was being touted around the Admiralty. This involved measuring the exact magnetic variation of the compass at a given latitude and locating it on a chart of all the variations observed on a particular ocean. Vancouver tested this cheap and easy solution, and found it foolhardy and dangerous. That the Admiralty should be promoting it at all, so late in the navigational day, says a lot about the dubious reliability of the Harrison clock.

There remained an ingenious and reliable method known as 'lunar distance'. Because the sun and the moon travel around the earth on different orbits and at different speeds (it is the navigator's necessary fiction that the sun, like every other heavenly body, circles the earth, and not vice versa), they can be thought of as a pair of clock hands. By calculating the distance between them at any given moment, you can find the exact time at Greenwich, and therefore your longitude.

The working of a lunar distance was the navigator's pièce de résistance. It required very accurate sights with a quadrant or sextant, followed by some horrible arithmetic. Midshipmen dreaded the exercise, and few captains were confident of their mastery of it. George Vancouver excelled at lunar distances, their finical quadrant-handling and abstruse mathematics. When he wrote about his 'lunars' in his *Voyage*, he did so in the tone of an evangelist. 'I hope to see the period arrive, when every sea-faring person capable of using a quadrant, will, on due instruction, be enabled by lunar observations to determine his longitude at sea.'

All the young gentlemen aboard *Discovery* were drilled by their captain in the lunar method; it was his great claim to intellectual prowess, and he enjoyed berating his better-educated juniors as they got lost in the miserable thicket of secants, cosines, and tangents.

Vancouver had learned how to work lunars when he was a midshipman aboard Captain Cook's *Resolution* ('a Quiet inoffensive young man', as Cook described him then), and had attached himself to William Wales, the expedition astronomer. Wales – a gifted teacher who went on to take charge of the Mathematics School at Christ's Hospital, where his pupils included Leigh Hunt, Charles Lamb, and S. T. Coleridge – had taken young George in hand, coaching him until he was as proficient in celestial navigation as any officer on the ship. Wales had been Vancouver's one-man university, and Cook his ideal model of captaincy.

So when the washed-out moon began its steady climb through the eastern sky, Vancouver's good humour brimmed over. Here was a Heaven-sent opportunity to teach these boys a much-needed lesson. He waited patiently for the moon to attain a sufficient altitude for a good sight, then set his young gentlemen to work.

At nearly noon, ship's time, the moon bore (096° T). Its observed altitude, by quadrant sight, was 29°04'. The sun bore 179°, at an altitude of 54°50'. Now came the brain-cudgelling part. (*Pay attention, Sykes! Are you listening, Humphrys?*) You had to solve a devilish spherical triangle. Your ship lay on a latitude just short of 49°N. The sun, reduced to its zenith point on the earth's surface, lay on a spot in mid-Pacific, roughly 2,700 miles west of Costa Rica. The moon lay – more roughly still – somewhere close to Providence, Rhode Island. Your job was to calculate the distance between those two geographical points, along with all the angles in the triangle formed by the ship, the moon, and the sun.

$$\tan \theta = \tan b \cos c$$
$$\cos c = \cos b \cos (a - \theta) \sec \theta$$

Poor Sykes. Poor Humphrys. But Vancouver scribbled for a couple of minutes, and had the answer.

Some work on the nascent, partially drawn chart, with soft pencil and boxwood parallel ruler – and there you were. Latitude: 48°13′N. Longitude: 235°59′E (Vancouver always measured his Pacific longitudes by going eastabout from Greenwich). Most important of all, the time at Greenwich when the observations were taken turned out to have been exactly 8.13′.06″ p.m. After thirteen months at sea, *Discovery's* main chronometer, made by Larcum Kendall of London, was running fast by 45 minutes and 46 seconds.

Flushed and ebullient with his textbook demonstration, knowing now precisely where he stood, Vancouver was in high form, strutting the quarterdeck like a plump rooster fluffing out his feathers. Fine on the starboard bow, a long sandspit topped with thin grass projected out for a mile or more from shore, its beach littered with dead pine trees thrown up by the westerly storms. The tide boiled past the end of it, where the water was marbled with rips and eddies. Vancouver proclaimed that the spit bore a quite remarkable resemblance to Dungeness as it reaches out a long, shingled arm into the English Channel from Winchelsea and Rye. This likeness was lost on most of the gentlemen on deck, but they nodded in polite agreement when Vancouver ordered the name New Dungeness to be written on the chart.

In the next few months, he'd find a thousand names. The established ritual of colonial possession required that every mountain, bay, promontory, pass, and headland be given an English name; and it was the privilege of the captain to leave his private fancies on the land that he explored. Vancouver named his land- and sea-marks after high-ups at the Admiralty, whose goodwill might lead to his promotion; after old friends and mentors, like William Wales; out of the *Royal Kalendar*, a much-thumbed, fusty red book of dates and personages that Vancouver kept in his cabin; after his ships, his officers, and his family; after incidents on the voyage; and after his own bipolar mental states. Most of his names stuck. Two hundred years later one could read the charts of the Northwest coast as a candid diary of Vancouver's expedition; a map of his mind, in all its changing moods and preoccupations.

Now his mood was one of serene if strangely elevated nostalgia, and his officers were foxed by this sudden new aspect of their captain's character. The next seven days, of uninterrupted sunshine and light airs, seemed a reflection of Captain Van's unprecedented internal weather. The quarterdeck remained wary. Some saw a bad omen in the captain's impervious sweet temper – the calm before the storm, the uncanny stillness in the air before the crack of thunder and the lightning bolt.

In 1797, when he was a half-pay captain living in the Thames-side village of Petersham and writing up his journals for publication, Vancouver recreated these first days as an idyll. He was in a state of dazzled infatuation with the land into which he'd sailed. Everything he saw, he praised, and in terms that gave a great deal away about his character.

With *Discovery* and *Chatham* at anchor inside the sheltering arm of New Dungeness, the small boats – two cutters and a yawl – were lowered and the officers set out on a sailing tour of the nearby coast. Vancouver reclined in the sternsheets of the yawl: in knee-breeches, silver-buttoned yellow waistcoat, wig, and cocked hat, he was the picture of a genteel Englishman, equipped for a pleasant Sunday ramble around his estate. Six and a half miles east of the anchorage, the yawl grounded on the sandy beach of a steep-sided island, and the party scrambled up the cliff to get a better view of the surrounding countryside.

'Our attention,' wrote Vancouver,

was immediately called to a landscape, almost as enchantingly beautiful as the most elegantly finished pleasure grounds in Europe. The summit of this island presented nearly a horizontal surface, interspersed with some inequalities of ground, which produced a beautiful variety on an extensive lawn covered with luxuriant grass, and diversified with an abundance of flowers. To the north-westward was a coppice of pine trees and shrubs of various sorts, that seemed as if it had been planted for the sole purpose of protecting from the N.W. winds this delightful meadow, over which were promiscuously scattered a few clumps of trees, that would have puzzled the most ingenious designer of pleasure grounds to have arranged more agreeably. Whilst we stopped to contemplate these several beauties of nature, in a prospect no less pleasing than unexpected, we gathered some gooseberries and roses in a state of considerable forwardness.

Still red-faced and out of breath from the climb, his wig (he wore it habitually, to hide his balding skull) a little askew, Captain Van picked wild roses, to the astonished amusement of his companions.

Just inshore of this delightful island opened a deep bay, and the yawl sailed to investigate it. Once inside, Vancouver was again enraptured by what he saw. A reliable supply of water was 'the only great object necessary for constituting this one of the finest harbours in the world'. The yawl picked its way along the edge of the beach while Vancouver searched for the outlet of a creek. 'Almost despairing of success, I suddenly fell in with an excellent stream of very fine water.' Next morning, the ships weighed anchor and sailed the nine miles to the bay, to which Vancouver gave the name Port Discovery.

The passage took three enjoyable hours.

The surface of the land was perfectly smooth, and the country before us exhibited every thing that bounteous nature could be expected to draw into one point of view. As we had no reason to imagine that this country had ever been indebted for any of its decorations to the hand of man, I could not possibly believe that any uncultivated country had ever been discovered exhibiting so rich a picture.

The captain was no great shakes as a writer. He loved the hard clarity of numbers and disliked the arbitrary, indefinite quality of words. He had to sweat to make them say what he believed he meant, and his grammar had a habit of wriggling out of control. (One of his midshipmen, Robert Barrie, would dismiss his great *Voyage* as 'one of the most tedious books I ever read'.) Struggling to hit the right lyrical note in his Petersham lodgings, Vancouver aimed high, and fell short.

The land . . . rose . . . in a very gentle ascent, and was well covered with a variety of stately forest trees. These, however, did not conceal the whole face of the country in one uninterrupted wilderness, but pleasingly clothed its eminences, and chequered the vallies; presenting, in many directions, extensive spaces that wore the appearance of having been cleared by art, like the beautiful island we had visited the day before. As we passed along the shore near one of these charming spots, the tracks of deer, or some such animal, were very numerous, and flattered us with the hope of not wanting refreshments of that nature, whilst we remained in this quarter.

A picture so pleasing could not fail to recall to our remembrance certain delightful and beloved situations in Old England. . . .

From someone still under forty, writing at the very end of the eighteenth century, Vancouver's way of looking at landscape was old fashioned to the point of being fogeyish. His vocabulary belongs to the Augustan and Palladian years early in the century; harks back to the landscape gardens of William Kent and the poetry of Alexander Pope. Vancouver made the Western wilderness conform to an idealized sylvan scene of glades and groves, of chequered shades and green retreats, in an attempt to conjure a landscape like that of Pope's *Windsor Forest*, written in 1713 –

> *Here Hills and Vales, the Woodland and the Plain,*
> *Here Earth and Water seem to strive again,*
> *Not Chaos-like together crush'd and bruis'd,*
> *But as the World, harmoniously confus'd:*
> *Where Order in Variety we see,*
> *And where, tho' all things differ, all agree.*

In landscape, as aboard ship, Vancouver's preference was for order and subordination. Views with a receding perspective. Everything balanced and in its place. 'Nature' was all well and good, but to mould it into a pleasing hierarchy of colours, forms, and spaces required 'art'. Gathering rosebuds on the 'lawn' atop Protection Island, Vancouver saw a landscape that needed only the addition of a few urns, an obelisk or two, some classical statuary, a pagoda, and perhaps a temple of Apollo to bring it into line with the pleasure grounds of Hampton Court and Chiswick House (both, as it happened, within walking distance of Petersham).

No wonder he was so at odds with the young gentlemen, with their hopeless arithmetic and their loose talk of the Sublime. They were excited by the modern rage for wilderness and solitude, by landscapes that inspired feelings of awe, dread, or, in Edmund Burke's phrase, 'delightful horror'. Such ideas were anathema to Captain Van, who saw in them the seeds of insurrection and chaos. They threatened the good order of his ship, as of the world.

Isolated from the crew by his narrow and conservative taste, Vancouver at thirty-four might as well have been seventy. Yet in this mild and sunny first week of May, officers and midshipmen alike were stirred by the new landscape, even though they understood it in very different terms.

Vancouver saw Old England, miraculously recreated in the reign of George I. To the urns and obelisks, he added church towers of chipped Norfolk flint; busy ports with blazoned customs houses; a handsome manor on every barbered eminence; a thriving agriculture, with sheep on the hillsides and fields thick with wheat. His articles of commission charged him to assess the land for possible settlement. Now a grandiose plan took shape in his mind, as he dreamed into being a paradisal New Albion: an orderly green redoubt of his own ancestral Toryism.

Archibald Menzies, botanizing in the woods, saw a wide-open frontier of scientific exploration. His job on the voyage was to extend the enormous taxonomic enterprise begun by Linnaeus, and each day he returned to the ship with more specimens destined for the royal gardens at Kew. (Most would wilt and die in the quarterdeck garden, or be eaten by the ship's goats.) At Port Discovery he found a new species of arbutus, with a prettily twisted trunk and papery red bark: he called it the Oriental strawberry tree, *Arbutus menziesii*. He also had a close, odious encounter with a skunk.

Peter Puget saw the wild habitat of Natural Man. Puget, a Londoner from a Huguenot banking family, was on nodding terms, at least, with the work of Jean-Jacques Rousseau, and he spent every spare moment trying to make contact with the Indians. He quizzed them, in sign language, about the meaning of certain peculiar wooden structures at New Dungeness, about their food and clothing, about their marital and funerary rites. Puget was no intellectual – Menzies, thinking him a metropolitan lightweight, tried to block his promotion – but he was bright, even-tempered, popular on all decks, and as comfortably abreast of his times as Vancouver (only eight years older) was behind them. As an amateur anthropologist, Puget was thoughtful, imaginative, and zealously modest in his observations. In Port Discovery he found a canoe burial, and puzzled over its meaning in his journal.

> *This . . . argues Strongly, that the Indians believe in a future State, or else why bury with them Eatables with their Weapons for procuring more & place the Body in a Canoe suspended in the Air, which we may reasonably suppose is to prevent its being damaged by Insects or Animals, that it may be of Service to the*

Deceased hereafter. However at present our knowledge of the Language is so very Imperfect that it would be impossible to form from it any Idea of their Religion or of the Deity – nor do I ever think from the very Short time we remain at any Place either in the Ships or Boats, that we shall ever be well acquainted with their Manners or Customs.

This is the late-night scribbling of an instantly likeable, alert, and open-minded man. Puget stands out among his colleagues for harbouring no grudges, being always in good spirits, and nearly always having fun.

In morning fog, and a rising wind from the south-east, the small boats felt their way gingerly along the shore until, six miles to the east of Port Discovery, they came to the entrance of an important inlet, to judge from the speed at which the tide swept them through. At noon the fog lifted, and the explorers could see they were at the seaward end of a great inland waterway: a broad channel, several miles wide, trending southward past a fringe of substantial islands.

To starboard, sequestered from the main channel, lay a 'more capacious harbour than Port Discovery'. Far to the south, a gigantic snow-cap appeared to float above the clouds like an inverted blancmange, its colour an unearthly shade of pale violet. Vancouver named the mountain after Captain (soon to be Rear Admiral) Peter Rainier. For the harbour he settled on Port Townshend, after Marquess Townshend. Midshipman Thomas Manby, whose acquaintance with the Townshends secured his place aboard *Discovery*, got out his penknife and carved into the trunk of an ancient cypress:

Anne Marie Townſhend
T.M. 1792

Whoever Thou Art, Traveller,
Know That ſhe Poſſeſſes
Every Beauty As A Woman
This Unequaled Cypreſs

Poſſeſſes As A Tree,
Without Fault Or Blemiſh.

Was this, perhaps, why the marquess had busied himself to find a berth for Manby – to put 20,000 miles between Anne Marie and this breathless young romantic?

Meanwhile, Menzies emerged, flushed, his topcoat bespattered with pink petals, from a deep bosk of rhododendrons new to science.

Puget was dispatched in a cutter to take soundings in the main channel. It was a rough and splashy ride, with the six oarsmen rowing hard upwind and the waves breaking short on one another's backs. Driven south on the tide, Puget's boat was soon out of sight of the Port Townshend shore party. He began sounding in mid-channel.

The sounding line, of three-quarter-inch hemp, lay stacked in coils on the bow thwart. Strips of ribbon, pulled through the braid of the rope, marked off the depth at five-fathom intervals. The conical fourteen-pound lead had a hollowed-out base, which the leadsman 'armed' with sticky tallow to pick up samples of the sea floor. With the boat stopped, the leadsman, wearing leather gloves, allowed the hemp to feed steadily through his fingers, coil after coil of rope snaking its way off the thwart; the lead sank, and sank, and went on sinking, the line bellying out in the turbulence below and thrumming in the leadsman's hands as violently as if a big fish were on the end.

'Sounded with 100 fth. line. Found no bottom,' wrote Puget in his notebook. His handwriting is all fluency and dash. The upright strokes of his terminal *d*'s rise in cheerful swirls and billows, the pencil taking flight from the word in an impulsive doodle.

To recover the lead from its fruitless journey to the deep took several minutes. Puget ordered the rowers closer inshore. Again, the same result. 'Sounded but had no bottom.' Apparently, the land sloped gently to the water's edge, then fell away into a submarine abyss.

From behind the headland to the south came a drift of smoke, blown flat by the wind, from an Indian campfire.

If the surrounding countryside sometimes gave Puget the

illusion of being back home, or in some greener, wilder England, this unfathomable water reminded him sharply otherwise. It was as deep as America itself.

My dawn was damp, still, gauze-gray. The inked needle on the barograph drum had fallen steadily overnight and now was sinking past the 1,000-millibar line into the foul-weather 990s. Waiting for the kettle to come to the boil, I turned on NOAA Weather Radio and listened to the forecast for Juan de Fuca Strait.

'Small craft advisory: winds, west, ten to twenty knots, rising to twenty-five to thirty knots in the afternoon; rain changing to showers.' The affectless male voice might have added that by afternoon, with the ebb tide running full tilt into a near gale, the sea would be heaped and growling, every wave baring its teeth. The vernacular translation of *small craft advisory* is: 'You will be cold, wet, and scared. You will curse yourself for having been fool enough to leave home.'

I'd planned that day to sail up Admiralty Inlet and cross the strait, meeting Vancouver's expedition as his small boats made their way south into the sound. Now I'd have to take another route through the labyrinth – sneaking up the sheltered backside of Whidbey Island while Puget & Co. came down the front. Maybe playing cat-and-mouse with the eighteenth century was a better idea than trying to confront it head-on.

There was no wind when I left Edmonds. The smooth surface of the water was tooled with scrolls and curlicues of current, as the flood tide divided – the main stream going south while the branch line, on which I was riding, curled around to fill the northern backwaters. I steered the boat through the swirls, where an angry parliament of gulls shrieked and squabbled over foetid titbits turned up from the deep.

The sea had the same faint scent of putrescence that greets you upon opening the door of the fridge after a three-week absence. The water was thick and dusty. Always reluctant to mirror even the bluest sky, it had a stubborn residual colour of its own – a scummy, dark, greenish grey. It might have passed as soup at Dotheboys Hall.

But it was wonderful water. The immense depth of Puget Sound was interrupted in several places by shallow sills of rock, over which the tide poured in hidden undersea cascades. Great plumes welled up from the bottom, spinning off eddies, boils, meanders, spirals. One needed the technical vocabulary of chaos, with its fractals, Mandelbrot sets, strange attractors, and homoclinic tangles, to do justice to the disorderly ebb and flow of the tide in this basin.

Frigid, lightless, saline water from the deep was being continually churned up with warm, oxygenated, brackish water from the surface – making a perfect hatchery and habitat for every kind of plankton. The sea-drifters (from the Greek *planktos*: drifting) were true creatures of chaos.

Stowed away in a compartment under the couch in the saloon was a yard-sale microscope. Dodging work during a writing retreat on the boat, I would sometimes haul it out and lower a bucket over the side, to check out my fellow drifters under the 97× lens. A teaspoonful of Puget Sound water yielded a whole world of Hollywood monsters: copepods; rotifers; flagellates, their whips flailing on the glass. Each time I dipped the slide in the bucket, the cast changed: new wrigglies waved spiky antennae, inflated their balloon-like luminescent torsos, flexed their cilia, flapped rubbery watery wings, or gazed up at me with vacant soccer-ball eyes. They put me in mind of Hieronymus Bosch. Imported to Venice from Holland by some doge, Bosch was so impressed by the scampi from the Venetian lagoon that his painted Purgatory (in a triptych in the Doges' Palace) is administered by an officious bureaucracy of giant prawns. If plankton were a little bigger, they would figure in everyone's bad dreams.

The phytoplankton – diatoms, spores of green algae – provide food for the shrimp- and jellyfish-like zooplankton. Zooplankton are food for fish. Fish are . . . It takes only two or three links in the food chain to arrive at the killer whales, sea lions, bald eagles, black bears. At the bottom of the whole animal hierarchy lay the ceaseless tumbling of the water in the basin, as it answered to the drag of the moon.

In the morning calm, this productive turbulence was revealed in the snaking S-shaped lines of kelp and driftwood that collected on the margins between eddies; in finger-sized whirlpools; in windrows of slick water that ran in twisting paths across the surface; in threads and seams of current, like whorled fingerprints. The slightest breeze would wipe these legible signs of disturbance clean off the face of the sea.

The surest measure of the tumult that was going on below was the GPS, which kept up a running commentary on the boat's course and speed from its perch above the chart table. This clever instrument, the size and shape of a TV remote, tuned itself into a clutch of military satellites, measured the time that each satellite's signal took to reach it, and translated the times into a position, accurate to within a few yards, anywhere on the earth's surface. The Global Positioning System always knew how fast the boat was moving over the ground, and could make a reliable map of the turbulent motion of the sea.

From the compass and the knotmeter – which gave the speed of the boat through the water, measured by a small spinning paddle-wheel mounted beneath the bow – I could tell I was on a steady course of 005° at a speed of 5.9 knots. But when the water itself is moving, course and speed through the water are very different from course and speed over the ground. The GPS showed that the real speed of the boat was constantly changing. From 9 knots it dropped to 3.8, climbed to 7.5, dithered for a while around 6.0, went up to 7.2. Likewise the course. The lubberline on the steering compass stayed more or less glued to 005°, but the simulated compass card on the GPS was swinging through a 25° arc. The boat's true progress was revealed as a tipsy foxtrot over the sea, as it was seized by gyres, thrust suddenly sideways, sped along by an onrush of current, brought nearly to a standstill by the countervailing force of the next eddy.

The arrival of the $250 GPS set had been a revelation. Before, I'd been lulled by the compass card, barely stirring in its bowl, and by the even ticking away of miles on the knotmeter. I professed to know where I was headed, and how fast I was getting there, when all the time I was lurching waywardly about, veering off on one tangent after another, my illusion of a steady career given credence only by the random reversals and corrections built into any chaotic system. Eventually, detours tend to cancel each other out, as chaos itself appears to cohere around a 'strange attractor'. But at any given moment you're probably going in quite the wrong direction, and at a speed that would certainly surprise and might frighten you. As $250 lessons in the navigation of life go, this one seemed cheap at twice the price.

Nursing a mug of coffee in the cockpit, I left the steering to the autopilot and watched the world slide by in fifty shades of grey. A tug was hauling a low island of logs crabwise across the tide. An epic freight train supplied the only trace of green in the entire landscape as it inched along the trestles at the edge of the beach, on the Burlington Northern line to Vancouver. The chimneys of Everett's derelict pulp mills stood out against the trees, and the miles of waterfront subdivisions, condo blocks, and gated retirement communities showed as a disfiguring rash of pale spots in the hills.

Yet from this sea-distance it was extraordinary how little the land had altered since Captain Van projected onto it his vision of a genteel Augustan future; even now one could see how the addition of a few obelisks, gazebos, and classical temples might set it off to its best advantage. After a hundred and fifty years of white settlement, it still looked like a forest – a badly vandalized forest, it's true, but a forest nonetheless.

In this moist and temperate climate, fir, salal, alder, fern, and salmonberry swarm over every inch of unattended ground. The gardeners of the Northwest spend a great deal of their time trying to fight off the encroaching forest. As I know well, whenever you clear a fresh space for a rosebush in one part of the yard, snakelike tendrils of camouflage-green will busily be colonizing another patch behind your back. If some disaster hit the people here – if Boeing and Microsoft both went bust – it wouldn't be long, a few months at most, before the advance troops of vine and bramble took over the highways and strip-malls, closely followed by an occupying army of young Douglas firs. In less than half a human lifetime the place would be back to wilderness again. Bears and cougars (who even now are regular summer visitors to the outskirts of Everett, where they upend trashcans and breakfast on household pets) would make their dens in the urban ruins.

Here, more than anywhere else I know, the tenure of civilization appears unexpectedly provisional and insecure. It didn't take to this soil as it took elsewhere. The Indians had lived on tiptoe, in small numbers, on the extreme fringe of the forest, barely grazing the surface of the water. Then the great self-important juggernaut of American capitalism rumbled through the Pacific Northwest, clearing it with chainsaws, paving it with asphalt, building bridges, banks, insurance towers, tract housing, and all the rest. Yet on this overcast morning, only a mile offshore, you'd hardly notice, so modest seemed its impact, compared with the urgent press of the forest and swirl of the tide. Squint a little and you might, for all intents and purposes, be back in 1792, looking out on a nature that still awaited men with grandiose designs on it.

Mukilteo, Darlington, Everett dissolved into the woods astern. *Unreal cities* . . . Abreast of Gedney Island, the entrance to Tulalip Bay opened up to starboard, with a faded red marker posted at the end of Mission Beach. The mile-wide bay was like a lake enclosed between the jaws of two low fir-encrusted headlands. Deep inside, the spire of the old white-painted Catholic mission church marked the location of the tribal dock and its huddle of small gill-netters. The bay was glassy. No boats were moving, and neither, though I scanned the dock closely through binoculars, could I see any people.

The reservation economy had turned away from the sea to the six-lane highway, where the Tulalips ran a round-the-clock casino. Fishing and salmon-smoking had lost out to bingo, blackjack, poker, keno, and roulette. Tulalip Bay was largely unvisited by whites because the channel leading to the dock was a narrow, crooked pathway through submerged rocks and gluey shoals. Their beautiful but forbidding harbour ensured for the Indians a lonely privacy that would be the envy of any pretty seaside village, and they had conspicuously refrained from buoying the channel, to make themselves less accessible to strangers.

On the hill behind the church, I could pick out the red-and-black killer whale motif on the wall of the longhouse, the tribal court, the crescent of plain grey wooden bungalows. The 'res': half tax haven, half open prison. Even at this remove, one could catch its uneasy quiet – a listless, Sunday-afternoon air that lingered on the reservation all through the week. A pickup with a broken muffler went snarling along the coast road. A cat's-paw of wind, passing over the mirror-surface of the bay, made the inverted reservation shiver for a moment, then smash to bits.

One mild Saturday afternoon in January 1992, I was one of two white guests invited to Tulalip to watch a night of spirit dancing. After driving out to the reservation, I found there'd been a hitch in the arrangements. The dancing, which usually took place by firelight in the timber longhouse, had been shifted to the Teen Center, whose fierce strip-lighting would rob it, I was warned, of some of its atmosphere. 'You'll have to use your imagination,' said my hostess, a tribal elder. 'It won't be quite the same tonight.'

Visiting dancers from the Swinomish reservation, forty miles up the highway, were pulling up in rust-bucket pick-ups and pink-and-aqua-painted clunkers from the age of chrome and tail fins. With one tribe paying a courtesy call on another, the event was as much a potlatch as a dance. Tulalip women were cooking up a feast in the kitchen at the back of the Teen Center, while in the main body of the hall, piles of ritual gifts had been laid out for the Swinomish visitors.

In the nineteenth century, ceremonial cloaks were an important unit of currency between tribes. The most highly prized, made by the Tlingits of the Queen Charlotte Islands, were known as Chilkat blankets. Woven from cedar bark and the wool of mountain goats, with an elaborate chequerboard design of faces, eyes, fins, beaks, claws, and hands, they were worn by chieftains on formal occasions, and were a valuable part of the community treasure chest. 'Blankets' was a misnomer, but the English word, applied by early travellers, had stuck fast. So, in honour of the word rather than of the thing itself, nylon blankets, still in their Kmart cellophane, were stacked on the floor of the Teen Center.

An elder made a speech of welcome in Lushootseed, the local tribal language. Although no native speakers remained, a revival of the language was under way in evening classes, guided by anthropologists from the University of Washington. 'Anthros', as Indians called them, taught tribes how to build canoes in the old way, and to reconstruct such lost rituals as the First Salmon ceremony and the winter dances.

When everyone was seated in a wide semicircle around the floor, the dancing started with a sudden howl from a pear-shaped man in his thirties, wearing a burgundy-coloured windbreaker with TULALIP BINGO on the back. Eyes squinched shut, twitching and moaning, he writhed in his chair, possessed by a spirit, then stumbled blindly to his feet and began to chant his spirit song in a glossolalic tongue, neither English nor Lushootseed. His head, arms, and upper torso quaked violently as he gave vent to a long dirge of nonsense syllables.

The rhythm of his song was taken up by men with rattles and drums. The drums – deerskin stretched over octagonal fir hoops – gave off a dull *thump-thump-thump-thump-thump*. The rattles were sticks with eagles' heads carved on their tops, further decorated with deer's dewclaws bunched together like clusters of mussel shells. The drums thumped, the rattles clacked. The man with the spirit did his dance, circling the floor in a series of ponderous and clumsy jumps, encouraged by the audience's chant, 'Kiro-k! Kiro-k! Kiro-k! Kiro-k!' To my profane eye, the dancer looked like an obese frog with the jitters.

In 1794, at the head of Nootka Sound, George Vancouver watched a tribal dance mounted for him by Chief Maquinna: 'an exhibition, that consisted principally of jumping in a very peculiar manner'. In 1859 James G. Swan witnessed a similar dance by the Clallam Indians: 'a series of spasmodic jumps, displaying neither grace nor agility'. In 1887 the missionary Myron Eells wrote of the Skokomish version in Hood Canal: 'white people would not call it dancing, for it is simply a jumping up and down'. Two hundred and five years later, the dance still amounted to jumping, though it was now accompanied by frenzied trembling and a tuneless guttural warble.

Early observers of Indian winter dancing believed that they were seeing a secular entertainment. James Swan was impressed by the life-like impersonations of bears, wolves, and lizards, as masked dancers assumed the characters of wild creatures. But he saw no spirits.

Like 'blanket', the word 'spirit' is a dubious piece of trans-lation. Anthropological and folkloric literature is full of spirits. At puberty, the Northwest Indians, girls as well as boys, were said to go on 'spirit quests', capturing the spirits of natural powers like the whirlpool, the orca, the grizzly bear, the loon, and the wolf. One young man went on a spirit quest and came back with the spirit of a steam locomotive.

But according to Wayne Suttles, a veteran ethnologist of the Coastal Salish, and the most reliable authority on their language, 'There is no precise Native equivalent of "spirit".' He found little evidence to suggest that Indians had 'worshipped' any deities before white contact. In his broadly suggestive essay 'On the Cultural Track of the Sasquatch', Suttles argued that in Northwest Indian cosmology no distinct line, or bead curtain, separated 'natural' and 'supernatural' domains. A rare beast such as the two-headed flying serpent (*s'inetle-quy*) existed in the same temporal dimension as frequently seen animals like bears and whales. So 'spirit', with its connotation of the supernatural, was a Eurocentric dualistic imposition on a monist culture and language. Whatever the elusive quarry of a 'spirit quest', it certainly wasn't the incorporeal wraith of Western religious lore.

The strip-lit dancers in the Teen Center were clearly miming pos-session by post-Christian, Western-style spirits. Sometime between the 1850s and the 1990s, the assumption of animal consciousness had turned into a religious rite, the dancer going into an ecstatic trance and speaking in tongues.

During the 1880s, Shakerism – with its frenzied bodily communion with the Holy Spirit, amongst others – swept through the reservations of the Northwest, much to the consternation of old-guard Catholic, Methodist, and Presbyterian missionaries. By then the Indians spoke of 'the Great Spirit' as their one-god creator – a Victorian invention put about, with no evident basis in aboriginal beliefs, by the mission churches. Shaker worship, trance states, and holy shivers caught on. What I was seeing was a curious mixture of animist tribal custom, Shakerism, and Pentecostalism, all refurbished for service in the late twentieth century by white American anthros.

One after another, the dancers took turns to howl, shake, jump, and chant their spirit-songs, while the drums banged, the rattles clattered, and the audience shouted '*Kiro-k! Kiro-k!*' as if cheering on a basketball team. Feeling a pounding headache coming on, I sneaked a glance at my fellow guest, a producer from the local PBS station: her chin cupped in both hands, her eyes wide, her mouth framing a faint, reverent smile of approbation. I guessed that she was dreaming of some mini-series on Native American Spirituality.

The bluish, deconstructive glare of the strip-lights afforded no cover for my growing boredom. I ached for shadows; for the log fire burning in the hearth of the longhouse, where I might have decently kept my indifference to myself. I tried cupping my chin in both hands and affecting the TV producer's rapt gaze. *Thump! Moan. Thump! Moan. Aiyeeeeee! Kiro-k!* I twisted my wrist, trying to glimpse my watch. Only an hour and a half had passed – of a session that would likely last, I'd been promised, at least five hours.

At 8:30, the din quieted, and the feast was served: sliced turkey and cold mashed potatoes served up on paper plates, with cups of bright-red Kool-Aid. I'd imagined something more along the lines of smoked salmon and wild berries.

My hostess came to quiz me about what I'd seen.

'Very, *very* interesting,' I mumbled with my mouth full. 'Extremely.'

She explained that the spirit-songs came in two groups: 'black-paint', or 'saltwater', songs; and 'red paint', or 'freshwater', songs. Black-paint songs were rough, warlike, and frightening. Red-paint songs were gentle and healing. Rough ones, she said, outnumbered the gentle by a ratio of six or seven to one.

After ten minutes, the dancing started up again. Attuned now to what I ought to listen for, I concentrated on distinguishing between the red songs and the black – which gave me an idea. I had close to $100 in my wallet. When the dancing finally ceased, I would stop by the casino and try my luck at the roulette table. I had fond memories of late-night visits to casinos in Monte Carlo, Venice, and elsewhere; I enjoyed the intense, temporary society that forms around the wheel, under the presidency of the croupier, and to which a few dollars' worth of chips grants admission. Never placing a chip on an individual number, I bet on blocks. A couple of chips on *rouge* and another couple on *impair* was my fallback position; though it rarely showed a profit, it kept me in the game. I lost modestly or, once in a blue moon, made a killing – as in one memorable session, in the small hours, seated among whiskey-swilling sheikhs in the Cairo Hilton casino, when I somehow managed to parlay an initial stake of $20 into a grand haul of just short of $1,000. For the next two weeks I walked the streets of Cairo with a swollen billfold, feeling like a sheikh in my own right; though the sheikh sitting next to me at the table had looked on my enormous pile of chips with disdainful amusement.

Thinking of roulette put the dancing and the drums at a soothing distance. I heard the songs as spins of the wheel. *Noir. Noir. Noir. Rouge.* I bet on which colour would come next and lost surprisingly often, given the huge bias in favour of blacks against reds. I looked forward keenly to the casino, thinking I might find some revealing parallel between the grave folk ritual of roulette – the most stylized and ceremonial form of gaming – and the strange ritual now taking place in the Teen Center. Roulette addicts, each with his or her secret, superstitious numerology, certainly believed in the spirit of the wheel, and in the gifted player's ability to commune with it . . .

It was after 11:30 when the last dancer finally subsided into his chair. Getting up to leave, I was asked if I could give one of the dancers a ride home to Seattle. No roulette for me.

I was wary of my passenger. Only minutes before, I'd watched Ron shuddering and groaning as he came out of his spirit-trance. I needn't have worried. When I opened the door of the car for him, he slung his rattle and regalia in the back, climbed into the seat beside me, said, 'Good party, huh? Lot of fun,' and lit up a Marlboro.

As we drove away from the reservation, I wanted to put a question to Ron, but couldn't think quite how to phrase it. 'What's your spirit, Ron?' would be too breezy by far. 'Do you have just one spirit, or can you have several?' I was in the same plight as Mr Salter, the city editor in Waugh's *Scoop*, who sits in the train from London to Boot Magna, trying to hit on a suitably knowing question with which to address his unmet rural host. Mr Salter's best effort is 'How are your roots, Boot?'

Fearful of that example, I kept things on a level of careful sociological generality, while the glowing casino receded behind us and the rainswept highway dazzled. As shy of me as I was of him, Ron spoke of the importance of spirit dances to young men his age. Most of the dancers were out of jobs, like Ron himself. Most had had trouble in the past with alcohol or crack cocaine. The dances helped to repair their self-esteem by putting them in touch with 'olden-day traditions'.

'You get to explore your creativity,' Ron said. 'Like you find your own song, and make up your own dance. It's real creative.'

When I stopped the car outside his Queen Anne Hill apartment, Ron showed me his rattle. To sculpt its fierce eagle's head must have taken him days of patient penknife craftsmanship.

I drove the streets aimlessly for a while, in blessed quiet and solitude. Queen Anne had gone to bed; our neighbourhood raccoons had the place to themselves, and raised startled blood-orange eyes at this invasion of their territory. I felt sorry for my boredom with the evening. I shouldn't have accepted the invitation. Yet what I'd seen was revelatory, in its jumble of long-disused customs, ecstatic Christianity, careless translation, ethnic pride, anthropology, New Age mysticism, and Oprah Winfrey-style therapy. I had gone in the hope of finding a true fragment of the lost maritime culture of the Coastal

Indians. Fat chance. Cast a leadline now into the turbid water of the Salish tribal past, and it would never touch bottom.

Basic Mazecraft. When in a labyrinth, keep one hand on the wall. However tortuous your route, you will eventually find your way out.

This was Vancouver's technique of exploration. He was under orders from the Admiralty to finally ascertain that the fabled Northwest Passage between the Pacific and Atlantic oceans did not exist. It was a grim commission. No serious geographer still believed that a navigable route was to be found, but so long as ships from France, Spain, Russia, and the newly minted United States continued to nose around the Pacific coast in search of the apocryphal channel, Britain couldn't afford to stay out of the unicorn hunt.

George Vancouver was the ideal candidate for the job. Unlike Cook, he cut no corners, went strictly by the book, and carried out instructions to the letter. Sailing through the maze of islands and dead-end inlets, he kept his right hand firmly on the wall.

When he arrived in the Strait of Juan de Fuca, he named the land to starboard the 'Continental Shore'. From now on, the boats would hug the starboard coast, working their way meticulously around every bay and fjord to make sure that no gloomy, pine-hung avenue of water might conceivably lead eastwards through the mountains to the Great Lakes and the St Lawrence Seaway.

Captain Van gave Peter Puget command of *Discovery*'s launch and ordered him to explore a long southward-trending inlet. The boat was loaded with a week's provisions, firearms and ammunition, and a sack of trinkets. *Discovery* and *Chatham* had sailed from England with a bizarre cargo of knick-knacks and novelties. A full £10,000 – a dizzying sum, about £3m at 1990s rates – was allocated for the purchase of assorted tools, tin kettles, beads, bracelets, Scottish tartans, ladies' garters, feathers, buttons, sheets of copper, iron bars, calico, red baize, earrings, and fireworks. I wonder how many aggrieved taxpayers witnessed this spree through London shops, as the explorers haemorrhaged government funds on baubles for the Indians. (By comparison, Vancouver's own pay, as the expedition's commander, purser, and astronomer, was finally negotiated up from six shillings a day to eight shillings – about £40,000 a year in modern currency.)

On 20 May, in weak sunshine and with a gentle following wind, Puget sailed the launch south, down a mile-wide channel between the Continental Shore and a long cigar-shaped island. The holiday weather and easy sailing turned the labour of 'taking angles' into a pleasant distraction. Whenever a new landmark was sighted, Puget took a careful compass bearing on it, sailed a measured mile, and took its bearing again. The speed of the boat through the water was monitored every few minutes by trailing the chip-log and counting the knots pulled off the freewheeling drum as the log fell astern. With the launch travelling downwind at a steady four knots, a mile was covered every fifteen minutes. Each new bearing was transferred onto a page of the folio journal, which was pegged open on the thwart. A smudgy chart of the unfolding world, its cliffs, coves, promontories, river mouths, began to emerge from the growing cobweb of pencilled lines.

Every hour or so, Puget brought the launch up, head to wind, sail flapping, while the deep-sea lead was cast. 'Found no bottom,' he wrote in the small red-morocco-bound notebook in which he kept his rough diary. By now this was a monotonous refrain. In these waters, finding bottom at all was a rare surprise.

Meanwhile, everyone on board kept an anxious lookout for signs of movement on the shore. Loaded muskets were kept within easy reach. So far, the natives had been disconcertingly inscrutable, neither obviously friendly nor obviously hostile. They could be seen, at a safe distance, going about their ordinary business; fishing from canoes, drying salmon on wooden frames on the beach, apparently indifferent to the white intruders. But when a boat was steered toward them, they scuttled into the woods. The few Indians whom Puget had met at close quarters were 'low and ill made, with broad faces and small eyes', their black hair 'exceedingly dirty'. They wore rolls of copper in their perforated noses and ears, and the men's faces were painted with 'streaks of red ocher and black Glimmer'.

Down the eighteen-mile length of the passage, no Indians were spotted; a bad sign, Puget thought, sensing the presence of invisible watchers. He kept the launch in midstream, out of bow-and-arrow range, and raked the beach with his spyglass.

As the boat cleared the southern tip of the long island, the great white bulk of Mt Rainier came into view. The mountain kept on surprising the explorers with its unexpected appearances. Each time it showed itself, it appeared to have wandered many miles from its previous location; like a jack-in-the-box, it would pop up suddenly over the top of a wooded hill. Now it bore due south-east, and, for the first time since the mountain was sighted off Port Townshend, Puget was able to estimate its distance as between forty-five and fifty miles away.

A fast flood tide swept the launch southward toward a splinter of light between high cliffs. The mountain vanished behind a black wall of pines, and, as the passage narrowed, the water boiled around the boat in greasy swirls. The wind dropped. The launch pirouetted in a lazy circle on the turbulence, with Puget on the tiller, fighting to regain steerageway.

As soon as the boat was back under control, soundings were tried for – and found, for once, at thirty fathoms, though the water was so broken that it looked at most only a few feet deep. The launch was now passing over one of the shallow sills (at Tacoma Narrows) that generate the fertile submarine turmoil of Puget Sound.

The chute of disturbed water turned out to be like a door that opened, abruptly, on a sunlit panorama of low islands and serpentine channels. Steering for the shore to starboard, as per instructions, Puget saw two canoes floating close in by the beach. Two seated figures were in one canoe, four in the other. He ordered the sail of the launch to be scandalized and told his men to row slowly toward them. Immediately the Indians paddled hard away from shore, making for an opening in the islands to the south.

Puget stopped his launch. The Indians stopped their canoes. Fifty yards of water separated the two parties. From his coat pocket, Puget drew out a capacious white handkerchief and waved it at the Indians like a flag. They stared, but didn't bolt. *Smile!* Puget hissed at his crew, who dutifully grinned and waved maniacally. A tidal eddy drifted the launch closer to the canoes. The faces of two of the Indians were heavily pitted with what looked like smallpox. One had lost an eye. Noticing a small green branch from a fir tree floating alongside, Puget reached for it and then waved it from side to side in slow, pacific strokes. The Indians hastily paddled a few yards farther off, then waited to see what would come next.

It's a seduction scene. Puget is trying to fascinate the Indians as he might fascinate a girl. Sex is very close to the surface in these colonial encounters, with the Indians being thought of as irrational, impulsive, fickle, *feminine*. So Puget now tried to court them with pretty things that might please an eighteenth-century girl's eye.

The sack of baubles was close to hand. Puget found two looking-glasses, a dozen polished copper medals, a bracelet, and a silver spoon. A floating log provided a convenient showcase, and Puget piled his selection of bibelots on the two mirrors, which he tied to the log with twine. Then, hatless, sweetly smiling, his shoulders hunched forward in a gesture of submissive candour, he backed the launch away until the log was equidistant from the Indians and Englishmen. As the log swung around on the current, the heap of treasures flashed and glittered in the sun.

It worked. The Indians paddled cautiously forward, quickly removed the gifts, and paddled quickly back to their original position.

Now the launch was rowed back to the log. A peacock feather, a card of pearl buttons, a string of coloured beads, a tin kettle, and a metal brooch were laid out as bait, and again the launch backed off. As before, the Indians came forward to pick up their booty, then retreated, despite Puget's warmest efforts to persuade them to cuddle up alongside the launch.

After the third pass in this floating tango, the Indians came close enough to the launch to receive their fourth instalment of gifts hand to hand over the water; but they wouldn't meet Puget's eye, and their faces were knotted in swarthy scowls. Far from being bedazzled victims of the lieutenant's boyish charm, they had the manner of heavies dunning cash from a persistent debtor. They pointed at the sack of presents and demanded more, shouting at the Englishmen in a language of popping glottal stops.

As often happens with disappointed suitors, Puget's mood of tender expectancy curdled quickly into bored distaste. He couldn't wait to get away from the importunate savages with their bad skin and filthy hair.

Later, when the tents were set up on shore, and an armed guard posted, Puget wrote up the incident by candlelight:

> *Nor could all the signs emblematical of Friendship, such as a white Handkerchief – a Green Bough & many other Methods induce them to venture near us. . . . However I did not like to quit those Indians altogether without giving them some evident Proof that our Intention was perfectly friendly & an Expedient was hit on that soon answered our Purpose. . . . By the subsequent circumstances I am of Opinion that they had the Ingratitude to impute our Friendship to a fear of their Power. . . .*

The sea in Saratoga Passage frosted over, as the forecast wind began to fill in from the south. The wrinkled skin of the water became ridged with breaking wavelets; in less than half an hour the waves were steep, regular, well formed, hard-driven by the building wind. With the headsail out to starboard, the boat skidded through the sea – the winched sheet bar-taut, the sail moulded into a white parabola as rigid as one of Frank Gehry's curved concrete walls. The wind keened in the steel rigging. At my back, I could hear the forward rush of each new wave, then its sudden, violent collapse in a crackling bonfire of foam. Hauling on the wheel, driving the boat downwind as it tried to slew broadside-on, I was on a jittery high. I hadn't had such sailing in many months. The three-step waltzing motion of the boat, the throbbing, strings-and-percussion sound of wind and water on the move, came back to me as an old, deep pleasure. But a pleasure tinged, as always, with an edge of incipient panic.

At thirty-five feet, the boat was as small as I could comfortably live in, as large as I dared handle on my own. The stronger the wind, the bigger it seemed. Like a novice rider gripping the reins of a runaway mare in heat (not a fancy simile; I fell off – very painfully – when she took a flying leap over the first of three hedges that separated her from the stallion), I stood, legs braced, at the wheel, nursing first the bedroom, then the bathroom, then the kitchen, lounge, and study down the long reach of growling sea.

A new sound entered the orchestra: the explosive *chuff!* of a Dall's porpoise surfacing alongside the boat. *Chuff! Chuff! Chuff!* Six black-and-white torpedoes, in close formation, went scissoring under the bow, came up to exhale, then shot astern, where they wheeled around in unison before launching another mock attack. Bantamweight, pure muscle, they whizzed past on the beam, just a few inches below the surface, in a show-off wriggle of exultant flesh.

The company of dolphins was a daily event in these waters – another by-product of turbulence and plankton. The animals would show up in a troupe, use the boat for five minutes' worth of target practice, tire rapidly of the exercise, and swim off in search of alternative amusement. It was like being temporarily adopted by a teenage street gang.

They appeared to bask in human attention. One could often prolong their stay by going up front, leaning over the rail, and showing an exaggerated interest in their under-the-bow manoeuvres. Unable now to leave the wheel, with the boat trying to imitate the writhing motion of a demented snake, I remembered a tip picked up from a Key West charter captain who claimed he could always drum up dolphins for his customers' entertainment by going below and doing a hornpipe, heel and toe, on the cabin sole. So I loudly stamped out on the teak grating of the cockpit floor the only rhythm I could think of: the silly drumroll that goes 'Pom tiddley-om pom – *pom! pom!*' or, as Julia had learned to chant it in preschool, 'Shave and a haircut – *two bits!*' I would have done better to make some subtler sign emblematical of friendship, such as waving a white handkerchief or a green bough, for the porpoises immediately fled. Not for the first time, I'd spoiled a relationship with my leaden-footed dancing.

To steer a straight course was impossible. Overpressed, and unbalanced by its single sail, the boat corkscrewed downwind at 7.6 knots, held to that speed by the braking force of its own bow wave, which peeled away from the hull in a long, curling moustache of surf. The mizzen-mast behind me shuddered with the strain taken by the rigging, and I was frightened that something up there was about to break. If one thing broke, so would a whole lot of things, in extremely rapid and disconcerting succession. It was a relief to gain the shelter of Strawberry Head on the Whidbey Island side, where the wind was reduced to muffled gusts and skirls, and I took in a half-dozen rolls of sail and let the boat saunter, gently, through a seascape so changed that it belonged to another nation.

The buoyed channel had shrunk in depth from around three hundred feet to barely thirty, and narrowed to a winding trail that hugged the island shore. To the east, the tide thinly covered several miles of mud flats, where the water was a streaky violet, the colour of a ripe bruise. Beyond, the Continental Shore showed as a level apron of low-lying land whose churches were taller than its trees.

As Vancouver had imagined a reborn Tory England rising on the foothills of the Olympic Peninsula, so Dutch immigrants had happened on the delta of the Skagit River and seen it as the new Holland of the Far West. Quite improbably, their vision had been realized with something close to total success. There were Dutch names on the mailboxes; Dutch barns in the fields; gloomy Dutch churches; Dutch poplars fringing long straight Dutch country roads. The flat fields were fenced and ditched in the severely rectangular Dutch style, and in the fields the descendants of the original immigrants grew tulips for the cut-flower trade. Seen from a plane in spring, on the Seattle–Vancouver shuttle, the whole valley looked like a gigantic Mondrian of coloured squares, black-bordered with dykes. Seen from any angle, the place was a startling *trompe l'œil*, a measure of the power of strict Dutch Calvinism to replicate itself in a strange land.

From the water, it looked uncannily like the north side of the

Scheldt estuary between Flushing and Dordrecht – Beveland and Overflakkee – where I'd sailed ten years before. It was lacking only a Dutch barge, with a house and garden at its back end, a family of bicycles stacked against the wheelhouse, and a Volkswagen parked on the afterdeck.

The great difference was that in Europe the Dutch had ingeniously stolen their land from the sea. Here they'd stolen it from the Skagit Indians. Immediately to the north of the rich floodplain stood the dark, loaf-shaped hill of the Swinomish reservation – really an island that the sea had failed to surround. The tulip growers had gotten miles of moist brown soil, whereas the Skagits' end of the bargain consisted of crags of grey rock, fir trees, salal, food-stamps, rehab clinics, and, from the tangled summit of their almost-island, a panoramic view of the wonders of Dutch horticulture.

Lieutenant Whidbey, who sailed this way in *Discovery*'s cutter, noted with excitement that the ebb tide ran north out of Skagit Bay. He'd thought he was following yet another dead end to its muddy conclusion, but the north-going ebb promised an alternative exit from the labyrinth. He followed the drift of the tide, expecting to find a passage through which the two parent ships could sail back into the open sea.

The ebb was running, for me as for him. Toward its northern end, the broad bight of ruffled water was studded with islets – irregular chunks of rock, each one just big enough to support a blackberry bush, a peeling madrona, a stunted pine. Cormorants, who used the rock as fishing platforms, had whitened almost every inch of bare stone with their droppings. The tide ran hard between these islets, and I sailed past their miniature cliffs with nine knots showing on the GPS.

To port, Whidbey Island ended in a low, gnarled finger of rock that jutted out into the stream. As the boat rounded the point, Lieutenant Whidbey's anticipated passage slid around the corner into view. He must have found it difficult to believe his eyes.

The tide poured westward down a funnel-shaped corridor, steep wooded bluffs rising on either side. At the far end, a little over a mile off, a hairline crack showed between the bluffs like a white thread in a bolt of dark cloth. At least fifty square miles of sea were somehow draining through a slot that looked hardly wide enough to squeeze a rowboat between its rocky jaws.

I turned back from the gathering surge of disturbed water and circled the approach, waiting for the ebb to weaken. Whidbey, already late for his rendezvous with Vancouver, went ahead in the cutter to take a closer look at his unwelcome discovery. He reported back that he had been duped by the tide: the passage was shallow, fouled with large boulders, turbulent in the extreme, navigable only by the smallest boats, and then only at slack water. Captain Van named the place Deception Pass.

I spent much of the 1970s trying not to buy a lava lamp – coloured chaos in a bottle. A prisoner of my insecure good taste, I feared the snobbish derision of friends if one were suddenly to appear in my sitting room. The lamps became fixtures in English pubs, and I consoled myself by perching on a bar stool and furtively communing with those iridescent, endlessly mutating lemon-yellow, green, and puce globules as they rolled tumescently behind glass. 'Obscene' was the usual adjective, but I found them beautiful; an addiction I kept under my hat.

Deception Pass was like a lava lamp on a heroic scale. As the tide entered the funnel, it felt the tightening constraint of the land; the bottom shallowed, and house-sized boulders tripped the water up and made it tumble. With far too much sea trying to escape through far too small an aperture, liquid panic broke out in the pass. The obstructed tide welled up vertically in mushroom-topped boils a dozen yards across or span impotently around in great saucer-shaped eddies. The surface of the water was pitted with small travelling whirlpools. Everything was on the move on its own eccentric curvilinear track. Keeping even a small patch of water in focus for more than a few seconds was like trying to hold in the mind's eye the sum of movements made by couples doing the quickstep in a crowded, old-fashioned ballroom, as they dodged, twisted, swerved, twirled, and went spinning off at tangents to each other.

The tide table reduced this spectacular confusion to a dry set of numbers. Maximum ebb was at 1437. Speed 7.4 knots. Direction 270° T. That *T*, for *true* (270° measured by true, not magnetic, north), was a blithe fiction. The tidal predictions applied to some theoretical net transport of water through the pass. But inside the funnel, where water jostled violently against water to gain the freedom of open sea, the theory came hopelessly unstuck. The actual flow was in every conceivable direction at every conceivable speed. Where the edge of a boil met the edge of a strong eddy, the tide might easily be going due east at fourteen or fifteen knots.

Better than the tide tables was a sentence I had culled from the 1930s WPA guide to Washington State:

> *The narrow, high-walled gorge of DECEPTION PASS spills 2,500,000,000 gallons of water hourly at ebb tide into Rosario Strait.*

I liked the suggestion of armies of men with buckets but had no idea where the writer had found his modest string of noughts. One might usefully tack on another three or four, to make the essential point: anyone who tries to enumerate exactly what goes on in Deception Pass when the tide is running should make a prior booking for a long stay at a comfortably appointed madhouse.

In the dwindling afternoon light, the water looked as black and thick as tar, its surface lumpy with boils and cratered with eddies. At ten past five, with fifty-five minutes to go before slack water, I fed the boat gingerly into the stream, running the engine at full blast to give it maximum steerageway through the turbulence. It was like driving a car on ice. Each time the boat's head met a swirl, it went into a sideways skid, and I had to spin the wheel violently to maintain any semblance of control. At this stage of the tide, the net current should have been running at little more than 2.5 knots, but this diminished flow made little impact on the mass of tumbling water in the funnel, as it piled up behind the narrows in its rage to escape. Too busy steering to keep my eye on the GPS, I could only snatch glances to check the boat's speed over the ground. It was 0.0 one moment, 13.5 the next.

A Gothic bridge spanned the bluffs ahead – a very short bridge, as I now could see. The water it soared over might have made a respectable trout stream, but as an arm of the sea it was grossly deficient. Seeing its steep downhill slope, I realized the chaos of waters was a product of simple gravity. The level of the sea in Skagit Bay was two or three feet higher than the level of the sea in Rosario Strait: a multibillion-gallon turmoil was provoked by a slight inequity of height.

A log the length of the boat was twirling slowly around on the starboard bow. I hauled the wheel to port and passed backward under the bridge – a pity, since there were half a dozen pale faces up there, and I was sorry to find myself suddenly turned into a happy spectacle of nautical incompetence. I got the boat facing the right way, yawed on a boil, slewed on an eddy, and slammed into a line of low, breaking overfalls. Somewhere, as I came out of the pass like a cork expelled from the neck of a champagne bottle, I found room in my head for the thought that I would not at all like to be doing this in a motorless cedar canoe.

The European explorers had a low opinion of Deception Pass, but it was an important locus in Salish culture: as a famous navigational hazard, a setting for stories, and a source of arcane knowledge. All these aspects conjoined in a single story, first collected by Franz Boas at the turn of the century, that crops up in several versions.

A young woman (in one version she is given a name, Kokwalalwoot) was gathering clams on the beach, or she was on a quest for a *sklakletut* (a 'spirit', in its suspect English translation). The usual method of gaining intimacy with the powers of the sea was to go diving for them, and diving into whirlpools was a widely recommended way of getting a *sklakletut*. My hostess at Tulalip told me that her auntie obtained a 'whirlpool spirit' in this manner. After ritual fasting and bathing, the adolescent boy or girl would go out alone into the woods or on the water, and, like a college graduate, return to the village in possession of a *sklakletut* – a useful qualification, and a mark of adulthood. So Kokwalalwoot was pursuing her study of whirlpools in the accredited Salish fashion.

In Deception Pass, one vigorous whirlpool manifested itself to her as a lithe young man, and Kokwalalwoot fell in love with him. She left the beach and went to live underwater with her whirlpool-lover. When she went back to announce her marriage, the villagers quailed at the sight of her – skin encrusted with barnacles, kelp growing from her eye-sockets, ears, and mouth. Her family and friends condemned this grotesque sea-being to submarine life in the pass, where she became an established navigation aid, guiding canoeists to safety through the rips and eddies. In one version, the scrolls and curlicues of current are the waving tresses of Kokwalalwoot's hair – though for me this detail has the ring of a white folklorist's embellishment.

All Indian stories are bedevilled by the fact that they generally have been lumped together indiscriminately and labelled 'myths'. Some are clearly meant as fiction – light entertainment with human and animal characters. Some were meant for adult audiences, others for children. (It's always interesting to note the gender of the original teller; many women's stories have a distinct flavour of *Clifford the Big Red Dog* about them.) There are creation stories, tribal histories, allegories, gossipy anecdotes. To label all these as 'myths' is to impute to the Indians a degree of naive credulity that makes them seem quite unnecessarily remote.

I'd prefer to read the story of Kokwalalwoot as a cautionary tale, not far removed in tone from Hilaire Belloc's 'Matilda, Who Told Lies, and Burned to Death'. It is about dangerous intercourse – a favourite subject in a society obsessed with the fine-print rules of kinship and status. Doing it with a whirlpool is like doing it with a wild beast, or doing it with a member of a tribe so alien to your own that it is beyond the reach of lawful exogamy. It is also a story about the dangers of education, especially for girls. To show an interest in whirlpools (or any other branch of physics) is all very well, but when it turns into a passion, dreadful things happen to the schoolgirl. Bluestockings threaten the social fabric. Kokwalalwoot, beautiful at the beginning, ends up by looking, literally, a fright. Be warned.

Like many other stories from up and down the Inside Passage, this one spells out the importance of whirlpools as great powers of the sea. Power was always associated with motion (which was why a man could go on a quest for the 'spirit' of a steam locomotive). Of all the turbulent movements of water, the sucking, spinning, vagrant whirlpool, like a disembodied hungry mouth on the lookout for a meal, comes closest to having a human shape and personality. At the top of the ebb in Deception Pass, a string of big whirlpools formed just above the bridge; they could ingest a twenty-foot log and spit it out again, and easily swamp a mismanaged canoe. As one of these great suckers veered out crabwise across the stream toward you, you'd readily credit it with volition, malignity, desire. As Catherine Earnshaw could fall in love with Heathcliff (himself another version of chaos in nature), Kokwalalwoot could fall in love with her whirlpool and, like Catherine, be destroyed by him.

In twilight I let go the anchor in Cornet Bay, just around the corner from Deception Pass; a scoop-shaped hollow in the bluffs, it was protected by a jagged reef that blocked most of the entrance. A heavy sea was running in Juan de Fuca Strait, and a good deal of slop was finding its way past the reef and into the bay. The saloon filled with noises. The anchor chain grumbled as it shifted, link by link, on the hard-sand bottom. The contents of the lockers rattled. Each incoming wave broke against the hull with, first, a muffled thump, then a long sibilance, like a sack of spilling rice. A loose halyard whanged against the mast. The lamps tipped in their gimbals, sending beams of light racing from ceiling to floor.

Out of practice at living on the boat, I had forgotten its enormous complaining repertoire of creaks and groans, its capacity to make even a placid anchorage feel like a continuous small earthquake, up in the high fours on the Richter scale. This isn't to disparage it. Being afloat gives me, at least, a heightened sense of being alive moment to moment. As small earthquakes do, it keeps you properly aware of your precariousness in the world.

I cooked up a forlorn bachelor's supper of dried linguine and Paul Newman's marinara sauce, and uncorked a bottle of wine from the cellar in the bilges. Never before seriously homesick on my travels, I now was afflicted by pangs of anxious disconnection from the house on Queen Anne Hill. I badly wanted to talk to my daughter.

I called the marine operator on channel 28, but my radio signal bounced off the high cliffs of the cove and went nowhere. My only answer was a throaty purr of static.

As much for my own consolation as for Julia's eventual entertainment, I slotted a fresh microcassette into the tape recorder and told it a bedtime story – a revisionist version of the tale of Kokwalalwoot ('Kokwalalwoot. Kokwalal-what? Nobody could say her name. They called her Koko for short . . .'), the girl who loved water.

III. SAILING INTO THE SUBLIME

The early morning was paint-white veined with streaky pink, like the inside of a mussel shell. Rosario Strait was ribbed with swell left over from the previous day's gale in Juan de Fuca, and the boat rolled badly in the airless calm as I made the crossing to the San Juan Islands. Downstairs, all the loose bits of my life were on the move: books spilling from their shelves, a stack of dinner plates slithering back and forth inside a locker, the drumbeat slamming of an unfastened wardrobe door. It sounded as if a poorly executed robbery were going on down there.

Feet planted wide apart, I leaned into the chart table in the shelter of the doghouse and tried to plot my courses for the day. Persuading the parallel rule to do its crabwise march from the pencilled course-line over to the nearest compass rose required some patience and cunning under these conditions, and being able to inscribe the number 283 beside the course was a small triumph. I measured off the miles with a pair of heavy brass antique-shop dividers (one minute of latitude is a nautical mile). I factored in the distortions that would be caused by tidal current, for the sea on which a vessel rides is always itself in motion; it's like trying to walk in a straight line from A to B across a giant travelator.

None of this was really necessary. My labours were mocked by the push-button, digital face of the GPS mounted above the chart, its stubby black antenna summoning a continuous stream of signals from the heavens. The GPS knew exactly where the boat was at any given moment, could lay a course to any point on the globe, altering it as necessary for the vagrancies of tide and leeway, could reel off the distance travelled, the distance still to come, and the estimated time of arrival to the nearest minute. The affectless GPS – whose brand and model, a Garmin 45, made it sound like a handgun – was the midget omniscient narrator of my voyage.

Yet I went on ruling lines with a freshly sharpened HB pencil. On one particularly nasty roll, the dividers leaped from the chart table and came within an inch of impaling my foot. The 'hockey-puck' hand-bearing compass, worn round my neck, thunked me in the chest at metrically regular intervals. The pencil point broke twice. Doing navigation the old way in a running sea was no fun, and carried a distinct risk of painful bodily injury.

I did it because the activity had a magical importance for me. It was a way of warding off bad things, from wind squalls to blocks in the fuel line. I had a deep, unshakeable superstition that failure to honour the sea with this daily morning ritual would cause the sea to rise up and drown me. Using the old-fashioned instruments, hefting brass and boxwood in my hands, gave me courage and reassurance. I felt like a craftsman working at a real trade. Proud of my clumsy skills at the chart table, I considered them my entitlement to be at sea; and if I lost them, surely I would come to a bad end.

Every half-hour, on the dot, I took bearings on three widely spaced landmarks and transferred them to the chart, where they converged in a triangle known as a 'cocked hat'. In theory, the position of the boat had to be somewhere inside the cocked hat, which usually covered about a quarter of a square mile of sea.

Then I'd look to the Garmin 45, whose latitude and longitude readings were spelled out to the second decimal place of a minute, putting the boat about sixty feet of where it truly was. This made my efforts with magnetized needle and parallel rule look so approximate, so hit-or-miss, as to seem worthless. As omniscient narrators tend to, the Garmin rendered the hero of the story as a foolish, purblind creature, unaware of the surprise in store for him at the next twist of the plot.

Once upon a time, people made their way across the sea by reading the surface, shapes, and colours of the water. On clear nights, they took their directions from the stars; by day, they sailed by the wind and waves. In the Homeric world there were four reigning winds: Boreas blew from the north, Notus from the south, Eurus from the east, Zephyrus from the west.

Wind made itself most useful for navigational purposes by generating swells. Whatever the fickle gusts of the moment, the prevailing seasonal wind was registered in the stubborn movement of the sea. Swell continues for many days, and sometimes thousands of miles, after the wind that first raised it has blown itself out. Islands, because they deflect the direction of swell, can be 'felt' from a great distance by a sensitive pilot. As the depth of the sea decreases, the swell steepens, warning of imminent landfall.

Sailing by swell entailed an intense concentration on the character of the sea itself. Wave shape was everything. A single wave is likely to be moulded by several forces: the local wind; a dominant, underlying swell; and, often, a weaker swell coming from a third direction. Early navigators had to be in communion with every lift of the bow as the sea swept under the hull in order to sense each component in the wave and deduce from them the existence of unseen masses of land.

David Lewis, a New Zealand born doctor who gave up his London practice to become a freelance ocean adventurer, sailed in the 1960s with some of the last traditional Polynesian navigators in their outrigger canoes. *We, the Navigators* is his firsthand report, from the Pacific Ocean in the mid-twentieth century, on how sailors like Odysseus crossed the Mediterranean circa 700 BC, before the invention of the magnetic compass. Most importantly, Lewis's book conveys how the open sea could be as intimately known and as friendly to human habitation as a familiar stretch of land to those seamen who lived on its surface, as gulls do, wave by wave.

Sea*men*. For the testicles were, Lewis wrote, the instruments best attuned to picking up slight variations in the rhythm of a swell – a sudden steepening, an interlocking of two opposed wave-trains. Rest your balls lightly on the top of the stempost and feel the jaunting upsurge of the bow, then its sudden, precipitous collapse into the trough . . . As a four-year-old, I keenly anticipated the approach to humpback bridges in my mother's lightly sprung 1938 Ford. Taken a mile or so too fast, each bridge induced a moment of exquisite, unmentionable pleasure; it was like finding a small but energetic tree frog trapped inside one's scrotum. Had I been blindfolded on these car rides in 1946, I believe I could have identified half the humpback bridges in Norfolk by my genitals alone.

So did Lewis's Polynesian friends feel their way across the hump-backed ocean. On these voyages, Lewis – a vastly experienced small-boat sailor – often found himself totally disoriented, as the wind changed direction, the sea got up, and the underlying swells became confused or imperceptible. Yet his guides could sense a regular grain in the roughest, most disorderly sea. Time and again they'd sail through fifty or more miles of murky overcast, without sight of the sun, and make a perfect landfall at – in one instance – a narrow passage between islands, breaking into sudden visibility less than two miles off.

Sailing with no instruments, the primitive navigator knew his local sea in the same unselfconscious way that a farmer knows his fields. The stars supplied a grand chart of paths across the known ocean, but there was often little need of these since the water itself was as legible as acreage farmed for generations. Colour, wind, the flight of birds, and telltale variations of swell gave the sea direction, shape, character.

Here, where you feel the intersection of two swells, each deflected by islands far over the horizon, you make your turn . . . Now you search for *toake*, the tropic bird, and follow its homeward flight until the sea begins to brown with sand . . . In *Polynesian Seafaring and*

Navigation Richard Feinberg, an anthropologist, includes a sequence of interviews with navigators from the island of Anuta in the Solomon Islands. One of these, Pu Maevatau, says of sailing under a cloudy sky that 'the expert navigator . . . will make his bearer the ocean'.

That sense of being borne along to your destination by the ocean itself is strong in Homer, whose voyagers are seen as creatures of nature assisted, or impeded, by the gods. When the gods are with you, the winds and the sea conduct you onward, like thistledown blown from wave to wave. For Odysseus, as for the Polynesian navigators in the books of Lewis and Feinberg, the ocean is a place, not a space; its mobile surface full of portents, clues, and meanings. It is as substantial and particular, as crowded with topographical features, as, say, Oxfordshire.

The arrival of the magnetic compass caused a fundamental rift in the relationship between man and sea. Europeans were sailing with compasses in the eleventh century, and may have used them even earlier. Once the compass became established on the quarterdeck, snug in its wooden binnacle, the whole focus of the helmsman shifted, from the sea itself to an instrument eighteen inches or so under his nose. Suddenly he no longer needed to intuit the meaning of the waves; he had become a functionary, whose job was to keep the ship at an unvarying angle to the magnetized pointer with its scrolled N. First he steered by letters, E by S, W by N; later, by numbers assigned him by the officer of the watch. Holding the bow to the sea at a steady 195, the helmsman was performing a task that eventually would be done more efficiently by a machine.

Such a simple invention, or discovery, the compass. One wet Saturday afternoon, I made one for Julia: we rubbed the eye of a sewing needle against a magnet on the fridge door; slipped the needle into a sawn-off drinking straw to make it float; and launched it in a water-filled salad bowl. Breasting the resistance of the surface tension, the needle obediently swung slowly around to align itself with the earth's magnetic field, pointing 21½° east of true north. With the sofa to the south, TV to the north, bookshelves to the east, and dining table to the west, I set Julia to walking the room on a succession of compass courses. Preschool Navigation: Lesson One.

Possibly we were merely replicating, by mechanical means, a piece of equipment that we both already possessed somewhere in our bodies. A recent study conducted at the University of Auckland in New Zealand shows that rainbow trout have built-in sensors composed of magnetite cells, with nerves connecting the sensors to their brains. With a Pavlovian regime of rewards and punishments, the experimenters were able to persuade the fish to swim on any given compass course; for the food pellet, take 195. When last heard of (on the BBC World Service), the scientists were busy dissecting migratory birds, hoping to isolate similar magnetic sensors, and speculating that humans, too, might be born with such navigational devices, at least in vestigial form. If so, the classic description of Columbus, as a man implanted with a compass rose inside his head, will turn out to be a statement of literal fact.

But the external compass – the magic gizmo in a box – put man at a remove from his surroundings. A compass course is a hypothesis. It has length, but no width. It can't be seen or felt (though once, perhaps, we could feel it, as the rainbow trout appears to). It cannot even be steered. The autopilot on my boat leaves a cleaner, straighter wake than I can manage, yet it keeps 'on course' – as I do – only by making continuous mistakes. Each time the vessel falls sufficiently away from its heading for the autopilot to notice the error, the machine administers a corrective turn of the wheel which points the bow to the far side of the notional course. The wheel, attached to the autopilot's motor by a strop, spins now to port, now to starboard, now to port again, making a monotonous *hee-haw, hee-haw* sound, like an ailing donkey. The real track of the boat through the sea is a weaving zigzag path whose innumerable deviations define the idealized pencil line of the course as it appears on the chart. Steering a compass course, by machine or hand, it is by indirection that one finds direction out.

So the helmsman looked away from the sea, wedding himself instead to a geometrical abstraction that had no tangible reality in nature. Possession of a compass soon rendered obsolete a great body of inherited, instinctual knowledge, and rendered the sea itself – in fair weather, at least – as a void, an empty space to be traversed by a numbered rhumb line.

Too little has been made of this critical moment in the history of navigation. Because the compass has been with us for a thousand years, we've lost sight of the mental revolution it caused. The figure of the helmsman, his eyes glued to the tilting card in its bowl, turning the spokes of the wheel to keep the assigned number on target against the lubberline, is an early avatar of modern man. The compass has turned him into a steering machine. He is the direct ancestor of Thomas MacWhirr, the dim, unimaginative son of an Ulster grocer who captains Nan-Shan in Conrad's *Typhoon*.

Bound for Fu-Chou, on a north-easterly course through the South China Sea, MacWhirr (whose name gives the game away) drives his ship straight through the eye of a hurricane. He has a timetable to meet, and a steam engine with which to meet it; and so he refuses to budge from the course of 040 that leads across the chart to the approaches to Fu-Chou. To MacWhirr, the compass course has become a blind imperative; he cannot deviate from it for a spot of what he calls 'dirty weather'. Jukes, the chief mate, urges him to turn the ship's head to the east, to meet the huge cross-swell that is the first sign of the coming typhoon.

> 'Head to the eastward?' [MacWhirr] said, struggling to sit up. 'That's more than four points off her course.'
>
> 'Yes, sir. Fifty degrees . . . Would just bring her head far enough round to meet this . . . '
>
> Captain MacWhirr was now sitting up. He had not dropped the book, and he had not lost his place.
>
> 'To the eastward?' he repeated, with dawning astonishment. 'To the . . . Where do you think we are bound to? You want me to haul a full-powered steamship four points off her course to make the Chinamen comfortable! Now, I've heard more than enough of mad things done in the world – but this . . . If I didn't know you, Jukes, I would think you were in liquor.'

MacWhirr is Conrad's archetype of the modern technological mariner, blithely, ignorantly divorced from nature. His sea is a placid vacancy, its terrors conquered by the compass and the engine. *Nan-Shan*, built of iron at a great industrial shipyard on the Clyde, crosses the globe in inflexible straight lines, reducing the ocean to a neutral medium for the commercial enterprises of men as literal-minded and mechanical as MacWhirr himself. The whirling cyclone that Conrad brews up to engulf the stupid captain and his crew is the ocean's revenge for the hubris of the steam turbine and the ruled line on the chart.

Aboard *Discovery* and *Chatham* were the latest Admiralty-approved compasses, quadrants, chronometers, artificial horizons (trays filled with mercury to catch the reflections of sun, moon, and stars), peloruses, engraved horn protractors, dividers, rulers – all the instruments necessary for reducing the globe to a two-dimensional mesh of intersecting lines. White invaders from the Age of Reason burst into an Indian world of primitive, animist, sensory navigation. Naval ships and cedar canoes, though afloat in the same water, were sailing on two different seas. Whites and Indians inhabited parallel universes, and the behaviour of each was a source of mystified anxiety to the other.

From the quarterdeck, as from the launch and cutter, movements of canoes were closely watched and logged, though no one could figure what they were up to. 'Canoes passing and repassing,' noted Captain Van, when *Discovery* lay at anchor not far from a big Indian village. The native craft were as inscrutable as water beetles in their multitudinous comings and goings. Full of obscure purpose, they paddled out to an arbitrary point in midstream, stopped for half an hour, then paddled off at another angle. They darted and scuttled, continually changing course for no apparent reason. Their insect-like motion, observed through the officers' spyglasses, gave rise to many alarms: the Indians were preparing to attack; they were just being curious; they were fishing; they were visiting their neighbours;

they were on some kind of aquatic picnic; they were mounting an ambush.

Many sleepless nights befell the surveying expeditions in the small boats. Armed guards were posted around the tents to keep watch for canoes in the dark, and rarely did an hour pass without the muffled splash of paddles, low voices, stealthy silhouettes. Peter Puget spent half his time trying to seduce the canoeists into friendship, the other half trying to frighten them away. Often, scaring the Indians off wasn't easy. One evening, camped on the shore of what is now Carr Inlet in Puget Sound, Puget was troubled by the presence of two canoes lying motionless in the water a hundred yards from the beach.

> *They still kept hovering about the Boats & being apprehensive they would be endeavouring to commit Depredations during the Night, I . . . ordered a Musquett to be fired, but so far was it from intimidating or alarming them, that they remained stationary, only exclaiming Pop at every report in way of Derision.*

Many years later, when white settlers and missionaries began to travel aboard Indian canoes as passengers, they were baffled and irritated by the strange, slow, halting progress of even the simplest voyage. The natives apparently had no idea of how to get from A to B without making detours to L, P, and Y along the way. The whites, who conceived of the sea as an empty space, expected their canoe to go in a straight line, a compass course, from departure point to destination, and could not fathom why Indian pilots should insist on frittering away precious time in a succession of stops, starts, and unnecessary diversions. A lot of ink was expended by settlers on the theme of Indian laziness and superstition – for why else should a passage of a few miles, in sheltered waters, be habitually protracted into a whole day of intermittent paddling, talking, and unscheduled visits ashore?

The Bostonian James Swan built a cabin on Shoalwater (now Willapa) Bay in 1852. Bluff and easygoing, he greatly admired the seamanship and boat-building skills of the Quinault Indians with whom he settled, and from whom he bought a dugout canoe forty-six feet long and six feet wide. 'These canoes are beautiful specimens of naval architecture,' wrote Swan. 'Formed of a single log of cedar, they present a model of which a white mechanic might well be proud.' Yet even the tolerant Swan grew impatient with the stop-go style of Indian navigation. He described a typical day aboard a canoe:

> When in the canoe, all hands will paddle vehemently, and one would suppose the journey would be speedily accomplished, the canoe seeming almost to fly. This speed will be kept up for a hundred rods, when they cease paddling, and all begin talking. Perhaps one has spied something, which he has to describe while the rest listen; or another thinks of some funny anecdote or occurrence that has transpired among the Indians they have been visiting, that has to be related; or they are passing some remarkable tree, or cliff, or stone, which has a legend attached to it, and which the old folks never can pass without relating to the young, who all give the most respectful attention. When the tale is over, the steersman gives the word 'Que-nuk, que-nuk, whid-tuck' (now, now, hurry), when all again paddle with a desperate energy for a few minutes, and then the same scene is again enacted.

There were innumerable deviations from the course:

> I noticed that the Indians were all heading in towards the beach instead of proceeding at once to Gray's Harbor. I asked the Indians why we were going ashore, and received for reply the invariable 'Klo-nas,' or 'I don't know'; a term which is fully as expressive and as often used as the Mexican Quien sabe.

Swan resigned himself to the fact that 'hurrying [Indians] up continually only vexes them to no purpose' and took comfort in his whiskey flask and waterproof bag of cigars.

Myron Eells – the costive Methodist missionary and humourless teetotaller who sermonized long and tediously on the evil effects of tobacco – was a frequent passenger in the canoes of his Skokomish parishioners. As Swan attributed the breaks and detours in the voyage to the canoeists' passion for gossip and storytelling, so Eells put them down to unregenerate paganism. Whenever his Indians stopped the canoe and began to talk among themselves, he believed they were 'doing tamahnous' (Eells's word for what later anthropologists usually transcribe as *tamánamis* – variously 'secret knowledge', 'special power', or 'guardian spirit'). A contrary wind prompted a halt for 'tamahnous'; so did a steepening sea, or a passage past a whirlpool, tide race, or dangerous rock. When the myopic gospeller lectured them on the folly of persisting in their old heathen ways, they paid him no particular attention. Rather, they took to lecturing him.

> Water monster. *They believe that there is a great water animal, which has overturned canoes, and eaten up people, but which cannot be killed. I have noticed that they seem to think it dwells at places where naturally the navigation for canoes is more than ordinarily dangerous, as at Point Wilson, near Port Townsend, where the tide rips are very bad, and at a dangerous place near Duckaboos, on Hood Canal. When passing these places in canoes, I have often been told to keep still and not say a word for fear of arousing the monster, and have also been told how he has sucked under whole canoes in these places.*

Myron Eells was no sailor. In a canoe, he had to do what he was told. So the minister, famous for his garrulous moralism, was silenced, made to crouch, stock-still, holding his breath, so as not to wake the monster.

More than fifty years later, the Reverend Eells was still clearly remembered by old people who had been children aboard those canoes. In 1934, a student of anthropology at the University of Washington, William W. Elmendorf, interviewed a Skokomish elder, Henry Allen, who spoke of Eells as 'that awful man'.

People didn't like him very well. He was collecting Klallam words from some Klallam Indians who were visiting here one time. I had to translate for him. So he would ask them for words like father, mother, house, dog, and so on. And those people didn't think much of Eells, so they would give him all sorts of dirty, nasty words, and he would write them down in a book. Then he would try and use some of those words, thinking he was talking Indian, and people would just about bust trying to keep from laughing.

Allen's most cheerful memory of Eells was of watching the minister and his family become miserably seasick in a canoe on passage up Juan de Fuca Strait, from Neah Bay to Port Townsend:

It got so rough that the minister's family all huddled together under a blanket and got sick. They emptied a basin regular from under that blanket.

Often sick and frightened, and nearly always impatient with the slow and convoluted progress of the journey, the whites were feeble observers at sea. On land, they took copious notes on almost everything the Indians did, from cooking to basketwork. They painstakingly described the construction of cedar canoes and fishing gear. But once the canoes were afloat, some affliction descended on these industrious amateur ethnologists, who suddenly went blind to the details of native navigation, except to complain about its failure to acknowledge the self-evident supremacy of the straight line.

Most accounts of nineteenth-century voyages contain hints of disagreement and bad feeling on the canoe. Some escapades are unwittingly comic, as when the Belgian missionary Father Augustin Brabant described how a heavy sea got up off the entrance to Clayoquot Sound, on the west coast of Vancouver Island, and his benighted crew first tried to calm the waves by smacking them with the flats of their paddles, then tried to appease them by throwing food into the water. For this they got a severe talking-to from their priest, who deplored their primitive superstitions. Father Brabant had the true solution. 'I put the matter into the hands of Saint Lawrence,' wrote this master of higher magic. The canoe landed up safe, but swamped, on an outcrop of serrated rocks. 'I named the place St Lawrence Reef,' said Father Brabant, with proprietorial smugness. The Lawrence Islets (they look like a set of jagged black molars) lie on the north side of what is now Brabant Channel.

Two world-views were in collision; and the poverty of white accounts of these canoe journeys reflects the colonialists' blindness to the native sea. They didn't get it – couldn't grasp the fact that for Indians the water was a place, and the great bulk of the surrounding land mere undifferentiated space.

The whites had entered a looking-glass world, where their own most basic terms were reversed. Their whole focus was directed toward the land: its natural harbours, its timber, its likely spots for settlement and agriculture. They travelled everywhere equipped with mental chainsaws and at a glance could strip a hill of its covering forest (as Vancouver does, again and again, in his *Voyage*) and see there a future of hedges, fields, houses, churches. They viewed the sea as a medium of access to the all-important land.

Substitute 'sea' for 'land', and vice versa, in that paragraph, and one is very close to the world that emerges from Indian stories, where the forest is the realm of danger, darkness, exile, solitude, and self-extinction, while the sea and its beaches represent safety, light, home, society, and the continuation of life.

The civilization of the coastal Indians was centred on a thin ribbon of shoreline between the water and the woods. Their grandly substantial wooden houses, with family crests painted on their fronts, flanked by carved totemic posts and poles, faced out to sea, their backs turned to the forbidding land. Going into the forest was distinctly more dangerous than going to sea: its hazards were more unpredictable and less easily avoided than the maelstroms and krakens of the deep. Wolves, cougars, and grizzly bears lurked in the woods. The tangled overstorey blocked out the sun, and people quickly became disoriented as they were forced to double back around snags and fallen trees, to clamber through the head-high undergrowth of fern, bramble, and salal.

Into the near forest ventured hunting parties, trusting to safety in numbers. Adolescents, on a ritual quest for *sklakletuts* or *tamánamis*, went alone, to test themselves in an alien and scary environment, much as their Anglo counterparts might run off to sea. Beyond the forest rose the mountains, in jagged planes of bare rock and ice – the habitat of the universally feared thunder-eagle, and of other fantastic, legendary creatures known for their casual, jocose brutality to mankind. The deeper one went into the woods, the closer one came to the nightmare domain of cruel superpowers whose parts were enacted by masked dancers at fire-lit winter ceremonies: the horned and snarling double-headed *sisiutl*; *kwekwe*, the earthquake maker; *bookwus*, the forest giant; *hokhokw*, a bird-monster. Adepts at metamorphosis, such beings could manifest themselves in the humble guises of a frog or a river otter, could soar on wings as powerful as those of eagles, could tear apart human flesh with the claws and teeth of bears. They belonged to the haunted netherworld of fearful imagination – a place Indians readily identified with the depths of the forest and the unscalable mountains above the timberline.

Reading through Franz Boas's monumental collection of tales from the Kathlamet, Kwakiutl, Salishan, Bella Bella, and Tsimshian tribes, it's striking how consistently the terms 'inland' and 'seaward' are used by the storytellers. When characters go 'inland', it almost invariably signals a dangerous adventure in unknown territory. 'Seaward' marks the return to safety and home.

The relationship between land and sea is nicely glossed in the opening lines of a Tlingit story, 'The Man Who Entertained the Bears', collected by Swanton in 1904:

A man belonging to the Raven clan living in a very large town had lost all of his friends, and he felt sad to think that he was left alone. He began to consider how he could leave that place without undergoing hardships. First he thought of paddling away, but he said to himself, 'If I paddle away to another village and the people there see that I am alone, they may think that I have run away from my own village, from having been accused of witchcraft or on account of some other disgraceful thing.' He did not feel like killing himself, so he thought that he would go off into the forest.

While this man was travelling along in the woods the thought occurred to him to go to the bears and let the bears kill him. . . .

The sea is too social for this lonely outcast. His canoe would be noticed, his presence become an object of gossip. For him, the sea is not the void, the ultimate anonymous refuge, of white culture; he can no more escape to sea than I can escape to my suburban mall. It is to land, to the obliterating darkness of the forest, that he must go for solace or suicide.

The sea was the canoe-Indians' workplace, their open market, and their battleground. Intertribal marriages were brokered there, where friends met and deals were struck. It was the front doorstep on which visitors were formally greeted, as the Nootka Indians greeted Captain Cook off the entrance to Nootka Sound, standing up in their canoes, throwing feathers and red ochre into the sea, and making speeches, followed by a song. 'After the tumultuous oration had ceased,' Cook wrote, 'one of them sung a very agreeable air, with a degree of softness and melody which we could not have expected.' Here, on the exposed coast, where the invariable westerly swell heaps up alarmingly as it feels the shallow bottom at the entrance to the sound, you'd have to be a Nootka Indian to stand upright in a canoe, let alone make speeches and sing tunefully on your feet.

The sea provided the Indians with a neighbourhood, around which they loitered, scuffed their heels, and traded small talk. While its lower depths harboured beings, like Komogwa, as dangerous and mercurial in character as those of the deep forest, the water's surface was a broad public arena on which most of daily life took place.

George Vancouver, keeping an anxious watch on the comings and goings of the canoes, their apparently random, zigzag routes, might usefully have cast his mind back to his native town of King's Lynn, where on the Saturday market in the long shadow of St Margaret's he must have seen the same patterns, advances, retreats, crossings-over, and deviations that sociable pedestrians practise everywhere. Indians were moving on the sea exactly as whites moved on dry land; but the whites steadfastly failed to wise up to this basic transposition of land and sea, place and space.

When the German geographer Aurel Krause was working on an Alaskan survey for the Bremen Geographical Society in 1881, he took time out to research and write an anthropological monograph on the Tlingit tribe. He was scathing, in a heavy, schoolmasterish way, about the dim intellect of his subjects. 'Their power of understanding is limited. . . . The tales of the origin of things are full of lively imagination, but lack all sensible understanding and scarcely show any comprehension of the universe.' Krause illustrated this tough judgement by describing the Tlingits' pathetic grasp of geography:

> *In spite of the fact that the Tlingit is constantly surrounded by nature, he is only acquainted with it as it offers him the necessities of life. He knows every bay that lends itself to fishing or the beaching of a canoe . . . and for these he has names; but the mountain peaks themselves, even though they are outstanding on account of their shape or size, are scarcely noticed by him.*

This unwittingly revealing observation suggests that the mountains, in Tlingit cosmology, occupied the same space as the ocean does in the cosmology of Europeans like Aurel Krause. They represented the formless and primordial flux, 'that state of barbaric vagueness and disorder out of which civilization has emerged and into which, unless saved by the efforts of gods and men, it is always liable to relapse', as W. H. Auden wrote of the ocean. They were utterly inhospitable to mankind. The terrible thunder-eagle, chaos incarnate, had his eyrie there. The mountain peaks, in all their meaningless variety, were unnameable. But the Tlingits had a thousand names for the sea.

Thatcher Pass was a hole-in-the-wall aperture between islands. Riding the flood tide, the boat slipped through the crevice and entered a nearly landlocked basin of water, smooth as oil, silvered in the diffuse and misty morning light. A deer stood motionless, spindle-shanked, on a shelf of black rock at the south-western tip of Blakeley Island, as if posed there for deliberate scenic effect. Nine or ten of the San Juan Islands were strewn negligently about the place, the smaller like crumbs of fruit cake, balanced on their exact reflections, while the bigger ones – Blakeley, Lopez, Orcas, Decatur – lent their inky, ever-green colour to the sea at their feet.

Motoring into the San Juans, I felt I'd trespassed rudely into the middle of a painted canvas. A luminist waterscape by Martin Johnson Heade or George Caleb Bingham? Not quite. Too manicured and self-consciously pretty for that, it was clearly the work of a later and more sentimental artist. With its mirror-still water, rocks, and fir trees, its view of distant snowcapped mountains, this was an authentic Bob Ross.

I'd seen him paint it one Sunday afternoon on channel 9. It took him twenty-five minutes, start to finish. On his PBS series, 'The Joy of Painting', whose name nicely put art on a par with other *Joy of* activities like cooking and sex, Ross showed one how to turn scenes from wild American nature into paintings that would grace the walls of any discriminating Chinese restaurant. The programs were aimed at elderly viewers with little or no experience of paints and brushes, and the words that cropped up most frequently in Ross's titles for his works – Serenity, Solitude, Golden, Quiet, Retreat, Hideaway, Seclusion, Lonely, Autumn, Winter – were all descriptive of the state of retirement itself.

For this particular painting, Ross laid on mountains of Prussian Blue and wreathed them deftly in Titanium White mist, chatting companionably as he went along. 'These gorgeous things . . . Just gorgeous! You can see a range of mountains like this, it looks like God was certainly havin' a good day when he made it.' His slight southern accent, exaggeratedly soft and slow, was a large aural dose of Valium. Fiftyish, bearded, with a great fuzzy thornbush of hair that some topiarist had trimmed to a perfect globe encircling his friendly face, Ross had the manners of a middle-aged boy – the sweet, capable son who never misses his Sunday visit to the old folks' home. On his palette he swizzled up a mixture of Midnight Black, Alizarin Crimson, and Satin Green, then conjured a low promontory of second-growth firs, reaching out into the water from the right-hand side of the picture. The trees, skinny and evenly spaced, less than twenty years old, were the kind that tugboatmen, rafting them up and down the Inside Passage, derisively called 'pecker poles'.

I skirted the promontory, smashing reflections as I went. The foreground trees, paler and more detailed than the rest, were picked out in Sap Green and Yellow Ochre. Slabs of rock, breaking the surface of the water along the shoreline, were set, bricklayer-style, by Bob Ross with a palette knife loaded with Van Dyke Brown.

'Just remember,' Ross said, 'the canvas is your very own world. You can do anything you like with it. Use your imagination.'

He piled drift-logs up along the beach, flicking his brush lightly along the water's edge. 'In one stroke, you can make all the little goodies here.' He added a dab or two of white for sparkle, then he was done. 'What a gorgeous scene!' Artist and viewers together gazed at the finished canvas: several hundred square miles of dream retirement-and-vacation real estate. Here was a Pacific Northwest in which nature had been spayed and declawed, robbed of all its power to threaten or surprise. Bob Ross pointed with his paintbrush to where the merely decorative forest met the merely reflective sea. 'That's where I'd put *my* cabin.'

Deep inside the gorgeous scene, I lit a Marlboro and added another hundred revs of engine noise as the boat ploughed through the looking-glass, past Upright Head and into Harney Channel. This picture wasn't actually unpeopled, as it had appeared on the TV screen. Looking closely at the ochre, green, and dark sienna woods along the shore, you could see the stilted waterfront properties, like overgrown tree houses, that perched over the beach with enormous, view-hungry windows, their attendant cars discreetly hidden in ivy-clad timber garages. Million-dollar weekend cottages and golden-age retreats peeked slyly through the trees, doing their best to camouflage themselves in the general tangle of Douglas fir, feathery cypress, and twisty-limbed madrona. The native woods had been teased and primped, as if with brush and palette knife, to create veils and vistas.

The snag about every waterfront property in the San Juans was that its chief view was of a lot of other waterfront properties. Since the whole point of this picture was, as the Ross titles put it, *Quiet Woods, Majestic Mountains, Secluded Waters,* and *Evening Solitude,* the homeowners had to camouflage their dwellings in order not to damage the illusion. The few bold modernist exceptions looked like pariahs.

Beyond and behind the precious waterfront, as property prices sank toward the lower six figures, the artsy-crafties took over: jewellery designers, potters, painters, quilters, wood carvers, weavers; makers of wind chimes, dream-catchers, weathercocks, seashell-encrusted bibelots, poems, screenplays, and little embroidered bags of home-cured potpourri. The Friday Harbor gift shops were stacked solid with the works of local artists, many of them in the school of Bob Ross.

The islands – once known for the Pig War against the British in 1859, the pig being the sole casualty – had lately made the front page of the *New York Times* as the site of the PWC War, a major skirmish in the annals of modern American class warfare. The dividing issue was a jet-ski rental business in Friday Harbor, which provoked an outraged alliance of waterfronters and artsy-crafties, who protested that personal watercraft, or PWCs, as the aquatic snowmobiles were called, were dangerous, loud, and incompatible with the tranquillity and natural beauty of the island environment. The well-orchestrated roar of complaint led the county legislature to pass an ordinance banning the use of personal watercraft in the San Juans. Then the storm broke.

The measure was immediately interpreted as an attack by the middle classes on the taste and culture of the lower orders – of which jet-skis were the metonymic symbol, and the thin end of the wedge. The ban was really a pre-emptive strike against baseball caps worn backwards, six-packs, hot-dog stands, Kool-Aid-purple pick-ups with jumbo tyres, cigarette smoke, pull-tabs, boom boxes, prefeminist body art, MTV, nose rings, crack vials . . . The jet-ski operator was introducing the wrong kind of people into the picture and spoiling the composition. If young proles on PWCs were allowed to carve up island waters with their seething wakes, then the pretty artifice of the San Juans would soon be wrecked beyond recognition. The ordinance struck a blow for social and aesthetic hierarchy, and was denounced as elitist and unconstitutional.

As I passed through, an appeal was on its way to the State Supreme Court. I grudgingly agreed that the appellants (backed by the jet-ski manufacturers) probably had natural justice on their side; but I had my own bone to pick with PWCs, and was keeping my fingers crossed for the county.

That morning, mine was the only personal water craft on the move. A car ferry, too big for the islands, went trundling from dock to dock like a white hippopotamus in a dew-pond. In the sheltered bays, a few tenantless sailboats and motor-cruisers rode to their mooring buoys. Many of the waterfront houses had a still-padlocked-for-winter look, their lawns beginning to run wild, their dark windows dead to the world. Out of season, the picture presented by the San Juans was unimprovable. An iconic eagle dipped and corkscrewed on a thermal overhead. From the deep, seals put forth whiskery faces with wide enquiring eyes, and obliging porpoises revolved like cogwheels. I steered through trees, around rocks, past little fir-topped islets, an appreciative tourist in this miniature resort-archipelago.

The charm of the San Juans was lost on Captain Van. Having spotted 'islands of various sizes' in the distance, he sent Lieutenant

Broughton to survey them in the *Chatham*. Broughton's report, after a five-day visit, was wearily dismissive: dangerous submerged rocks, foul anchoring grounds, no wind, hopeless fishing (every afternoon, the *Chatham's* crew hauled a seine-net along the beaches without success), heavy overfalls, fast and baffling tides. Broughton lost a sounding lead and twenty fathoms of line to a crevice in the rocks, which didn't improve his temper. The larger islands were 'well Cloath'd with wood', but this was no special recommendation, given the abundance of timber everywhere else in sight. Even the Indians appeared to avoid the place: during the cruise, Broughton and his men met only six natives in two canoes. They traded them beads and hawks-bells for venison, and brought aboard a live fawn. Thereafter, Vancouver gave the islands a wide berth.

Two hundred years on, Captain Van might have been astonished to discover that the San Juan Islands now came closer to his Augustan ideal of landscape than any other spot on the 2,000-mile reach of coastline he charted on his expedition. In the late twentieth century, here was a North American equivalent to Pope's Windsor Forest, abundantly equipped with sylvan groves and chequered shades. Here, though all things differed, all agreed – shadow and reflection, rock and tree, seal and porpoise.

People who scoffed at the tameness of the San Juans missed the point. They were more works of art than of nature; a pleasure ground, a version of pastoral, a cleverly contrived Elysium. Pope's poetic vocabulary fitted them beautifully. They were verdant isles, adorning a purpled main, where, interspersed in lawns and opening glades, thin trees arose that shunned each other's shades.

> But now secure the painted vessel glides,
> The sun-beams trembling on the floating tides
> . . . .
> Smooth flow the waves, the Zephyrs gently play –

Sunbeams were in short supply, but everything else was pretty much in place. Coming up to Pole Pass, a fifty-foot squeeze between great mossy boulders overhung by craggy firs and alders, more grotto than navigable channel, I doubled an ornate gazebo on a kelp-girt rock and spotted a statue of Pan, cast in alabaster-white cement, deep in a sculpted clearing. This was the Pacific Northwest Vancouver had first dreamed into being at Discovery Bay, in his exalted mood. Indeed, he could have been happy in his retirement here; a choleric old sea captain, busying himself with letters and petitions, focusing his telescope on the bizarre excesses of the modern world as it floated offensively past his window. Fuming about PWCs might have kept him alive a few years longer (he would be dead at forty).

The only wrinkle was that no half-pay captain could possibly afford waterfront in the San Juans. Captain Van had long ago been priced out of the land he discovered.

The smell of paint and contrivance faded in the Spieden Channel, where the flood tide, backed by a breeze, ran hard against the boat. Getting out of the San Juans was a lot harder than getting in. I inched over the ground, forcing my way upstream against the incoming sea. Ahead, the Gulf Islands – the Canadian continuation of the San Juans – stood out against the long flooded mountain range of Vancouver Island, as dark and shadowy as an advancing storm front. The border ran north to south down the middle of Haro Strait. To reach customs at Sidney on the Vancouver Island shore, I had to claw crabwise across the grain of the tide in the strait, pointing the boat south-west to make a course of west-by-north. Gooch Island and the South Cod Reef buoy sidled slowly toward me at an oblique angle; floating islands, steaming purposefully at around three knots across a motionless sea.

Only five miles wide, but more than a hundred fathoms deep, Haro Strait was a saltwater river of great power and volume. It filled and drained the 2,000-square-mile basin of the Strait of Georgia. It divided the nations. It flowed with languid, weighty self-importance, its surface barely scored by the tribulations of its fast current. One had to watch the land hard and continuously to avoid being swept away north by the stream.

When the Garmin clocked up the meridian of 123°15′W, the boat entered Canadian waters. A subtle boundary, it was not at all like crossing the Rio Grande or the Dover Straits. But the pecked line on the chart marked a cultural fissure that was all the more vexed for being so ambiguous and indistinct.

Raked with binoculars, Canada looked like a different country. The Gulf Islands were shaggier and wilder seeming than their American siblings. They suffered from traumatic alopecia, with irregular bald patches in their pelt of firs. Gulf Island residences didn't peep coyly through fringes of combed and scissored greenery, but glared from wedges of bare hillside. One could see the outlines of vegetable plots, with strings of bird-scaring tinfoil; monkey bars and slides from Toys R Us, in splashes of poppy-red and forsythia-yellow; the winking panes of a greenhouse; the brown half-moon made in the dirt by a chained guard dog. One difference was of money and title. In Canada, the foreshore was Crown property, open to the public, which took the exclusive edge from waterfront ownership and frustrated the efforts of lands-end gardeners. Incomes were generally lower, and taxes higher, than in the US. Many Gulf islanders were retired civil servants, Captain Van characters making do on fixed pensions. They lived in plain wood-frame houses, not million-dollar retreats.

Nearly all of Canada's long border with its fat and promiscuous neighbour consisted of a chain link fence broken, at intervals, with roadblocks. When the language spoken on both sides of it is the same, a roadblock is a very inadequate reflection of intensely felt national differences. The rigid parallel of 49°N, ruled across the western half of the subcontinent from the Great Lakes to the Strait of Georgia, had been drawn in aloof disdain of the topography of mountain ridges and river valleys that might have lent a visible dimension to the division of Canada from the United States.

So this curving line through the sea, a graceful arabesque that ran between the San Juans and the Gulf Islands, then swung east, then west again, out through Juan de Fuca Strait, taking the same route as the ebb tide, was a frontier to be cherished. Here nature and politics appeared – for once – to coincide. Here Canadians could look out on America across a stretch of water that corresponded to the metaphysical gulf of history, taste, and sensibility that, as every Canadian I knew believed, separated the two countries. Whenever I crossed over I met that gulf as an anxious question. *Don't you see how different we are? What do you notice?* Often I noticed too little, feeling the Canadian differential more as absence than presence. It was a Canadian fate to wish, forlornly, that America lay elsewhere, across a palpable vacancy, a cordon sanitaire. Canadians ached for sea room – and here, for a hundred and thirty nautical miles, America was blessedly overseas. On some days, when atmospheric conditions were at their friendliest, the crass, overbearing empire faded completely out of sight.

At Sidney, I tied up to the empty customs dock and reported my arrival on the courtesy phone nailed to a piling. The mouthpiece smelled of stale dutiable items – the fruity breath of a cigar smoker, a woman's scent, a whiff of sour-mash whiskey. They were weekend smells, and two or three days old. I declared my wine cellar – eleven bottles – and was told to stay with the boat; an officer would be with me shortly.

There were no boats or people at this end of the marina. Bare pontoons, meant for the summer hordes, reached out across the harbour like a dozen giant bleached fish spines. Two berths down from mine a blue heron stood at the end of a slip, its accordion neck folded on its shoulders, a trickle of watery green guano leaking from beneath its tail onto the white concrete. Infected by its air of patient boredom, I wanted to be off among the islands for the remains of the day, not stuck in Sidney waiting for customs. I put together a cheese sandwich and sat up in the cockpit, munching irritably. Twenty minutes passed. An otter swam splashily between the pontoons, unafraid, tamed by fishermen's titbits. I threw what was left of the sandwich but the creature altered its course, shunning my American Cheddar. The heron went on staring at the water with an unillusioned button-eye. The tide turned. I joined the heron in its tedious vigil, watching the ebb make strings of finger-sized vortices, little cones of turbulence, as it ran out past a tarred piling.

'Penelope?'

'Yes?' I hated answering to my boat's name, which I'd meant to suppress in this narrative.

Two officers, a man and a woman, both too young for their blue-serge uniforms and black attaché cases, hoisted themselves ceremoniously aboard at the shrouds and came aft to join me in the cockpit.

'Sorry to keep you hanging about. We've been busy out at the airport.' '*Aboot . . . oot.*' The pursed Scottish *o* gave the British Columbian accent a soft, owlish, *to-whit-to-woo*ing sound. The past lingered longer in Canada than it did in the US, and British Columbians still spoke in lilting voices that had changed little since Victorian lowlanders, from Stirling, Falkirk, Motherwell, Kilmarnock, had first settled here.

I rolled back the carpet in the saloon, pulled up a floorboard, and exposed my meagre stock of wine.

'We're going to conduct a routine search,' said the male officer, pink with bureaucratic self-importance. This was Canada making the most of its sea border. The Americans were relaxed to the point of ennui when it came to small boats entering the US. Coming into Canada, I had been searched and questioned several times. Either I was on some kind of official hit list or Canadian authorities liked to make as much of a fuss as they could, drumming it into American heads that theirs was, indeed, a foreign land.

'You are the only person aboard the vessel?'

'I am.' There was no joking with these two.

My accent and British passport counted for nothing. I was in command of a US-registered vessel – a little floating America, an ark, an emissary from the land of indulgence and excess. Through the eyes of these border guards I saw the boat lying low in the water, weighed down by easy-to-come-by firearms, cheap liquor and smokes, porno-graphic videos, the whole corrupting cargo of American culture.

'Do you want me to show you where things are?'

'No. We'll find our own way around.'

From the cockpit, I watched them at work, a pair of young proctologists in rubber gloves, poking and probing into the boat's private parts. One climbed onto the double bed at the front and rummaged through a closet full of socks and pants; the other could be heard prying things open in the head. They lifted floorboards, thrust their arms shoulder-deep into every crevice, shone their flashlights into the dark corners of my life.

I had no contraband, had declared my only dutiable goods, yet felt despondent with guilt and anxiety. I was a wrongdoer, I was sure of that; and these clinical investigators would somehow find me out.

They moved back into the saloon. From the bookshelves, the woman pulled out a row of my own paperbacks and heaped them on the table. For a moment I thought she was going to say, 'Oh, you're the author!' and all would be well. But her interest was in what lay behind the books, their illicit subtext; and here, I feared, she might be on to something. As she felt along the vacant space for the hidden 9mm semiautomatic or the stacked cartons of Camels, I could practically feel her fingers graze my vitals.

I began to ransack my memory for forgotten violations. A summer night . . . stirring the phosphorescent water with an oar and raising shovelfuls of pullulating green light, swarming *Noctiluci*. We were smoking joints. What happened to the butts? And, more to the point, what happened to that small zip-topped freezer bag of grass?

But that, surely, was on the Orwell estuary in England . . . at Pin Mill. Not this boat. Not even this decade. The luminous plankton, alarmingly vivid a second before, faded abruptly from view.

For twenty-five years I've been visited by a recurrent bad dream. I am the owner, or the tenant, of a warren of rooms in a city that usually seems to be London. It's a strange apartment, where the dividing line between my property and that of my immediate neighbours is unclear, and they occupy at least one room that is legally mine. Somewhere in this dusty no man's land, in a closet, or buried under the floorboards, is a body, long decomposed. Though not the murderer, I am guilty of knowing about this body and keeping silent, and I'm about to be apprehended.

They were pulling up the floorboards now.

The young man's face appeared in the hatchway. He raised a plastic bag. Exhibit A. 'Potatoes,' he said.

Three large baking potatoes rimed with white mould. Each had grown pallid shoots, like trails of candle wax, searching for light in the dark of the bilges.

'I'm sorry – I'd forgotten those. They must've been left over from last year sometime.'

'We'll have to confiscate them.' He scribbled on his clipboard.

'You're welcome to them.'

He climbed the companionway steps and started to rootle through the cockpit lockers, while his colleague squeezed past me and lowered herself into the aft cabin.

'Can you tell me why I've been singled out for this sort of search?'

The officer paused in his excavations. 'Just the luck of the draw.'

I wasn't so sure. A couple of years before, a friend, dining in a downtown Seattle restaurant, had pricked up his ears when he heard my name mentioned at the next table. A long-haired man in his mid-thirties (I couldn't identify him from my friend's description) was telling his companion that he knew me well, and that I supplemented my income from writing by smuggling liquor aboard my ketch to a BC Indian reserve. 'That's how he can afford to keep that boat of his.' If this wild flight of fancy had found its way into the computer files of Canada Customs, then I could be grateful that the officers weren't conducting their enquiry with chainsaws and power drills. One day I hoped to meet a customs man old and wise enough to confide in – but these young zealots were clearly the wrong audience.

The woman came up from the aft cabin, looking mildly baffled by her researches among the soft toys, charts, pilot books, and assorted works of Dr Seuss and A. A. Milne. I caught the pair exchanging *no luck* glances.

For my eleven bottles, I paid as much in duty as it had cost me to buy them in the supermarket. The boat was given a clearance number. In the end, I was convicted only of coming from the United States, and of being in possession of three elderly American potatoes.

The light had gone out of the day and the ebb was now running south at full tilt. With the odium of official scrutiny in my clothes and on my skin, jittery and out of sorts, I untied from the customs dock and shifted moorings to a slip on the next pontoon. I would make my escape from Sidney at dawn.

In the Phoenix, an underpatronized shoebox-like restaurant boasting 'Authentic Cantonese Cuisine', I poked with chopsticks at a bowl of stir-fried beef and wrangled with myself in the pages of my notebook. The border crossing . . . the deep but narrow gulf – call it Haro Strait – that yawned between Canada and the United States . . . that slick, deceptive water, so easily misconstrued, needed careful navigation.

People liked to say that if America was a melting pot, Canada was a salad bowl. In Canada, immigrants kept their original identities and flavours, while in America they were assimilated into the cultural stew. If you came here as a spring onion, you could stay a spring onion, without anyone trying to turn you into a tomato or a cucumber.

There was some obvious truth to this. The Chinese cooking at the Phoenix was more authentic than in most of its American counterparts. Newcomers here were under relatively little pressure to 'Canadianize', to adapt their styles and manners to those of the host country; more easily than in the United States, they could go on doing things much as they'd done them at home. The English stayed English, the Chinese stayed Chinese. America was a land of immigrants, Canada a country of émigrés.

This blunt distinction fitted nicely with a subtler one made by Russell Brown, a Canadian literary critic. Trawling a broad net through American and Canadian fiction, Brown suggested that one essential difference between the two cultures lay in the characters of Oedipus and Telemachus. In the States, a society founded on revolution, the mythic hero was the runaway son, the patricide; Oedipus as

Huckleberry Finn. Escape, rebellion, the cult of the new life at the expense of the old, were the commanding American themes. Up north, in a society founded on the refusal to rise up against its parent, the mythic hero was the loyal son of Odysseus, Telemachus; the voyager in search of the lost father. Americans broke with their ancestral pasts, whereas Canadians honoured theirs.

The customs people (I wrote) were right to see through my accent and my passport and nail me as an American from across the water. I was Oedipus, not Telemachus – an escapee, a new-lifer, a rainbow-chaser. An immigrant, not an émigré. Leaving Britain for the United States was an attempt to make a clean break with my past, as going to Canada never could have been. In Seattle, I thought, I could shake off the dust of England and make a fresh start. Late in my day as it was, I heard America's old cracked siren-call and believed that *over there* I might yet accomplish something new and unexpected.

Sirens tempt sailors to their ruin, but we forget the whole story all over again once they start singing. No music came out of Canada for me. I saw the Queen's head on the currency, the frowsy post-Gothic colonial architecture, the displaced Britishers with their rowing and rugby clubs, their London papers two and three days out of date; a national demeanour of peevish modesty; a public life of reasonableness and fair play. Canada was for realists, and I was no realist. When I took my seat on the plane at Heathrow, I was an ageing Huck Finn in search of a territory to light out for. I couldn't have lit out for Canada; that would've felt uncomfortably akin to lighting out for the Isle of Man.

'Gorrenny lie cheesevyu?'

The voice came from the table over by the door. The speaker was an Englishman, from the stuffed-nose urban Midlands – Walsall, perhaps, or Dudley . . . not far from where I spent five years at boarding school. He was asking the waitress about dessert, but it took me a moment or two to decode what he was saying.

'Gorrenny lie cheesevyu?'

'Wah!' The waitress gave off a small, explosive puff of sound, baring her teeth in an exasperated grin.

'Lychees!' he said, putting the matter in bold block capitals.

'Ngha! No!'

Canadian language difficulties. Enforced bilingualism had burdened Canada with twice as much writing as most nations. Cereal boxes, cigarettes, the tide tables – everything came in parallel texts, English and French. This grossly fattened all official publications; pamphlets became books, books stout tomes, and the simplest notice turned gabby and verbose. Everything was a translation of something else. Far from reinforcing each other, one version tended to cast doubt on the other, making its meaning tentative and provisional.

On the back of the Canadian twenty-dollar bill was a handsomely engraved portrait of the common loon, a fleet of which I'd shouldered through on my way into Sidney. COMMON LOON, it said; and, just above the English caption, HUART A COLLIER. But a *huart à collier* is a collared diver. There was an English and a French way of seeing the same bird in the same picture. In French, your eye went straight to the collar – an arresting necklace of white feathers interleaved with black – and you saw it *dive*, a disappearing trick leaving a neat circle in the water where the bird had been a millisecond before. In English, it was the loon's gregarious commonness that first seized one's attention, its maniacal laughter, its plump bath-toy figure.

This kind of thing made one self-consciously alert to the Canadian language – continually on the lookout for contradictions, ambiguities, loopholes. In particular, I hoped to find a brand of Canadian cigarettes that would kill you when smoked in French but only damage your health when smoked in English.

When I crossed to Canada from the United States, this betwixt-and-between character always struck me immediately. The country seemed disconcertingly prone to drift from its anchorage in space, time, and language; here one moment, there the next. Just a few weeks before, I was dining alone one Sunday evening in a much grander Chinese restaurant in Vancouver, where I was the only Caucasian in sight. The meal, selected for me by a helpful waiter, was full of surprises, all good. The only drawback to this selfish feast was the continuous plastic-canary chirrup of two dozen cellular phones, going off singly and in chorus. Sometimes several male patrons at the same table could be seen engaged in separate conversations, heads averted from their feeding bowls as they snapped and barked into their leather-clad Motorolas.

This frenetic sociability, at eight o'clock on a Sunday night, was a puzzle easily solved. It was high noon on Monday in Hong Kong, and these expatriate businessmen were enjoying their Canadian family weekend while tyrannizing their office peons in the middle of a Hong Kong weekday. Floating somewhere in mid-Pacific, between time zones and datelines, with these yakking businessmen, I thought that perhaps Vancouver's low specific gravity was its most Canadian attribute. The city was so lightly tethered to its coordinates of latitude and longitude that you could easily imagine you were in Glasgow, or Portland, or Hong Kong. In seven years of visiting the place, I still couldn't put my finger on its essential Vancouverishness. The city had no smell. When I left it, no picture remained in my mind, and sometimes I wasn't entirely convinced of its existence.

After hard-edged America, Canada seemed out of focus. As it resisted ideology and national myth-making, so did it resist definition. In this land of chronic translation, there was no national translation for the American Dream – an idea too grandiose for a country that had inherited the English tradition of pooh-poohing empiricism. Canadian Dreams would be met with the phrase used in the title of Alice Munro's story collection *Who Do You Think You Are?*. In America, people were expected to get above themselves. Over the border, it was a social transgression, and people learned to mask their ambitions with a show of jokey diffidence, infected by English gentility and nervous English party laughter, which made them seem diffuse and evasive by American standards.

I paid the bill and made my way up Sidney's modest main street. The night was mild and damp. A halo of refracted light bloomed from each street lamp. The street itself was gimcrack-Western, with single-storey businesses constructed of cinderblocks and timber lining a too-wide carriageway. At the grocery store, spotting jars of Marmite on the shelves, I added one to my basket. That fierce-tasting sandwich spread, gluey and mahogany-coloured, staple of the English nursery tea, had never made the border-crossing into the States, and I was glad to see that it was thriving still in Canada. I bought three grizzly-bear postcards, and mailed them to Julia at the post office.

Sidney was Alice Munro territory. Several of her stories were set on the urban southern tip of Vancouver Island, between Sidney and Victoria. At the centre of each was a woman stifling like Emma Bovary in a dull, prosperous marriage. The women did things on the fringes of the arts, worked in bookshops, starred in amateur dramatics, wrote, gave talks on local radio; they escaped into hazardous sexual adventures with unsuitable men. And here the border came into play. Seattle figured prominently in Munro's stories as a reliable source of treacherous lovers, including a friendship-wrecking red-haired deep-sea diver; an all-American Pan, with the oddly un-American name of Miles. In another story, set in the Kootenay Mountains, a character called Dorothy 'had a lover in Seattle, and she did not trust him' – a nice piece of grammar, in which the man's hometown is turned into a sure-fire guarantee of his interesting untrustworthiness.

I slightly knew Alice Munro's first husband, who owned the handsome, dark-panelled bookshop, once a bank, on Government Street in Victoria. I enjoyed spotting him, or bits of him, in the husband-figures in her fiction. At his grey-stone house on a hill overlooking Juan de Fuca Strait, I had, or so I fancied, met many of the women characters, twenty-five years on; grey hair swept back and tied with Indian scarves; ruefully bright talkers. They still did things on the fringes of the arts; and as I sat smoking in a wicker armchair on the porch, the black strait glittering below in starlight, I wondered if they still looked south across the border for their dangerous men – like Miles, showing up from Seattle on his motorbike, a human bomb designed to blow marital life apart in tame Victoria.

Across the street from the post office, a bookstore was still open. A pale and dusty shadow of Munro's, it nonetheless had a few new books from England, as yet unavailable in the US. I browsed through them, searching for the work of friends and acquaintances. I bought

The Times – for its crossword, which I missed – and a reprint of *The Adventures and Sufferings of John R. Jewitt, Captive of Maquinna*, the ghost-written tale of an English seaman taken prisoner by the Nootka Indians in 1802, which also went under the jaunty title of *White Slave of the Nootka*. It was a book I'd been hoping to add to the boat's library for some time – a strange concoction, in which the romantic embroideries of Jewitt's ghost, an untravelled Connecticut journalist named Richard Alsop, were at least as interesting as the dubious memoirs of Jewitt himself. Paying by credit card, I was grateful for the clerk's glance of recognition as she filled in the slip.

'I heard you read last year at the festival,' she said. 'What are you doing in Sidney?'

'Sailing to Alaska. Slowly.'

And 'slowly' would be the word for it, I realized, when I stepped out to the empty street. At the top of the hill was an ominously swollen glow, from a stoplight that hung in the sky above Sidney like a fuzzy green moon.

I walked back to the boat, the Marmite jar clinking in my shopping bag, *The Times* tucked under my arm. Arrival in Canada had made me feel, as I hardly ever did in the United States, suddenly and painfully in exile.

By 6:00 a.m. the fog had enclosed the boat in dense, clammy, frogspawn grey. Waking to the electronic beeping of the alarm, I could hear the hollow, unrequited blare of a diaphone, a long way off on some rockpile. I sat up and peered through the cabin window into the gloaming: the customs dock, at sixty feet, was vague but recognizable; beyond it, nothing existed. The wooded cliff, the marina, and the town of Sidney were gone.

The process of advection, which had gone on steadily overnight, had not missed the opportunity afforded by the clothes I'd left hanging in the saloon. There was fog in my shirt, fog in my trousers, fog in my socks. I fired up the cabin heater, set the kettle to boil for coffee, and found a CBC station on the radio. The morning news was fittingly dismal.

A plane carrying Ron Brown, the American Secretary of Commerce, was missing in Croatia. Trying to land at Dubrovnik in heavy rain and near-zero visibility, it had lost contact with the airport and was presumed to have crashed somewhere in the mountains of Dalmatia.

In Moscow, President Boris Yeltsin denied that his troops were overrunning the Chechen Republic, which wasn't the story from Grozny, where there were reports of Russian tanks and sniper fire in the streets.

In Britain, the price of beef had been slashed in an attempt to win back customers frightened by mad cow disease.

In British Columbia, the provincial government had announced a scheme to buy back the licences of commercial salmon fishermen, in order to cut by half the already diminished BC fishing fleet. An industry spokesman explained that the collapse of Canada's west coast fishery, from the Fraser River to the Skeena, on the Alaskan border, had been caused by the reckless greed of the United States. American fishermen, stationed off the Washington coast and around Dixon Entrance, were ambushing millions of salmon born in Canadian rivers and trying to return from the ocean to their homeland.

Talks between the governments on this issue had broken down. The Canadian Coast Guard promised a clampdown on American fishing boats transiting Canadian waters. Seattle-based trollers and gill-netters using the Inside Passage would be seized for any technical infraction of Canadian regulations. A vessel that failed to stow all movable fishing gear below decks, or to report on the dot as it crossed the frontier, would be taken into custody by armed patrol boats. Canadian fishermen were planning to blockade the American-owned passenger ferries that ran between Prince Rupert, BC, and Alaskan ports. In this war I wanted to claim neutral status.

Stowed in the bilges was a can of midnight-blue enamel for touching up biffs and scrapes on the hull. I thought I might usefully spend part of this fogbound morning painting out the name of the boat's port of registration. I also had a ragged, sun-bleached red ensign rolled up at the back of the cutlery drawer. I rarely flew a flag of any colour. The precise and delicate legal position of a seagoing vessel is that it is a detached fragment of the nation under whose flag it sails. I was pleased by the notion that by going flagless I could pass the boat off as an independent political entity – a sloppy, liberal, bookish, agnostic republic of one. In Canadian waters just now, the last thing I wanted was to be a floating chunk of the US.

From the bottom of a cockpit locker I dug out an old jackstaff, left there by the boat's previous owner; tied on the British ensign; and mounted it in the holder on the stern taffrail. While this would cut no ice with officialdom, it should deceive the average passer-by. While I set up the flag, the customs dock faded out of sight. All around the boat, helical twists of vapour drifted like puffs of smoke, as the air, chilled by the sea, mutated into water-dust.

That the region wasn't more permanently fog-shrouded surprised me, for a dominant feature of the local weather was the Pineapple Express: moist, warm air from the subtropical Pacific, blowing from the south-west over the frigid channels of the Inside Passage. The gauzy stuff that now festooned the rigging came hot from Honolulu, air with a dewpoint so high that a minimal drop in temperature changed it instantly to water.

The crossword offered half an hour's distraction. Crouched over the saloon table, in thick fog, in a far-western outpost of the Commonwealth, under an illegal British flag, it was nice to find that the cricketing allusion required to turn 'Bring down deliveries worth circulation (9)' into 'overthrow' still came readily to hand. 'Language once spoken in Yorkshire or Kent areas? (5)' was 'Norse', of course. And 'Sound transport poet provided for birds (9)' was 'lorikeets'.

I was roused from 'Nymph involved in more adventures (5)' by the sound of heavy footsteps on the dock. At the end of the pontoon stood a burly, shaven-headed man in an oilskin jacket. Eyes moving intently from left to right, he seemed to have found something worth studying in the nothingness.

'It will burn off by noon. So they say.'

He spoke English with a ripe French accent. Built like a hooped cask, nut-brown, seventyish, he exuded an infectious, gloomy hilarity. He and his English-born wife had sailed to British Columbia in their catamaran from the Isle of Wight, via South Africa, the West Indies, the Panama Canal, and Hawaii. They, too, were headed for Alaska. A lifetime as a wheat farmer in France, he said, had turned him into a philosopher when it came to weather.

'I expect nothing. So I am not ever disappointed.'

He waved at my newly installed ensign. 'I fly the same flag. I am a grand admirer of your Mrs Thatcher.'

'Are you?' That wasn't the message I'd meant to convey.

'Yachts are full of socialists nowadays.'

'Really? Socialists?'

'But yes – socialists! You are varnishing your boat and the guy says, "May I have some of your varnish?" You know? It happens all the time. They want your paint, your wine, your coffee . . . Socialists.'

'Ah, that kind of socialist.'

'I detest socialism. So I am glad to meet another admirer of Margaret Thatcher.'

We shook hands warmly in the fog. 'You have such a pretty boat – please don't tell me you are a socialist.'

Oread was the adventurous nymph.

Shortly after noon, a shining slab of rock, topped by a madrona tree, appeared in the sky overhead. A few minutes later, the lamppost at the head of the slip began to cast a stunted shadow and Sidney emerged looking pale and bright, as if in convalescence after a high fever. I got the engine started and unwrapped the ropes from the cleats on the dock.

To the south, a low fog bank, brilliantly white in the sun, and as solid-looking as the chalk cliffs of Kent, blocked the channel. The masts and top deck of a multi-storey ferry showed above the fog, moving fast. To the north, rags and patches of fog clung to the islands, snagged in the trees. To reach one of the two broad channels that ran north through the Gulf Islands, I had first to thread the boat through an eight-mile obstacle course of islets, kelp beds, rocks drying and submerged, and a confusing thicket of buoys and markers. The exact direction of the flood tide, as it swept at three knots through these rock-strewn shallows, was doubtful, but it would be more help than hindrance, though likely to drag the boat sideways from its plotted course.

Half an hour and three miles out from Sidney, I was passing a rusty iron cross, not marked on the chart, that was attached to a drying rock the size and general shape of a hippo taking a mud bath. Fifty yards off, the rock sank abruptly from sight, but the iron cross remained, mysteriously, in view. It took me several moments to figure that a long white scarf of fog, only four or five feet high, was now trailing through the islets and had already covered the last buoy on my route, which I had passed, in good visibility, five minutes before.

Fog, says Lecky's *Wrinkles in Practical Navigation* (1881), is 'so very embarrassing at sea' – and never more so than when it suddenly enfolds you in a narrow channel littered with obstructions and in continuous use by ferries, tugs, fishing boats, and pleasure craft. As the iron cross faded out to starboard, I swung the wheel to port and brought the boat onto a reciprocal course of 170°, trying to grope my way back along the path I'd taken on the way out. The long bleat of my masthead horn went unanswered, and I raced downstairs to switch on the radar.

The radar, which had come with the boat, was elderly, slow to warm up, and tricky to use properly when I was sailing alone. The set was tucked into the aft starboard corner of the saloon; to read the screen, I had to leave the wheel, dodge down the companionway steps, jam my head into the rubber hood, then race upstairs again, holding on to the memory of what I'd seen. In water as tight as this, with radar-echoes cluttering the screen in every quadrant, its use tended only to add to the embarrassment of disorientation in fog. But it was a comfort to know it was there: if the worst came to the worst, I could stop the boat, map the echoes on the screen, then match them to the chart up in the doghouse.

For now, though, I concentrated on trying to glue the number 170 to the lubberline on the compass as the tilting card shifted and wobbled in its bowl. From its mounting over the chart table, the Garmin reported that the tide was sliding the boat westwards; 170 through the water was more like 190 over the ground. I was relieved, though, to see that, running against the flood at a reduced speed of about four knots, our real speed over the ground was only 1.5 knots, which should soften the bump if an unexpected rock loomed under the bow.

Inching down-channel on apprehensive tiptoe, I had to steel myself against the tempting deceptions of the fog. The boat was turning to starboard in a circle, with the compass card apparently stuck on a piece of grit – no, trust the compass! The fog was swirling, not the boat. More than half a mile off, by my eye, a distinct horizon became visible – a dark threadline joining air and water. But a common loon, or *huart à collier*, coming up close under the port side, faded into grey within a boat's length. The perceived horizon was a wishful fantasy.

I strained to listen over the mutter of the half-speed engine, and watched the water for the betraying ripple of another vessel's wake. My feeble horn was joined by several deeper blasts, but they sounded consolingly far off; probably ships moving in the Haro Strait, three miles and more to the east. Though lightning visits to the radar screen revealed no alien blips in the sea immediately ahead, I kept on seeing things: rivets and bleeding gobs of rust on the immense brick-coloured plates of a freighter bearing down on me at a distance of around thirty feet; the dark stain in the water of a ragged shelf of rock, thinly covered by the tide. I steered, heart in mouth, between fog-chimeras, waiting for the crash.

I could hear the warning howl of the diaphone on Danger Shoal in Haro Strait. In one of the Alice Munro stories I'd been reading, a character described a foghorn, heard from inside a house in suburban Vancouver, as 'the sound of a cosmic boredom'. I had news for that woman. The only time I've ever heard a foghorn exactly replicated in nature, it was at a branding at a ranch in North Dakota. Just at the instant when the red-hot iron was thrust into the calf's flesh, a nanosecond before the puff of barbecue-smelling smoke rose from its fur, the animal did a pitch-perfect imitation of a diaphone in fog. There wasn't a trace of boredom in it.

A moving blip resolved into the shadow of a fishing boat, faintly imprinted on the fog, but at a reassuring distance of about a hundred yards. Watching the depth-sounder, checking the radar, I felt my way cautiously inside the sheltering arm of Sidney Spit – a mile-long drying sandbar that ran out from the northern end of Sidney Island. Using the depth-sounder like a blind man's stick, I tap-tap-tapped around a broad apron of ground in a steady fourteen feet of water, where I let go the anchor, switched off the engine, and found that my hands were incapable of striking a match to light a cigarette. They blundered about in the air, a pair of shaky fists, obstinately declining to take orders from the brain.

With the boat swinging nicely to its anchor, I sounded the horn. A mushy echo came back five seconds later from the invisible woods on Sidney Island, half a mile away.

Sound travels through the air at around 1,100 feet per second – a fact to cling to in this foggy and steep-sided part of the world. Indian navigators were expert at using voice-radar: letting the canoe drift in silence, they yelled into the vacant grey; the returning echo gave them their distance from shore; its sound quality told them if they were passing bare rock, a timbered hillside, or a cliff of sand and shale. In home waters, they could paddle from point to point in zero visibility, knowing exactly where they were over distances of many miles.

Until the 1970s, when radar came into general use, white fishermen emulated the Indians whenever fog closed in. In 1961, my friend and mentor Mike Wollaston went north for the first time aboard the gill-netter *Alaska Seas*, owned by Bob Kohlase. The two men, both in their early twenties, learned to navigate long stretches by ear and nose. Every ten minutes, they'd shut down the engine and sound the Cunningham air whistle. Each second taken by the echo to bounce back was reckoned as two hundred yards – a cable . Then they tried to match the character of the echo to the topography shown on the chart, guessing at a forest here, a sheer bluff there. They followed the advice given in *The U.S. Coast Pilot*: 'In narrow channels with steep shores the vessel can be kept in mid-channel by keeping in such a position that the echoes from both shores return at the same instant.'

Every so often, they'd get a welcome confirmation of their position from noxious or noisy features ashore. 'You'd get the whiff of a cannery or a pulp mill. Woodsmoke from a logging camp . . . Waterfalls give good fixes. They're precise on the chart, and you can hear them from a long way off.'

Fog breeds an anxious hyper-alertness of the senses. The continuous danger of grounding and collision wakens you to powers and instincts you barely knew you had. Ears cocked, nose twitching, eyes peeled for the slightest movement, darkening, or differentiation in the grey, you find yourself moving like a wild creature. This is how the badger must feel as it prowls through the darkness.

On *Alaska Seas*, as on every fishing boat of that time, the Hansen *Handbook* was kept propped open on the shelf beside the wheel. Mike had lent me his copy to take on my own trip north: bound in bottle-green leatherette, the 1951 edition looked like an old family hymnal. First published in 1917, Captain Sofius Hansen's *Handbook for Piloting in the Inland Waters of the Puget Sound Area, British Columbia, Southeastern Alaska, Southwestern Alaska, and Western Alaska* was used by every fisherman and towboatman on the Inside Passage, before radar made it obsolete. Captain Hansen reduced all the major routes between Seattle and the Bering Strait to lists of landmarks, compass courses, and exact mileages. His book gave you Alaska by numbers. Using Hansen and dead reckoning, you could safely ditchcrawl your way along 2,500 miles of chronically fog-ridden coast.

For his 865-mile route between Seattle and Juneau, Hansen gave some three hundred and fifty changes of course. Here we are in Haro Strait, for instance, with Kellett Bluff half a mile off on the starboard beam. A carefully measured run of two miles on a course of NW ¾ N, or 323° Magnetic, will put us two miles abreast of the bell-buoy (as it was then) on Danger Shoal. And so it goes: past Turn Point Light, Pelorus Point, Canoe Rock Light, Mouatt Point . . . The margins of the text are crammed with the captain's pen-and-ink sketches of the lighthouses, islands, headlands, waterfalls, cliffs, and rocks that mark the passage to Juneau, mile by annotated mile.

In rough weather and thick visibility, Hansen was the ancient mariner at one's elbow in the wheelhouse. His voice was gruff and calming. 'Start turn when light is 2 points forward of beam.' 'Change course when light is 045° on bow.' His drawings of the passing land-scape took a seamanlike, no-nonsense view of nature, as a string of signposts conveniently engraved on the hills. He boiled down John Muir's romantic wilderness to postage-stamp-sized outlines, severely cross-hatched, with little arrows pointing to their distinguishing marks. The sea in each picture was shown by four lines, closely ruled in parallel.

Hansen's sketches gave his *Handbook* its engaging personality: they were dogged, painstaking, and free of any facile touches of art. Looking at them, I could see the captain squinting, breathing heavily, his fist bunched around the pen, as he peered through the wheelhouse window. Small wonder, then, that people were fond of Hansen and kept it on their shelves at home, as they kept no other, more official, pilot-book. Wanting a copy for myself, I posted an ad on the notice board at Fishermen's Terminal. I got half a dozen calls in reply, from retired fishermen and fishermen's widows. Each caller said that I could look at his or her copy, and perhaps borrow it for a few days, but it was too precious to sell. Years after the boat had been broken up for scrap, the Hansen *Handbook*, its pages crinkled with damp and ringed with coffee stains, remained as the last evocative memento of the annual voyage north; opening it at random could set off a flash flood of memory. Every second-hand bookstore in Seattle carried bashed-up copies of *The U.S. Coast Pilot* and *The British Columbia Pilot*, but none carried Hansen. The friend of one's youth, he was not for sale.

Meanwhile, I was stuck in fog that thinned and thickened but would not lift. The beacon on the islet at the end of Sidney Spit made a brief, ghostly visitation, then faded out. The wake from something large rolled smoothly through the anchorage. I listened to it break, close by, on sand, the splash of the waves defining the shape of the beach. The town of Sidney was only two miles across the water, and I could easily have tapped my way back to the boat harbour, the Chinese restaurant, the gift shop, the next back issue of *The Times*. But the boat was safe here, displaced from the world in its cocoon of fog, and I was glad to stay.

I kept house: tidied the cabin, swept the floor, wax-polished the saloon table. By the time the last of the daylight drained out of the fog, leaving the boat in thick, furry darkness, there was a casserole, loosely based on Elizabeth David, bubbling on the stove. A cone of primrose light from the bulkhead lamp fell on the pages of an open book. I could hear the mooing of the traffic out on the strait, and the links of my anchor chain rearranging themselves on the sandy bottom as the boat swung to the tide. With the boat sashaying gently on a swirl of current, I poured a drink and settled down to read.

In this dreary and comfortless region, it was no inconsiderable piece of good fortune to find a little cove in which we could take shelter, and a small spot of level land on which we could erect our tent . . .

Sailing north, the crew of *Discovery* again felt the weight of their old cargo of bad feelings. The elation that swept through the ship when it arrived in the Northwest had evaporated, as the survey trips in small boats grew more repetitive and exhausting, contact with the natives became routine, the supply of fresh food dwindled, and the surrounding land steepened forbiddingly, offering ever fewer prospects of future settlement. The winds were fitful and contrary. The expedition hauled itself slowly forward through a blur of mist and rain. Spirits were low, tempers short. On the quarterdeck, the short, fat, florid captain put an increasingly frigid distance between himself and his officers and midshipmen, and the air was charged with acrimony.

Six months had passed since Vancouver ordered the flogging of Midshipman the Hon. Thomas Pitt, in January 1792, when *Discovery* and *Chatham* lay at anchor in Matavai Bay, Tahiti. The incident, festering in the memory of the ship's company, wasn't the cause of the bad feelings so much as the nucleus around which they cohered. When the gentlemen aboard *Discovery* tried to justify their dislike of Captain Van, their minds instinctively went back to Matavai Bay: to the moored ship rolling uncomfortably in the swell; the steam bath heat; the full complement of officers and midshipmen formally assembled in the captain's cabin; young Pitt, stripped to the waist and spreadeagled on a gun-carriage; the lash in the hand of John Noot, the boatswain's mate.

Pitt had joined *Discovery* at Falmouth, the ship's last English port of call, from the family seat at Camelford in Cornwall. Vancouver had looked forward to having him aboard: the sixteen-year-old was heir to the Camelford barony and a cousin to William Pitt, the Prime Minister. He hoped to inspire in the well-connected young aristocrat the kind of devoted admiration that Captain Cook had roused in the midshipmen on *Resolution*, twenty years before. As his naming of the Pacific Northwest betrayed, Captain Van had a middle-class weakness for lords and ladies, especially when their titles were linked to political clout in Parliament and the Admiralty. As a career naval officer, without a private income, without relatives in high places, Vancouver was mournfully conscious of the loneliness and vulnerability of his position. In 1796, he would complain in a letter to Lord Chatham that he was 'as it were insulated, from all connections with persons of consequence. . . . I know no friend in power, on whom I can call.' So on paper, at least, Midshipman Pitt seemed quite a catch.

But Midshipman Pitt in person was not at all what Vancouver had in mind. The boy, at six feet plus, towered over the man: languid, willowy, with a Roman nose and a petulant curl to his upper lip. Vancouver had fondly anticipated a manner of well-bred deference – head becomingly tilted downward, eyelids at half-staff, in the presence of a superior officer, et cetera. Instead Pitt (along with an objectionable quantity of luggage) came up the gangway as if he owned the ship, and spoke as if he'd absentmindedly mistaken his captain for a tenant farmer. Vancouver, always prickly, and too quick off the mark at divining signs of insubordination, loathed what he interpreted as the boy's loud, braying insouciance. The lieutenants on *Discovery*, who saw more of Pitt than Vancouver ever did, didn't think him particularly difficult or disobedient. The general view was that he was larksome, a little wild, good company but sixteen.

During the voyage south to Cape Town, Tom Pitt emerged as the spokesman for the midshipmen – a further irritant to Vancouver, who suspected that his young gentlemen were being set against him, and corrupted, by this gangling, arrogant, offensive boy. Pitt, he believed, was behind every outbreak of juvenile rough-housing, as he was at the centre of the games of whist and loo played for insolently high stakes. He had only to set eyes on the midshipman to feel obscurely taunted by him.

Pitt on the quarterdeck, talking to his cronies in his born-to-rule voice, set Vancouver's teeth on edge. In every interview with the boy, Captain Van felt his own want of inches, money, social standing, and natural authority; and he conceived of Pitt as a danger to the good order of the ship.

Pitt fell asleep on watch.

Pitt, ragging late at night with two other midshipmen, broke the glass of the steering compass.

Pitt, on watch in the forecastle, failed to answer his captain when hailed from the quarterdeck.

The multiple offences of Midshipman Pitt became Vancouver's haunting obsession.

Discovery and *Chatham* reached Tahiti (then known as Otaheite) in December 1791. Vancouver had last seen it fourteen years before, as a midshipman on Cook's third voyage. Nearly all the islanders he met on that visit were now dead, and the Tahitian women – remembered for their loveliness – now appeared to Vancouver as gross, unattractive, riddled with syphilis. 'The extreme deficiency of female beauty on these islands', he wrote, 'makes it singularly remarkable, that so large a proportion of the crew belonging to the *Bounty*, should have become so infatuated as to sacrifice their country, their honour, and their lives, to any female attachments at Otaheite.'

George Hewitt, the surgeon's mate on *Discovery*, tartly remarked that in 1777 Vancouver had been 'a Young Man but that not being now the Case the Ladies of course were not so attractive'. Vancouver's conviction that syphilis was rife was based on a mistake made by Cook, who confused the symptoms of syphilis with those of yaws – which was endemic in the south Pacific, and not venereally transmitted. Whether because he'd lost his own libido, or because he feared the spread of infection aboard his ships, Vancouver made the hugely unpopular decision to deny shore leave to anyone below the rank of lieutenant.

This was a violent break with naval custom. The rest-and-recreation facilities of Tahiti and Hawaii were the chief attraction of voyages to the Pacific. English sailors would cruise the native villages in search of girlfriends, and at nightfall, women would swim out to the anchored ships, selling sex for a handful of nails. Iron, in any form, was the usual pay for a prostitute. Tender tropical nights in the arms of an obliging girl were an expected perk on any South Sea expedition.

Vancouver ordered shore parties on ship's business to avoid fraternization with natives. Almost everyone aboard the two ships thought the ban cruel in the extreme, and many sought sex on the sly.

While on an official shore party, Captain Van spotted Midshipman Pitt talking with a woman and put him under immediate arrest. He was found to be in possession of a piece of iron, part of an old cask-hoop bent into a zigzag shape and used in the midshipmen's quarters as a griddle.

The twisted scrap of metal gave Vancouver the excuse he needed. The iron hoop was technically part of the ship's stores; ergo, Pitt had committed theft. Vancouver sentenced the midshipman to two dozen lashes for 'purloining'.

As Joseph Whidbey, master of *Discovery*, later wrote, 'If such a construction as *Purloining* is applicable to the cutting up of an Iron hoop I am afraid that there are few Officers in the Navy, that are not guilty of *Purloining*.'

The usual punishment for an errant midshipman was to be 'mast-headed' – sent aloft for a few hours with an improving book. None of the lieutenants backed Vancouver's judgement; and in the ward-room the sentence was thought the outrageous revenge of a mad captain on his unfortunate *bête noire*.

Vancouver, feeling goaded by Pitt beyond forbearance, was too unimaginative to look ahead into the likely consequences of what he was now doing. He knew he had to assert the power of rank over the insidious power of class; had to humiliate Pitt for the sake of his own captaincy; had to show the ship's company that his rightful authority, as per His Majesty's commission, was not to be undermined by an insufferable young lordling.

Of all the officers on board *Discovery*, the first lieutenant, Zachary Mudge, was the most upset by the sentence. Mudge owed his own position to the patronage of the Pitts; and Lady Camelford had made a point of entrusting her son to Mudge's personal care for the dura-tion of the voyage, an unenviable assignment. Subsequently, Sir Joseph Banks would describe Mudge as a man 'who appears to have born but a moderate Character'; he was certainly an ineffectual go-between. Whenever he tried to approach Vancouver on Pitt's behalf, he exposed himself to the captain's impatient fury; and when he tried to approach Pitt, he met only with the midshipman's inflated sense of his name and social station.

At six bells in the forenoon watch (eleven o'clock), all officers and midshipmen were ordered to present themselves, in uniform and wearing swords, in the main cabin. The fifteen marines aboard were mustered on the quarterdeck under their lieutenant, standing at attention with muskets shouldered. The boatswain's mate carried the cat-o'-nine-tails in his ceremonial red-plush bag. (Hence 'to let the cat out of the bag'.)

Archibald Menzies, as ship's naturalist, claimed the privilege of a civilian and kept to his private cabin, where he still could hear the intolerably long-drawn-out administration of the punishment. The drumlike construction of the ship's hull made the sounds of John Noot's footsteps, and each crack of the lash, reverberate between decks.

After the first dozen lashes was an interval. Blood trickled from the welts on Pitt's narrow back; his body looked like a carcass hanging in a butcher's shop. Mudge detached himself from the line of officers and went up to the boy, saying that if Pitt would vow to behave better in the future, he would plead with the captain to remit the final dozen lashes.

With what was left of his voice, the midshipman said something about 'honour', and then that he 'would not be begd off by Mr Mudge'.

Noot laid on twelve more strokes of the cat.

When news of the flogging filtered back to London, brought there by fur traders who had stopped in at Nootka Sound and Hawaii, some of the papers reported that a mutiny had taken place on *Discovery*. That wasn't true. *Discovery* wasn't *Bounty*, and naval discipline held, both during and after the punishment of Thomas Pitt. Yet after Matavai Bay, the ship's command structure came to rest on rank and regulations alone. Captain Van could no longer count on the affectionate respect of any of his officers. They obeyed his orders. They trusted his expertise as a navigator and surveyor. They acknowledged his professional experience. But that was as far as they went. Even Joseph Whidbey, Vancouver's favourite, couldn't respond to him with any warmth. An atmosphere of stiff correctitude reigned on the quarterdeck as *Discovery*, a tiny, crowded wooden world, rolled uncomfortably across the North Pacific.

Every so often, the Matavai Bay skeleton would rattle the door of its closet.

On the King's birthday, 4 June 1792, Captain Van proclaimed a twofold celebration: the survey of the Puget Sound region was complete, and next day the expedition would sail north into the Gulf of Georgia (now Georgia Strait). The loyal toast would be observed with a double issue of grog for the men, and a vinous feast in the main cabin. Tom Pitt's closest friend aboard the ship, the Honourable

Charles Stuart, son of Lord Bute, got himself boisterously drunk. In a moment of weird alcoholic theatre, he pulled a razor from the pocket of his waistcoat and made a vainglorious speech to Vancouver. 'If, Sir, you ever flog me, I will not survive this disgrace: I have this ready to cut my throat with.'

In Sir Joseph Banks's account, based on Menzies's firsthand report, 'Mr. Stuart experienced much inconvenience from the Captains Revenge from the beginning of the Quarrell he was often sent to the masthead as a punishment for trifling or supposed offenses & kept there an unreasonable time but his Spirit never gave way he did his duty to the utmost of his Ability & bore the injustice he received patiently.'

Like puffs of dust, the reek of ancient class snobbery still rises from these pages. The 'disgrace' feared by Stuart was clearly the disgrace of being sentenced to be flogged by someone he regarded as a common little man – and most of the people who left some written record of the voyage shared the young Honourable's opinion of Vancouver as a coarse-grained parvenu. Another young gentleman, Robert Barrie, referred to Vancouver as 'a mere sailor not an educated man' (he was comparing him with La Pérouse). That the Grand Tour aspect of the voyage should have attracted such a bevy of disdainful young swells – boys born to expose his every solecism and insecurity – was Captain Van's bad luck. Trying to resolve his social difficulties, he only made them worse.

Writing to a friend in 1793, from Monterey, California, Midshipman Thomas Manby described the nasty mood on the quarter-deck:

We are my good fellow spinning about the Globe like a Worligig, seldom in a place, and as seldom like true Seamen contented with our situation. Good health continues in our little squadron, though I am sorry to add not that good fellowship which ought to subsist with adventurers travelling these distant Seas, owing to the conduct of our Commander in Chief who is grown Haughty Proud Mean and Insolent, which has kept himself and

Officers in a continual state of wrangling during the whole of the Voyage.

Following the undercurrents of Vancouver's voyage, through the lavish footnotes and appendices of W. Kaye Lamb's Hakluyt Society edition, I felt a growing kinship with the man. I was annoyed to overhear his midshipmen talking of him as their natural inferior. The Lords of the Admiralty thought well enough of Vancouver to entrust him with one of the great expeditions of the age. They saw him as the logical heir to Captain Cook; he knew the Pacific, he had studied astronavigation under a leading astronomer and mathematician, he had an unblotted record as a midshipman and lieutenant. Yet his failure to win the respect of a scornful band of teenage patricians wrecked his captaincy.

His ship was a little floating England, in a period of great class upheaval. Vancouver, rising on his own merits, was a new man, and a lonely one. He possessed every necessary technical skill, though without any leavening of charm or humour. His very existence aboard *Discovery* was a threat to the old aristocratic order – people brutally expert at cutting outsiders down to size. The customs collector's son, with his mangled Dutch name (originally van Coeverden) and root-vegetable features, was forced to endure the supercilious mockery of his juniors.

He tried to rise above his unpopularity, keeping himself increasingly aloof. Or *a-luff.* When a ship 'keeps aloof', it sails as close to the wind as possible, trying to avoid being driven onto a lee shore. He withdrew into his superior rank like an injured hermit crab into its shell. Coming out of his private quarters, he aimed to present to the world a façade of inscrutable gravity, but it kept on crumbling before the force of his ungovernable temper.

He 'behaved like a Madman raged and swore', wrote George Hewitt after one of Vancouver's outbursts. 'His salutation I can never forget, and his language I will never forgive', wrote Thomas Manby after another. 'It was no unusual thing with him to be passionate and illiberal in his abuse', wrote Menzies.

Dignity eluded Captain Van. His meltdowns were triggered by the slightest affront to his authority. An unpunctual rendezvous, smoke from a bonfire set by natives, a flicker of insubordination from a midshipman, a mention of Menzies's accursed quarterdeck greenhouse – and Vancouver would explode, scalding everyone around him with the lava flow of his rage. Yet when it came to the tedious and frustrating business of nautical astronomy, an eerie calm came over him: setting up the observatory tent, waiting patiently for the low clouds to disclose Antares or Polaris, taking sights by the score, then working them out on paper and transferring them to the ever-growing chart, Vancouver was alone among his officers in his methodical placidity. So quick to blaze up at any man-made impediment to his will, George Vancouver was benignly tolerant of the vagaries of the weather and the stars.

There was no dawn for me, only a slow dwindling of the darkness into oatmeal-grey. I struggled out of bed into the nimbus cloud that had taken possession of the cabin and draped itself around the unwashed dishes and half-emptied glass of wine. Vancouver, in four volumes, sprawled untidily over the settee, the table, and the floor. On the VHF marine weather channel, shore stations on the mainland coast of Georgia Strait were reporting visibility in miles, which was promising. As the morning wore on, I fretted through the hours, making repeated visits to the cockpit, trying to shift the fog by mind-power. The top of the mainmast was lost in fog, the bow-pulpit an indefinite shadow of its former self. My bronchial cough sounded mildly alarming as it came rattling back to me from the invisible shore.

Past two o'clock the fog suddenly evaporated, revealing a world of misty unexpected distances. Sidney showed as a substantial city, many miles off; the rocks and islands to the north looked limitless as they trailed away into the haze. I got the engine started, winched up the anchor, and clawed into the archipelago against a smooth, fast river of tide.

Meringue-like gobbets of fog were caught in shady, northward-facing hollows, but otherwise the coast was clear. It was a slow, sunlit wriggle through the islands, ticking off the marks as they crept by on the beam. In Satellite Channel I was overhauled by an elderly wooden purse-seiner, Seattle-registered and painted up to the nines, as if off to Ketchikan on a blind date. Her hull was a brilliant moss-green, with red and white trim. The final touches were still being put on; much of the deckhouse was clad in grey primer, and on the afterdeck, in the lee of the house and just out of sight of the skipper at the wheel, a man stood smoking, paint bucket at his feet. He lifted his cigarette in salute as he was carried past, and for a moment I thought I'd met him before – the pale hair tied back in a ponytail, the childish stare, the greasy, flyblown tartan jacket.

Rounding Musgrave Point, at the entrance to Sansum Narrows, I slowed and let the boat drift in neutral past the tiny cove at the foot of a steep overgrown meadow on Saltspring Island. A ramshackle jetty ran out from the beach. This was where the ketch *Tzu Hang* was moored in the 1950s, when it wasn't being pitchpoled and dismasted off Cape Horn, or visiting Japan, the Hebrides, or any of the other spots around the globe to which Brigadier Miles Smeeton and his wife, Beryl, used to sail on the flimsiest of pretexts. They gave themselves rational destinations – Melbourne, to see the 1955 Olympics; Tokyo, to return a ceremonial sword to a Japanese general – but these were just excuses for them to indulge their addiction to big waves, nautical emergencies, and huge doses of undiluted solitude on the ocean. I had some of Miles Smeeton's books on board – *Once Is Enough*, *Sunrise to Windward*, *The Sea Was Our Village* – and I'd hoped to catch a glimpse, at least, of Musgrave, the Smeetons' farmhouse. If the house still stood, it was securely hidden by the trees above the meadow.

The Smeetons had been a famously daunting couple: crusty, Spartan, quarrelsome, tough as a pair of old boots, and resolutely happy. Leaving India and the army in 1947, the year of Indian independence, they had shrunk from the prospect of a life of tame restriction in Clement Attlee's postcolonial socialist Britain. Sight unseen, they'd bought Musgrave – a ruin, half-smothered in blackberries and salal – out here in the Western wilderness. Then, like many other ex-officers at the end of the war, temperamentally at odds with peacetime life, the Smeetons had gone poking around the muddy ports of England in search of a mothballed boat in which they could escape to sea. *Tzu Hang*, found in Dover, became their 46-foot ark, in which the Smeetons' unfashionable code of values was enshrined. The central character in Miles's books, it becomes an emblem of personal liberty, self-sufficiency, thrift (Beryl, at a pinch, would serve her guests curried cat food for a grandly presented dinner), and the romantic quest for hazardous adventure.

Tzu Hang was a counter-world, sailing on the reciprocal course to that taken by post-war Britain. As a child of that time, I quailed at the idea of the Smeetons and what they stood for. I knew very well that if the brigadier and I had ever come face to face, he would have immediately nailed me as a ninny and a wet – a typical produce of the welfare state he so despised. In turn, I'd have thought him a ferocious dodo. But I read his books with pleasure, and travelled as a vicarious stowaway aboard *Tzu Hang*, admiring the hardihood and bravery of the Smeetons from a safe distance, without having the least desire or ability to emulate them.

In 1968, the ageing Smeetons sold *Tzu Hang* to a friend. Several owners later, she was carrying large cargoes of marijuana on the Colombia–Chesapeake Bay run, and in 1988 she was impounded by US Customs agents. In 1990, a Puerto Rican ship-breaker bulldozed her to bits.

The sun, blocked by the mountains on Vancouver Island, had already left the cove, and the water on which *Tzu Hang* used to swing was turning fast to pitch. The Smeetons were gone – Beryl died in 1979, Miles in 1988 – and the remains of their beloved boat were now interred in a San Juan landfill. Miles's godson, Miles Clark, whom I came to know when he was working on their biography, had very recently killed himself, aged thirty-two. The last I'd heard from him had been a cheerful fax describing his plans to sail into the heart of Russia via the Black Sea and the Volga; it was an expedition that I envied, though I hadn't bothered to send Clark a letter in return. His suicide happened soon after he came home from his Russian expedition. It was a horrible end to a bright young career. Passing Musgrave now, its dock fallen in, its fence in need of repair, I was taken aback by how powerfully it gave off the too-intimate stink of the Reaper.

Twilight perhaps made Sansum Narrows seem more sepulchral than it really was: the black cliffs on either side of the passage interlocking with each other like pieces of a loose-fitting jigsaw puzzle; the name Burial Islet attached to a low grassy hummock in midstream; the priestly cormorants on a line of pilings by the shore. In the narrows between Sansum Point and Bold Bluff the broken water burbled like a pebbly brook, though the chart showed it to be three hundred feet deep. A fishing boat, southward-bound, riding the tide, came rocketing out of the pass as I went in, to labour hard against the current, the shallow-sounding water tinkling and spitting around the hull.

Six miles on, wreaths of pale steam from the tall chimneys of the pulp mill at Crofton drifted across the dark sky. It was just possible to make out the low-floating islands of logs in the booming grounds, a fair-sized forest stripped and peeled, ready to be ground up and cooked in the mill. Moving slowly, watching out for the dangerous silhouettes of escaped logs in the water ahead, I eased into the cluster of fishing boats at the government dock, where an amiable pyknic type took my lines and tied me up. The fenders of my boat had barely kissed the dock before Mr Pyknic was talking my ear off.

He was a self-appointed one-man chamber of commerce for Crofton and its glories. A shift-worker at the mill, he commuted from his home on an island a few miles away, in a new white 21-foot motorboat, his own marine sport-utility vehicle. With a family across the water and a little Filipino darling in Crofton – who even now was fetching him a bowl of hot noodles – he was, he said, as happily placed as anyone in the province.

Mr Pyknic, like many outgoing innocents I'd met, valued cunning above all other virtues. He was proud of his own, and generously appreciative of other people's. He drew my attention – as if it needed to be drawn – to the steepling mill chimneys that rose more than three hundred feet above our heads.

'You know how that steam smells?' he said.

I did. Steam from a pulp mill in full production reeks like the intestinal gas of a giant on a badly balanced diet.

'Well, the way they designed it, you never smell it in Crofton. Those chimneys carry it right up and over the hill there, so it all gets dumped round Cowichan Bay, where the rich and fancy live. Cunning, see?'

He was keen to show off his boat, a marvel 'made right here in BC'. He led me through the engine controls, showed me how the seats in the back folded into a double bed, and said, 'Now, watch this.' He slid aside a panel to reveal a sky-blue plastic receptacle. 'My little flushing shitter,' he said fondly. 'Cunning, isn't it?'

I was glad to see his Filipino friend gingerly descending the cleated walkway in high heels, carrying the promised noodle bowl in both hands. Grabbing Vancouver, volume two, I took flight into town.

Crofton was a very Western settlement in the way that its great expectations had not been granted historical reality. The founding fathers had laid out a broad grid of streets on a cleared hillside over-looking Stuart Channel, but after more than ninety years of occupation the grid was still thinly sprinkled with fewer stores and houses than would have comfortably filled a single street. Most of Crofton was oily grass. While its fine view over the Gulf Islands might have attracted the tourist and retirement industries, the cathedral-like dominance of the pulp mill and the proletarian aspect of the surrounding houses made the town invulnerable to the northward march of chichi development on Vancouver Island. One couldn't possibly mistake it for a fishing village ripe for prettying-up with a lick of paint, a tourist kiosk, and a few antique lamp standards. Crofton looked like a place where working people worked, smoked, tinkered with engines, and put forth gouts of noxious steam.

At the Dockside Motel-Pub-Cafe, I ploughed happily through the $8.95 turkey dinner. Vancouver was propped open between the ketchup bottle, verso, and the mustard-squirt, recto. Discovery and

Chatham were moving up the mainland coast, about twenty miles due east of Crofton, following the mazecraft rule and keeping the starboard shore in sight. Vancouver's mood – even as he tried to gloss it in his Petersham lodgings three years later, turning his logbooks into a literary production – was grim, and getting grimmer.

He idolized Cook. His whole idea of captaincy was modelled on Cook's example. Yet Vancouver was as far from being Captain Cook as I am from being Miles Smeeton.

Part of Cook's extraordinary appeal lay in the heroic obscurity of his social origins. The son of an itinerant agricultural labourer, James Cook at seventeen was working behind the counter in a haberdashery and grocery in Staithes, Yorkshire. He went to sea in a Whitby collier, then joined the navy, where at twenty-seven he was a boatswain, at twenty-eight a master, at thirty-nine a first lieutenant, at forty-two a commander, at forty-six a post-captain – rising through the ranks by the force of his own maritime genius, a word often used in reports on Cook by senior officers.

Portraits of Cook by various artists all agree on his great scimitar nose, his square-cut chin, the austere set of his lips, his large, deeply recessed eyes. It is a raptor's face, like that of an osprey given human features; a useful visage on the quarterdeck.

Cook had the knack of being able to simultaneously enthral and terrify his juniors. He handled the stern mask of command like a talented actor, occasionally lifting it a few inches to disclose the face behind – a move calculated to inspire awe. One of George Vancouver's fellow midshipmen aboard *Resolution*, James Trevenen, has left a sketch of Cook on a shore-excursion with his young gentlemen:

> *Capt. Cook also on these occasions, would sometimes relax from his almost constant severity of disposition, & condescend now and then, to converse familiarly with us. But it was only for the time, as soon as we entered the ships, he became again the despot.*

Poor Vancouver: too young, too short, too plain, too lacking in self-control to act the part of Captain Cook. Yet that totemic figure – 'that distinguished character', 'this great man', with 'his profundity of judgement' and 'pre-eminent abilities' – haunts his disciple's *Voyage*. Captain Van saw himself as cast in the same mould, and it was with deep injured chagrin that he came to realize that no one on his expedition could share with him this lofty self-image. The harder he tried to promote it – frowning darkly, exactly as Cook had frowned darkly – the more the midshipmen sniggered behind his back.

Cook had the grace to come from nowhere; Vancouver the misfortune to come from a too easily identifiable somewhere. Cook's rise in the world was a fabulous occurrence – a phoenix, born in smoke and ashes – and his high rank something the aristocracy could regard with complacent pride. Cook proved that there was room for wild untutored genius in the upper echelons of eighteenth-century England; he also proved that such genius, being extremely rare, was no threat to the system.

Vancouver was a different matter. His tax-collecting father was prominently involved in local politics, in the Tory interest, and was known around King's Lynn as Little Van; his mother, a younger daughter from a landed East Anglian family. The trouble with Captain Van – viewed from the acutely class-conscious angle of the quarterdeck – was that he was both too little and too much a gentleman. Issuing from the dangerous margin of genteel society, he was neither fish nor fowl. He had only to handle a sea otter pelt for a superior midshipman to murmur 'Trade!' – the most damaging epithet in the class lexicon. Thomas Manby, himself striving for the hand of the Marquis of Townshend's daughter, had Vancouver's number:

His Language to his Officers is too bad, and I am sorry to say what with his pursuing business, and a Trade he has carried on, are unbecoming the Character of an Officer in his Honourable and exalted station.

Yet Cook bought skins at Nootka and always kept a weather eye out for likely opportunities of personal enrichment. Trade interested him keenly: he hadn't worked in the shop in Staithes for nothing. After his death, his widow, Elizabeth, lived in much discussed grandeur in Clapham, complete with a liveried footman. But what Cook could get away with was no guide to what Vancouver's junior officers would allow him. People warmed to the pirate in Captain Cook; the same people turned up their noses at what they saw as the money-grubbing vulgarity of Captain Van.

Working slowly up the coast, Vancouver wrote that he was 'disappointed' by what he saw: it was 'rugged', 'barren', 'dull', 'sterile', 'gloomy', 'dreary', 'comfortless'. Each of these words is used again and again. They were all the colours available on Vancouver's verbal palette for the month of June 1792, and seem to describe the captain's internal geography at least as much as they describe the mainland coast of British Columbia. The dripping precipice, the black firs, the mist and rain, the tumbled shale and rock, the powerful but irregular tidal currents might be the evergreen landscape of depression itself, the natural habitat of Black Dog, with whom Vancouver had a more intimate relationship than he did with any human being.

Beneath the payphone at the Dockside was a blue Naugahyde couch that had died of stab wounds several years before. Sprawled among its bushy extrusions of stuffing, with a mug of beer at my feet, I dialled Seattle.

There was an echo on the line. Though we were separated by only a hundred miles as the gull flies, it sounded as if we were talking across an ocean.

It took some time for Jean to persuade Julia to come to the phone. 'Hi, Daddy, we goed to Coe Park, I had spinach pie, I'm watching Mowgli on TV, you can talk to Mommy now, 'bye—' and she was gone.

'She's distracted,' Jean said. 'She's got *The Jungle Book* on the video.'

'Am I in bad odour with her?'

'No, she's just distracted right now. I'm distracted too. There's a whole bunch of crazy shit going on around here.'

A violet fog of cigarette smoke eddied round the Dockside pool table, throwing the players into soft focus.

'Where are you, anyway?'

'Oh, a mill town on Vancouver Island. A lot of logs, some fish boats, a Canadian pub—'

We talked baby-sitters. Jean's job, as dance reviewer for the *Seattle Times*, required her to go out to concerts three evenings a week, and then to sit up over her computer, often till four in the morning, when the paper went to bed, hacking her overnight piece out of a chaos of phrases. For help with Julia she was raiding the pool of teenage girls who staffed the checkouts at Ken's, our local supermarket. The girls tended to beg off at the last moment, because they had dates, or colds, or homework, or forbidding parents. That night, Jean had been scheduled to review a concert, but the baby-sitter had called at seven to say she couldn't make it.

And where was Julia's father in all this? Jean's tone implied. Out at the pub, with all the other deadbeat dads.

'I'm sorry,' I said, to her tone of voice rather than to any particular accusation. My presence at the Dockside, on the slaughtered couch, seemed to me, too, to be an inexcusable defection.

'Well, have a wonderful time,' Jean said, as if Crofton were Waikiki. 'How's the weather?'

'Fine,' I said miserably, and we rang off without endearments.

In a hangdog mood I went back to the boat. Crossing the railroad tracks in the dark, I stumbled and turned my ankle. Vancouver took a flying leap into the grass. Hobbling painfully to the wharf, I saw that Mr Pyknic's boat was still tied up there, with a light showing through drawn curtains. I crept past, dragging my bad ankle behind me as quietly as I could. Hauling myself aboard my own boat at the shrouds, I disturbed an owl perching on the mainmast crosstrees. It clattered off into the night sky on creaking wings. From the Pyknic floating lovenest came the sound of muffled laughter.

I was up soon after dawn, with a slight limp and a jumpy eagerness to put Crofton far astern. The fog was back. Mr Pyknic's boat was gone. I took my coffee mug out to the cockpit to watch the ferry leave and gauge the visibility on the water. With a long, sorrowful blast, the ferry pulled away from the dock and headed for Saltspring Island. Inside sixty seconds its colours paled, and its outline began to fuzz; in two minutes it was a grey ghost, and in three it was gone. At my best guess, visibility was roughly half a mile – just enough, so long as it got no worse.

On the far side of the pontoon, a man and a boy were readying a gill-netter for departure. Since there was no net on the big aluminium drum, I asked the man if he was off on a pleasure jaunt.

'We're going beachcombing,' he said.

His gill-netter, its powerful winch dominating the stern, was now a makeshift tugboat, and he spent his days cruising through the islands in search of logs that had escaped from rafts and booming-grounds – the floaters and deadheads that bedevilled my navigation of these waters. When he was in luck, he could assemble a sizeable raft of truant timber, which he towed back to the pulp mill and sold by the metre-length. A single big fir fetched $150.

'It pays the wages,' he said. 'There's more money in logs now than there is in fish.'

With his spectacles and close-cropped hair, he looked like a lean, tanned high school teacher, and he took a detached, teacherly view of what had happened to the fishing. Glancing at my limp and soggy British ensign, he said, 'We like to blame the Americans, but that's just trying to shift the responsibility. We're all to blame for it. We were too greedy for too long. We wrecked the fishery. And now we're beachcombers.'

It wasn't just in old men's memories – of boats laden to the gun-wales, sinking under the weight of their catch; of the entire surface of Juan de Fuca Strait torn and white with the splashes of leaping fish – that the great salmon runs of the past were now preserved. In the summer of 1990, a few months after my arrival in Seattle, Jean and I, on passage to Vancouver, ran into the salmon fleet off the mouth of the Fraser River. Trying to thread our boat between the floating nets of several hundred gill-netters was nightmare pilotage. For more than an hour we zigzagged, at half speed, through openings barely wider than the boat, sliding hull-to-hull past the fishermen, with Jean up on the bow yelling warnings, as we inched through a sea of white corks. I thought then that a salmon would have to be Houdini to evade the miles of suspended nylon mesh that barred its access to the spawning grounds upriver.

I never again saw the inshore fleet in full fig. Most of those boats were now rotting to death in harbours up and down the coast, with FOR SALE signs glued to their forlorn windows. In Puget Sound, Juan de Fuca, and Georgia Strait, the sea had been fished clean out.

'It's the boys at the back of the class that I feel sorry for,' the beachcomber said. 'They were never going to be rocket scientists, and fishing was their one big chance. They could make something of themselves when the fishing was good. It's all right for people my age – we'll make out somehow. But for him –' he nodded his head in the direction of his own boy – 'it's his future, gone, just like that. Round here, kids of his age, they've got nothing to look forward to now. That's sad, and maybe dangerous, too.'

'You were a teacher,' I said.

'Yes. How did you know?'

'It wasn't exactly an inspired guess.'

I waved goodbye as they left on their scavenging. In seven minutes the gill-netter had dissolved into the fog. Then I followed them out, clinging to the massive chimneys of the pulp mill as a landmark and looking to starboard for ghosts.

On the morning of 22 June, in a hazy calm, Captain Van was seated in the sternsheets of the cutter while the men pulled at their oars, rowing south to Birch Bay, where *Discovery* and *Chatham* lay at anchor. He was on the return leg of a ten-day survey trip that had taken him more than eighty miles to the north and deep into a succession of gloomy, dead-end inlets. The days had been long and weary; hour after hour of sounding, taking sights, charting, naming.

The world we live in is the words we use, wrote Wittgenstein — and the world through which the cutter now moved under oars was one freshly recast in English words, and a *Who's Who* of the 1790s King's navy. The 'extensive sound' with its 'rugged snowy barrier' to the north was now Burrard's Channel, named for Sir Harry Burrard. The 'dreary and comfortless' reach beyond it was Howe Sound, after Admiral Earl Howe. Another 'equally dreary' fjord, fifty miles farther north, had taken the name Jervis Inlet, after Admiral Sir John Jervis.

Even in exhaustion and depression, Vancouver was understandably complacent. In ten days he had brought a great lonely tract of dark and foggy wilderness into the orderly ambit of English civilization. He now trained his spyglass on Point Grey, named nine days earlier after Captain George Grey, the younger son of General Grey, later Earl Grey. The low, thickly wooded promontory ended in a pale, curving bluff, off which lay two strange European ships, a small schooner and a brig.

Trespassers.

The cutter altered course. The captain snapped at Peter Puget to get the oarsmen to increase their striking-rate. Nearly ten minutes passed before Vancouver was able to make out, through the glass, the flags of the Spanish navy.

It was a devastating moment. Captain Van had known, of course, that the Spanish were on the outer coast; indeed, part of his commission was to reclaim the Spanish garrison at Nootka on behalf of His Britannic Majesty, in accordance with the treaty signed in 1789 at the Nootka Convention in Madrid. But he hadn't expected to find Spaniards poking around in his 'Mediterranean ocean'. Since entering the Strait of Juan de Fuca in May, he had been secure in the sense of his own originality, as the first white man ever to burst into this particular silent sea. Now the spyglass revealed that he was just another European visitor to a land already discovered, and by a foreign power.

As he would find out later that day, the Spanish had already sounded, charted, and named the very waters that Captain Van had been exploring for the last week and a half. Point Grey showed on their charts as Punta de Langara.

The world we live in is the words we use.

Point – Punta. Grey – Langara. Vancouver's names were suddenly robbed of their authority by their Spanish alternates. Where they had sounded natural and inevitable, they now seemed pert and capricious. In his *Voyage*, he confessed the humiliation caused by the first true discoverers of the Strait of Georgia:

> *I cannot avoid acknowledging that, on this occasion, I experienced no small degree of mortification in finding the external shores of the gulf had been visited, and already examined a few miles beyond where my researches during the excursion, had extended. . . .*

Yet aboard the brig *Sutil* and the schooner *Mexicana*, Vancouver found unexpected balm for his prickly soul. The two Spanish lieutenants in charge, Dionisio Alcalá Galiano and Cayetano Valdés, met Vancouver with a show of elaborate deference to his superior rank. Galiano spoke English, and laid on a fine breakfast in the main cabin of the schooner. The beautiful drawing-room manners of the Spanish officers, their quickness to concede Vancouver's every point, were in sharp contrast to the treatment he was used to receiving aboard his own ship. Over breakfast, Galiano expressed polite surprise that Captain Van had failed to discover the Fraser River, known to the Spanish as Rio Brancho, and Vancouver appears not to have noticed that his diligence as an explorer was being subtly called into question.

He loved being in the Spaniards' company – both here and, later in the voyage, at Nootka and in Monterey. As a man from the uneasy middle of English society, he was chronically uncomfortable with countrymen who came from grander backgrounds than his own – especially when they were under his command. But in a mess room full of foreigners, bound by the rules of international naval protocol, Vancouver flowered. He even managed to charm his hosts, though he couldn't speak a word of Spanish. To the Spaniards, Captain Van was the commander of the British expedition, and the designated representative of William Pitt and King George. They were not interested in his accent, or his father's occupation, or his failure to get along with his highborn midshipmen.

In the evening, when Vancouver was back on *Discovery*, a Spanish rowboat arrived in the British anchorage to present a sack of cabbages and a churn of milk from Juan Francisco de la Bodega y Quadra's farm at Nootka, with the compliments of Lieutenants Galiano and Valdés. These tastes of home were much enjoyed at the officers' long table on *Discovery*, though some of the diners were able to interpret the barbed message in the gift.

The cabbages and milk announced that the English were trespassers here, where the Spanish had already established a successful farm. Quadra, governor of Nootka, Knight of the Order of Santiago, was a famous bon vivant who had made a big splash on the outer coast. He liked to be greeted with expensive and deafening twenty-one-gun salutes. In return, he threw lavish dinner parties for visiting ships' captains and their officers: venison on crested silver platters, vintage Spanish wine in silver goblets, followed by toasts and after-dinner speeches. Naval explorers and fur traders were dazzled by the amenities of Quadra's country seat in the far West. At Friendly Cove he raised cattle, hogs, sheep, goats, and chickens. His extensive gardens were planted with European vegetables. His servants ran a bakery near the house. Each morning, Quadra sent out a boat to deliver hot rolls and milk to all the ships in the cove.

Under the terms of the Nootka Convention, he was required to hand over his estate to the British, whose claim to Nootka, though legal in the narrow sense, seemed tenuous when set against Quadra's industrious and popular occupation of the land. The milk and cabbages made the point, with refined irony. How could Captain

Vancouver presume to evict the hugely hospitable and courteous Governor Quadra from his fruitful acreage?

But Captain Van was not tuned to nuances. He drank his milk and ate his cabbage, then went off to write of 'these new and unexpected friends'.

The lifting fog uncovered Kuper and Thetis islands, and their offlying string of sawtooth reefs and islets. A mild southerly breeze blew into the face of the weakening ebb, chipping the surface of the water into small, flint-grey waves. Trying to make Dodd Narrows before the flood tide turned it into a breakneck slalom run, I had the headsail out and the engine running hard.

As one travelled north and west, the tidal passes grew more numerous, more turbulent, and more interesting. Dodd, where the sea spilled through the two hundred and twenty-five yard gap between Vancouver Island and Mudge Island at speeds of up to nine knots, was faster than Deception Pass, but little more than a premonition of the horizontal cataracts of Seymour Narrows (fifteen knots) and Nakwato Rapids (eighteen knots). The names of the passes – Arran, Yuculta, Dent, Hole-in-the-Wall, Greene Point, Whirlpool – were for me the most evocative by far of all the names on the coast. Each set of rapids had its own haunting character. If I went through a pass once, the whole face of the water left its features printed on my memory, from where it was likely to sneak into my dreams.

Also filed in memory, under the same rubric as the passes, was a painting by Lucian Freud of a dripping tap on the wall of his London studio. The form taken by the water in the painting was of a disorderly braid – a badly tied pigtail of escaping wisps and strands. I'd seen the picture in two exhibitions of Freud's work and been arrested by it for many minutes at a time. It answered beautifully my own obsession with the chaotic motion of fluids when they meet an obstruction – whether a defective tap-washer or the giant leg-and-boot of Portland Bill as it dangles into the English Channel and kicks up a maelstrom in which many ships have foundered. Freud, who works with legendary patience, must have spent weeks gazing at that twisting thread of water as it leaked into the sink below in a spindly, dishevelled double helix. Unique to that tap, that wall, that sink, Freud's Drip was a natural wonder as unreproducible as Seymour Narrows or the Arran Rapids; an exquisite domestic Niagara.

I reached Dodd Narrows in good time, the last few minutes of the ebb tide still in hand. From the south the pass showed as a tapering funnel, leading to a low, impenetrable tangle of brambles and alders at the far end. The water was laced with greasy boils and eddies, in which big chunks of scum, like pieces of yellowed foam upholstery, revolved slowly. The air stank of salty putrescence.

Out in the middle, a slovenly army of herring gulls was snacking on titbits thrown up by the flux. They yelled and jostled, fighting over whatever loose body parts had been left behind by such submarine scavengers as the dogfish and squid: an old anemone tubercle, half a flatworm, a bit of decayed starfish arm, a fibrous morsel of rancid crabmeat.

Dodd Narrows had a shallow, uneven bottom. When the tide was going at full tilt, even the heaviest objects trundling along the sea floor would be flung to the surface as they were sucked into the turmoil of the race. Stay long enough around Dodd Narrows and all kinds of pale, submerged horrors would no doubt come to light.

So the bickering gulls stabbed at shadows and leapfrogged over one another's backs to snatch at any lump of solid matter that boiled up from the bottom. Did gulls ever gag on what they ate? Was there some final, repulsive stage of decomposition at which a herring gull would draw a fastidious line?

A tug suddenly materialized out of the bushes, followed, seconds later, by its attendant raft of logs. The channel – which had a dogleg in its narrowest part – evidently lay a good hundred yards to the left of where I'd placed it. I hung back in the tail of the race, waiting for the tug to clear the approach and the tide to turn in my favour.

Then, taking aim on a notional gap in the alders, I drove the boat into the palpitating mass of gulls. Outstretched claws hanging straight down, wings throbbing, the birds rose to the level of the cock-pit coaming, screaming and fixing me in the indifferent glare of their yellow button-eyes. 'Hi ya! Hi ya!' It was like pushing through a mob of lager louts. Dead, I would've made a fine feast for the gulls, but as it was they could only sink resentfully back into the boat's wake and continue their pursuit of tastier, more seasoned flesh.

When I reached the alders, the flood had picked up speed, and I was poured smoothly through the neck of the pass by the new tide. The rank, low-water smell of Dodd Narrows lingered in my nose long after I had left the place astern. I tried lighting a cigarette, but the week-old-fish taste of the tobacco was too much, and I had to flip it overboard.

Dodd greatly impressed me, winning a secure position in my private pantheon of tidal passes. That it lay five miles downtide of the city of Nanaimo, and a mile and a half downtide of the Harmac pulp mill, accounted for much of its memorable personality: it was a gargantuan flush toilet.

I had thought of stopping for the night at Nanaimo, but with five hours of daylight still to go, and a friendly wind from the south-east, it seemed silly not to go on and catch up with the Vancouver expedi-tion on the far side of the Strait of Georgia, twenty-five miles to the north. I cranked up the mainsail, made a late lunch of cheese and Marmite sandwiches, and loafed in the cockpit, watching the shore of Vancouver Island fade into the haze at six miles' distance. To be out of sight of land at last, with a force 3–4 wind in the sails, an easy swell, and the boat, under autopilot, weaving around its set course of 323°, was a pleasure. I had a circle of sea, twelve miles in diameter, entirely to myself.

The ten-day exploration along the mainland coast of Georgia Strait sharpened the division between Vancouver and his younger officers and midshipmen. Probing the great steep-sided inlets of Howe Sound and Jervis, with their high snow-caps, thundering waterfalls, and stunted pines on rocky ledges, Captain Van saw a landscape that was ugly, intimidating, inhospitable, and useless. He instinctively recoiled from the sight of the dizzy precipice and the toppling crag: affronts to his taste for order. In Discovery Bay and Puget Sound, the low hills and forest clearings fitted nicely with Vancouver's conservative pre-conceptions of how nature should be arranged. But in the wild – and getting wilder – geology of the northern end of Georgia Strait, he was lost. He deplored the 'unfathomable' depths, complained that the roar of the cascades drowned out the birdsong, and was disappointed by the scant, dwarfish vegetation.

In this, as in much else, Captain Van was out of step. The land-scape he found merely depressing roused great excitement among the Grand Tourists, who felt that they were actually entering the awe-inspiring realm of the eighteenth-century Sublime – a word never far from the midshipmen's lips as they rowed, in a perpetual dank twilight, between beetle-browed cliffs, while the sun lit up snowfields thousands of feet above their heads.

On the conventional Grand Tour, the Alps had an important place on the route, as the gentlemen and their tutors went south in search of the Italian Renaissance. For Swiss excursions, the recommended reading was Edmund Burke's 1757 essay 'On the Sublime and the Beautiful', in which he carved out an intellectual space for wild nature, as one might encounter it in the English Lake District, the Alps, a tempest at sea, or vast uninhabited tracts of desert and prairie. According to Burke, appreciation of the Sublime began in terror.

Whatever is fitted in any sort to excite the ideas of pain and danger, that is to say, whatever is in any sort terrible, or is conver-sant about terrible objects, or operates in a manner analogous to terror, is a source of the sublime; that is, it is productive of the strongest emotion which the mind is capable of feeling. I say the strongest emotion, because I am satisfied the ideas of pain are much more powerful than those which enter on the part of pleasure.

The ocean – especially in a storm – was the archetype of sublimity in nature.

> *A level plain of a vast extent on land, is certainly no mean idea; the prospect of such a plain may be as extensive as a prospect of the ocean: but can it ever fill the mind with anything so great as the ocean itself? This owing to several causes; but it is owing to none more than this, that the ocean is an object of no small terror. Indeed, terror is in all cases whatsoever, either more openly or latently, the ruling principle of the sublime.*

Burke went on to describe how physical pain and mental terror combined to induce feelings of sublimity in 'The Finer Organs'.

> *They are capable of producing delight; not pleasure, but a sort of delightful horror, a sort of tranquillity tinged with terror.*

Burke's essay was useful because it gave a name and an explanation to a new response to wilderness that was gaining ground in mid-century writing and painting. In 1739 Thomas Grey and Horace Walpole visited Grand Chartreuse, a mountaintop monastery near Grenoble. Grey wrote to a friend:

> *In our little journey up to the Grand Chartreuse, I do not remember to have gone ten paces without an exclamation, that there was no restraining: Not a precipice, not a torrent, not a cliff, but is pregnant with religion and poetry. There are certain scenes that would awe an atheist into belief, without the help of other argument. One need not have a very fantastic imagination to see spirits there at noon-day. . . .*

The young poet's unbridled enthusiasm for torrents, cliffs, and precipices would have shocked his elders. Burke's theory of delightful horror, of commingled pain and pleasure, allowed one to take the old-fashioned view of mountains as 'frightful', 'barren', and 'monstrous' –

the words of Daniel Defoe, describing the Lake District in 1726 – even as one revelled aesthetically in their most horrid qualities.

By the 1770s, the rage for the Sublime was in full swing in the English countryside, where landscape gardeners contrived delicious terrors for their patrons. Sir Richard Hill, lord of Hawkstone in Shropshire, finding himself in possession of a newly fashionable precipice with a six-county view, turned his estate into a Sublime theme park. The ocean made its appearance, far inland, with a statue of Neptune seated inside the ribs of a whale, and with a 'Scene from Otaheite' based on illustrations in Captain Cook's *Voyages*. A mobile waxwork druid resided in a grotto. But the great draw remained 'the precipices'. Dr Johnson lugged himself up to the summit, where he drew on Burke's essay to describe his excited state of mind.

> *He that mounts the precipices at Hawkestone wonders how he came hither, and doubts how he shall return. . . . He has not the tranquillity, but the horror of solitude, a kind of* turbulent *[my emphasis] pleasure between fright and admiration. The Ideas which it forces upon the mind, are the sublime, the dreadful, and the vast.*

This was the movement that had passed Vancouver by. Here on the Northwest coast, where the ocean sucked and grumbled at the bottom of precipices many times the height of those at Hawkstone, Captain Van was nearly at the heart of the modish Sublime, but nothing in the landscape stirred him to poetry. He found it simply alien, and ideas of the Sublime suspect and pretentious.

In the same months that the English were sailing up the coast, an American fur trader, Joseph Ingraham, in command of the seventy-two-ton brigantine *Hope*, was sailing southward through the Queen Charlotte Islands, buying skins from the Indians to sell in China. (Vancouver and Ingraham would soon meet, at Quadra's table in Friendly Cove.) Four years younger than Captain Van, Ingraham was in boyishly high spirits, cruising for his own pleasure and profit. On the night of 31 July, he sounded his way around the Copper Islands and into the lee of Burnaby Island – a heart-in-mouth passage even with an engine and a modern chart. According to his journal, Ingraham worked his ship through the darkness in a state of exalted aesthetic wonder:

> *There was something awfully sublime in entering this dreary port at this hour of the night. The surrounding high mountains threw an additional gloom over the face of the deep whose vast silence was at times interrupted by the hollow surge of the sea on the surrounding rocky shores or the gamboling of immense whales. On shore the scene afforded a subject which I lament my inability to do justice to. It seemed to inspire a reverential awe for the Almighty, Who presides in all places; but none I believe display His grandeur, power, and elegance more conspicuously than occurrences of the mighty deep.*

If only Ingraham could have supplied a few grams of whatever he was on to poor Vancouver, *Discovery* would have been a very different vessel. Ingraham's commonplace delight in sublimity was a necessary precondition for explorers of this coast, and Vancouver didn't have a trace of the stuff.

This was probably what his juniors meant by twitting him for not being 'an educated man'. The accomplished nautical astronomer, fogeyish about the ordinary manners and fashions of his time, could not connect with the bizarre enthusiasms and catchwords of the midshipmen, to whom he appeared cloddish and philistine, a grey man of numbers, a body without a soul.

The midshipmen's own response to the landscape is read most clearly in their drawings. Because no official artist had been assigned to the expedition, John Sykes, Thomas Heddington, and Henry Humphrys were kept busy with their soft pencils and watercolour boxes, under orders to supply a visual record of the country as it unspooled past the ships. Unfortunately, the London engravers tampered with the midshipmen's originals, making the illustrations to Vancouver's *Voyage* look more conventional than the sketches on which they were based. A drawing by Harry Humphrys, of towering black mountains rising from an empty sea near Port Dick, was improved by the engraver's addition of a fleet of thirty-eight native kayaks, turning a scene of lonely and romantic vastness into a Saturday afternoon regatta. But even in their touched-up state, the illustrations – especially those by Heddington – are full of images of the Sublime: gaunt crags and precipices; snowcapped mountaintops wreathed in coronae of swirling mist; lone eagles in the sky; the brooding ocean. The ghost of Salvator Rosa, hugely popular in England at the time, hangs over the midshipmen's efforts as they labour to translate the giddy heights and vacant solitudes of the Northwest into familiar pictorial terms.

Even Vancouver couldn't escape the use of the word 'sublime', but he handled it as though he were picking it up, unwillingly, with a pair of tongs. Writing about his grim excursion up Howe Sound, with the fashionable chatter of the young gentlemen still in his ears, he admitted that he'd seen 'a sublime, though gloomy spectacle'.

Lasqueti and Texada islands were fifteen minutes late, by my reckoning. There was a clear horizon where the southern tips of both islands should have been, so I switched on the radar and left it to warm up. Under sail and engine, the boat rolled in the swell as the dying wind came in fitful puffs and wheezes. In the distance, about five miles off, a large ocean-going tug was pulling a pair of barges across my path.

When I went downstairs to check the radar screen I found three blips of light, well inside the one-mile ring. Fooled by fog again. The tug wasn't big, just much closer than I'd thought; and when I stepped up into the cockpit, I could hear the *whump-whump-whump* of its diesels across the water. For the next ninety minutes, in thickening fog, day fading into night, I played blind man's buff with a string of unseen islands – shuffling over the sea at three knots, using the radar, the Garmin, and the depth-sounder for a white cane. Visibility was down to less than a quarter-mile as I groped toward a cleft in the bluffs on the mainland shore. The fog suddenly parted around a wall of black rock to reveal cormorants on a ledge, a madrona clinging by its toes to a niche, and a dripping pinnacle surmounted by a happy navigation mark – a large board on which *SECRET COVE* → was painted.

I was just in time for dinner at the Jolly Roger Resort. A whimsical developer must have sometime passed this way, scattering names like Buccaneer Bay and Pirate Cove on the chart. This coast had a perfectly good history of its own, but its own evidently wasn't good enough: it craved for the sentimental yo-ho-ho of Captain Kidd, and the skull-and-crossbones, and revenue men in cloaks and tricorn hats. The homesick preference for the ersatz-European over the far-Western real was, I thought, more a Canadian than an American affliction, producing pubs with horse-brasses and plastic Tudor beams. So the eighteenth-century explorers and fur traders were passed over in favour of pirates and smugglers from the banal imaginary history of Merrie England. Done with a giggle and meant to be cute, it betrayed the everlasting provincial anxiety that one's own experience, one's place and one's past, are somehow less real than those of people nearer to the centre of the big world.

I was paying the bill for my Pirate's Platter when a couple, close to retirement age, stopped at my table.

'We saw you come in. All on your lonesome in that big sailboat?'

They exuded an air of comfortable self-possession, like a pair of busy chickadees. Some people are more married than others, and the Schmales (they told me their name within seconds of our meeting) were more married than most. For either of them to use the first-person singular was rare; everything they did, apparently, was done together, and their first concern with me was where I'd left my wife. To the Schmales, it was inconceivable that I might not have a wife.

'She's back in Seattle, with our daughter.'

'Oh dear,' said Mrs Schmale.

Guided by Mr Schmale's flashlight, we walked down through the firs to the marina.

'We've got a Bayliner 25—'

'We've just been tooling around the islands—'

'We're in the mineral business—'

'—in Vancouver. We've been away for the week—'

'We needed the holiday—'

Theirs was an intercontinental marriage. Her voice was West Country English, his Canadian. Her burr and his twang were their chief distinguishing characteristics, but they sang an identical song.

Like the Schmales themselves, their boat was short, plump, and cosy. A bottle of Drambuie was found in a locker. We drank it in glasses decorated with vintage-car transfers. I got the Bugatti.

They had no instruments except a compass. Their only chart was of Vancouver and its approaches. For the last six days they'd been touring the sea with a folded road map of Alberta and British Columbia.

'Our only problem's been the fog.'

'How on earth did you manage to find the entrance here?' I said.

'Oh, we just sort of bounced our way from rock to rock.'

'I'm a born seafarer,' said Mrs Schmale. 'I'm from Plymouth, right by the Hoe.'

'I worked on a towboat once,' chipped in Mr Schmale.

I had taken 'the mineral business' to mean something to do with gemstones, but it was more prosaic than that. The Schmales dealt in sand. Their chief customers were the golf courses of suburban Vancouver. He did the heavy lifting, she made the calls and handled the accounts. Whenever demand flagged, they ran away to sea and went jouncing, chartless, over the wave-tops in their little white fibreglass cocoon. They liked it best when it was rough, they said, and I saw that their marriage was a boat: tubby, sea-kindly, built for rough weather. I could see them riding out storms and getting off the rocks with barely a scratch. For all their disregard of the usual rules of navigation, they knew how to stay afloat.

'Go on, have another one,' said Mrs Schmale. 'We will!'

It was nice to sit on for a while in the warmth of their good marriage. Though I felt a twinge of Vancouver's 'mortification' upon meeting Galiano and Valdés: the Schmales' slapdash, happy-go-lucky way with the sea took a little of the shine off my own more ponderous expedition.

Their curtains were drawn when I untied next morning. While I could see no fog, the air was uncannily still. The splash of a belted kingfisher plopping into the cove a hundred yards off sounded as if someone had chucked a brick into the water. A curdled grey sky was draped across the treetops. Moving as quietly as I could, I pushed the boat out; but when I looked back, both Schmales were on the dock, waving goodbye.

In Malaspina Strait, between Texada Island and the mainland, the sea was covered, shore to shore, by the glossy membrane of its surface-film. One could see stretch marks on it caused by the current, but it was distinct from the water on which it lay like an enormous sheet of Saran Wrap. Motoring into it, I made a long ragged tear in the film, and my roiling wake stretched back as far as I could see.

As the sky began to lift and clear, a hesitant breath of air came wafting up the strait from the south, crinkling the surface tension without breaking it. A minute or two later, a more confident gust drove two lines of ripples angling away on both sides of the wind, creating a crisscross pattern on the water. The film, still intact, now showed as a dimpled mass of small lozenges of light – each one catching something distinct from the sky – and the water was suddenly alive with its myriad of indefinite reflections.

In the making of waves, first the air 'deforms' the water, which then begins to 'perturb' the flow of air across it; and it is out of this delicate intercourse between the elements that the wave is born. As the ripple turns into a wavelet, its slight convexity gives the wind something to shove against, and soon the wavelet develops a leeward face and a windward back, with a growing differential between the weak air pressure in front and the strong air pressure behind. The unstable air, given these sudden inequalities of pressure, helps the wave (as it now is) to climb: the water's line of least resistance is to go upward as the energy in the wind is transferred to the sea.

That morning, after a few experimental zephyrs, the wind blew down the long funnel of the strait with mounting, purposeful acceleration. I had no sooner unfurled the genoa than I was struggling to reef it down to half its full area. Waves barely formed were suddenly breaking white all around the boat. (The toppling crest of foam returns to the air a tithe of the energy given by the air to the water.) It took only minutes for the waves to find their natural periodic rhythm and build into a short, steep, lumpy sea.

'Lumpy' was the operative word. Seen from the cliffs, the sea might have looked as evenly arranged as the strings on a harp – the lines of white-caps running parallel at intervals of sixty feet or so. Seen from the wheel of a small boat, it presented quite a different aspect. Each wave in the train carried a multitude of smaller deformities – nascent waves bulging, heaping, trying to break as they rode the back of the senior wave in the system. Many-angled, climbing every which way, they turned each square yard of water into an unruly brew of shifting planes and collapsing hillocks. Wherever the wind found an exposed surface, it raised tiny wrinkles of waves awaiting birth. Big waves have little waves upon their backs to ride 'em; and little waves have littler waves, and so ad infinitum.

I couldn't safely run before the wind, but had to angle the boat so that the wind was securely on the port quarter, blowing over my left shoulder. Under the reefed genoa, the boat fitted itself reasonably comfortably into the waves – or, rather, it seemed, the wave, for I was kept company by the continuous crackle of foam, as a running wave broke around the stern. To the noise of the foam was shortly added the tomcat-yowling of wind in the rigging, which put the wind speed at about thirty-five knots.

This was hardly the stuff of *Typhoon* or *Moby-Dick* – the waves were four feet high, with an occasional rogue five-footer. The six-mile width of Malaspina Strait ensured that any tempest here would be in a teapot. But it was plenty rough enough for me. I had no choice but to stick to my course. The Texada Island shore was a long unbroken cliff. And to make a dash for the inlets on the mainland side would mean an hour, at least, of serious violence, both wind and sea on the beam: everything on board would get slopped about like cement in a mixer.

It greatly heartened me to see, about two miles ahead, a small open fishing boat with two men aboard. Mostly they were lost in the breakers, but every so often they were lifted above the level of the horizon. Their black silhouette, rising and falling, became my friend. We were in this together – and if they could take it aboard that walnut shell, then I, on a boat designed for open-ocean sailing, should be thoroughly enjoying myself. I aimed to pass them by close enough to wave. They couldn't know how glad I was to share the water with them, but I wanted to signal my gratitude to them for being there.

A mile on, I was in a hugely improved mood. The wind in the stays and shrouds had lost its power to hex. The boat was sluicing through the sea at seven knots under its meagre triangle of sail. The sun, breaking through the clouds, shone through the wave-crests at my back, turning them a luminous Pernod-green in the second before their powdery explosion into white. With my safety-harness clipped tight to its U-bolt on the cockpit floor, legs braced, spinning the wheel to keep time with the waves, I felt a sudden rush of adrenalin. *I like it here.*

Just as I lifted my hand to salute the fishermen, the sea raised them high into the sunlight on the gathering crest of a big wave. The boat was not a boat but the sawn-off bole of an enormous old-growth Douglas fir. Two man-sized amputated stumps projected from the trunk. Waterlogged, blackened, with a trailing skirt of roots, this serious hazard to navigation could have sunk a tugboat. As I veered away, I saw it go right underwater in a wave-trough and stay submerged for many seconds before it again broke the surface, like a turtle coming up for air.

You'd never know what hit you.

When I looked back, five minutes later, there were the fishermen, uncannily lifelike, one at each end of the boat, enjoying their morning at sea.

Texada Island, long and thin, was roughly boomerang-shaped. At North Point, a little more than halfway along its leading, eastern edge, the island bent away to the west. So far, the wind had been blowing from the south-south-east, following the line of the strait. If this wind continued, shelter should be waiting beyond North Point. Or the wind might bend with the strait, promising a steadily worsening sea for the next eighteen miles, after which I could duck into the shelter of Blubber Bay at the north-western tip of the island. I tried to form no opinion about what would happen at North Point: having just made friends with a dead tree, like George III in his madness, I had good reason not to trust my own judgement.

The wind stung. I was soaked through with spray. The boat was beginning to crash into the troughs, going too fast for its own good.

The motion of a ship in a seaway is conventionally broken down into six components, known as the six degrees of freedom – pitch, roll, sway, heave, surge, and yaw. With the wind pinning the sail to starboard and keeping the boat heeled at a steady 25° angle, its freedom to roll and sway was mercifully inhibited, but it was taking every other liberty on the menu. It yawed, heaved, surged, pitched – serially and in combination. Trying to stay deaf to the pandemonium that was raging downstairs, I heard an odd sound coming from behind me, like the gnawing of a rat behind the wainscoting. I glanced back and saw the jackstaff and ensign being wrenched from their socket on the taffrail; they touched down briefly on the roof of the aft cabin, then made their way over the side, rather to my relief. The unfamiliar snapping of the illicit red duster in the wind had been one of the annoyances of the morning.

As headlands go, North Point wasn't much: a bluff that slightly protruded from the long straight run of land and blocked the view of what lay beyond. But the wind was incensed by it. Half a mile short of the point, the life suddenly went out of the headsail. It flapped limply in a strange pocket of calm. Two or three minutes passed. Then the wind reappeared in a new guise – a gale-force blast from the west, blowing right off the point, that laid the boat over, flattened the waves, and turned the water into froth. Caught in this aerial whirlpool I yanked the genoa-sheet off its cleat and let it go free, not greatly caring if the wind tore the loose sail to rags.

I could now see what I had not dared hope for: west of the point was a broad stretch of spitting waves barely a foot high, a sea of white-flecked jade. I could safely cross the shallow bar at the entrance to Vananda, just eight miles farther down on Texada's north shore.

The hills around Vananda had been gouged out by quarrymen, and stone dust from the marble works was in the wind as I came into the cove. Inside the steep rock walls, eddying gusts chased one another around the harbour and I hung back from the dock, waiting for a calm interval in which to go alongside. Two men left their sport-fishing boat to take my lines.

'Thanks.'

'Right you are?' The voice rose at the end of the phrase, though no question was being asked.

'It's rough out there,' said the second man. I took them for brothers; both in their forties, dark, tousle-headed, unshaven. 'It's been blowing a hooligan.'

'Yes,' I said. 'It came out of nowhere. One moment flat calm – the next, it was as if someone had switched on a hair-dryer. Whoosh!'

The man squinted at me, eyes narrowed against the whirling dust. 'Where you from?'

Warned by his tone, I said, 'Seattle.'

'You're *Umurrican*?'

'Yeah, sort of. I mean, originally I'm from' – and thought for a moment before I said it – 'London.'

Additional space had suddenly grown between us. The brothers treated me to a stare of chilly, unamused scepticism and went back to their boat.

Their accent and mine were ancient enemies. They spoke in the accent of Catholic Northern Ireland, the voice of Derry and The Falls Road. I spoke in the accent of colonial rule. If you listened a certain way, you could hear in my voice the long roll call of English oppressors from Oliver Cromwell to Margaret Thatcher and John Major. Nothing I actually thought or said about the current situation in the

Six Counties would mitigate the bad impression made by the way I pronounced my vowels.

I had been here before. Leaving a Belfast cinema in 1969, I'd been summoned back by an angry yell from the woman in the ticket booth, who shouted that my offence was underpaying by sixpence. I handed over the coin without argument. The woman, speaking not to me but to her rolls of tickets, said quietly, in a voice of world-weary contempt, 'Focken Proddy.'

So, on the dock at Vananda again, I found myself a *focken Protestant*; or, worse, a snooping Englishman, with the likely ring of Sandhurst and the army in his voice. I went below, to restore the fallen books to their shelves and sweep up the remains of two smashed glasses and a broken dinner plate. Then, wanting to show the brothers I had nothing to hide, I left the boat unlocked, its companionway open to inspection, and set off to find a bank and grocery store.

Vananda, pretty in the spring sunshine, was a village of looping paths and dirt roads, lightly sprinkled with wooden cabins. Flowering shrubs ran wild over the common ground. Every garden had an upturned boat on chocks, hummingbirds at the feeder, and a collection of auto parts on the lawn. From the open door and windows of one cabin came a further blast of Ireland – a fiddle, a penny whistle, a concertina, and a recorded voice singing –

> *The pig is in the mire and the cow is in the grass:*
> *A man without a woman through this world will sadly pass.*
> *Me mother likes the ducks, and the ducks like the drakes,*
> *And little Biddy Mulligan, I'd die for her sake . . .*

Whoever lived here was apparently trying to broadcast his national affiliation to the Canadian mainland on the far side of Malaspina Strait. Only the profoundly deaf would be able to tolerate the noise of the record inside the house.

> *Acushla mavourneen, married we will be,*
> *And be happy in the valley*
> *Winding down to the sea.*

The song's many choruses followed me up hill and down dale, along the forking paths of Vananda.

The bank was located in a trailer, where my accent went down a great deal better than at the dockside; the teller was from Chipping Sodbury, in Gloucestershire, and we had a moment of reminiscent Englishness as she counted out my money.

'You seem to have quite a contingent of people from Northern Ireland here . . .'

Her hands stopped moving on the bills.

'You get people from all over on Texada Island,' she said.

Around the next loop, a very large Irish tricolour was flying from an improvised pole set in the front yard of a ramshackle cottage, on whose roof a trio of other flags – German, Swedish, and Norwegian – rippled in the breeze. A roughly lettered shingle proclaimed HENRI-ETTA'S LAND. Henrietta herself – or so I assumed – was tending several small piles of burning rubbish in the road. The smoke from her activities made it hard to see the paving. I climbed the grassy verge, trying to keep out of the way of the smoke, which smelled putrid.

'I'm just doing my recycling,' Henrietta said.

'That's OK,' I said, hurrying on.

'Don't I know you?'

On second glance, I thought that perhaps we did know each other – or had done, long ago. She was my age and, in the phrase, my type. She was wearing a mini-length wool-knit dress, filthy now, but once expensive; it might have been King's Road, *circa* 1960-something. Her bony legs were bare, grazed with scratches, soil-stained. Her grey hair, lately blonde, looked as if she cut it herself, with garden shears. Years of bad sleep showed in the bruise-coloured bags under her eyes, yet her face still held something of the koala-like coquettishness that she must have had when last we met, if meet we ever did. She put me suddenly in mind of Lulu, the pop singer, long forgotten, at least by me, until that moment.

'How do you like our new country?'

The crazy shingle, the fires, the flags, the ruinous cottage were irrationally, unexpectedly depressing to me. It was as if we really had known each other and, thirty years on, I'd stumbled on her living in this squalor. I was afraid that she would speak my name. I hunted for a Henrietta in the junk room of my memory, and came out empty-handed.

'I *do* know you,' she said. But her face was vague; she was looking beyond me, at someone else altogether. 'I'm being harassed by the government, you know.'

'Which government?'

'The BC government. The *provincial* government,' she said. 'This road – look here, it encroaches nine inches on my land. I've got the title deeds. I've proved it to them. But they sent their agents here. Last week. They shot my goat . . .'

'I'm sorry.'

'He's in there.' She pointed through the smoke. 'I want to give him a proper burial. I need to cremate him. But I'm not strong enough to carry him, you see? Now, you – you're strong. If you could just—'

'No. I'm sorry. I can't.' I edged past her. 'I'm late. I'm meeting my wife—'

'You could *help* me.'

I kept walking as her voice pursued me from behind the pall of drifting smoke: 'Help . . . it's not much to ask. You've got the build for it, you see.' Her tone was composed and good-humoured, as if we were conducting a flirtation. 'It wouldn't take a minute.'

I found the grocery store, then, laden with shopping, stopped at the wharfinger's house to pay harbour dues for the night. 'I can't deal with you now,' the woman said. 'I'm waiting for the Lotto on TV. You'll have to come in.' Her bungalow was full of cats: strolling cats, squirming cats, cats draped over chair-arms, cats asleep, cats bickering. The moment I entered, the entire pack was after the contents of my two bags of groceries, which I held up to my chest. The television blared.

'It'll be on in a minute or two,' the wharfinger said. 'Six forty-nine.'

Her Lotto tickets – evidently a major investment – were laid out on the floor in front of her chair.

It was local news time; though viewed from Vananda, the news from the Vancouver area looked as if it came from some foreign capital.

'That clock must be fast,' she said, then, at seven o'clock, she realized she had the wrong day for the Lotto results and turned off the television.

'Henrietta's Land . . .' I said.

'*Her*. She's not been taking her medicine.'

'Where's she from?'

'Somewhere back east. She used to be a schoolteacher.'

'England?'

'Maybe. It was back east somewhere, I know that.'

'You seem to have a lot of Northern Irish people in Vananda.'

'Yes. We got them. We got a lot of Newfies, too.'

Newfoundlanders – fugitives from another stricken corner of the world. Leaving the wreckage of the inshore fishery on the Grand Banks, they must have arrived in British Columbia just in time for the collapse of the salmon fishery here.

I settled up, and the wharfinger opened her front door on a welcome draught of air that didn't smell of cat. 'And that's another thing,' she said, stepping out with me. 'Him in there –' she pointed to a weather-beaten trailer, with KEEP OUT scratched into the paint on its door – 'I haven't heard anything of *him* in the last few days. We're on the same water, and I hear him every time he uses it. He's not had the water going, not since Tuesday.' She looked up at me, head cocked, to see if I was catching her drift. 'Someone ought to take a look,' she said.

First a dead goat, now a dead man.

'I'm sorry. I'm late.' I wanted very badly to get back to my boat, and stay on it, out of harm's way. 'You'd better find one of his friends.'

'He doesn't have no friends that I know of.'

Some guy is lying dead in there, and you are going to do nothing about it?

'Sorry!' My feet had control now, and were marching me past the trailer and into the road that led down to the harbour. Vananda was altogether too interesting for comfort. I had planned to go to the scruffy pub-motel for dinner but had a strong premonition that some new relationship was awaiting me there, and that my immediate future would be greatly simplified if I spoke to no one and went early to bed.

Everything on the boat was as I had left it. I sat out in the cockpit, glass in hand, watching the light die in the cove. 'Vananda' would be, I thought, a useful word:

vananda, n. A place where loose ends naturally collect, and where lost objects are likely to be found. A port in a storm; a bolt-hole, an asylum.

Shortly before eleven, in the pitch dark, I heard the crunch of car tyres on the stone chips of the harbour road. Whoever it was had stopped on the long mole overlooking the floats and was raking the water with a powerful flashlight. The roving beam came to a halt on my boat and stayed there for the best part of a minute. I listened for voices and heard nothing. Probably it was only the wharfinger checking on her domain, but it put sleep abruptly out of reach.

I kept the reading lamp in the forecabin on all night, and dozed uneasily over Evelyn Waugh's *Put Out More Flags* – his funniest novel, and the one I thought most likely to provide distraction from the anxieties of the moment. But Basil Seal, a genial terrorist, fighting his private war on the home front, kept fading out on me, replaced by images of men in berets and balaclavas with Armalites. At first light, I rose groggily and cast off my lines. I liked Vananda best as it fell securely astern.

Twists of steam from the chimneys of the Powell River pulp mill climbed straight up into a windless sky. The sea, scored with current-lines, was like an ice rink imprinted by the tracks of figure skaters. This northern corner of Georgia Strait was choked with islands – from big, bold, wooded hills like Harwood, Savary, and Hernando, down to unnamed chunks of bare granite used as fishing platforms by ospreys and bald eagles, stained white with birdshit. Vancouver called it a 'very unpleasant navigation . . . on every side encompassed by islands and small rocky islets; some lying on the continental shore, others confusedly scattered, of different forms and dimensions.'

Discovery and *Chatham* sailed out of Malaspina Strait in company with *Sutil* and *Mexicana*. The Spanish thought that a passage to the ocean probably lay somewhere ahead, in which case the mountains to the west would prove to be an island. Indians interviewed the previous year had said this was so, and there was a more doubtful rumour that Robert Gray, the American fur trader, in the sloop *Lady Washington*, had found a route through the mountains to the open sea.

From here, it seemed improbable. The Strait of Georgia appeared to end at a black wall of mountainous country. Peaks crowded thickly on peaks. In the far distance, the snowline looked unbroken. Nor did the tide – as yet – suggest that an opening to the sea might be concealed there. That the ebb continued to flow east and south, back to Juan de Fuca Strait, tended to confirm the explorers' fears that they were up another blind alley.

At dead low water, running before a light wind from the east-south-east, the four ships passed inside of Harwood Island (named by Vancouver for Edward Harwood, a naval surgeon who served under Captain Bligh) into a tricky and deceiving reach of sea. The surface was sprinkled with isolated rocks, as if these were boulder-strewn flats, barely covered by the tide. Yet the leadsmen went on calling bottom at sixty and seventy fathoms, even as the rocks drew alarmingly close. Double lookouts were posted at the masthead and the bows to watch for submerged reefs. But the dull light and wind-ruffled water made this an impossible assignment. The rocks appeared to sprout from nowhere. Their cousins might be anywhere, a few inches out of sight. The ships reduced their sail and crept forward yard by yard, waiting for the crunch.

My Canadian Hydrographic Service chart showed a weird underwater topography of hidden cols, pinnacles, and crevasses, the blue contour lines a busy scribble of loops and whorls. Any fool could now safely plot a course through here, but before sonar chartmaking this must have been a hideous passage, capable of driving the coolest navigator to fits of nervous panic. Captain Van was not the coolest navigator. On the quarterdeck of *Discovery* no one dared speak. Except for the creaking of ropes in the blocks and the whisper of water around the hull, the ship moved on in a tense bubble of apprehensive silence.

I got the jitters, too, but for a different reason. A few feet off the port bow, I saw a circle in the water, like the dimple of a rising fish. I slammed the engine into reverse, and the thing slid by along the beam – a huge deadhead, the waterlogged trunk of a tree, floating vertically in the water, its top end grazing the surface. This wasn't a Puget Sound peckerpole, a foot to eighteen inches in diameter. An old-growth Douglas fir, four feet across, it might well go down sixty feet into the sea. Hit it and you'd sink as surely as if you had impaled your boat on a pinnacle of solid rock. I had missed it by inches, and for the next hour or so my lookout was as anxious as that of Vancouver's men up in the yards. Every small fish was a deadhead. Seals were deadheads. The hole left in the water by a diving loon was a deadhead. I carefully steered wide of them all.

The tows that came steaming out of the mountains at half-hour intervals kept me vigilant: the logs that made up their rafts were all of a size to match my monstrous deadhead. In British Columbia, unlike Washington State, timber companies were still hacking down ancient forests; a measure of the power of the provincial government to resist the calls for environmental restraint that came down from Ottawa. The British Columbians saw the Western wilderness as their property, to dispose of as they pleased. Paul Bunyan, quietly dropped from the pantheon of American heroes, appeared to be enjoying an active retirement up here in BC. His blue ox, Babe, had been replaced by the orange twin-rotored helicopter I saw en route from Powell River to some luckless old-growth patch up a remote mountainside; its garish lifeboat colour was presumably meant to make its wreckage easier to spot.

Picking their route through the rocks and islets, the ships sailed so slowly that it was 9:30 p.m., nearly dark, and sixteen miles on when the flotilla arrived at a gap in the mountains a mile and a half wide. The leadsmen had been calling ever-increasing depths, and the water was now fathomless. A thin, persistent drizzle had fallen since mid-afternoon, thickening the visibility and dampening the spirits of the explorers. *Discovery* was the first to ghost through the entrance, which opened on a strange, watery crossroads of black precipices and inky canals, leading off in every direction like the arms of a starfish. The ship drifted more than sailed to within a cable of the continental shore, under a towering cliff. No bottom was found. I could see, as they could not, that they were floating over a sheer-sided submarine valley 1,500 feet deep.

The landlocked wind, confused by the mountains, came in feeble scurries – now from the north, now from the east, now from the south – and repeatedly took the ships aback. 'The night was dark and rainy', Vancouver recalled, 'and the winds so light and variable that by the influence of the tides we were driven about as it were blindfolded in this labyrinth.'

This labyrinth. When Vancouver wrote the sentence – or at least polished it for publication – his lodgings at Petersham were a pleasant four-mile walk from the famous labyrinth at Hampton Court. The hornbeam hedge-maze, planted in 1690 for William of Orange, the scourge of the Irish and the Protestant victor of the Battle of the Boyne, had, by the 1790s, taken on a kind of legendary antiquity. A controlled theatre of disorientation, the maze was an allegory of the operation of chance and choice in human life, and a tourist attraction with which Captain Van was certainly familiar. Like other ornamental mazes of the time, it was known as 'the wilderness'. Trying to convey his helplessness as he drifted through pitch darkness in eerily deep water at the whim of the tide, Captain Van saw the bleak Pacific Northwest wilderness dissolve into the maze at Hampton Court –

that play space in which people liked to lose themselves, on sunny afternoons, for fun.

He was rescued from his distress by the Spaniards. Galiano, on *Sutil*, had been patiently sounding around the high conical island, and its two satellite islets, at the centre of the crossroads. On its north side he found an uneven rocky shelf at depths of thirty to fifty fathoms. Here, at midnight, the four ships gathered to drop anchors. The cables rattled down from the capstans into nearly two hundred feet of water – an uncomfortably deep anchorage by normal standards, but a solace in this miserable darkness walled in by looming, shadowy mountains. With each ship laying out six hundred feet of cable, the vessels spent the night wandering in vague circles, the watches calling to one another over the water as they came close to collision, then drifted safely off again.

At daybreak on Tuesday, 26 June, Vancouver was able to see the true character of the maze. In the sullen morning light, it appeared no friendlier: the sides of the channels, black with pines, were nearly vertical, rising to heights of close to 6,000 feet; the water, starved of sunlight, looked peculiarly dark and dead, as it borrowed the furry, tenebrous colour of the trees. The whole place dripped. Small cataracts, pouring from rock overhangs, echoed monotonously inside the canyon-like walls. A landscape of appalling, ungraspable dimensions, it belittled the ships floating like toys on the lip of the submarine abyss.

Two major channels led away from the crossroads – one to the north-west, the other to the east-north-east. But from the deck, Vancouver could see bifurcations in both channels that might take them anywhere in this serpentine conglomeration of mountains and islands. Survey boats would have to be sent up every arm and corridor, leaving no possible opening unexplored; and it looked as if they might usefully be equipped with a clew of thread, the standard maze-craft accessory to guide the lost traveller back to his starting point.

Lieutenant Broughton went off in *Chatham*'s gig to find a better long-term anchorage. Puget, Whidbey, Johnstone, and Swaine (the most senior of the midshipmen) were put in charge of the four survey crews. Captain Van himself declined to participate, explaining in his journal that he couldn't leave *Discovery* because he needed 'to produce some observations of the longitude'. He was visibly unwell. Menzies was concerned about the deep bronchial rattle of his worsening cough. Unable now to sleep without heavy draughts of laudanum, the captain, whose habitual manner was of close, secretive abstraction, sometimes appeared to be close to dementia.

As arrangements for the survey expeditions were being made, under a sky that promised only rain and wind, Vancouver spoke of the urgent necessity of setting up an observatory tent onshore so he could take lunar distances. Yet almost anywhere on the coast would have provided a better site for the calculation of longitude by astronomical observation: here, the view of the sky – if the clouds ever cleared – was badly obstructed by mountains. But Captain Van, lost in his own black maze, turned instinctively to astronomy, as he always did when he felt his grip on reality starting to weaken. Lunars would show him where he was. When the boats were gone, Vancouver would use his quadrant to find himself.

At noon, it began to blow hard from the south-east and the ships, catching the brunt of the wind, strained against their anchors, lifting a hundred feet of cable and more off the bottom. Broughton came back in the gig to announce a better, more protected anchorage six and a half miles to the north-west. He had barely pointed the place out to Vancouver before *Discovery* dragged her anchor clean off the shelf, the cable now dangling uselessly into the abyss. Scudding before the wind, with the men at the capstan still recovering the anchor, the ship ploughed up-channel to her new quarters at the foot of a vast, shaggy cliff of tobacco-brown rock-faces and stunted evergreens. In Vancouver's opinion, the anchorage was 'equally dreary and unpleasant', though it had one merit. Half a mile across the water, to the south, an apron of level land skirted a nodule-like point: a good place to pitch a tent, find Greenwich time, and fix the longitude.

One by one, the launches and cutters were lost to sight in the rain squalls. Valdés went off with a crew of Spaniards, aboard *Mexicana*'s launch. Vancouver and Galiano remained behind. Their friendship had its rough edges and the two commanders continued to name jointly discovered land in rival languages. Vancouver called the points on each side of the labyrinth's entrance after his sisters; Sarah to the east, Mary to the west. Galiano promptly redubbed them Punta de Sarmiento and Punta de Magellanes, allowing only the initial letters of the sisters' names to survive.

Yet Galiano, with his strongly accented, diplomatic English, was the one human being to whom Vancouver could now turn for company. For the next two and a half weeks, the ships anchored under the forbidding precipice, Vancouver took his meals alone, locked in his private cabin on *Discovery*, emerging from his den only when Señor Galiano came visiting. He accepted invitations to dine aboard *Sutil*, where they drank and conferred together, commander to commander. With Galiano he was able to share the multitude of 'observations' that he was making in the tent ashore.

Though the sky was rarely clear enough for nautical astronomy, Vancouver was eventually able to take ten sets of lunars, dragging the images of the sun and moon down from the heavens to kiss their reflections in the mercury pan of the artificial horizon. On average, the readings gave him a longitude measured eastabout from Greenwich of 235°5'30" – accurate to within less than a third of a mile to the position of what is now Joyce Point as it juts out into Lewis Channel. Given the terrain, the weather, and the difficulty of the calculations, this was a brilliant result.

There was nothing crankish in Vancouver's fondness for the lunar-distance method. While he worked away in his tent, the fur-trading Joseph Ingraham, charting the Queen Charlotte Islands for his own purposes, was also getting his longitude by lunars, even though he was no great mathematician. It's a fact worth repeating that in 1792, this far out from Greenwich (or any other port where chronometers could be synchronized), the sky still provided a more reliable clock than the one devised by John Harrison.

Vancouver wasn't happy with his Joyce Point lunars. He thought ten insufficient, and the results disagreed with the longitude suggested by the ship's chronometers. Not knowing which to trust, the quadrant or the clock, Captain Van found himself doubting his own accuracy. He talked to Galiano. And, when drawing his position on the chart, he went by the chronometer and put himself more than ten miles farther inland than he actually was. This mistake – made after a feat of textbook navigation – was a measure of his shaken self-confidence.

Next he tackled the usually simple problem of finding the local magnetic variation, measuring the azimuth angle between true north and magnetic north as it was shown on the ship's compasses. With correction tables and a series of good sights of the Pole Star, a competent midshipman should have been able to come up with a reasonably precise figure. But again Vancouver couldn't get his results to agree. He took angles from *Discovery's* quarterdeck, then from the observatory tent ashore. The numbers were all over the place. The easterly variation lay somewhere between 14½° and 23° – a wide discrepancy. Vancouver had to settle for two fudged averages, 16° aboard the ship and 19° ashore.

But the tides troubled him the most. He daily watched the water's movements, sailing the gig point-to-point, marking tide levels on rocks, and following the passage of twigs on the stream. The more observations he made, the more baffled he was by their meaning. For a seaman in coastal waters, time and tide are synonymous: he plots his day by the predictable rhythm of tidal stages and currents. Mysteriously, these labyrinthine tides had no discernible rhythm at all.

> *The irregularity of the tides was such that no correct inferences could well be drawn. . . . In the course of some days there would not be the least perceptible stream; and in others a very rapid one, that generally continued in the same direction twenty four hours, and sometimes longer. The time of high water was equally vague and undefinable.*

The essential logic of nature had somehow come unstuck here. In Vancouver's mental world, the fundamental constants were the stars, the tides, and the earth's magnetic field; he was at home with them as he was in no human society. William Wales's devoted pupil now doubted the celestial clock, was foxed by the tides, and mistrusted the compass.

He remembered his seventeen days of incarceration:

Our residence here was truly forlorn; an awful silence pervaded the gloomy forests, whilst animated nature seemed to have deserted the neighbouring country, whose soil afforded only a few small onions, some samphire, and here and there bushes bearing a scanty crop of indifferent berries. Nor was the sea more favourable to our wants, the steep rocky shores prevented the use of the seine, and not a fish at the bottom could be persuaded to take the hook.

Most of the midshipmen were away on survey boats, so Captain Van was at least spared the misery of listening to them prattle about the Sublime grandeur of the situation. He hated the 'stupendous rocky mountains', the habitual dank overcast, the confining walls, the lifeless silence broken only by the sound of water dripping. The turbulence and disorder of this place brought him to an intolerable vision of chaos, in nature as in his own storm-ridden character. He named the water Desolation Sound.

IV. POTTS LAGOON

Like a childhood home revisited after many years, Desolation Sound appeared to have shrunk. In hazy sunshine, its forested walls were green, not black, and its forked paths of water glittered. Yards from the boat, a silver salmon hoisted itself three feet into the air, shook itself vigorously from head to tail, and fell back into the sea with a loud smack. Far from being dismal, dreary, awful, lifeless, or even stupendous, Desolation Sound was a picture-postcard image of rugged prettiness.

In April, the log tows and migratory fishing boats had the place to themselves; mine was the only pleasure craft. But in high summer, Desolation Sound would turn into a vacation resort; for boating families in the Pacific Northwest, it was a favourite destination for the annual two-week cruise. In Refuge Cove and Squirrel Cove, mooring floats were attached to seasonal stores, padlocked now, that would soon be doing a hectic trade in ice, beer, fishing tackle, sunglasses, frozen rib-eye steaks, and Desolation Sound T-shirts. From June onwards, scheduled seaplane flights from Seattle and Vancouver would plop into Refuge Cove, bringing fresh supplies and tourists, in shorts and deck shoes, eager for a taste – however diluted – of wilderness, grand scenery, and whatever romantic solitude could be found in crowded anchorages richly scented with the smoke from a dozen taffrail barbecue grills. By day, the paths of Captain Van's grim labyrinth would be dotted with small boats, moving slowly – on the foredeck of each one, a lightly clad figure with a video camera, capturing the majestic sweep of the precipice, the awesome plunge of the waterfall. I'd once sailed to Desolation Sound in August, and fled; it was uncomfortably like Hampton Court on a sweltering long weekend.

This was not a new development. In 1792, several members of Vancouver's crew were similarly enchanted by Desolation Sound. Archibald Menzies, staying behind on *Discovery* when the survey boats left, spent his days botanizing on the slopes above the ship for the quarterdeck greenhouse. His busy comings and goings were conspicuously ignored by the captain, who would have been gratified to see Menzies and his damnable garden go overboard and be for ever lost in the inky depths. Vancouver was greatly irked, when he deigned to notice, that Menzies was plainly enjoying himself in this Stygian, infinitely depressing place. Cloistered with his instruments inside the mildewy canvas tent, Vancouver was enraged to have his calculations interrupted by the merry plash of oars, as Menzies sauntered about in the gig, pleasure-boating again.

Menzies noted in his journal:

> *Near the bottom of a deep Cove which obtained the name of Cascade Cove about a mile & a half to the North East of the Ship there was a beautifull Waterfall which issued from a Lake close behind it & precipitated a wide foaming stream into the Sea over a shelving rocky precipice of about thirty yards high, its wild romantic appearance aided by its rugged situation & the gloomy forests which surrounded it, rendered it a place of resort for small parties to visit during our stay. On the Banks of this Lake I found several species of Plants. . . .*

Menzies and Vancouver, aboard the same ship at the same time in the same place, were on separate journeys through two landscapes. Their

Desolation Sounds were leagues apart. They couldn't even agree on the weather – Menzies's all sunshine and shadow, Vancouver's only overcast and drizzle.

Menzies revelled, mildly, in the mighty cataract and the deep romantic chasm. Tumult in nature roused his fancy. Reading him, one is in the company of an averagely clever university-educated man in his thirties; a lot less interesting than his captain, because he is so cheerfully at home in his own time, as he was in Desolation Sound.

The wooded promontory of Joyce Point, where Vancouver pitched his tent, blocked my view of Menzies's waterfall at the head of Teakerne Arm. Hardly a view worth having anyway, I thought, and didn't bother to detour around the point to see it. Two centuries of romanticism, much of it routine and degenerate, has blunted everyone's ability to look at waterfalls and precipices in other than dusty and second-hand terms. Motoring through the sound, watching for deadheads, I sailed through a logjam of dead literary cliché: snow-capped peaks above, fathomless depths below, and, in the middle of the picture, the usual gaunt cliffs, hoary crags, wild woods, and crystal cascades.

When *Discovery* was anchored here, William Wordsworth, at twenty-two, was the same age as some of the more senior midshipmen, like Thomas Manby. Manby's own appetite for the picturesque – revealed in the journal he kept secretly during the voyage – was akin to the manner of Wordsworth's earliest poems. The young sailor who wrote (in Discovery Bay) of his bark skimming over the surface of the deep, on a morning that had more the aspect of enchantment than reality, would have read Wordsworth's 'An Evening Walk' (1793) with a quickening sense of listening to a new voice speaking in the language of his own generation.

During the next dozen years, Wordsworth wrote nearly all the poems that would eventually redefine the way in which English-speaking readers learned to perceive wild nature. In *The Prelude*, finished in 1805, he described the undergraduate walking tour of the Alps he had made in 1790. Though the setting is Switzerland, it might as well have taken place in Desolation Sound.

Wordsworth and his Cambridge friend Robert Jones set out for the Simplon Pass, but missed the trail. When the lost travellers found a helpful peasant, he disappointed them profoundly with the information that they had unknowingly crossed the Alpine divide and that the pass was already behind them. Chastened, Wordsworth and Jones began the long descent towards the Italian border.

> *downwards we hurried fast,*
> *And entered with the road which we had missed*
> *Into a narrow chasm. The brook and road*
> *Were fellow-travellers in this gloomy strait,*
> *And with them did we journey several hours*
> *At a slow pace. The immeasurable height*
> *Of woods decaying, never to be decayed,*
> *The stationary blasts of waterfalls,*
> *And in the narrow rent at every turn*
> *Winds thwarting winds, bewildered and forlorn,*
> *The torrents shooting from the clear blue sky,*
> *The rocks that muttered close upon our ears,*
> *Black drizzling crags that spake by the way-side*
> *As if a voice were in them, the sick sight*
> *And giddy prospect of the raving stream,*
> *The unfettered clouds and region of the Heavens,*
> *Tumult and peace, the darkness and the light –*
> *Were all like workings of one mind, the features*
> *Of the same face, blossoms upon one tree;*
> *Characters of the great Apocalypse,*
> *The types and symbols of Eternity,*
> *Of first, and last, and midst, and without end.*

This is one of the great epiphanies of Romantic literature: an intense experience of chaos and derangement in nature, which at last brings Wordsworth face to face with his pantheistic demiurge – a being whom the Kwakiutl Indians might well have recognized as their own lord of oceanic misrule, Komogwa. The tumbling, vertiginous landscape is a place where liberty (the 'unfettered' clouds) is barely distinguishable from madness (the 'raving' stream), and where exaltation verges on nausea. It is a place of moral, mental, and physical extremity; above all, a gloomy *strait*, a liquid region in which air ('winds thwarting winds') and water (the crazy brook, the cascades, the 'drizzling' crags, the 'torrents' that 'shoot' from the cloudless sky) are in a state of chronic, turbulent recombination.

Of the several Desolation Sounds on offer, Wordsworth's is the one to cling to, for the comprehensive seriousness of its vision. There's room there, too, both for Vancouver's mortal horror, and Menzies's aesthetic pleasure. It provides a human footing in a nature seen to be inherently unstable, whirling, contradictory; and discovers, against all odds, meaning and order, even in aberrant tides and disorienting stars.

This was nature as painted by J. M. W. Turner, five years younger than Wordsworth and the exact contemporary of the Honourables Pitt and Stuart. Wordsworth's experience on the Simplon Pass is mirrored by Turner's on a pass thirty miles to the east, where he stopped on the Devil's Bridge to sketch his version of a natural world chaotically inverted. In *The Pass of St. Gothard*, the lines of conventional perspective have been canted ninety degrees downwards so as to meet in the abyssal depths. Far beneath the painter's feet, tumbled clouds are trapped in a chasm: below the clouds, eagles wheel on a thermal. Even now, in the age of the familiar aerial view from the window of a Boeing 747, the painting – at the Birmingham City Art Gallery – has a dizzying effect as it leads the viewer's eye down into the crevasse, past the lower edge of the frame, into unpainted space.

Turner's rock-faces are painted as a geologist or mountaineer might see them, with precise attention to every plane and outcrop. The painting (sketched in 1802, finished and exhibited in 1804) is a work of scrupulous realism, but it also represents that mystical Abyss, the great deep, the primal chaos into which reason itself might topple. It's a painting designed to make you lose your balance and fall into it, through the circling raptors.

The Pass of St. Gothard was painted near the beginning of Turner's career, before his obsession with turbulence and upheaval took a more and more expressionist form. In the late, wonderfully titled *Snow Storm – Steam Boat off a Harbour's Mouth Making Signals in Shallow Water, and Going by the Lead. The Author was in this Storm on the Night the Ariel left Harwich* (1842), Turner painted his greatest picture of pure turmoil.

What one sees at first, from a distance, is a single catastrophic vortex – a hurricane-force wind made manifest in whirling snow and spume. As one steps closer, the vortex resolves into a nest of multiplying vortices with, at their centre, not so much a ship as bits of a ship: a defiant mast, a signal flag wrenching at its halyard; the blades of a spinning paddlewheel; a flattened billow of smoke from a tall funnel. Before these bits cease to cohere, and the dismembered ship dissolves into the liquescent swirl, appears to be only a matter of moments.

Like Ishmael, Turner is escaped to tell the tale. Not only is the title of the picture stuffed with documentary reference, but Turner also said that he'd been lashed to the ship's mast for four hours, sketching the maelstrom, and had fully expected to drown.

Art historians have pounced on Turner for this. No *Ariel* appears in the shipping lists of the time, and Turner was nowhere near Harwich when the storm broke. Yet he wasn't boasting deceitfully of his own bravery so much as making a modest, if metaphorical, statement of fact. In this fictional tempest, the steamer is going by the lead and making the correct signals, while the artist, bound to the mast, is going about his usual business with pencil and sketchpad. *This is how the world is. We live with chaos as the encompassing condition of our lives. We learn to work through it. With luck, we emerge from it.*

In the 'Turner and the Scientists' exhibition (1998) at the Tate Gallery, James Hamilton, the curator, hung *Snow Storm* alongside James Faraday's magnetic-field experiments, in which iron filings were sprinkled on sheets of paper, below which a magnet, or magnets, had been placed. The filings, arranging themselves around the attractors in drifts and squirls, made vortical patterns that exactly resemble the painting's composition. The play of randomness and order in Faraday's experiments excited Turner, and led him, as Hamilton suggests, to the radical design of his portrait of chaos at sea. *Snow Storm* uncannily anticipates the Mandelbrot set and the fractal cluster, as his iron ship performs the function of a Lorenz attractor.

Turner was sixty-seven when he completed the painting. His courage, implied by his story about being lashed to the mast, was real enough. At an age when he might have taken to his slippers and easy chair, Turner chose to face the Abyss with heroic artistry and composure.

The great early Romantic artists such as Wordsworth and Turner created a basic grammar, in which responses to the wild North American West could be phrased by later writers and painters including John Muir and Thomas Moran. Muir, travelling in Alaska, strained in prose to be a born-again Wordsworth, ravished at every turn by what he read in the glorious pages of 'Nature's Bible'. Moran, in *The Grand Canyon of the Yellowstone*, strained to paint in the manner of Turner *circa* 1800. Moran's swirling clouds and liquid mountains look like Turner with a dose of flu. The land itself was an original subject – the West outdid the Alps in its thrilling and tumultuous geology – but the painting is a grandiose imitation.

As a post-Romantic tourist, I felt that entering a landscape like Desolation Sound was uncomfortably like wandering over a famous battlefield left over from someone else's war. That it had been a scene of such heightened emotion in the past only made me feel more keenly my own absence of feeling in it. 'Enbosomed in scenery', as John Muir put it, I instinctively fought its old, mothball-smelling embrace. The tidal atlas advised that here the tides were 'weak and irregular' – a fair description of my response to Desolation Sound, as I flipped a cigarette butt into it and made an anxious calculation as to whether I could still make slack water at the Dent and Yuculta rapids, fourteen miles ahead.

The orange helicopter, seen earlier that morning, was at work high in the bluffs on the north shore of West Redonda Island. Inside the steep walls of Lewis Channel, the air thumped and shook to the heartbeat of the rotors, as the machine hovered within a few feet of the trees. Moving with the ponderous daintiness of a fat man on a dance floor, it plucked a single log from a scarred patch on the mountain, whisked it aloft in a sling, then inched fastidiously down a 2,000-foot column of air. In Redonda Bay, the water of the booming-ground swallowed the log without a visible ripple.

A show-off demonstration – for an audience of no one in particular – of the loggers' dangerous skills, it was lovely to watch. The fallers and 'copter pilots, the men on the baby tuglets, or 'boom-boats', who formed the rafts, were precision craftsmen. One small misjudgement of angle or distance could easily cost them their lives. There were more deaths and serious injuries in the timber industry than in any other except commercial fishing. Until lately, loggers were seen as romantic figures; brave, self-reliant woodsmen in touch with the wild. In old sepia postcards from the Pacific Northwest, the logger figured as the heroic, blue-collar *genius loci*: a nonchalant type, with Robert Redford looks, in a broad-brimmed hat, perched like a steeplejack halfway up the trunk of a cloud-scraping Douglas fir. But since the 1960s, he had come down in the world. He was now more likely to be thought a spoiler and a vandal in need of moral rehabilitation and retraining.

Even Julia, who was down on nobody, was down on loggers.

She came back from her preschool one afternoon, armed with an epic, breathless sentence. 'Do you know? It's bad to cut down trees: trees are alive, and trees make air, and we breathe air, and when people cut down trees, they kill all the fish!'

Reverence for the forest was on the preschool curriculum in the urban Northwest and drummed into the heads of adult newcomers. When I first moved here, all I saw was trees – a thick pelt of forest, denser, darker, and more extensive than I'd seen anywhere on the face of the earth. Then I was told, severely, that this was not a forest at all, but a patchwork of 'tree farms' – fir plantations, sown over the ruins of the actual forest, which long ago had been clearcut. I soon learned to look at trees with the critical eyes of a consumer-connoisseur. Second-growth was no good. Only old-growth would do, and it must have a spreading canopy, a crowded overstorey, a floor littered with fallen snags – habitat for the bugs and small animals essential to a true, organic, *grand cru* forest. It should harbour spotted owls as proof of its purity. It should never have been contaminated by the presence of loggers.

I learned to dismiss as fake whole mountainsides. The seeming-forests were not, according to the nature zealots, nature. The birds, bears, mountain lions, and bobcats lived there under a mighty misapprehension, tricked into accepting as real a false habitat created by the timber companies.

Having come from a country logged out completely by the mid-sixteenth century, I realized I'd been living under a considerable misapprehension myself. By the new standards I was trying to master, England had no nature at all. The consuming activities of my childhood – bird's-nesting, fishing, butterfly hunting, pressing wildflowers between the pages of old books – had been, as Mary Baker Eddy would have said, a case of Error. The countryside I had mistaken for nature was in fact so managed and cultivated as to amount to nothing more than a sprawling allotment or pea-patch.

My Englishness, in part, made me a poor reader of such modern Northwest writers as Gary Snyder, Barry Lopez, and Richard Nelson, who celebrate their at-oneness with the habitat of the wild. They owe more to Emerson than Wordsworth – and to Emerson at his most vatic. In 'Nature', what Emerson wrote of the forest –

Here is sanctity which shames our religions, and reality which discredits our heroes. Here we find nature to be the circumstance which dwarfs all other circumstance, and judges like a god all men who come to her.

– might serve as an epigraph to a long shelf of books about the prayerful relationship between the writer and the woods. Rooted in Native

American lore and Zen Buddhist teaching, the Northwest school's dominant tone is solemn, lyrical, minutely observant. In wilderness it discovers not chaos but transcendental order. Watching the riddled surface of the McKenzie River as it drifted past his Oregon forest home, Barry Lopez wrote, in 'The Whaleboat':

> *Sunlight flexes too rapidly, too completely, on the river's skin for the eye to spot a recurrent pattern in it, from bench or window, but I believe one is there. It's not anything I feel compelled to find; I don't believe I must know its meaning. I know that the design inherent in such things is orderly according to some logic other than the ones I know. It is akin, I think, to the logic that makes one's life morally consistent.*

Lopez was too good for me. Perhaps I was disqualified from following him because I had led a morally inconsistent life. Turner's whirling abyss seemed to me a true picture of reality as I generally experienced it; Lopez's version struck me as improbably tidy and benign. A 'design inherent' in nature implied a designer, in whose existence I had no faith at all. 'Logic' was, I thought, a useful word so long as it *meant* logic, not some vapoury, intuited life-force. That there might be many coexistent 'logics', as Lopez suggested, was news to me, knowing only one. I saw chaos where he saw order – a 'pattern' with a discoverable 'meaning', whose actual discovery could be put off to another day, another essay.

Reading the Northwest nature writers, I found myself an agnostic in their church; embarrassed, half-admiring, unable to genuflect in the right places. I wished there were more jokes. But humour was not their line. I liked the microscopic particularity of much of their writing, their intent and well-informed gaze, as they tried to penetrate the veil of the natural world. I thought individual passages were beautiful. But I couldn't join in their hymns, and after a few pages I grew restless and began to ache for more profane company.

The survey boats came back from their labyrinthine wanderings with crucial information. A few miles beyond where the ships lay at anchor, the ebb tide ran out to the north-west, proving that the explorers were on the inside of an enormous island. The tide gushed at tremendous speed through several narrow ravines, in a mass of rips and whirlpools. Indian villagers had shown the Englishmen how they could safely transit the rapids in canoes at slack water – though the water there was never truly slack, with mushroom-boils and fierce eddies lasting through the end of one tide into the beginning of the next. The surveyors reported that the Indians not only had iron-tipped spears and arrows but also carried muskets, pistols, and cutlasses for which they had traded furs with a man in a ship from Boston. So the rumour of Robert Gray's passage through the straits in *Lady Washington* was now confirmed.

At first light on 13 July, *Discovery* weighed anchor and sailed out of Desolation Sound on a breath of wind from the north. *Sutil* and *Mexicana*, their commanders still asleep, rode to their cables, while the foredeck crew of *Chatham* wrestled with a snagged anchor, slackening the cable, then quickly jerking it in on the capstan – an exhausting business that went on for nearly four hours before the anchor was freed and *Chatham* able to follow *Discovery* out of the sound. The night before, it had been agreed that the British would go through the pass nearest to the big island, while Galiano and Valdés, known as the Dons for short, would make their way seaward via passes closer to the mainland.

Vancouver escaped Desolation by the same entrance through which he had come in. He was at last on the move again, in a fair wind, the hateful waterfalls and precipices receding behind him. The oyster-pink sunshine at six o'clock penetrated his psyche, and he was able to smile for the first time in weeks. He enthused about the landscape of low islands and sandspits fringed with pleasant, familiar trees – alder, poplar, maple, hazel, willow, silver fir. 'They presented an appearance infinitely more grateful than that of the interior country.' He was even charmed by the local marine wildlife. 'Numberless whales enjoying the season, were playing about the ship in every direction, as were also several seals.' From Captain Van, this was a rapturous appreciation of nature.

All sails up, *Discovery* ghosted through a deep-water gap between islands that Vancouver named Baker Passage, after his third lieutenant, toward a long headland trending southward like an extended forefinger; this he called Cape Mudge, after his first lieutenant. When he put away the *Royal Kalendar* and the Admiralty list and began naming things in honour of his own officers, it was a sure sign that the captain's spirits were rising steeply. The officers themselves had learned to be wary of Vancouver's fits of twinkling bonhomie. When he prattled sentimentally about the antics of whales and scattered his shipmates' names over the surrounding land, the response on the quarterdeck was to run for cover.

Eight miles up Discovery Passage (Vancouver was feeling warmly toward his ship as well) the tidal pass now known as Seymour Narrows lay on the inside of Cape Mudge; a dark gorge, half a mile wide, between nine hundred foot bluffs, where at mid-tide the water boiled and broke in fleecy overfalls. *Discovery* and *Chatham* took advantage of the north-going ebb and hurtled through the rapids, whose entire surface was bomb-cratered with whirlpools. Thomas Manby described how the two ships 'stood through the narrow pass, the tide rushing along like Lightning, it running at least ten knots an hour'.

As soon as the passage widened and the tide slowed, canoes put out from shore to approach the visitors. 'A great many skins were bought by the rich Merchants on board,' Manby wrote, 'and from a party of Fishermen we purchased Two hundred Salmon, at the price of two buttons each.'

Several miles further on, the ships stopped at a large village, where more than a hundred canoes awaited them, each with a cargo of sea otter pelts for sale. Here Manby gave vent to his loathing of his captain:

a vast quantity of all kinds of skins were purchased, those
people who were intrusted with the various Articles sent out

> *by Government, made to their disgrace an amazing harvest –*
> *Bales of Cloath and blankets were sold with lavish hand for*
> *Skins, at a time when many . . . of our own Crew were shivering*
> *with cold from the want of woolen cloathing.*

Vancouver was purser of the expedition as well as its commander, so 'those people' are really one person. The 'disgrace', Manby implies, was Vancouver's alone, as he heartlessly feathered his own nest, at tax-payers' expense, while his crew shivered in rags.

This episode also fuelled Manby's condemnation of Vancouver in a letter he wrote to a friend, six months later, from Monterey. 'I am sorry to say what with his pursuing business, and a Trade he has carried on, are unbecoming the Character of an Officer in his Honourable and exalted station.' The word 'trade', first attached to him by Manby, would stick permanently to George Vancouver's public reputation.

In Gillray's 1796 cartoon of the scene in Conduit Street, when Vancouver was thrashed by Midshipman Thomas Pitt, now Lord Camelford, trade cuts right to the heart of the matter. Captain Van – fat, popeyed, blubber-lipped – has stepped out of a shady-looking establishment whose sign reads: THE SOUTH SEA WAREHOUSE, *From China! Fine Black Otter Skins (No Contraband Goods Sold Here).* Crucified pelts hang in the door and window. Vancouver's curious cape is labelled, *This Present from the King of Owyhee to George III forgot to be delivered.* The tall young baron, whose clean-cut features contrast wholesomely with his former commander's ugly pudding of a face, towers over the dwarfish captain, his stick raised over his shoulder. In the balloon issuing from Camelford's mouth, the words are: 'Give me Satisfaction, Rascal! – draw your Sword, Coward! what, you won't? – why then, take That, Lubber! – & that! & that! & that! & that!'

Gillray's reactionary satire holds that Vancouver amply deserves his thrashing for the simple reason that he is no gentleman. The cartoon is dedicated 'To the Flag Officers of the British Navy' – those admirals who unwisely promoted the parvenu, and whose reputation has been besmirched by the low, money-grubbing behaviour of their ill-bred protégé.

Yet Vancouver – in this, as in other things, the earnest disciple of Captain Cook – saw no shame in his trading activities. In the *Voyage*, he mentions the incident in passing: 'Our visitors . . . brought us the skins of the sea otter, of an excellent quality, in great abundance, which were bartered for sheet-copper, and blue cloth; those articles being in the highest estimation among them.' Only the use of that passive verb betrays a hint (if hint it is) of embarrassment.

For a man with no fortune of his own, soon to be retired on half-pay, the pile of sea otter pelts in his cabin was a hard-earned pension fund. Their soft, thick, chocolate fur meant comfort and security in his old age. On the Chinese market, a single pelt, properly cured and with its guard-hairs removed, fetched $100, about £25. As purser and commander, Vancouver was eventually paid at a rate of eight shillings a day, so a prime otter skin equalled two months' salary. He cannot have sold many; a year after *Discovery* returned to England, Captain Van was in debt and harassed by duns.

The trade he fails to mention is one that went on continuously as the expedition moved slowly up the coast. Manby (writing here about the Kwakiutl Indians, met in Discovery Passage) described it in his journal:

> *The women . . . wore a narrow strip of skin tied round their middles, some wore twisted rushes in its stead, tho' barely sufficient to conceal their sex, some of them were tolerably featured, and could they have been cleansed from their filth and dirt, might be termed passable. When absent from the eyes of the men, they readily accepted the embraces of anyone, that would bestow a glittering trinket for the favour.*

That the women of the Northwest coast were 'filthy' was an old complaint from English sailors, who themselves must have stunk like polecats. In 1778, when Cook's *Discovery* was anchored in Nootka Sound, David Samwell, a surgeon's mate, gave a gloating account of how the young gentlemen bathed Nootka girls before having sex with them:

> *Hitherto we had seen none of their young women though we had often given the men to understand how agreeable their company would be to us & how profitable to themselves, in consequence of which they about this time brought two or three girls to the ships; tho some of them had no bad faces yet as they were exceedingly dirty their persons at first sight were not very inviting; however our young gentlemen were not to be discouraged by such an obstacle as this which they found was to be removed with soap & warm water; this they called the Ceremony of Purification, and were themselves the officiators at it & it must be mentioned to their praise that they performed it with much piety and devotion.*
>
> *Their fathers who generally accompanied them made the bargain & received the price of the prostitution of their daughters, which was commonly a pewter plate well scoured for one night. When they found that this was a profitable trade, they brought more young women to the ships, who in compliance with our preposterous humour spared themselves the trouble of laying on their paint & us of washing it off again by making themselves tolerably clean before they came to us, by which they found they were more welcome visitors and thus by falling in with our ridiculous notions (for such no doubt they deemed them) they found means at last to disburthen our young gentry of their kitchen furniture; many of us after leaving this harbour not being able to muster a plate to eat our salt beef from.*

Sailing up Discovery Passage and into Johnstone Strait, where Kwakiutl villages crowded along the shoreline, the men on the quarterdeck were contented summer tourists. The weather stayed fine. The captain's manic good humour at least meant that he made no attempt to interfere with the young gentlemen's amusements, on board and off. They got laid as often as they pleased. Each day they dined on fresh salmon or venison, finishing the meal with wild strawberries and blackcurrants. They stashed away sea otter pelts by the score, and became avid collectors of native artefacts: baskets and conical hats, woven from twisted threads of the inner bark of the cedar and quaintly decorated; painted chests inlaid with abalone shell; masks, rattles, clubs, charms.

Meanwhile the currency given in exchange for these services and souvenirs – iron tools, beads, buttons, fabrics – provided the means for a spectacular explosion of Kwakiutl art, as the carvers and weavers incorporated European techniques and materials into their work. The iron chisel, in particular, enabled the Indians to do fast and easily what they had achieved only slowly and with great difficulty using tools of bone, shell, and stone. With their new technology, and with copper, mirrors, sacks of coloured trade-beads, Kwakiutl craftsmen were liberated into a new world of imaginative expression.

The Indians were equally impressed by the arts of the visitors – especially by the carved and painted figureheads on their ships, whose meaning and totemic power were much discussed. Interestingly, no one on the Vancouver expedition mentioned seeing a totem pole, nor is one shown in any of the midshipmen's drawings of native villages, though carved house-posts were observed almost everywhere. The fur trader Joseph Ingraham, cruising the Queen Charlottes in 1791, was taken to see 'two pillars . . . about forty feet in height, carved in a very curious manner indeed, representing men, toads, etc.' But the Haida Indians on these islands had been regularly visited by American and European traders for more than seventeen years by the time Ingraham arrived; they were the most cosmopolitan of the Northwest tribes. By the 1820s, totem poles were seen everywhere along the Inside Passage: a product of fur-trade wealth and leisure, iron chisels and gouges – and possibly the example of figureheads on white men's ships.

While all these transactions between the two cultures were taking place, the crews of *Chatham* and *Discovery* were keeping afloat on their newly matured supply of spruce beer, brewed ashore during their stop at Desolation Sound. Sprigs of fir were boiled in a vat for several hours; the bitter, greenish residue was strained through cheese-cloth; then water, molasses, and yeast were added, and the mixture was left to ferment in the cask for a week. I haven't tested this recipe, which comes from the late Admiral Bern Anderson of the US Navy; I'm still waiting for the right mood, of cheerful self-destruction, to descend on me. The appeal of spruce beer was that, unlike the daily rum issue, it was freely available to the sailors whenever they fancied. Since it was medically recommended for its power to ward off scurvy, a pleasant sense of virtuousness attended the experience of getting drunk on it.

It was a balmy interlude in a spooked voyage, these days of unrestricted sunshine, food, drink, sex, and fur trading, with deep water to sail in by day and comfortable village-anchorages at night. An air of vague, beery good humour infects the narratives of everyone on board between 13 July, when the expedition quit Desolation Sound, and 7 August, when *Discovery*, soon followed by *Chatham*, ran aground in the rocky shallows of Queen Charlotte Strait.

I took the Dons' route, through the jumbled mosaic of islands to the north and east of Discovery Passage. As the channels narrowed and the tide began to quicken, the windless water changed character. Sinewy, fibrous, braided, gathering itself for the rapids ahead, it had the colour and apparent consistency of black molasses.

Where Stuart and Sonora islands squeezed up against the British Columbian mainland they formed a slender Y-valve through which an immense quantity of water had to pass on its way to and from the open sea. To the north-east, Bute Inlet – more than thirty miles long and 2,000 feet deep – drained, on the ebb, through the Arran Rapids, a two hundred and fifty yard gap between Stuart Island and the mainland. From the south came nearly all the water in the Desolation Sound labyrinth, funnelled through the Yuculta Rapids between Stuart and Sonora. The two streams met and mingled in a cauldron-like basin of violent rips and whirlpools, before they shot, in consort, through the Dent Rapids into the broad reaches of Cordero Channel and Johnstone Strait, and out into the ocean at the north end of

Vancouver Island. Arran, Yuculta, and Dent, named like a firm of attorneys, were the Scylla and Charybdis of the region – though far more ferocious and powerful than the modest swirls to be found in the real-life Strait of Messina, and famous for gulping down canoes, tugs, and fishing boats. At any time other than slack water – a five-minute pause in the turbulence – these rapids could upend even large craft, then swamp them by the stern or hurl them into the rocks with their serpentine ten-knot currents.

Mexicana and *Sutil* waited for slack water at the northern entrance to the Arran Rapids, called by them Angostura de los Commandantes, surrounded by a troop of excited advisers in canoes. The Indians pointed to a distant mountaintop and indicated that the safest time to run the rapids would be when the sun was in transit over the peak: four o'clock in the afternoon, ship's time. José Cardero, the expedition artist, was almost certainly the author of the anony-mous published account of the voyage, in which the frightening passage through Arran and Dent is described.

> *The extreme rapidity which the waters attained was a phenom-enon worthy of the greatest attention. The current of Angostura de la Esperanza in the Strait of Magellan is seven and a half miles an hour near the shore, and its velocity is much greater in mid-channel. Nevertheless, the difference between the two currents, which can be noticed at once, is so great that it is no exaggeration to say that the current in Angostura de los Commandantes has a velocity of twelve miles. The sight is most strange and picturesque: the waters flow as if they were falling from a cascade; a great number of fish are constantly rising in them, and flocks of gulls perch on the surface to the entrance to the channel, allowing its rapid flow to carry them along, and when they have reached its end, they fly back to their original position and repeat the experience. This not only amused us, but it also supplied us with a means by which to gauge accurately the force of the current.*

A few minutes before four o'clock, the Indians paddled ashore to watch the foolhardy Europeans from a safe distance. Galiano and Valdés were overcautious; waiting for the tide to slacken, they missed the null, and when the brig and schooner pulled into the jaws of the narrows, under oars and studding sails, the ebb was already running fast. *Mexicana* hugged the mainland side, and was swept clean through; *Sutil*, running close to Stuart Island, got caught in an eddy and 'was turned around three times with such violence that it made those of us who were in her giddy'. Her hull scraped the rocks on Arran Point. *Mexicana* clawed her way over to a mainland cove, half a mile from the rapids, and began to lower her anchor, but *Sutil* couldn't cross the stream and was carried out of sight, spinning on the whirlpools.

> *The continual cross-currents and eddies, sometimes in favour and sometimes against the schooners, now driving them back and now driving them forward, making it always impossible to control them and leaving them at the mercy of the waters, alternately raised and mocked our hopes of making a creek which was very near. The Sutil attempted to reach with the boat a point which was to the east, but at that moment was caught by another violent whirlpool and again carried along, breaking the end of the cable which was just being made fast.*

Skidding wildly in a series of involuntary pirouettes, the ships were flushed through the cauldron of rips and eddies, and out through the long chute of Dent Rapids, from where their shaken captains managed to lead them to shelter, of a sort, under what is now Burnt Bluff. They anchored in forty fathoms, with stern lines tied to trees on the shore. Cardero, half sailor, half artist, was torn between seaman-like concern for the ships' safety and romantic relish for the sublime aspects of the night that followed:

> *Later the wind increased in strength, so that we heard it whistling through the plants above us and through the trees on the mountain. At the same time the violent flow of the waters in*

the channel caused a horrible roaring and a notable echo, this producing an awe-inspiring situation, so that we had so far met nothing so terrible.

I reached the entrance to Yuculta Rapids, the southernmost arm of the Y, thirty-five minutes before slack water. In the lunar cycle of the rapids, it was a very tame moment, a day of neap tides, called 'soakers' by towboatmen, as opposed to the big 'bull-tides' of fortnightly springs. Yet the ebb was still running hard. I turned the boat on the current and motored at four knots, facing back the way I'd come. At this speed I was able to keep a madrona tree on Sonora Island fixed in position between the starboard shrouds. In midstream, the flow was smooth and laminar: the only visible turbulence was my own wake, which trailed out behind the boat, strangely narrowed and attenuated, as the tide swept it away into the distance. When I began to gain on the madrona, I slackened off on the throttle until, at just two knots, the tree held in place. Then I turned and ran with the dying stream.

Off Big Bay, great curds of yeasty scum marked the sites of rips and whirlpools that were now nearly extinct. A few logs and uprooted kelp stems continued to revolve in patches of broken water. But the surviving eddies were flaccid, and there was no real heart in their attempts to wrench the steering from my hands. The boat sauntered, at eight knots going on nine, through Gillard Passage and Dent Rapids – a scene of spent turmoil, like the tumbled sheets of an empty bed, with an appropriately salty, post-coital smell of bladderwrack drying on the rocks.

Few seaways in the world have been named after artists. Cordero Channel, where I met the infant flood, had been Cardero Channel until Victorian chartmakers, ignorant of his painstaking watercolours and pen-and-ink drawings, took to casually misspelling it. This deserves to be put right. Both as writer and painter, Cardero, a short man nicknamed Pépé, paid closer attention to the arts of the Indians, and was more deeply stirred by the mountains and inlets than most of the Englishmen on Vancouver's ships.

On the VHF, Environment Canada had just put out an updated forecast of an imminent south-easterly gale: thirty-five to forty knots in Georgia Strait, fifty to sixty knots on the outer coast. The afternoon now had the dead stillness of the calm before a storm. Since lunchtime, the inked line on the barograph had sunk below 990 millibars, and the inert air felt thin and vacuous, as if someone had extracted it from the islands with a pump. Even with the engine going, I could hear birds in the trees – the show-off, quick-fire cannonade of a sapsucker drumming up a mate; the monotonous, squeaky-hinge keening of a chickadee.

The only motion was that of the incoming tide, stealing smoothly through the forest at one knot. Where fallen branches obstructed the current near the shore, they sprouted whiskers of turbulence that were steadily maturing into braided beards. The water was moving just fast enough to feel the abrasion of the air against it, and its surface was altering from glassy to stippled with the strengthening flood. Soon the false wind, brushing against the tide, created a trellis-like pattern of interlocked wavelets, their raised edges only a millimetre or two high; just deep enough to catch, and shape, a scoop of light.

I went up front to photograph the water ahead of the bow, but the action was too quick for the shutter. For the space of an eyeblink, each wavelet held a distorted scrap of a reflection, then it was gone. There, for a millisecond, was a bit of sky – a bit of tree – a bit of dark-hulled boat – a bit of my own face. The myriad fragmentary images flashed, stretched, contracted, and dissolved. Pursuing them with a camera, I was on a fool's errand; it was like trying to catch globules of mercury in a shrimp net. But I went on snapping, hoping to take the photograph I needed by accident.

I was trying to prove a point. The fundamental design-unit in the art of all the Northwest coastal tribes is a shape more easily sketched than described:

In a full-blown composition like a Chilkat blanket, a wall-hanging, or a carved and painted bentwood chest, you can see dozens of these lozenges, sometimes packed as tight as bricks in a wall. They vary in size and shape; they can be stretched out into a long, curvaceous boomerang, or squashed up until they're very nearly square. Often they contain smaller lozenges, just as the ripples I was trying to photograph contained concentric ellipses of light and shade.

José Cardero noticed the lozenges, which crop up in several of his drawings of Indian clothing and decoration. The Haida Indians, Judge Swan noted, identified them with the spots on the skin of a young skate. Franz Boas called them 'eye designs'. Bill Holm, the leading modern authority on Indian art of the Northwest coast, calls them 'ovoids'.

I've watched ovoids form, in their millions, in almost-still water, under a breath of wind, or by the friction of the moving tide. The canoe Indians, living on this water as their primary habitat, saw ovoids in nature every day of their lives; and when they combined them in a design, they made them do exactly what capillary waves do – reflect the world in smithereens.

The ovoid's 'formline' (Bill Holm's useful word) typically frames a dismembered body part: an eye, a claw, a jointed wing, the bladelike dorsal fin of a killer whale, the front teeth of a beaver. The whole picture, with all manner of interlinked ovoids, teases the spectator into trying to solve it like a puzzle. You find yourself instinctively reconfiguring its constituent pieces into a single creature or narrative sequence – yet the winged and finned creature is usually beyond the ken of conventional zoology, and the story proceeds by strange and contradictory leaps and bounds.

Turn-of-the-century Indian commentators on these designs were wonderfully ingenious and assured in their interpretations, though rarely did one commentator ever agree with another. Franz Boaz achieves a moment of rare comedy in *Primitive Art* when, trying to decipher the patterns of Chilkat blankets, he consults two ethnologists, George T. Emmons and John R. Swanton, each with his own native experts in tow.

The blanket shown in figure 203 represents, according to Emmons, a female wolf and young. . . . According to Swanton the blanket represents a young raven.

The blanket shown in figure 204 shows, according to Emmons. . . . a brown bear sitting up . . . According to Swanton the design represents a halibut.

The blanket in figure 103 represents, according to Emmons, a diving whale and the lateral fields a raven sitting. . . . According to Swanton the same blanket represents a wolf with young.

Boas then turns to bentwood chests; and here he is able to draw on the firsthand experience of the Haida artist, Charles Edenshaw, who obliges him with a frame-by-frame (or ovoid-by-ovoid) reading of the four sides of a painted box. This is Boas's drawing of the box in question:

And Edenshaw's gloss:

The design [shows] four interpretations of the raven as culture-hero. The upper right hand rectangle of the first side he claimed to represent the head of the raven surmounted by the ear; the large eye to the left of it, in the left hand upper corner, the shoulder and under it the wing and the tail. The design in the right hand lower corner he interpreted as the foot; the toes are clearly visible in the lowest right hand corner of this field. He claims that the

head turned upside down in the left hand upper rectangle of the
second side represents the head of the raven and under it the
hand; the raven being conceived as a human being. . . .

Forewarned by the Emmons–Swanton controversies, Boas wrote of this exegesis, 'I consider it entirely fanciful.'

The point, surely, is that these compositions are infinitely amenable to interpretation, no version of which can be counted final and authoritative. With marvellous stylistic assurance and control, the Indian artists have rendered a world inherently fluid, fragmentary, elusive, and chaotic. Look, it's a bear; look again, it's a halibut. This is nature as one meets it in the distorting mirror of the water. It's no coincidence, I think, that Boas's drawing of the painted chest bears an uncanny resemblance to the photograph I was trying, and failing, to take of the marbled, endlessly shifting, random chiaroscuro of Cordero Passage.

The maritime art of these mostly anonymous Kwakiutl, Haida, and Tsimshian craftsmen appeared to me to grow directly from their observation of the play of light on the sea. Trailing through the museums of Seattle, Vancouver, and Victoria, then, later, through the Northwest Indian galleries of the American Museum of Natural History in New York and the Menil Collection in Houston, I saw a water-hauntedness in almost every piece. This was an aspect of the art the descriptive literature ignored. Thousands of pages were given over to discussion of its shamanistic symbolism, and, since Bill Holm's landmark *Northwest Coast Indian Art: An Analysis of Form* (1965), its abstract design. What I found, touring the museums, was an art in thrall to ripples and reflections.

The simplest way of retrieving order from chaos is to hold a mirror to it. The scraps of coloured plastic in Julia's kaleidoscope, given a random shake, yielded a perfectly symmetrical pattern. In the sheltered inlets of the Northwest, the Indians faced constant daily evidence of the mirror of the sea as it doubled and patterned their untidy world; and it's no wonder that their art is possessed by a rage for symmetry. It's full of spatchcocked animals – ravens, wolves, whales – sliced down the middle and laid out flat so the left half of the creature is an exact reflection of the right. In most boxes and blankets (Boas's chest is atypical in this respect), an invisible seam runs from top to bottom down the centre of the composition, the two sides mirroring each other like a butterfly's wings. Totem poles, at least viewed from the front, have the same rigid, reflective symmetry.

Sometimes, especially in early morning, the water of the inlets is as still as a pool of maple syrup, its surface tension unblemished by wind or tide: then it holds a reflection with eerie fidelity, with no visible edge or fold along the waterline. Capturing the Indian sea in this mood, my amateur photographic efforts were a lot more successful.

The previous year, I'd been up at 5:30 a.m. in a lagoon-like nook, deep among the fjords on the west coast of Vancouver Island. At high-water slack on a spring tide, about two feet of earthen bank showed above the water. A welter of roots and rocks protruded from the dark soil, and the whole length of the bank lay on its exact reflection. Moving carefully in the cockpit so as not to make ripples, I took a dozen pictures. The long, low bank and its watery double came out perfectly, with no give-away seam showing where earth stopped and reflection began.

Turned sideways, the photographs showed precisely what I'd seen: a pillar of strange faces. Doubled, every random feature of the bank took on meaning and expression. The curved root became a pair of eyebrows; the narrow wedge of rock, lodged slantwise in the earth, turned into a grinning mouth; a stone was the flared nostrils. In a few yards of crumbled bank one saw a jostling crowd of gargoyles.

I framed four of the pictures and hung them on the kitchen wall – four blackened pillars standing in a jungle of greenery. Whenever a visitor eyed them, I supplied a single clue: 'The paint's worn off – they're very old.'

'Oh, I see. Totem poles.'

It worked every time. The experiment proved nothing in particular about totem poles, but it did show how instantly legible a random string of marks becomes when doubled with its mirror image. Boas thought the taste for symmetry in primitive art was 'difficult to understand', but surely it wasn't difficult in the Northwest, where, more days than not, at dawn and dusk, everything on land was rooted to its watery reflection. The split creature – a favourite motif – was a simple fact of visual life: the wading heron joined by the ankles to its twin; the twinned loon; the black bear at the edge of the lake, lapping up its own image with its tongue.

Water plays tricks on whatever lies within its reach. It distorts and dismembers, then restores an extravagant wholeness, making two of one – which is exactly what the Indian artists of the Northwest were doing in their designs. Living on water, as aquatic in their habits as sea otters, the coastal tribes couldn't help but see in the water's playful games a true reflection of their own instinctive worldview. Rippled surfaces exposed a restless and inconstant nature, in which things continually swapped places and sudden, mysterious trans-formations abounded. Carving a box or painting a muslin curtain, the artist was, in effect, recreating scenes from the water's never-ending picture show.

At twilight I reached the summer resort on Blind Channel, its line of finger piers deserted. Preparing to pull into a slot, I saw the tide was swirling through the piers like a river in spate. The fenders gasped as the water pinned the 14,000-pound weight of the boat against the dock, and the protesting chuckle of the current against the hull was loud in the dead air.

The picture windows of the waterside restaurant framed bosomy snowdrifts of furniture, dust-sheeted for winter. The shop-cum-post office was dark, and no lights showed in the nearby house. The only sign of life was the drone of an electrical generator in a whitewashed shed. In the gloaming, it took a little while to detect the object of my visit, a BC TEL satellite payphone shrouded in bushes up a dirt path.

Most likely, the owners were sunning themselves on the beaches at Waikiki and that evening I was the only inhabitant of West

Thurlow Island. My big problem was the distance – no more than a hundred feet – that yawned between me and the phone, on which I had promised to call Jean and Julia.

I've always been scared of large mammals – in England, cows; in the Northwest, bears and cougars. West Thurlow, out of season, looked to me like prime bear country. My instincts were to stay with the boat, but I meant to keep my promise.

One of the US Coast Guard's many antiquated regulations was that every vessel above a certain length was required to carry a ship's bell, for use in fog. I unhooked my bell from its mounting on the coach-house roof and advanced slowly up the path, clanging the bell like a medieval leper and listening, between each mournful tintinnabulation, for the sound of heavy crashing in the brush. A panicked wren fled a patch of salal. The only other wild inhabitant I met was a fat banana slug.

At the phone I dug into my pockets for change with one hand and shook the bell at the wilderness with the other, thinking as I did so that this was probably not quite how Barry Lopez or Richard Nelson would handle the situation. Like a triton shell, the phone had the sound of the sea in it. I fed a fistful of quarters into the slot and punched in the 12.06-billion number of home. The surf continued to break on the faraway coast.

'Hello? Operator?'

But no one was hiding in the static.

I tried again a dozen times and got nothing but the lonesome sea. I walked back to the boat, jangled the bell morosely and cursed BC TEL, as Blind Channel lived up to its name and the water darkened to the colour of the surrounding fir forest. Remembering stories of how bears in these parts regularly boarded boats, lured by the tantalizing scent of domestic garbage, I slid the companionway hatchboards into place and locked the hatch against ursine burglars.

The wind arrived at midnight, waking me with the sudden, urgent hammering of a loose halyard against the mast and, inches from my left ear, the brushlike sound of waves collapsing against fibreglass. In the drumskin interior, the vibrating halyard took on a thunderous resonance. With each gust it whanged louder and faster, until I was forced to fix it. Throwing a parka over my naked shoulders, I went out barefoot with a knife and a coil of shock-cord. Stubbing a toe on the steel cleat amidships, I added a wolfish howl of my own to the varied noises of the night.

I was awake again at dawn. Through the ovoid of scratched perspex that served as a porthole, I watched a demented limb of alder trying to detach itself from its parent tree, against a background of sky that looked like cold grey porridge. I twiddled my way through the wavelengths on the bedside radio, but it was as empty of voices as the satellite payphone. Hemmed in by high islands, I was in a radiophonic black hole.

But the wind snuck through. Fierce squalls raced across the width of the whitening channel and heeled the boat hard against the dock, where it shivered from masthead to keel at each new gust. The fenders squealed. The mooring ropes, sounding thin and taut as ukulele strings, sawed against the fairleads and wrenched at the cleats. Safely tied up, with nothing much to do and nowhere to go, I settled down to enjoy my enforced leisure on this wild morning. I lit the lamps, put the kettle on to boil, and, to counter the noise of the discordant ship's orchestra, plugged in a tape of Mozart's clarinet quintet in A – the Amadeus Quartet, with Gervase de Peyer on clarinet.

First the violins, joined by cello and viola, made a hesitant, exploratory descent into the bass, where they discovered the clarinet, sounding as fresh and wild as the pipes of Pan. In 1789 the clarinet was still a vulgar novelty, and Mozart was breaking new ground by writing such a star part for the instrument. In this piercingly beautiful recording, de Peyer gave every note a liquid, experimental quality, as if sounding out a course through uncharted territory.

Mozart – just eighteen months older than Captain Van – was another figure living on the cusp of the Romantic revolution. Hearing his music framed by all the noises of the boat in a small gale, I found I was listening to the clarinet as the symbol of that unfettered liberty to which Mozart's late work seems always to be gesturing, pointing the way to Beethoven and beyond.

With the saloon full of music and the smell of coffee, I began translating the previous day's forecast into an intelligible weather map. An intense low (infuriatingly, its depth in millibars wasn't specified) was bearing down on Vancouver Island from the west, with an associated front trailing southward from its centre. The front had been predicted to cross the island, raking it from north to south, overnight; but my barograph was still falling and the wind was blowing out of the east-south-east, which suggested the system had stalled on the outer coast. Once the front passed, the wind ought to slacken off and veer to the south-west, while the drooping arm of the barograph should begin to climb back toward the horizontal. The inked line now touched 981 millibars, and its downward slope gave no hint of having yet bottomed out.

De Peyer took flight in an arpeggio of woodnotes. The wind harped in the shrouds. I exercised the pretty rule of thumb known as Buys Ballot's law. If you stand facing the wind (in the northern hemisphere), the low-pressure centre lies somewhere between eight and twelve compass points to your right. That put my low in the general direction of Cape Scott – a hungry void spinning counterclockwise, sucking great draughts of air into itself as it came trundling inland from the ocean.

On a fresh page of the logbook, I sketched the coastline and drew a nest of whorled isobars on top of Vancouver Island, the winds draining into it like bathwater going down a plughole. In a pleasant daze of Mozart and mapmaking, I took several moments to register that an intruder was thumping purposefully on the hull. Bear! I thought, and leaped for the now-open companionway.

A man in a yellow rainslicker stood by the cockpit: the resort's owner, demanding the $15 fee for overnight moorage. So certain was I of my solitude here that I could only gape in silence at this Man Friday apparition.

'I'm sorry. I thought—'

I mumbled about no-lights-on-in-the-house and didn't-realize-anyone-was-here, but could see this wasn't cutting much ice. The man's eyes were looking not at me but at the cockpit seat, where I had parked my leper's bell.

I went downstairs to hunt for my wallet. The trio section had just begun. I switched de Peyer off and resolved to reappear as an ordinarily personable being, in full possession of his wits. But nothing I said seemed to dent the impression made by my bell-ringing activities the night before. The man's expression condemned me as a nutcase, to be handled at cautious arm's length. His manner, as he wrote out the receipt, was studiedly remote. When I plied him with questions, he answered with uninflected monosyllables. I asked where he and his family had come from before setting up shop on West Thurlow Island.

Out of long habit, he nodded in a southerly direction. '—Vancouver,' he said.

I'd never heard the name pronounced with such a charge of disapproval that 'Vancouver' came out sounding like Sodom, Gomorrah, Babel, and the Great Wen rolled into one.

So he was an urban type, supporting his wilderness retreat by opening it to boatloads of other urban types for three months a year. Not only was I the madman with the bell, but out of season to boot. An unwelcome intruder on his solitude, I felt doubly unpopular.

'Can you open the store for me?'

He checked his wristwatch and said, regretfully, 'Noon.'

'Can I mail stuff from here?'

'Mailplane. Tomorrow.'

'Thanks,' I said.

'Welcome,' he said.

Pining for conversation, I found myself an outcast on the island, where my unsavoury reputation had got abroad. A woman on a bike, pedalling between the house and the resort, abruptly changed course at the sight of me and found urgent business to attend to in her vegetable patch. At noon, in the store, the owner stood guard over the till, drumming his fingers lightly on the counter while I browsed through the few items remaining on the shelves. I bought half a dozen bear postcards for Julia, stamps, some food in cans and packets, then begged to make a phone call. The owner let me use his cellphone to access the BC TEL satellite system.

'This is Jean,' lied the comb-and-paper, magnetically encoded replica of Jean's voice. 'Please leave a message.'

I told the machine I was gale-bound on an island, virtually out of contact with the rest of the world, that I hoped Julia's bear postcards had been arriving in a steady stream, that I'd call again as soon as I got the chance, that 'I so miss you both. I—'

'Ping-pong,' said the two-tone doorbell chime of the machine, telling me my time was up.

'Nine dollars,' said the resort owner, who'd been pricing the call with the second hand on his watch.

Defeated in all my efforts to make contact with another human being, I walked back to the boat to commune with the waves, now breaking in regular formation across the passage. The driving wind remained obstinately in the east-south-east, though I thought I saw a distinct levelling of the barograph needle on the 980-millibar line.

The waves came hissing at the transom. Only a few minutes old, born as wrinkles eight hundred yards away across the channel, already they were mature and grizzle-bearded. Blocklike, lumpy, they packed a big wallop for their size. Pale ribbons of dissolving foam streaked the inky water, and the boat was being jostled with sufficient force to make me double up the mooring ropes. It was now hard to stand upright on the floating dock, which pitched and rolled underfoot like a Boston cakewalk.

According to Mircea Eliade, the earliest known form of decoration, the zigzag pattern rimming a Neolithic pot, represented a wave train in profile. On this coast, the undulating line of the waves, their interminable cycle of growth and collapse, ran through the art of the Indians as the essential shape of life itself. Waves chase each other around woven hats and baskets. Beautifully chiselled waves edge a goathorn ladle, a wooden feasting bowl, a maple-wood mortar. The swooping calligraphic brushstroke, as it defines the outlines of an extended composition, mimics the curve of the wave, from trough to crest and down to trough again.

Waves have always been emblems, full of sombre meaning. 'I hear the waves!' cries out the six-year-old Paul Dombey in his delirium, a few moments before his death. Philip Larkin, at the seaside, meditates on 'the small hushed waves' repeated fresh collapse', conjuring a multitude of small hushed lives going to their deaths. Shakespeare, in Sonnet 60, sees in the waves the futile brevity of life:

> *Like as the waves make to the pebbled shore,*
> *So do our minutes hasten to their end,*
> *Each changing place with that which goes before,*
> *In sequent toil all forward do contend . . .*

The wave's urgent and dramatic expenditure of energy to no significant effect makes it a natural symbol of human self-importance and mortality. Watching waves break is a pastime designed to induce reflective melancholy, and I doubt if the wave processions that march through Northwest Indian art were meant to be any jollier in their significance than their deathly cousins that course through English literature.

Down in the saloon, I laid the postcards out on the table, numbered them, and tried to write Julia an upbeat story about a wandering bear named Emily. It was tough going. The conventions of talking bears (hats, gumboots, honeypots, etc.) seemed as formal and strict as the rules governing the Petrarchan sonnet. Emily's dim adventures kept being invaded by bear stories collected by Boas and his colleagues, in which the bears' sexual intercourse with humans, and its social consequences, usually provided the climactic narrative event. Perhaps A. A. Milne and Michael Bond were similarly tormented, trying to stop Winnie the Pooh and Paddington from molesting children in the nursery. I feared my bear story was broadly comparable, in its entertainment value, to a tale recorded by Boas, entitled 'Mucus of Nose' and reading, in its entirety: 'It goes down mucus – It goes up mucus – It goes down mucus – It comes out.' Meanwhile the waves went on breaking at my back, ploughing into the stern with a crackling-bonfire sound and jolting my living quarters so hard that it was like trying to write on a shunting train.

Late in the afternoon the wind shifted decisively into the south-west, swinging around the channel until it came off a wooded point within a hundred yards of the dock. The noise of the waves shrank to an amiable chuckle along the waterline; the barograph needle was up to 982; the line of the front had passed overhead on its way inland. Then the rain arrived – a warm downpour that fell into the water like granulated sugar from a chute.

Clad in full-dress orange storm gear like a member of some chemical-warfare unit, I mailed my postcards at the store, flicking them one by one under the door in the hope they eventually would make it to the mailplane, then went back to the boat and took refuge from the rain and growing darkness in a pile of Indian texts.

> *A chief lived in the middle of a very long town. His daughter was fond of picking berries. Once she went for berries with her father's slaves, and while picking far up in the woods she stepped upon some grizzly-bear's dung. 'They always leave things under people's feet, those wide anuses,' she said. . . .*

The offensive bear ('you with the big hole at each end') changes itself into human form and seduces the young woman. In the grizzly's den she becomes a bear; and when she tries to return to the human world, she is hunted by the angry grizzly-bear tribe.

> *She began crying for her life. She came out on the edge of a lake. In the middle of this big lake a canoe was floating wearing a dance hat. It said to her, 'Run this way into the water.' Then she ran into the water towards it. She was pulled in, and it went up with her into the sun.*

It's another warning story about the fragile and precarious nature of human identity, and the danger of tangling with such forces of the wild as bears and whirlpools. Stay in the town, or on the safe surface of the water. In the depths of the forest, and beneath the sea, false lovers abound. When means of escape present themselves, like the canoe wearing a dance hat, they can be relied on to conduct you from the frying pan into the fire. (When the canoe carries the woman aloft, she is gang-raped and impregnated by the sons of the sun.)

The moral of these stories would seem merely sensible and commonplace if it were not for the sentimental myth of Indians living in a state of idealized harmony with nature. Nature, as described in their literature, is quick to take offence, vengeful, sexually predatory, and generally ill-disposed to humankind. Civilization – the canoe, the house, the village – exists as a tiny circle perpetually threatened by a greedy and rapacious wilderness, and can be destroyed by one careless move. The bear-woman's troubles begin with an act of impoliteness, when she rudely makes fun of the grizzly's big anus.

The trouble is that the Indians' oral literature has been systematically eroded by several generations of Dr Bowdlers and Mrs Grundies – starting with the first late-Victorian collectors, who tended to flinch at the stories' bawdy relish for the details of sex and evacuation. Swanton, not an obvious prude, resorted to turning the dirty bits into Latin:

> Bear asked Raven, 'What do you use for bait anyhow, my friend?' *Corvus respondit, 'Testium cute ad escam praeparandum utor.' Ursus aeiebat corvo, 'Licetne uti meis quoque?' Sed corvus dixit, 'Noli id facere, ne forte sint graviter attriti.' Paulo post ursus aegre ferens aiebat, 'Abscide eos.' Tum corvus cultellum acuens aiebat, 'Pone eos extrema in sede.' Postea corvus eos praecidit, at ursus gemens proripuit circum scapham et moriens incidit in undas extreme cum gemitu.* *
>
> After a while Raven said to Cormorant, 'There is a louse coming down on the side of your head. . . .'

*The Latin translates roughly as:
Raven replied, 'The skin of the testicles is the best bait to use.' Bear said to Raven, 'Would mine be useful too?' But Raven said, 'They wouldn't do – they're all worn out.' A little while later, the sickly bear said, 'Cut them off.' Then Raven, with a little sharp knife, said, 'Lower your rear end.' Then Raven lopped off the bear's balls, and Bear, roaring, dragged himself round the canoe and, dying, put his ass in the waves, with terrible groans.

Not quite a bedtime story for Julia, but hardly XXX-rated either.

If *that* had to go into Latin, one wonders how much of the story must have been unprintable in any language. Later folklorists, trying to gain a larger, younger audience for Indian 'myths', bled the stories dry of all remotely unseemly references, until all that was left behind was a milk-and-water residue of Native American Spirituality and a cast of animal characters who would not disgrace themselves in *The House at Pooh Corner*. The popular books – Ella E. Clark's *Indian Legends of the Pacific Northwest*, for example – were so thoroughly permeated by the wholesome tradition of folktales-for-children that their versions bear almost no relation to the harsh, startling, and scatological narratives heard by Franz Boas and the other early anthropologists.

As my own trip took me deeper into a region that looked, at least, a lot like wilderness, I found that Indian art and stories were becoming daily more meaningful, losing their tophamper of exoticism and grotesquerie and gaining a melancholy realism that was rooted in the physical landscape through which I was travelling. It was easy to feel a personal resonance in the many stories about the bad things that happen to people who wander away from home. Loneliness was a dominant theme. Characters were constantly being driven to madness or suicide by the death of a spouse or the desertion of their friends. A man loses his family to a deadly epidemic; alone, he entertains pieces of floating ice to a ceremonial feast. When a man's wife dies, he commissions the village's best carver to fashion her image in red cedar, which he then dresses in his wife's clothes and takes with him everywhere; the wooden statue begins to move, but only slightly, and never learns to speak.

No fate was worse than being an outcast or exile. The literature was rich in grim examples of people who, by bad luck or selfish actions, were excluded from the sustaining warmth of village and family life. Causes of exile included laziness, jealousy, offence to a powerful being, poverty, contentiousness, and having sex with the wrong person – or animal, as in the case of the young woman whose unseen lover turned out to be a dog, and who gave birth to a litter of puppies. The sole consolation of exile was that solitary people occasionally came into possession of shamanistic powers. Such rare, fortunate outsiders could enrich themselves with great hauls of fish or supplies of copper, and return to the village as persons of consequence.

The stories harped on the terrors of the unknown – the lonely island, the dark forest, the undersea grotto of the giant devilfish, the sky-domain of the thunder-eagle. You had only to dive a little too deep, walk a few steps too far, climb one hill too many, and you'd cross into the habitat of creatures to which the fire-lit masks at winter dance ceremonies offered a scarifying field guide.

I was beginning, at last, to put all this in its proper context. The stories reflected an imperilled social world, in which humans were laughably puny in relation to two hundred foot conifers, impassable 10,000-foot mountains, and tidal rapids resembling horizontal Niagaras. Here people were hugely outnumbered and outweighed by carnivorous wild animals.

Claude Lévi-Strauss once suggested that the 1,000-mile-plus stretch of coast between Puget Sound and south-east Alaska once held a population of around 150,000 Indians. The figure has been subsequently criticized for being too high, and 75,000 is probably nearer the mark – a good crowd for a baseball game, but tiny when set against this long straggled terrain of inlets and archipelagos. Coastal tribes lived in scattered villages, some of which, like the 'very long town' of the bear-woman, were very big indeed. Vancouver wrote of 'upwards of a hundred canoes' putting off from a single village to trade furs with the visitors.

Both the Spanish and British explorers sailed for days on end without seeing a sign of human life or habitation; though in some areas, around the Arran Rapids, for example, and along Johnstone Strait uptide of the Seymour Narrows, they met with large concentrations of population. Turbulence meant life as well as danger. The best fishing was where the tide ran fast; and the rapids attracted all the other creatures that fed on fish, from gulls and eagles to bears and sea otters. Between these magnet-centres lay great stretches where a grizzly bear might pass a lifetime without setting eyes on a human being.

No wonder that when they told stories to their children, Indians cast the animals in roles of arbitrary and malevolent power. Even small creatures – that cruel joker, the raven; the mink, the frog, the clam – could, if provoked, easily humiliate or kill a grown human. The animals were the ancestors of the tribes, but showed little compassion for their dim two-legged descendants.

Read simply as children's fiction, these stories describe a world of infinite danger and portent, where knowing one's place and following baffling rules of deference and etiquette are every bit as important as in Lewis Carroll's Looking-Glass House (or Captain Van's England). In the Pacific Northwest, humankind lived on sufferance, at the whim of a great multitude of untrustworthy and intelligent creatures. Tread with care, the stories warn; you are as nothing to the beasts of the forest and the monsters of the deep.

Most collectors tidied up their material, doing their best to squash it into the mould of Aesop-like fables. But in Boas's faithful transliterations, the strange narrative grammar of Indian storytelling is kept intact – and the grammar is sometimes as interesting as the eventful content. Quite often a story begins with the word 'Then' and finishes abruptly, with an open-ended sentence: 'Then he drifted down' or 'The warriors drifted about' or 'He had just been dead when he came down falling from the sky'. Frequently the plot is hard to follow, because things happen contingently, for no apparent reason, the story moving forward by means of a series of bolts from the blue. Just as you think you're getting the hang of it, a killer whale is likely to swim up and abduct the central character. A bad person suddenly comes into an unexpected fortune; a good and inoffensive one suffers inexplicable punishment. The world of these stories is turbulent and random: again and again, they show Indians as creatures moving through a landscape full of powers – hapless babes in the malevolent wood.

In Kwakiutl stories, masks, and statuary, two important characters recur: Komogwa, the submarine plutocrat, and his forest counterpart, Tsonogwa. Though operating independently, in different elements, they are a perfectly matched couple. Komogwa has a beak nose and protuberant, see-all eyes. Tsonogwa has huge pendulous breasts, and her eyes are usually shown half-closed, as if blind or in a stupor; her mouth is an insatiable O, with lips thrusting inches out from her face. Short-sighted, dim of brain, ferocious, Tsonogwa is close kin to the grizzly bear.

Both of these beings prey on humankind. Komogwa drags canoes under the surface. Tsonogwa, a thief and a kidnapper, steals young children from villages whenever a lapse in security allows her to make a raid. At winter dances, the masks of Komogwa and Tsonogwa were among the scariest, with Tsonogwa letting out her child-catching cry of '*Huu! Huu!*' through monstrous vermilion lips. Yet both figures were intimately associated with livelihood and wealth. Komogwa presided over his undersea treasure-stash of valuable copper. (According to Lévi-Strauss, the same word could signify both 'copper' and 'salmon', perhaps due to their similarity in colour.) Tsonogwa lived in a forest mansion stacked to the roof with skins, dried meats, berries, grease. Komogwa/Tsonogwa stories usually explain how lucky, or clever, Indians managed to return from the ocean or forest laden with riches from the ogres' dens.

So Komogwa and Tsonogwa embodied the wilderness that humans must brave in order to survive or prosper. They were no more given to friendliness than the killer whales and bears who were their familiars. In their carved and painted portraits, one can see bottomless reserves of greed, malignity, and power. They bear no resemblance at all to Mother Nature, the smiling goddess of the modern American preschool, though they do represent the best efforts of the Kwakiutl to put an intelligible face on nature as they knew it.

On that lonely, chilly evening in Blind Channel, the masks and stories made great sense as I studied them by lamplight, the trees groaning in the wind and the rain hammering on the coachroof. Too often, Indian life on the Northwest coast was pictured as an idyll – the tribes living at one with nature, in a region of unparalleled abundance – until it was violated by the white intruders. Nothing in their own art or literature gave credence to that guilty, sentimental notion. Rather, what rose from every page was the justified terror of living cheek-by-jowl with creatures far larger and more powerful than oneself.

You might go picking berries and find yourself – armed with no better weapon than a bow and a few arrows tipped with mussel-shell points – squaring up to an aggrieved bear. You might go fishing and find your canoe spinning out of control in the swirls as half a gale blows down the exposed strait. You were constantly made aware of your own physical insignificance by the girth of the fir, the rearing bulk of the grizzly, the crash of the whale, the massive turmoil of the tide.

Huu! Huu!

Komogwa and Tsonogwa were the rightful geniuses of this place.

Early white visitors – Cook, Vancouver and his troop of journal-keeping young gentlemen, Cardero, Joseph Ingraham – all wrote of how welcoming the Indians were, sometimes extravagantly so, as when Maquinna, the Nootka chief, laid on feasts and entertainments for the whites at Tahsis, his winter village. Very occasionally, the Indians tried to attack vulnerable survey boats or small ships like Ingraham's seventy-two-ton brigantine *Hope*; generally, however, the interlopers found the natives eager, confiding, vastly curious, and quick to catch on.

When a four-storey floating village of white men came ghosting into view under full sail, it was commensurate in scale to its surround-ings. *Discovery's* main topmast, with its fantastic cobwebbing of shrouds and spars, stood a hundred and twenty feet above the water – as tall as a well-matured forest tree. Lying alongside the ship, a canoe looked like a hazelnut shell. Moving silently, airborne, without the splash of paddles, the giant ship was an emblem of human power to match the powers of nature, a dizzying vision of what mankind could accomplish, given the tools and materials that the whites left scattered in their wake in exchange for fish and furs.

By the late eighteenth century, Indians had pretty well exhausted the possibilities of their technology. The artefacts that Cook picked up in Nootka Sound (now in the British Museum) are astonishingly ambitious and refined, when one thinks of craftsmen labouring to bring them into being with implements of bone, stone, and shell. Looking at the red-cedar Tlingit chest in New York's American

Museum of Natural History that is said to date from the seventeenth century, one imagines a fierce struggle between the carver's soaring imagination and his minimal toolkit: it is as if the chest itself were dreaming of what it might have been, if only the carver had possessed a better chisel.

The Indians needed no teaching. They fell on the tools, firearms, nails, iron, copper, and cloth as necessities long overdue. White ships had barely dropped anchor off the villages before Indians were using iron fishhooks and arrowheads. With muskets (denied them by Captain Van, but standard currency in the fur trade) and woodworking tools, the Indians were at last able to get on a more nearly equal footing with Komogwa and Tsonogwa.

Among the much later products of the new technology was a twenty-two-foot-tall sculptural effigy of Tsonogwa, photographed by Edward Curtis for volume ten of *The North American Indian*. She stands on the edge of a partially logged forest, her arms spread wide to receive a gift of property from the family of a bride-to-be. Her body is finely tooled, with special care paid to the realistic musculature of her arms and her blunt, big-fingered hands; but it's an odd piece of work. There is no threat, only pathos, in her collapsed breasts. Her painted head is carved in a quite different, cartoonish style. Jug-eared, with wide-open saucer-eyes, she stares out of the photograph looking like a shocked Minnie Mouse. Even her yawning mouth and out-thrust lips suggest little more than vague, senile bewilderment. This is a Tsonogwa who has lost her power to hex – who by 1900 or thereabouts, when the statue was carved, had become a harmless folk memory, no longer the guardian of forest riches but an antique figure of fun.

0645. Bar. 998, r. Sky like a grubby washcloth, draped low over the trees. Dead calm. Forecast wind: NW10–15.

In the chill of what passed in Blind Channel for dawn, the blood had bypassed the tips of three of my fingers, which made writing difficult, and gave my extremities the appearance of belonging to someone else's corpse. Gripping a mug of hot coffee to coax the pink back into my fingertips, I pulled away from the dock and began a stopwatch race against the tide. Greene Point Rapids, just around the corner, turned at nearly the same moment as Whirlpool Rapids, twelve miles further on. By taking the first set on the flood, an hour and ten minutes before slack, I hoped to shoot the second on the ebb, within an hour of the turn.

Greene Point Rapids was a long, straight, gleaming hill of water, where the tide surged through the gap between West Thurlow and the Cordero Islands. Seabirds had stained the cluster of spiky rocks to starboard a uniform white, and the usual foul-tempered mob was rioting over the bonbons cast up by the turbulent deep. The boat laboured against the gradient, barely gaining on the beacon where two sated cormorants were perched, digesting their breakfast fish. Seven knots through the water; two, at best, over the ground. The diesel snarled underfoot at maximum revs. Blue smoke swirled astern and came drifting back into the cockpit. The cormorants, hanging their wings out to dry, inched past the bow to the shrouds, then drew level with the doghouse: a pair of miniature black pterodactyls with prehistoric eyes.

I was surprised by the force of the tide as it drove deep inland, but was able to keep the boat more or less on course, with only an occasional sideways slew as it skidded on a boil. The gulls' clamour and thrashing wings made it hard to read the water surface and locate the back-eddies to the side of the main stream, but the beacon slid gradually astern and the current soon weakened to a manageable three and a half knots.

In the stories I'd been reading, the tide was the most nearly friendly to humans of all the powers of nature. Though it had not always been so: once upon a time, control of the tides had been in the hands of famously vindictive beings: South Wind (Puget Sound Salish); West Wind (Nootka); Thunder-Eagle (Coos and Tillamook); Wolf (Kwakiutl); or the Mistress of the Tides, the ancient hag who held the 'tide-line' in her hands and could let it out or draw it up at will (Tsimshian and Tlingit). In those days, the sea sometimes rose so high as to drown the mountains, or withdrew so far as to leave the whole country parched and dying. Then someone – usually Raven, though sometimes Halibut, Skate, or Mink – tricked or blackmailed the tyrant power into moderating the tide and putting it on a regular daily basis with strict limits to the extent of high water, so that Indians could safely gather shellfish from the beaches during an ebb tide, without fear that their villages might be inundated by the coming flood.

It was obvious why people thought the tides of the past much fiercer than those of the present: a bull tide, when the sun and moon lined up on one axis, came roaring through these narrow channels as if nothing short of miraculous intervention could ever stanch it. Most coastal tribes had stories of a great flood long ago, when the sea swamped the world and left canoes stranded on snowpeaks. The missionaries found Noah was a surefire hit on the reservations; one had only to see a spring tide in action here to start thinking of arks and Ararats.

In this habitually overcast country, where a week might go by without a glimmer of sun or stars, the best available way of telling the time was by tide. In Halkomelem, the language spoken at the south-east end of Georgia Strait, Wayne Suttles found terms to describe each stage of its cycle: 'flooding tide', 'be flooding', 'ebbing tide', 'be ebbing', 'high tide', 'be just high water', 'low tide', 'be in a period of half-tides', 'be slack water'. The continuous variations plotted the day as efficiently as any clock: one glance at the level and direction of the current and you'd know exactly how soon to begin paddling home for lunch. Under clear skies, the states of the tide could be synchronized with the movements of heavenly bodies – as the Kwakiutl Indians showed Galiano and Valdés the time of slack water at Arran Rapids, by pointing at the mountaintop over which the sun should stand before the Dons attempted the passage.

The tide – calendar as well as clock – mapped the Indian year. In the Pacific Northwest, the two lowest tides of the year occur at local noon within a few days of the summer solstice, when the moon is full, and at midnight close to the winter solstice, when the moon is dark. Both events were celebrated. Families swarmed over the beaches to harvest shellfish during the midday summer lows. On the midnight winter lows, men and boys hunted wildfowl by torchlight. Suttles found Halkomelem words for the seasons: 'shifts to daylight' meant the coming of spring, in March, when the big bull-tide lows, ideal for gathering clams, begin after sunrise; 'shifts to dark' meant October, when the lowest lows occur after nightfall; 'moon tide' described a low tide under a full moon, like the ones that signalled the summer clam-fest; 'dark tide' referred to a low in the moon's final quarter, like the December wildfowling tides.

Afraid of meeting whirlpools in Whirlpool Rapids, I watched the tide as keenly as an Indian. The tables were not to be entirely trusted, especially at this time of year, when rising temperatures in the mountains filled the rivers with snowmelt: the torrent of fresh water, escaping to the sea, could easily overmaster a weak flood and throw a spanner into the works of the tidal clock. Strong offshore winds or abnormal atmospheric pressure were also likely to screw up the computer-modelled predictions. In the last twenty-four hours, a fifty-plus-knot wind had been blowing off Cape Scott, and the pressure was way down in the barograph's bass register.

The scrolled current-lines grew lazier and more indistinct as the flood dwindled to a trickle. Off Lyall Island, eight miles short of the rapids, I could sense the brimming stillness of high-water slack – when the sea seems to draw breath, the land to be afloat on a painted lake. The Halkomelem word for it was *xtlúnexam*. According to Thom Hess's *Dictionary of Puget Sound Salish*, when a story began with an image of water in this moment of stasis – mirror-like, without a ripple – a happy ending was guaranteed. Of these upbeat calm-water stories, though, I hadn't yet managed to find one.

Within five minutes, the sea was on the move again; thimble-sized vortices slid diagonally across the grain of the emerging current, and the Garmin showed the boat to be travelling steadily faster over the ground than through the water. Riding the friendly tide, with the blood now back in my fingers, I could afford to take time out for a small diversion.

Where does the word 'nookie' come from? 'Prob. from *nook*,' opines Wentworth and Flexner's *Dictionary of American Slang*, in an untypically spiritless shot in the dark. Joseph Ingraham, cruising the Charlottes in 1791–2, compiled a rough-and-ready vocabulary of essential Haida words. The first and most important word on the list was for sea otter pelt: 'nuckky'. In 1907, long after the sea otter had been hunted to near extinction, Franz Boas noted that the Bella Bella word for fur seal was 'nukwe'. By the early 1800s, several thousand American sailors – always generous contributors to vernacular English – were using 'nookie' to mean something furry, soft, and precious. Captain Van would have gone from village to village, earnestly asking for nookie.

Far to the south, a tear in the sky exposed a ragged strip of blue behind the clouds; and a dog's-breath of air, from the south-east, not the forecast north-west, wrinkled the water. Whirlpool Rapids, now steaming into view, lay where the channel was blocked on its western side by a bold wooded bluff with an offlying cigar-shaped island, which squeezed the tide into a fire-hose jet.

The whirlpools formed at the downtide end of the pass, where the stream of fast water rubbed against the pools of slack on either side. A seven-knot current travels at nearly twelve feet per second – a fierce speed when applied to the rim of a baby vortex whose diameter is just an inch or two. This was like setting a gyroscope in motion with a long tug on a wound-up thread; the spinning vortex grew into a hungry, self-propelling eddy with a deepening centre – a Kansas twister made of water.

As tornadoes do, whirlpools wander on wayward and arbitrary tracks that make them seem full of inscrutable purpose. A whirlpool might suddenly lunge sideways to snatch at a canoe, or veer off as abruptly as a shark declining to accept the bait. Indian literature dwelled on the skittish humour of whirlpools, their taste for human flesh, and their extreme sensitivity to fancied slights. In exchange for a safe passage, they required to be fed. The Tsimshian whirlpool of

Getemnax, for instance, was partial to an offering of fat from the kidneys of a mountain goat. In one story, it was deeply offended by a group of young men who not only failed to provide the fat but also tried to smuggle past it an adolescent girl in the middle of her first menstrual period. They took the precaution of putting the girl and her grandmother in a separate canoe, and covering them with blankets, before towing them through the rapids; the whirlpool, undeceived, swallowed the men, breaking the towrope, and left the women safe but adrift.

In its emphasis on caution, respect, due preparation, and the consequences of bad timing, the story might have earned a place in Lecky's *Wrinkles in Practical Navigation*. I appeased the charted monsters by offering them hours of apprehension beforehand, by checking and rechecking the tide tables, and by allowing whirlpools to invade my dreams. Going into a tidal pass, I wasn't above crossing my fingers or touching the wood of the binnacle. On land, I was a hardline sceptic; afloat, something else. I never whistled on the boat. I noticed – with a faint tremor of anxiety – when a Friday was the 13th. On occasion I would've been reassured by the presence on board of the caul of a newborn or the feather of a wren killed on 1 January – a custom that led to the wren becoming an endangered species on the Isle of Man, so highly did Manx sailors prize their lucky feathers.

Racing into the jaws of Whirlpool Rapids, doing ten knots over the ground, I was sixty-five minutes into the ebb and just in time. A big bowl-shaped eddy had developed in the lee of the island, its swirling sides like tar in a mixer. But it paid no attention to the boat, and no sooner had I seen it than the tide had sucked the boat past, out toward Johnstone Strait and open ocean.

'Everywhere', wrote Lévi-Strauss, meaning on the Northwest coast, 'there emerges a parallelism between these natural disorders [like whirlpools associated with named monsters] and those which attack familial and social life.' But of course! The safe management of a canoe through tidal rapids and rough water was the first requirement for survival in these parts – an experience that supplied an inevitable metaphor for the conduct of life. Drowning in a whirlpool was probably the culture's single most vivid image of catastrophe: the sudden loss of control, the upset boat, the bodies in the water, the overpowering current, the sucking down into the abyss. If you tried to imagine the consequences of, say, killing your brother, or sleeping with your sister, they would naturally present themselves in terms of the whirlpool, the earthquake, the tsunami – just as the canoe was seen as the vessel of life, from the canoe-cradles in which babies were rocked to those used for air burials in the trees. Bad social behaviour was like careless canoeing, and got you into much the same kind of deep water. Here, where life was seen as a voyage through a multitude of natural hazards, it was hardly surprising that Lévi-Strauss should discover that the Indians' sea stories were really lightly coded encryptions of basic social rules, like the prohibitions against incest, murder, laziness, and egotism.

Maybe they order these things differently in French, but in English the fund of maritime metaphor goes very nearly as deep as it did in the Kwakiutl and Haida languages. We see things out to the bitter end (anchored in a storm, you let out all the cable you can to save the ship, and at last you reach the bitter end, the remaining length of chain in the locker, nearest to the bitts, around which it is secured; the ship eventually goes down, of course). When surprised, you are taken aback, caught head-to-wind; when things go easily for you, it's plain (correctly, *plane*) sailing. Your manner is aloof (or *a-luff*); you let things go by the board; you need a loan to tide you over; coming home from the pub, three sheets to the wind, you lose your bearings ... Both Robert Louis Stevenson, a Scot, and Elias Canetti, from Bulgaria and Vienna, observed that the Englishman has a deep-rooted habit of thinking of himself as the captain of a ship at sea; as Stevenson wrote, 'a man from Bedfordshire, who does not know one end of the ship from the other until she begins to move, swaggers [on a Channel packet] with a sense of hereditary nautical experience'. Taken by and large (as one assesses a ship in terms of her capacity to sail close to the wind, or 'by', and off the wind, with sheets eased, or 'large'), the English are in a good position to understand why Northwest Indians were inclined to see the whole of human life as something you do in a canoe.

In open water now, I killed the engine, unfurled the genoa, and let the boat coast quietly on the breeze while I tried to raise a marine operator on the VHF. Clicking through radio channels containing only static, I at last found a voice from the station at Alert Bay, the Kwakiutl reserve on Cormorant Island, and put through a call to Seattle.

Radio amplified the ringing tone, whose forlorn throbbing filled the boat. There's an audible difference between the sound of a telephone that will, in a few moments, be answered, and one that, at best, will say: 'This is Jean . . . please leave a message.'

The words had the volume and sound quality of an announcement echoing through the porcelain tunnels of the London Tube. 'Mind the gap, please. Mind the gap!'

In a calm sea, the first sign of turbulent water ahead is often a slight roughening of the horizon line, like the deckle edge along the top of an invitation card. Odd, you think, but pay it no special attention. Only later do you realize it was a signal to batten down the hatches.

The great outpouring of tide from the interior had smoothed the walls of Johnstone Strait, a gulley forty miles long and 1,000 feet deep, between Vancouver Island and the labyrinth of smaller islands to the north. The place had an unpleasant reputation as a wind funnel, but that morning the south-easterly was blowing at a gentle ten to twelve knots, just enough to keep the boat moving nicely under sail. With the sun now breaking through the clouds and silvering the water, the strait was a cheering sight after my string of lonely days: a broad marine highway on which orderly lines of coasters, fishing boats, tugs, and barges were following the posted route between Puget Sound and

Alaska. The skipper of a Seattle-registered purse-seiner stepped out from his freshly painted wheelhouse to give me a wave as he swept past; we were both of us now far enough away from our shared home port for the usual tribal hostilities between yachts and working boats to be forgotten.

The narrow entrance to Port Neville opened and closed again in what seemed like a flash, with the boat travelling much faster than the tide tables said it should. I was sailing at five knots, but the land was going past at eight, or so the GPS consistently reported. My best guess was that I was enjoying the benefit of 'slippery water'.

Seawater, laden with chlorides and minerals, is heavier than fresh. When a river meets the sea, it's liable to spill out in a wide fan across the top of the denser, saline water. So the brackish surface layer of an estuary can move independently of the saltwater tide below, sliding over it in a continuous ebb current, even when the deep tide is on the flood. Something like this was happening now on Johnstone Strait. The boat was riding on the fast surface current, while the true tide rolled sluggishly westward at a knot or less. I dipped a bucket over the side, and tried the water on my tongue: powerfully salty, not brackish at all. But I clung to the slippery-water theory, a useful explanation of all sorts of inconsistencies between the tables and the erratic behaviour of the actual tide.

I'd just stowed my bucket when a sudden rush of wind came down the funnel of the strait, like an unprovoked punch delivered out of nowhere. The boat corkscrewed. The genoa-sheet, bar-tight, groaned on the drum of the winch. I feared for the stitching of the sail as the fabric swelled under the impact of the wind, which had begun to yodel nastily in the rigging. In no time at all, the ruffled water changed to a short, steep, breaking sea.

Sunlit waves never frighten anyone half so much as the same waves under a sullen sky. These waves were full of light and life. The sun, shining clean through their tops, rendered them an opalescent milky green, which darkened, as the wave thickened around the middle, to the turquoise of a peacock's tail. Algae and phytoplankton gave them the colour of a coastal sea dense with vegetable matter, like frigid minestrone.

I had meant to go on to Alert Bay, to meet the Kwakiutl, but the wind nixed that plan. Thirty knots was more than I could safely handle. As the fetch of the strait lengthened, the waves climbed and the boat seesawed over them, crashing into each trough and trying to bury its nose in the wave immediately ahead. Drenched in spray, and by the occasional bucketful of solid green water, I hung on to the wheel, spinning it violently to keep to a more or less steady downwind course. I had too much sail up, but it was too late now to mess around with flailing sheets and furling-line. For more than an hour the boat ran away with me, rearing and plunging as if bent on trying to catapult its rider into the sparkling soup.

Even in high sunshine, I had no appetite for this. I had learned to sail too late in life to acquire a real seaman's instinct for what to do when the wind gets up and the sea growls. I had to listen to the creaking machinery of my own reason as I thought, not felt, my way through the rising waves, trying to figure out what on earth I'd do when the mast snapped off at the root, as it surely would, and soon. I remembered some book or other saying that heavy-duty wire cutters were essential onboard. I had none. So the forty-six-foot mast, now in the water, trapped by a cat's-cradle of steel rigging, would work on the hull as a battering ram, until it punched a hole amidships and the boat went down in a string of big bubbles. Wrenching the wheel to starboard, hoping to correct the boat's sideways slew down a wave, I could already hear the crunch of the severed mast breaking through into the gallery, smashing plates and glasses, letting the sea rush in. I was always the coward, who dies many times before his death.

Nine miles on from Port Neville was a merciful gap in the north wall of the strait, where the Broken Islands were strewn across the entrance to Havannah Channel. I ran for cover there, with the boat skidding into the lee on a crackling surge of foam. The mast still stood. The sun shone. A seal, basking on a rock, opened an eye at my arrival and slid soundlessly into the calm water, making not a ripple.

The 1965 edition of the *British Columbia Pilot* promised a hotel, general store, and post office at Minstrel Island, tucked snugly into the labyrinth a dozen miles to the north. A working phone was all I needed, and Minstrel Island sounded like telephone heaven. I lunched on cheese and Marmite sandwiches, and spent the afternoon idling, under sail, through a bunch of islands named after British officers aboard the frigate *Havannah*, a survey ship stationed here in the 1850s; Mist, Harvey, Hull, Bockett, Atchison, Malone . . .

The old Kwakiutl names had been precisely descriptive, as vivid now as they were before Messrs. Bockett, Atchison, & Co. came on the scene. Foam on Beach. Having Great Ebb Tide. Roaring Surf Inside. Tide Running Alongside. Having Wind. Sail-Tearing Place. Breaking Waves. Having Spider Crabs. Sound of Dripping Water. Shallow in Middle of Water. Having Waves. In his monograph *Geographical Names of the Kwakiutl*, Franz Boas covered their entire territory and restored to the map Indian names obliterated by the British when they turned the Inside Passage into a gigantic naval cemetery. The word for island, *mekala*, meant 'round thing on the water'. The generic name for a dangerous navigational hazard, usually a narrow pass featuring boils and whirlpools, was *nomas*, 'old man', a polite way of signifying a resident monster.

Following Boas's map of Havannah Channel, I sailed from Rocky Place Not Reached to Paddled Through On Beach, to Long Face, to Shelter Point, to Round Things On Water In Front Of Beach, to Having Devilfish, to Hanging Place, to Coming In Sight In Front, to Abalone On Back, to Having Fern Roots, to Round Thing On Water Inside – a graphic and memorable afternoon's cruise.

I liked to think of Boas here. He was an arresting anthropological specimen in his own right: short, wiry, with black eyes, black hair, an aquiline nose, and a bushy black moustache. His face was deeply incised with duelling scars, from his student days in Heidelberg (that must have interested the Indians). His personality was forbidding. He had an ascetic relish for physical hardship; detested frivolity in any form, but especially light opera; and his grim prose style reflects a mind of such flinty seriousness that one quails at meeting it on the page. The man was a research engine. Not a glimmer of warmth shows in his writing, which reveres the cold fact to a degree rarely seen since Mr Gradgrind made Sissy Jupe define a horse.

What can the Indians have made of him? He looms craggily over the field of Northwest ethnology, with his dictionaries and grammars, his collections of native myths and stories, his relentless tabulation of motifs in Indian art and oral literature. Somewhere there must be Kwakiutl or Tsimshian stories of Franz Boas – Scarface, with fountain pen and ledger, meatgrinding their whole world into volume upon volume of the *Columbia University Contributions to Anthropology*.

Strangely, Boas comes most to life in the moment of his death. He was eighty-four when, on 21 December 1942, he hosted a lunch at the Columbia Faculty Club for the French anthropologist Paul Rivet. With lunch over, he refilled his wineglass and lit a cigarette (a late-in-life luxury), delivered a two-sentence denunciation of the evils of racism, and fell back dead in his chair. This is a rare glimpse of Boas indulging himself in earthly pleasures, and it would be nice to imagine the aged dean of anthropology aboard an Indian canoe, blowing thoughtful smoke rings into the evening sky.

From Atchison Island (or Round Thing On Water Inside), the sun-starved gorge of Chatham Channel (otherwise Cormorant Place) led to Minstrel Island, where, with an Indian fisherman's help, I found a place for the boat in the huddle of skiffs and gill-netters.

'There's a phone here?'

'Yes,' he said, pointing up to the half-moon of buildings at the head of the cove. 'Right up there outside the bar.' After a calculated pause, he said, 'If you can make the sucker work.'

Minstrel Island was a roundish green thing on the water, about two miles in diameter, rising to a thickly timbered cone at fourteen hundred feet. The harbour was sheltered from the exposed north-west by the tarred hulks of lighters that had gone down at their moorings. The 'hotel' was a line of scabious cabins on fir stilts; a hunting-and-fishing resort presently being used as the bunkhouse for a logging crew. The carpets were rank, the light bulbs unshaded. On the veranda overlooking the harbour, a big, rheumy-eyed dog with a lot of German shepherd in it stood guard by the payphone.

'Don't mind him – he won't bite,' said the woman in charge of this amiably gimcrack establishment. 'You can try the phone. Somebody got through on it yesterday, or the day before.'

I fed in a pile of money but, as at Blind Channel, the satellites were in the wrong conjunction. All I got was the sound of surf, lazily collapsing on a faraway beach. I ached for Jean's and Julia's voices, especially at sunset, when distances lengthened like shadows and the city lights of Puget Sound now seemed as remote as if I'd left my family back in Liverpool or Valparaiso. I kept at it, trying to will a dial tone into being. No luck.

'We don't have much use for the telephone around here. We're all on radio, channel six. You want the roast-beef dinner?'

My beardlessness made me conspicuous in the bare formica cafe. I lacked even the minimal three-day stubble that might've enabled me to pass without comment from the loggers, who viewed my brown tweed jacket, khaki pants, and scuffed Docksiders with discomforting interest.

'You with the census?'

'Sorry?'

A lone yachtsman, it turned out, had lately been cruising the islands, his salary and expenses paid handsomely by the Canadian government. In an average day's work, he would seek out and register one married couple, stay for a free meal and bath, then retire to his boat. He was thought to have the most enviable job in the world.

'We figured you must be his pardner. You and he, you got the exact same boat.'

'How do you like your meat?' the woman asked me.

'Oh, rare as it comes—'

'Moooo!' said the spade-shaped tangle of black beard sitting opposite. 'Moo! Moo!'

The crew, who were helilogging a stand of old-growth cedar near the island's summit, were not great conversationalists. Each man gloomed privately over a broken-spined paperback or last Sunday's edition of the Vancouver *Sun*. Blackbeard was reading a seventh-hand copy of John Grisham, his eyes travelling at a leisurely pace from word to word; occasionally his lips moved, to frame a difficult trisyllable.

All I could find to read was the 'Fisherman's Chain Letter', a photocopied document pinned to the wall above my head.

> *Dear Friend:*
>
> *¾ of the earth's surface is water . . . and only ¼ is land. . . . The good Lord's intentions are very clear. A man's time should be divided . . . ¾ FOR FISHING. ¼ FOR WORK.*
>
> *This chain was started in the hope of bringing happiness to fishermen. Unlike most chains it doesn't require money. Simply send a copy of this to 5 fishermen friends, then bundle up your wife and send her to the fellow whose name heads the list. When your name reaches the top of the list you will receive 16,268 women and some should be dandies. Have faith, don't break the chain. One man broke it, and got his wife back!*

When the food came, it looked like Minstrel Island on a plate: a mountain of mashed potatoes flanked by cliffs of beef and Brussels sprouts. My portion was sufficient to feed several of me, with enough left over for two or three hungry dogs. The loggers methodically clear-cut their plates, in a gristle-chewing silence infrequently broken by the low one-liner, perfectly incomprehensible to me but answered with appreciative growls by the rest. Like a ship's crew, these men had spent so long in one another's company that they spoke in a close-fisted code. If you were in on it, a single phrase, 'camshaft', perhaps, or 'Mac's toenail', could bring the house down.

At the beginning of the century, logging crews were on the front line of organized labour in America. Big Bill Haywood's Industrial Workers of the World were headquartered in Seattle because so many of the Wobblies were loggers in the Pacific Northwest, marching to the songs of Joe Hill.

Working men of all countries, unite!
Side by side we for freedom will fight.
When the world and its wealth we have gained,
To the grafters we'll sing this refrain:
You will eat (you will eat), bye and bye, (bye and bye)
When you've learned how to cook and to fry (way up high).
Chop some wood (chop some wood) – 'twill do you good (do you good)
And you'll eat in the sweet bye and bye (that's no lie!).

Loggers were good candidates for conversion to revolutionary socialism. Working at their dangerous jobs in deep rural isolation, far from their fat-cat big-city employers, they created their own fraternal societies in the woods. The Wobbly Manifesto foresaw an industrial democracy 'where the workers own the tools which they operate and the product of which they alone will enjoy'. In the labour-intensive timber industry, the chief tool was the saw, and loggers were in a fine position to plot the overthrow of their absentee capitalist bosses. At the time of the Seattle General Strike of 1919, every remote logging camp was a soviet waiting to happen.

I wished I could talk with the Minstrel Island crew about such things, but had only to glance from beard to beard to know that my chances of persuading these men to open up about their political convictions were a good deal slimmer than those of beguiling them into a group discussion of *Swan Lake*.

At dinner's end, the proprietress came through from the kitchen to join us, and the addition of a woman to the equation instantly altered the room's tone. Books were shut, newspapers folded away, as we sat over coffee like Lutherans at a church supper. The chief topic of conversation was – in a cursorily oblique way – me.

Mrs Minstrel recalled that last summer 'a Seattle millionaire' came to stay for the fishing. In these parts, Seattle was a byword for extravagant wealth, and anyone from the city was held to be made of money. Mrs M's husband had been this grandee's guide and boatman. One day, at low water, a grizzly bear was sighted feeding on clams at the edge of the beach. The husband shut off the outboard and let the skiff drift inshore, to give his client a photo-op.

'They got so close in they could see the blood on the bear's mouth. He was dripping blood. You know how they cut themselves on the shells . . . This guy, his hands were shaking so much, he dropped the camera in the sea.'

The loggers snickered, all eyes on me.

'Then he got so scared he climbed right into Bob's lap. Bob thought they were going to both land in the water. The bear was about as far away as you to me.' She took a long drag on her cigarette before coming up with the payoff. 'Funny, that. You'd think, coming from a city like he did, he wouldn't be frightened of *nothing*.'

I could see myself, as she did, right there in Bob's lap.

Now we were chasing a theme. Everyone had a contribution to make on the alien character, and characters, of the city. We talked of wretched nights in motor-inns; of sleep ruined by elevators grunting and groaning in their shafts; of kids on Harleys revving up in the parking lot at 2:00 a.m.; of the grinding of truck brakes; of helpings of food so stingy that you could pay $12.00 for dinner and still go hungry; of muggings, murders, and chlorinated water. 'I gag on it. I don't know how people can drink it. You know what I look forward to most when I come back here? The first glass of water from the well. After city water, that first glass – it tastes like honey.'

To find myself the designated ambassador of violence, noise, excess wealth, chemical additives, cowardice, and stupidity was an unwelcome responsibility. I put the blame on my shiny jowls and Brooks Brothers jacket, and retreated, chastened, to the boat.

I had begun to write the story of the millionaire and the grizzly in my notebook when I was interrupted by a hesitant tapping on the hull amidships. The two youngest members of the logging crew were outside, looking unsure of their ground.

'We just wanted to see what kind of boat it was, that a guy could sail in up to Alaska all by himself.'

Delighted to see them, I fetched beer and wine and glasses while they poked approvingly around my quarters. Fellers, they'd worked as a pair for more than two years, flying from camp to camp. As long-established couples do, they had grown into the habit of completing each other's sentences. With the same beard, same plaid shirt and jeans, they were difficult to tell apart.

They asked what the barograph did; they peered, in turn, into the rubber hood of the radar; they read the labels on the panel of forty-three switches. But their serious interest was reserved for the two 1790s framed prints of birds that were screwed to the bulkheads.

'Rufous hummingbirds.'

'Tropicbird. Macaw.'

The fellers were birders. Only last week they'd seen their first spotted owl. 'Well, we think. I thought it was a barred owl at first.'

'They were spots, not bars.'

We talked bird guides – Peterson versus Audubon Society versus National Geographic. We agreed that painted birds won hands down over photographed ones, which put the Audubon in third place. They liked the clarity of National Geographic; I liked the writing of Peterson, his description of the raven's 'goiter-throat', or the appearance of a purple finch 'like a sparrow dipped in raspberry juice'.

The fellers were now busy destroying the habitat of the birds they loved to watch – a fact that made them rueful about their work, not least because toppling an old-growth forest was a far more skilled and satisfying business than mowing down peckerpoles on a tree farm. I said cheerily that they were in a great ornithological tradition: John James Audubon, a crack shot, had slaughtered the birds of America many times over in order to paint them, each exquisite coloured plate requiring a mound of small corpses for its completion. The fellers weren't much consoled by this analogy.

'You know the latest craze around here? Hunting grizzlies with bows and arrows.'

'Like playing at Red Indians?' I said.

'They've got high-tech bows – titanium, graphite, something like that. They go up to the head of Knight Inlet, where there's a whole bunch of bears in the summer when the fish are running. You have to get inside of thirty feet from the bear to kill it with an arrow . . . close enough to smell the breath on that thing. Most of them panic and loose off from a lot farther than that.'

'These guys aren't regular hunters. They're, like, bankers. Or they do software.'

'Testing their manhood. I hate that.'

'Then they turn them into sausages. That's the big thing – get the guys from the office round to breakfast and feed 'em grizzly-bear sausages. "I killed that bear, with my bow and arrow." '

'It's an ego trip. Killing to prove yourself. I don't think it should be legal.'

'They wound more than they kill. The guide's supposed to kill a wounded bear, but it all happens so fast the bear's usually back in the brush with an arrow sticking in its gut.'

Their beards were suffused with yellow lamplight. I liked the men's seriousness. Living out of a kitbag, working in the forest, always moving on from job to job had given them a distinctly higher specific gravity than most people their age. An enforced detachment from the daily chatter of TV and magazines had left them free of the usual *idées reçus*. They were comfortable with solitude, and their unfashionable expertise (not so unlike my own, which also entails the destruction of trees) set them at an oblique angle to the rest of the world, and they seemed content with that.

'You could go a long way in this . . .'

While we were talking, I'd watched the younger of the pair taking possession of the boat with his eyes: the books and pictures; the ICOM radio; the stainless-steel cooking stove in its gimbals; the perfectionist Swedish joinery; the brassbound clinometer by Kelvin, Bottomley and Baird of Basingstoke; the handbearing compass on its customary hook; the chart on the saloon table, folded back to expose the approach to Minstrel Island and weighted down by the navigational protractor. With his arms stretched wide across the top of the settee and his ruddy outdoors tan, he seemed an altogether more plausible captain of this boat than me.

'I wouldn't go to Alaska, though. I'd cross the ocean. I'd sail to . . .' He rolled his eyes, recollecting his geography. 'Borneo!' he said, with pleasure and surprise.

Groping, fog-headed, in the dank chill of just-past-dawn, I was slow to take in the implications of the latest marine forecast. I listened to it twice, making careful notes and drawing an isobaric sketch map in the log. The map looked like the whirlpool of Getemnax, roving free across the North Pacific. A new 'intense low', actual depth unspecified, was spinning eastward over the ocean, the Queen Charlotte Islands its likely destination. When it touched land, it was predicted to stall, and to dominate the weather for the foreseeable future, bringing storm- or gale-force winds to all sea areas. For Environment Canada, the foreseeable future meant five days. There'd be good sailing for the next twenty-four hours, with a wind out of the south-east at fifteen to twenty knots. Thereafter, all I could detect in the meteorologist's indifferent, Scottish-accented voice was horizontal rain and rearing hollow flint-grey seas.

I had a thoughtful breakfast. I was now just one day away from making the crossing of Queen Charlotte Sound, the short stretch of open ocean between the top of Vancouver Island and the bottom of the next string of protective coastal islands. This morning, the sea in the sound ('combined wind-wave and swell heights', as the radio announcer said) was running at four metres, which would translate into a forbidding amount of pitch, roll, yaw, heave, surge, and sway. Tomorrow, as the cyclone neared, the sea would start to climb. The waves would be as high as houses.

I'd hoped to get halfway to Juneau – to Bella Bella, BC, at least – before parking the boat and flying back to Seattle for a couple of weeks, to prove to Julia that she still had a father more or less in working order. The vile forecast put paid to that. Within the next few hours, I had to find a snug berth for the boat, someone to keep a friendly eye on it, and passage home for myself, before the coming storm swept through the archipelago.

I was in luck. A chance conversation with a woman named Wendy, her radio call to her husband (how I envied the casual ease of that), and I was on my way to Potts Lagoon on West Cracroft Island.

The entrance from Clio Channel (named after yet another British warship) was so narrow as to be invisible until the last heart-stopping moment, when a jagged sliver of light showed in the solid wall of foliage and angular grey rock. Trusting the chart rather more than my senses, I crept through the gap, trees brushing against the rigging, and came into a forest-girdled pool, silent except for a warbler of some kind that was singing in the branches overhead. Though it was blowing hard in the channel, the lagoon was smooth as oil, so sheltered that a hurricane would have barely ruffled it.

On the southern shore, a long raft of massive logs supported a cabin and half a dozen small outbuildings. Wendy's husband, John Walders, was waiting for me at his front door.

'You found us all right, then.' He took my lines.

'This is wonderful – it's like *The Secret Garden*.'

At the back of the raft, a cleared patch of forest held an orchard and a few rows of vegetables. Apart from a live-aboard crabber and his wife, the Walderses had the entire lagoon to themselves. Their closest neighbours were the black bears who raided apples from the orchard and sometimes boarded the raft in pursuit of leftovers from the Walders table, when they were shooed off by the family dog, a limping black Lab.

I followed Mr Walders inside. Bare but cosy, the house might have been a homestead from the century before. Waterlights danced on timber walls. A crocheted rug of many colours brightened the floor. The furniture was old and well cared for, exuding an air of austere yet reliable domestic comfort – the outward and visible form of a good marriage.

A dozen years before, John Walders had been working as a welder in a Victoria shipyard. 'I was thirty-five – I had my mid-life crisis early.' He disliked the city, and the noise and monotony of his job. 'I used to look at the older men and think, "That's you in twenty years." All the life was gone out of them. They were zombies.'

He spent all his spare time outfitting the sailboat in which he and his wife planned to escape. *Escape* was an intransitive verb – they didn't know where they might escape *to*. Walders – a reader, the cabin was full of books, in prettily carpentered shelves – lost himself in antique stories of adventure on the South Seas. Then, in 1985, he quit his job, sold up, and he and Wendy set off on a voyage to nowhere in particular, sailing up the Inside Passage on a shakedown cruise while trying to decide whether to shape a course for the Sea of Cortez, or Surabaya, or Tahiti. Instead, they'd found their way to Potts Lagoon.

He now made a not-too-strenuous living out of other people's marine mishaps. His welding shop on the raft drew a regular procession of fishing boats with mechanical troubles. He was a diver, expert at liberating seized-up propellers from crabtrap lines and fishing nets. As a tugman, he hauled broken-down vessels out of harm's way, and went beachcombing through the islands in search of escaped logs. Every few weeks he'd tow a pile of valuable driftwood over to a mill on Vancouver Island. Ten or fifteen logs – the beginnings of a new boom – were marshalled at the west end of the raft; easy money, if you could find it.

Fuel came from the forest; water from the roof, funnelled into a great galvanized tank by the front door; electricity from a generator in a nearby shed. The Walderses lived handsomely on fish, game, and whatever they could grow in the garden they shared with the bears. A trip to the bank, the supermarket, the hardware store, the hairdresser, meant a three-hour boat ride, in calm weather, to Port McNeill, twenty-six miles to the south-west – as long as it takes to fly from Seattle to Los Angeles.

I saw Walders, with his narrow, beaky face, his smile full of teeth, as Ratty in *The Wind in the Willows*. He might easily have been the source of the line that is Ratty's contribution to the language: 'There is *nothing* – absolutely nothing – half so much worth doing as simply messing about in boats.' A few strands of hair, like mouldy straw, clung to his skull. He had busy, avid eyes. Beachcombing suited his temperament, for he was a passionate collector, continually on the lookout for unnoticed treasures.

Every shelf in the cabin displayed the Indian artefacts that Walders claimed lay all around, in the soil and on the sand, but which were mysteriously invisible to everyone else, including his wife. There were stone arrowheads, beautifully flaked into shape; a powerful chisel made of malachite; a large quern; stone awls; bone halibut-hooks; a club, its handle gouged into the outline of an eagle's head. Many of the stone pieces looked as if they dated back to a period well before the arrival here of Cook, Vancouver, and the fur traders. As a twelve- and thirteen-year-old, I used to tramp in early spring along the edges of gull-patrolled fields in Sussex and Hampshire, looking for neolithic relics turned up by the plough. Occasionally, an odd glint in the wet soil would lead to a flint axe or the fishlike tip of an ancient Briton's spear. But their workmanship was inferior to that of John Walders's trove.

There were European artefacts, too – trade-beads that the early white visitors had brought in sackfuls to this coast. Walders poured several dozen into the palm of my hand. Most were tiny, like snip-pings of the plastic insulation sleeve on electrical wire, but translucent and still as brilliant in colour as they had been in 1792. Emerald, crim-son, azure, primrose . . . They felt strangely cool on my skin.

'Venetian glass,' Walders said.

I held one between forefinger and thumb, tilting it against the sun. It was the colour of a kumquat, and glowed like a small sun in its own right. The travels of this bead were worth reflecting on: from the factory on Murano to a haberdasher's in London, to Cape Town, to Australia, to the Northwest coast, to John Walders's floathouse and my hand. This bead might well have come on *Discovery* or *Chatham*, part of a scoop of treasure ladled out by Peter Puget or Captain Van.

Trade-beads were showered on the Indians in such vast quantities that they quickly lost their value. One 1790s fur trader reported that he'd seen dogs in Indian villages decked in beads from head to tail. Thrown like confetti at the launching of a canoe, they suffered from the same hyperinflation as German marks in the Weimar period – you'd need a full wheelbarrow to pay for lunch.

John Walders told me of a beach where I could easily find beads for myself. 'There are thousands there. You just have to walk, close to low water, on the ebb, when the sand's wet. Stand in one place and look down at your feet. You'll see them there, if you've got good eyes.'

I thought of Puget, trying to woo the Indians with pretty things, when what they really wanted were saws, chisels, copper, iron. In 1778, Cook wrote of the Indians of Nootka Sound:

> *Nothing would go down with our visitors but metal; and brass had by this time supplanted iron, being so eagerly sought after, that, before we left this place, hardly a bit of it was left in the ships, except what belonged to our necessary instruments. Whole suits of clothes were stripped of every button; bureaus of their furniture, and copper kettles, tin canisters, candlesticks, and the like, all went to wreck.*

Yet expeditions continued to dispense trade-beads. They were the chief symbol of the universal white assumption about natives, that they were childish and feminine; irrational lovers of worthless trinkets, governed by their foolish eye for anything that sparkled. In turn, the Indians gave the beads to their dogs or used them to court the favours of the irrational creatures of the sea.

I pored for a long time – too long, perhaps – over John Walders's collection, and finally put the little kumquat bead back among its several hundred fellows.

'You can keep it if you like—'

'This is the right place for it. I'd like to remember it here, on your windowsill.'

'Not many people take an interest. When the yachts come in here in the summer, it's always, "Are you Mr Potts?" Then, "Do you live here year-round?" Then, "But what do you do, all that time? What do you *do*?" *What do I do?* I do – this!' He spread his arms wide to include

in their ambit the woods, the rocks, the sea, the sky – a life too large
and various for any summer visitor's comprehension.

I saw the archipelagian bush telegraph in action when John
Walders arranged for me to be airlifted out of Potts Lagoon to Port
McNeill. He radioed his wife; his wife radioed the postmistress on
another island; the postmistress telephoned the seaplane outfit; and
word came back by radio that an air-taxi would pick me up from the
raft by five o'clock if the weather held.

Walders rode off in his skiff with his dog to go log hunting. I
tidied the boat, doubled the lines, packed my seabag, and sat on
an upturned fish crate, watching the winking ovoids in the water
assemble themselves into Kwakiutl designs.

With nothing to do but wait for the plane, I pursued a wistful
daydream. If only I were better with my hands. If only I weren't so
wedded to the comforts of university libraries and Italian restaurants.
If only Jean and I could bring up Julia in a floathouse on a Potts
Lagoon – *just for a year or two . . . just, say, between now and the time
she goes into first grade.*

Julia, born to the Northwest, lived within easy reach of a version
of nature, and of a regional past, that was utterly remote from most
people's everyday experience. Visiting the wild as a tourist, it would
be a mere spectacle, like going to the zoo. But a two-year stay – that
would involve isolation and depression, sure; much difficulty and
inconvenience for everybody. But there would also be, laid down in
the cellar of memory, a reserve of knowledge on which she could draw
for the rest of her life. She'd know, not just have seen, the mountain
goats and bears; the runs of salmon – cohos, kings, pinks, sockeyes;
the protean sea in all its moods. We'd gather winter fuel to feed the
tyrannous wood stove. Rain and wind would sock us into our cabin
for weeks at a time; and that would be part of it, too. We'd find trade-
beads and decode the meaning of rotting totems in the forest. We'd
fish for our supper. The only team I ever made at school was for rifle
shooting; we'd have venison.

It wasn't so impossible. I had a book to write, and could support
the three of us. Jean ached to write fiction. If we found the right

island, we could be in touch with London and New York by cell-phone. Was there such thing as cellfax? Presumably. We'd need a place where other young children were not so far away as to be unavailable for play dates and sleep-overs. We'd need . . .

A floatplane in scuffed blue-and-silver livery banked over the lagoon, came in low over the entrance, climbed sharply, and flew back seawards for a second attempt. This time its floats grazed the treetops, then it plopped into the water as gracefully as a descending swan, webbed feet outstretched, and taxied across to where I was standing on the raft. I climbed in with my gear and sat up front beside the pilot, shaking hands on the way with my only fellow passenger, a logger going home from a job in Knight Inlet.

'Your boat?' the pilot shouted over the throb and clatter of the engine.

'Yes.'

'Nice!' he yelled, and pointed at my camera. 'Want to take some pictures of her?'

'Sure!'

Growling, then roaring, we skidded over the dimpled surface of the lagoon. As the plane came unstuck from the water, it rose with the dizzy momentum of a cork exploding from a carelessly opened cham-pagne bottle. The forest went into a sickening roll. For a moment, John Walders's raft stood perpendicular to the plane, with my boat defying gravity like a daddy longlegs on a wall.

'You can open the window if you want!'

The air rushed past at hurricane speed, bringing tears to my eyes. I had trouble focusing on the image in the viewfinder. The late after-noon light had turned Potts Lagoon to a burnished olive-gold, the colour of carp scales. I snapped my boat and then the Walders's buoy-ant household, zooming in on its domestic details – the covered woodpile, propane tanks, twin chimneys, rainwater ducting system. Squeezing repeatedly on the shutter, I knew I was trying for a shot that was impossible, a picture so opulently detailed that my wife would see what I saw in it: a new life that we might yet lead together.

V. RITE OF PASSAGE

Twenty-four hours later, hot and dirty from my travels, I stepped out of another plane, the jet shuttle from Vancouver to Seattle. My small family was waiting for me at the gate, and Julia leaped into my arms. She clung fiercely to me, silent, her face buried in my shoulder, inhaling me in long deep draughts. From the alien potpourri of smells – the vile Port Hardy motel room, diesel fuel, sweat, the airline miniature of Johnny Walker – she was busy extracting a vital essence-of-father. The knowledge that I possessed this precious scent made me weak with love and pride.

'She hasn't napped today,' Jean said.

The pale sterile corridor of the main terminal stretched ahead of us, a dozen deserted departure gates.

'She's put on weight.' I wriggled my shoulder to investigate my daughter's face. She was fast asleep.

'I have to go to a dance concert tonight. Your proofs came. Your mother called.'

'I'll ring her tomorrow.'

Home was unexpectedly enormous after the doll's house of the boat. I rambled with pleasure through our warren of rooms: all those high ceilings! those views from the windows! two bathrooms! Jean had bought me a bottle of Oregon Pinot Noir, and we sat out on our third-floor deck, looking out across the Ship Canal to Ballard and

Phinney Ridge, while I riffled through the daunting pile of mail and faxes.

'Bob Silvers wants you to call him. He made it sound urgent.'

'It's a gift he has.'

'There's more stuff in your office.'

I couldn't stop smiling. The novelty of being home after less than three weeks away was overpowering. Before Julia was born, when I was fifty, it was never like this. Now, late in the day by any standards, I knew what home meant, at long last.

Next morning, after Julia was at preschool and Jean at her desk at the *Seattle Times*, I began marking up the proofs of my book *Bad Land*, about drought and disappointment in a dry country, 1,000 miles from the nearest ocean. I'd always conceived of it as a sea-story – the shipwreck of a hopeful fleet of wooden houses on the dusty shoals of Montana and North Dakota. It had been my passionate occupation for two years, but now, seeing it in severe print for the first time, I was embarrassed by it. This was the British edition, and a London copy-editor had helpfully translated my American prose into English English. Where I had written 'parking lot', it read 'car park'. 'Railroad' was 'railway line'. 'Store' was 'shop'. 'Windshield' was 'windscreen'. 'Trunk' was 'boot'. I spent a couple of hours erasing these corrections, yet their lingering presence tainted the whole book for me. All I could see were clumsy bits of narrative construction, as if the story had been cobbled together with hammer, nails, and two-by-fours.

Needing a break, I called my parents in England. My father came to the phone.

'Peter – hi! I'm back in Seattle for a couple of weeks. How are things?'

'Fair winds?' he said. The connection wasn't as good as usual; his voice was faint.

Full of my trip, I told him of my defeat by the storm forecast and the snug berth I'd found in Potts Lagoon; I rattled airily on about crags, precipices, cascades, whirlpools. I was trying to whet his appetite for spectacles of nature, for as soon as I returned from

Juneau, my parents were setting off on an American adventure of their own. My idea was that they should fly to Minneapolis, rent a car, and drive to Seattle along the minor highways of the West, taking the better part of two weeks. No interstates, I said; choose dirt roads over blacktops. Use the DeLorme state atlases, with their large scale and full contours. They'd put up for the night in one- or no-stoplight towns. I promised them that they would discover an America rarely seen by Americans. They'd cross the Plains, the Rockies, the Cascades. My plan was that they'd lose their ingrained British notions of 'the Yanks' and see something of the grand, complicated, and hospitable country that had made an immigrant of me. I saw them arriving in Seattle astonished at the country, all their preconceptions and prejudices gone by the board.

'You've got the state atlases now?'

'All in the study, old boy. And the what's it . . . the Rand McNally.'

'Forget the Rand McNally. The roads that you'll be taking aren't marked in Rand McNally.'

'One thing, old boy?'

'Yes?'

'Just a slight question mark's cropped up. Lately, I've been having a spot of tummy trouble. You know.' He made the noise – sniff, snort, chuckle – with which he usually greeted such nonsenses as the latest ruling from the Church of England Synod or daft goings-on in the town-planning department of Market Harborough.

Eighteen months before, he'd been through surgery and chemotherapy. 'Nipped it in the bud,' he'd said cheerfully, and never mentioned cancer again.

Now he said: 'Tests . . .' and 'Looks as if we might have to put our American jaunt on hold for a bit, I'm afraid, old boy.'

He was telling me that he was dying.

In London, people were frying in the May heat. The city was airless and thinly overcast, the sun showing like a pockmarked orange from behind its perpetual veil of cloud. 'Global warming' was the phrase of the moment, though I took the unseasonal heat to be just another of the vagaries of English weather. Jean, Julia, and I camped out in Brixton, in the tall, narrow, and mercifully gloomy house of an old friend of mine and her eleven-year-old son. Julia fell besottedly in love with Francis, resplendent in his Arsenal Football Club regalia and his coxcomb of gelled black hair. Asked if she liked her first taste of English ice cream, she said, approvingly, 'It's wicked,' in an earnest imitation of the South London whiffle.

Like any foreign visitor, I had rented a car at Heathrow; and as soon as we were settled, I drove alone to Market Harborough, stopping first at Fortnum & Mason's to buy candied ginger for my father.

'It's good for him,' my mother said over the phone. 'He can keep it down, you see. I have to build his strength up. So we can go to Scotland . . .' She had set her heart on one last holiday together.

I loaded the boot, not trunk, with an armful of jars of ginger, then let myself back into the car on the passenger side, wondering where the steering-wheel had gone – the beginning of a morning of jet-shocked strangeness.

I took my usual route north. I could do it in my sleep: Marble Arch to Seymour Place, to Lisson Grove and Abbey Road, with wedding-cake stucco giving way to serious oxblood-brick and then to pebbledash, concrete, and facetious mock-Tudor. At Brent Cross I fed the car into the grey chute of the M1, jamming my foot down hard on the accelerator to keep up with the crowd. We drove at 85 m.p.h., nose-to-tail, a streaming caravanserai of coloured tin.

At intervals of every mile or so, giant placards stood on the verge of the carriageway, saying KEEP YOUR DISTANCE! The signs were weatherworn, their lettering beginning to fade; but they were new to me, though I had driven this route less than six months before. We were going so fast now that the signs ran into each other, keeping up an impotent, repetitive chatter. KEEP YOUR DISTANCE!

KEEP ... YOUR ... DISTANCE! They might as well have been addressing the coupled carriages in an express railway train.

Keeping one's distance on this overcrowded island had always been a thorny problem. Within my own living memory, the vast and labyrinthine intricacies of the class system had helped to compensate for England's chronic absence of breathing space. In club or pub, drawing room or lounge, miles of distance could yawn between people once someone opened his mouth and spoke in an accent inappropriate to the setting. The country house, at the end of its rhododendron-guarded drive, lay at an immense remove, in language and manners, from the village that provided its postal address.

But in the last quarter-century or so, the class system had eroded to the point of almost total collapse. One of the lessons administered by Margaret Thatcher, during her long, despotic, and intransigent reign as prime minister, had been that money, not class, divided the English. It was a good lesson, and long overdue; but money was poor insulation by comparison, and everyone in England now seemed more tightly squashed up together, bumper-to-bumper, elbow-to-elbow, in a manner that – fresh from the wilds of British Columbia – I found surreal. There appeared to be no distance left to keep, as England sped north up the motorway in its new American-style sport-utility vehicles. My rental car – the cheapest on offer from Avis – made a poor showing against the mob of Jeep Cherokees, Nissan Pathfinders, Range Rovers, Ford Explorers, Mitsubishi Shoguns, and Toyota Land Cruisers.

The language had changed, too. Over the car radio came the dialect of the new England, a contrived accent known as Estuary English. BBC announcers, politicians, writers all spoke it. The estuary in question was the Thames, and the idea was that everyone should try to talk like a laid-back, street-smart car salesman from suburban Kent or Essex. The most determined Estuary-speakers were men who'd been to traditional boarding schools, followed by the universities of Oxford or Cambridge. During a newsbreak on Radio 4, I listened with bemusement to the leader of the Labour Party, Tony Blair (Fettes School and Oxford), talking in Estuary as if he'd just returned from a long, arduous, and not altogether successful session with the official New Labour elocutionist.

My accent had become a relic from another age, with its too-distinct imprint of an army-oriented boarding school in the 1950s, plus several generations of Anglican country vicars. I was unselfconscious about it on the west coast of North America, where I was usually nailed as an Australian; but in England it sounded offensively languid and plummy in my own ears, a lah-di-dah voice for which the Estuary word was probably 'poncy'. Though I had fallen so far out of touch, I realized, that 'poncy' would now almost certainly be thought poncy.

Unable to keep up with the frantic pace of modern Britain – the swerves from lane to lane, the cuttings-in, the disdain of signals, the great impatient free-for-all – I left the motorway just past Milton Keynes and entered an easier, more familiar world. Here was the England that every homesick exile conjures for himself on lonely evenings: rolling, green, deciduous; with dry-stone walls, thick hedgerows, tall church steeples, houses built of honey-coloured local rock, red pillar boxes with the initials *VR* ornately entwined above the mail-slot, pub signs on chains (the George & Dragon, Dog & Duck, Coach & Horses, Star & Garter, Pig & Whistle), footpaths through the fields, thatch on the (occasional) roof, cottage gardens, parish pumps, horses at pasture, hawthorn in bloom (a blackbird sings on the top branch of every bush), tottering signposts (LITTLE BRINGTON 3¼), manorial houses with ha-has and oak avenues, blind bends in the lanes (concealing from view the oncoming green Massey-Ferguson tractor), scarecrows, duck ponds, skylarks, hayricks, bells chiming the quarters – the whole sweet sentimental boiling.

This was the England that Captain Van had read into the raw coniferous land on Puget Sound. Two hundred years on, Captain Van's England was still visible here, as Bedfordshire bled into Northamptonshire and Leicestershire. The immemorial elms were gone, reduced to stumps, victims of Dutch elm disease in the 1970s. The old villages had grown 'outskirts' much bigger than themselves, of 1950s council-housing and newer, Crayola-coloured, vinyl-clad townhouses. Captain Van would have been flummoxed by England's new canary-yellow hillsides, where hundred-acre fields were now given over to the cultivation of oilseed rape. The yellow, far too fierce and brilliant for England, made half the landscape look as if it had been transplanted, wholesale, from Languedoc; it belonged in a painting by Van Gogh, not Constable.

Yet enough of the old still remained for one's eye to edit out the new. Driving through the Bringtons (Little and Great, both tiny), I could see how they had been in Captain Van's time, or in 1918, when my father was born, or 1942, when I showed up. After the here-today-gone-tomorrow settlements of the American West, they looked like for ever, even though the larger houses now probably belonged to London merchant bankers and villagers got CNN by satellite. The eye alone could be deceived: I was seeing only the surviving husks of a rural life that had withered long ago. But there was comfort in looking at the husks. At this particular moment, I was in need of the old churches, old houses, old trees, old walls; of a cultivated landscape that had long preceded, and would certainly outlive, the sparrow-flight passages of my father and myself.

I stopped at a pretty, low-beamed pub, its walls tricked out with horse-brasses, yards of ale, and sepia photos of dead cricket teams, and ate a 1990s lunch of microwaved steak-and-kidney pie and Bird's Eye frozen peas, whose green was as exotic a hue as the yellow of the rape outside. The pub was evidently a favourite watering hole for office workers from one of Northampton's outlying industrial estates; it was full of people, and all of them were laughing.

I had forgotten that laughter. No nation on earth laughs as loudly, frequently, and insincerely as does England: the land of *ha-ha-ha* and *haw-haw-haw*. In the pub, newcomers were greeting the already arrived with an exchange of hearty guffaws. Around the tables, the laughs were coming thick and fast, each performed in a studiedly personal style. The alpha-male trumpet-laugh. The wry, thin sneeze delivered through the nose. The Falstaffian explosion, beginning in the belly and aimed at the ceiling. The complicit chuffing sound of a steam locomotive getting underway. The nudge-in-the-elbow snigger.

The preferred women's laugh: an upper-palate, saliva-powered '*Ngh! hng! hng! hng! hng! hnng!*' that was capable of shattering glass.

Not that anything said – in my earshot, at least – was funny, but in this country humour was valued in abstraction, like love or honour.

'Laugh? I nearly died,' people would say.

'Well, it's good for a laugh.'

'There's nothing like a good laugh, I always say.'

'Give us a laugh.'

'He only did it for the laughs.'

Laughter was a serious business here. I badly wanted to tell the man sitting next to me that I was on my way up to Market Harborough to see my father, who was dying of cancer, just to listen to the jovial honking noise that I was sure would be his response.

And I would have been glad to hear it.

There was a strange car in the driveway of my parents' bungalow on Coventry Road, and a strange face at the door when I pressed the bell.

'I'm the district nurse!' confided the face, in a whisper, as if she were a burglar. 'You must be one of the sons.' From behind the nurse, my mother appeared, looking uncertain of her standing in her own house. Beside the unshapely largeness of the nurse, my mother looked tiny, an elf-woman, her eyes huge and exhausted.

'Jonathan! Are you all right? You're so thin. You're all skin and bones!'

We were each shocked by the sight of the other.

'I'm fine. I've been on the boat. I always lose a bit of weight at sea.'

I felt my mother's distress at finding a gaunt man in his fifties as her son. I saw that, in this novel period of life, when time itself goes weird, she had been prepared to greet me as a hulking teenager, or an assistant lecturer at a university in his pink twenties – not someone so promising a candidate for death in his own right.

I hugged her. She was all skin and bones.

'How's Peter?'

'Well, he was up this morning, but then he went to bed again . . .' The nurse still stood by with a proprietorial air, as if in charge of the both of us as well. I gave her the evil eye and she reluctantly stumped off toward the kitchen, where she began to rattle dishes, loudly, in the sink.

'He's got a touch of jaundice,' my mother said. 'The doctor says that's quite usual.'

A grey metal wheelchair stood in the hall, a plaid rug folded on one of its arms. I couldn't take my eyes off this alien contraption; its utility-issue ugliness, like the nurse's dowdy uniform, seemed somehow needless and cruel.

'I think he's awake. Peter, dear? It's Jonathan.'

I followed her into the bedroom.

'Hello, old boy.' From beneath the bedclothes, he extended his right hand.

I shook it, thinking that the oddest thing about this scene was that I couldn't remember ever seeing my father in bed before.

'Sorry about all this . . . kerfuffle.'

'How are you feeling?'

'Oh, pretty well. No pain to speak of. How are Jean and – uh – Julia?'

'Fine,' I said. 'They're fine. We'll all be here on Saturday for the party.' Planned long before, this was to celebrate my parents' wedding anniversary – their fifty-fifth.

'Good-oh,' my father said.

Jaundice had turned the skin of his face to the colour of an ancient legal deed. Every bone protruded from behind the skin. But his beard was in fine fettle, sprouting in silver tufts and curls and tassels, as if it had every intention of enjoying life long into the future.

'Well!' said the district nurse, announcing herself. 'I'm off now. See you in the morning, Peter!' she said with a professional twinkle.

'Thanks so much. Bye.'

'So you've got Big Nurse,' I said when she was gone.

'She's a perfectly decent sort,' he said – always quick to correct my knee-jerk negative opinions.

'Rather you than me.'

My mother wanted him to eat. She was feeding him with packets of nutritious powder dissolved in water. I retrieved the jars of candied ginger from the car.

'Fortnum & Mason's,' I said, trying to force a note of gourmet extravagance into my father's grim diet.

'Awfully kind of you, old boy. I hope you didn't go out of your way.'

'And I've brought back Colonel William's diary.' This was a calf-bound manuscript book from the 1830s, when Colonel William Raban, sailing to Madras, had run into a storm at sea. My father had thought it would interest me, but Colonel William had proved as dull a dog as most of my paternal ancestors.

'Oh, good of you to remember. Could you put it on my desk in the study, do you think? So it won't get lost in the . . . general commotion?'

A minute or two later, my father's eyes closed, and he drifted into sleep. I took the book into the study. The desk was largely occupied by US atlases. My father, who'd been an artillery officer from 1939 to 1945, had always planned our family holidays like army campaigns, and he had gone to town on the projected drive from Minneapolis to Seattle. His old gunnery slide rule was placed on the opened Rand McNally, and there were several loose passages of notes in his small, careful handwriting. He had been sketching several alternative routes. Names of towns big enough to sport a motel had been circled. Reading the notes and looking at the maps, I saw he'd got as far as Great Falls, Montana, in the plan of campaign. Halfway to our house.

I put the colonel's diary on top of the DeLorme atlas for Idaho and joined my mother in the kitchen.

'Do you take sugar, dear? I don't remember.'

'No sugar for me.'

'I think it's William who does. Or is it Dominic? I don't think it's Colin.'

'Whoever,' I said. 'Tell me what you can – what you know.'

'Well,' she said, her high voice rising in forced brightness. 'I talked to the doctor this morning. We both like him, Peter and I, we both like the doctor very much. And I said to him, "There will be a remission, won't there? If I can get him to eat properly – if he gets his appetite back? He will get up and about again, won't he? We might be able to go to Scotland?"'

Before her marriage, my mother had supported herself by writing romantic stories for women's magazines. Dialogue had been her forte.

'And the doctor said, "Well, Monica, I don't think I ought to raise your hopes *too* high. I'm afraid I don't think you ought to *count* on that." And I said to him . . . "How long?"'

Her voice was an appalled whisper.

'He said . . . he said, "One never can tell, but, perhaps, a few . . . weeks."' She gave a choking laugh, and in my mother's face I saw the abyss.

Market Harborough was a fox-hunting town: I passed a shop selling red coats and riding crops for the tally-ho crowd. Beyond the market square, and, on massive antique oaken stilts, the old grammar school, lay a shopping mall, of sorts. The architect had obviously visited America, but he hadn't got it quite right. In the Sainsbury's supermarket of this mid-Atlantic no-man's-land, I put together the ingredients for a chicken-and-coriander curry and bought a mixed case of wine. The cool of the aisles and the close-reading of wine labels, the ritual of getting cash out of the ATM machine, all felt preciously ordinary, and I spun out my trip away from the bungalow for longer than was necessary.

'Hi,' I said to the girl at the checkout. 'How you doing?'

She gave me a look, and reminded me of my Martian status here.

When I reached my parents' home, rain had begun to fall; the first in weeks. Big splashy globules were dropping from a windless grey sky.

'That's nice,' my mother said. 'It should perk up the garden for the party.'

I made an important fuss of chopping things on the kitchen table, pulling the cork on a bottle of red burgundy, ostentatiously sniffing it, then clinking glasses with my mother.

'I don't stop hoping. It's very wrong to stop hoping, don't you think? I just hope now that we can have this summer together . . . But he must *eat*,' she said with sudden fierceness. 'He liked your ginger. He had some when you were out shopping.'

With the curry bubbling on the stove, I went into the bedroom to talk to my father. He was awake, but dozy with morphine.

'Thanks again for the ginger, old boy.'

I sat in the chair by the bed in the darkening room, and told him about Julia – her ebullient sociability, her growing verbal dexterity, her happiness at preschool.

'Light of my life,' I said.

He nodded, smiled, and went to sleep.

My mother and I ate in the small dining room that opened onto a glassed-in porch overlooking the back garden. The bungalow was a modest brick affair, built in the 1940s, that my parents had moved into a couple of years before. A few steps from the town centre, it was conveniently opposite the old people's nursing home, to which, my father used to joke, they might eventually graduate, 'when we reach our dotage'. But only weeks before, dotage had lain comfortably in the twenty-first century, and the bungalow had been bought with a long tenure in mind. The camper, in which my parents had toured Europe, east and west, was parked out front. My father's researches into the history of Channel Island privateering, in which his Priaulx ancestors had been active in the eighteenth century, took him and my mother on regular jaunts to Guernsey, St Malo, Cherbourg, as well as to county record offices all over England.

The bungalow's one stab at grandeur was its lawn, which could have held a tennis court with ample room left over. In the last year, my father had been planting it with saplings, to break up the monotony of mown grass. In the half-dark, I could see their spring leaves hanging limp from the drought. To plant young trees, I thought, is tempting fate, an activity that ought to be reserved for children.

'I do hope this rain keeps on,' my mother said. 'Peter heard it, and he was *very* pleased. He's been worrying about the garden.'

I left to drive back to London after eleven that evening. Fearing the slippery wet lanes, I got onto the motorway at the nearest junction, a few miles west of Harborough. Traffic was thin at this time of night. I was dazzled by my own lights on the wet black surface of the carriageway. Heavy lorries sped south, big as cargo ships. To right and left, the darkness crowded in – a thick fir forest. By Newport Pagnell, where I stopped for petrol, I was seeing boils and whirlpools in the road. To rid myself of these marine hallucinations, I turned up the radio and got the news on Radio 4, followed by the shipping forecast.

'Dogger, Fisher, German Bight . . . Humber, Thames, Dover . . . Wight, Portland, Plymouth . . .' There were gale warnings for Fastnet and Irish Sea. South-west 7, rising to gale 8 later.

I was back among the whirlpools, passage-making through the forest.

Death is a wilderness in which everyone is lost for words.

Two days of steady rain transformed the garden, and by the Saturday of my parents' wedding-anniversary party the leaves on the saplings had recovered their bounce and the banks of flowers were in profuse bloom. On the lawn, Julia and her cousin Alethea, two months apart in age, raced screaming and naked while their thirteen-year-old cousin James chased them with a water hose.

Things were less simple at the lawn's east end, where the grown-ups were sprawled on the grass or seated in candy-striped garden chairs on the crazy paving. The four sons, ranging in age from thirty-four to fifty-three, looked like peas from one pod: dark, narrow-beamed six-footers. Only I had inherited the baldness on my mother's side of the family, a deficiency I tried to keep hidden under a baseball cap worn indoors and out. Our brotherly similarity of build was deceiving. We all had the same deep voice but spoke in different accents, and were riven by ancient slights and grievances, never explicitly spoken of, never resolved. As Arabs and Israelis, Belfast Protestants and Catholics, might warily exchange small talk at some unfortunately arranged cocktail gathering, so my brothers and I, glasses in hand, spoke to one another on topics carefully chosen for their neutrality. Three of us had a child apiece, and the partner of the fourth was expecting a baby. Three of us owned sailing boats. Three of us sported rival brands of cellular phone. Brought together now, for the first time in many years, by my father's cancer, each was doing his best to put on the family play; but we were drastically under-rehearsed in our parts, and our lines sounded wooden, even by the forgiving standards of a first reading.

Each of us had a long-standing alliance with one of the others, and the easiest thing for all of us, when we dried up onstage, was to fall back into two camps of four people apiece, with the female partners standing by their men. Jean, as the visiting American, carried the least baggage, and was the most socially mobile of the women, though still, she incurred the odium of having married me.

Yet we tried, as our mother, back-and-forthing it between our father in the bedroom and the drinkers in the garden, watched for the old signs of trouble, some of them dating back nearly half a century. I could see the worry on her face as she stepped out from the sunroom. Had she heard the Syrian say 'Golan Heights', or the Protestant 'Sovereignty'? No, she hadn't. But among the sounds of ice tinkling in vodka and the giddy frolics of the dripping three-year-olds, the danger was real.

We visited Peter in relays. Jean carried Julia in her arms when it was our turn. My father gave us a game smile, exposing the tomb-stone-teeth that were among my inheritances from him.

Julia stared. 'Is that my Grandad Peter?' she said.

'Having a good time?' my father said.

'Yes, thank you.' Her eyes were wide while she took in the strange colour of my father's skin, his sunken eyes, those teeth. 'Can I go play with Alethea now?'

'See you later, Peter,' Jean said. 'Say goodbye to Grandad . . . '

'Goodbye, Grandad Peter.'

When we were left together, my father said, 'Begonia and Alethea are looking well . . . '

'Jean and Julia,' I said. 'Can I get you anything? Ginger? A glass of wine?'

'Not right now, old boy. I'm quite comfortable as I am.'

I took his hand in mine. He looked surprised – and even, possibly, a little frightened. Things were not usually thus between us. I let the hand drop, but said: 'You're setting us all a hell of an example to follow . . . handling this with so much bravery. We're all very proud of you.'

A sudden, lively argumentative gleam came into my father's eyes.

'Oh, I don't know about "bravery",' he said. He was back in his *come-off-it-old-boy* voice – the one he'd used to debunk my latest, university-fed ideas in the days when I'd fancied myself a Marxist literary theoretician. What should have accompanied the voice was a long, considered exhalation of St Bruno pipe smoke. But my father had quit smoking in 1992. His first day off his pipe had coincided with the morning on which he'd taken captainly charge of the narrowboat that Jean and I had rented to tour the Oxford and Grand Union Canals.

'I don't know about bravery. I'd say it was more of a question of what kind of act you put on. Wouldn't you, old boy? Presentation of self and all that?'

This was an allusion. In the mid-1960s, when I was teaching literature at the University College of Wales in Aberystwyth, and my brother Colin was reading sociology at the University of Manchester, the three of us used to sit up till three and four in the morning, wrangling amiably over bottles of red plonk. Colin and I were both interested in 'role theory', and had made Peter read Erving Goffman's *The Presentation of Self in Everyday Life*.

'Well, if it's an act,' I said, 'it's a wonderfully brave act.'

'It . . . doesn't . . . take . . . bravery,' my father said, laying out the words between us, one by one. Then he made a mild, self-deprecating, harrumphing sound; a very English laugh.

At a little after three o'clock, my mother came out to say that Peter was getting up and would soon be joining us.

'Is he really strong enough for this?' I asked.

With a touch of anger in her voice, she said, 'Yes! He's feeling much better now, and he doesn't want to miss the party.'

Ten minutes later, my youngest brother, Dominic, piloted my father out to the sunroom door in the hideous wheelchair. Though the temperature was in the eighties, he was cocooned in blankets. Below the knees, the legs of his striped pyjamas fluttered round ankles that seemed little more than bare bones. The pyjamas themselves, with their convict pattern and extreme thinness, looked as if they might have survived from his boarding school days. He nodded and smiled, the cavernous black sockets of his eyes masked by glasses now. His hair had been brushed neatly back, and his silver beard glittered in the westering sun.

Glasses were raised. Someone said, 'Happy anniversary!' but it wasn't me.

My father got his right hand disentangled from the blankets and slowly raised it level with his head, first and second fingers erect, with the third and fourth held back by his thumb. The gesture was entirely familiar to me, though I couldn't quite place from where. I thought it belonged to the resurrected Christ in an Italian painting.

He's going to give us a benediction! This was strange. At theological college in the early 1950s, then for the next few years as a deacon and curate, my father, like his own, also a parson, had been a ritualist, an Anglo-Catholic. He had gone in for heavy vestments and incense; had said the daily orders – Prime, Matins, Compline, Vespers. Then, in the 1960s, under the influence of the Church of England modernists such as John Robinson, the Bishop of Woolwich and author of *Honest to God*, my father had dropped all the High Church trappings, even to the point, eventually, of never wearing his dog collar. Watching the raised hand, the skyward-pointing fingers, I thought: He's gone back to Anglo-Catholicism; and the benediction, when it comes, looks as if it may well be in Latin.

Yet he didn't speak. The hand was moving slowly from side to side. He wasn't blessing; he was counting.

'All my sons,' he said.

'Wine, Peter?'

'Oh, just a small glass. White. White would be nice.'

He held it, but did not drink. He grinned, in a vague, grand-fatherly way, at Julia and Alethea, who were struck mute, lemur-eyed, as if God himself had appeared to them in the middle of a burning bush.

We had return tickets to fly back to Seattle on the Tuesday after the anniversary party. 'Take Julia back,' I said to Jean. 'I'll wait. Until.'

'Don't you want us to stay?'

'This isn't a time for Julia. She needs to get back to normality, or she'll forget what normality is.'

But that was my cover. I wanted to be alone. If I were to properly play the role of son as my father lay dying, I couldn't manage the roles of husband and father too. I saw Jean and Julia on to the plane at Heathrow and drove direct to Jermyn Street, where I tried on a ready-made double-breasted charcoal-grey suit.

'A little bit on the heavy side, perhaps, sir, for this time of year?'

'I need it for a funeral.'

'Oh, I'm *very* sorry,' said the man, in a very unsorry sort of tone. Then a note of genuine anxiety showed. 'What day will you be need-ing it, sir?' I'd told him that I wanted the cuffs on the trousers removed (I had to kick myself into remembering they were called 'turn-ups' here), a slimming pleat taken in on the spine of the jacket, and a slight lengthening of the sleeves.

'You'll have time for the alterations. He's not dead yet.'

'I *see*.' He stared at me over the top of his half-moon glasses, trying to figure out if I was a ghoul or, as I thought, merely being practical.

I bought a black tie, a couple of starchy white shirts, and a pair of funereal shoes. Now that the costume was complete, I felt suddenly disburdened. I lunched with a publisher at an Italian restaurant on Curzon Street. We talked death. His father – another Anglican clergyman – had died a few years before, and I had gone to his memorial service. My parents had once gone to a party at Christopher's house in Islington.

'I need tips and clues,' I said.

'Will you be giving the address?'

'I suppose so.'

'Make it funny, if you can.'

I drove north and took a room, with a telephone, in a pub at Great Oxendon, three miles south of Harborough. With a base in London and another in Leicestershire, I hoped I could be everywhere at once, as required.

With some difficulty, my brothers and I drew up a roster so as to visit in rotation, without either intruding on the time that our mother needed to spend alone with our father or leaving them so alone that she might feel abandoned by her family. A fine line to draw, it was the subject of prickly dispute between us.

My father was surprised to find me at his bedside again.

'I thought you were supposed to be going back to the States.'

'Oh – stuff cropped up. You know, publishing stuff. I've just handed in the proofs of my new book.'

My father looked at me. The look said, *Come off it.*

In London, people were anticipating another event. John Major's Conservative administration was dead on its feet: Major himself had the hangdog, beaten air of a school Captain of Cricket whose team had lost ten matches on the trot. Everyone I knew was certain that a snap election would follow a last, desperate autumn budget, and that – whatever tax give-away was in the budget – the Labour Party would romp home. The dominant mood, over the dinner table and at parties, was of high, if slightly tremulous elation. After seventeen years of Tory governments hostile to the arts, to higher education, to people like us, *we* were going to be back in power at last. Several of my acquaintances were close to members of Tony Blair's shadow

Cabinet. A lot of first names were dropped and already there was talk of life peerages for contemporaries of mine who had served time on the anti-Thatcher barricades.

I felt my exile keenly. I wished the *we* included me. Watching Major on television, looking greyer and more unconfident with his every appearance, made me think of my father – a comparison that would have annoyed him no end. I looked forward to the moment when Major would finally fall off his perch, but knew that when he did so my father would certainly be gone too.

From my friend's house in Brixton, I borrowed a pile of books to keep me occupied in the pleasant, airy room I'd rented in the converted coach house of the Great Oxendon pub: John Lanchester's *The Debt to Pleasure*, Evelyn Waugh's *Work Suspended*, Richard Holmes's *Shelley: The Pursuit*, and a small-print Victorian copy of Shelley's poems.

Seated by the open window, with bees foraging in the flowers outside, waiting for the telephone to ring, I tried my best to stay in touch with the voyage, and the book, I had left behind at Potts Lagoon. It was hard to read, and hard to think. The word 'metastasis' was too much on my mind. *Rapid transition from one point to another.* The bees metastasized from flower to flower. I metastasized from Waugh to Shelley. The cancer, running wild inside my father, brought with it a new vocabulary for unruliness and disorder . . .

Come off it, old boy. Day by day, as my father weakened, he fell back more and more on the conversational protocol that had served him well as an experienced parish priest. 'Good to see you,' he'd say. 'Nice of you to drop in.' He was dealing with his own death patiently, tolerantly; a trained professional at dealing with bad news.

At the vicarage, the bell would ring in the middle of lunch. 'Oh, drat! Another parishioner!' my mother would say. But my father would go to the door, assembling his vicar's face as he went. 'Oh, hello there! Not at all! Do come in!' and he would escort the visitor into the drawing room. Just before closing the door behind them, he'd turn and make a face at my mother. His range of faces was as wide as a ship's wardrobe of signal flags, from the face that said *I'll be rid of this pest in a couple of minutes* to the one that said *Cancel all my afternoon engagements, and bring us tea and sandwiches in half an hour.*

Until the early 1960s, at least, the Anglican vicarage was the officially designated receptacle for any tale of woe. The bereaved, the destitute, the depressed, the crazy made a beeline for our house. Young men in trouble with the law parked their motorbikes against the porch. Young women, then known as 'unmarried mothers' in need of 'moral welfare', showed up in droves.

From behind the closed door came the sounds of distraught sobbing, fantastical narratives of hard luck, expostulations of aggrieved innocence, insane cackles, and, sometimes, screams. These were punctuated by my father's voice, as regular and predictable as a metronome. 'Uh – huh. Yup . . . yup . . . yup. I *see* . . . Uh – *huh* . . . I've got you . . . Hmmmm . . . '

Sitting at his bedside, I was the parishioner now. He was trying to offer all his visitors the solace in the presence of death that it had been his job to dispense as a parson. He must have conducted, on average, three or four funerals a week during his working life. He knew the rigmarole. In the face of his own death, he sought to project an air of calming professional reassurance. He struggled to be jokey, upbeat, *nothing to it*, and *carry on as usual*. Sometimes I saw the fear in his eyes, but it would be gone in a flash; he was boxing it away from public view, as a good priest must.

My mother told me that the morphine was giving him bad dreams.

I read Shelley, and for good reason.

Shelley was mad about boats. He loved to write about water; and died at the helm of his own wildly over-canvassed miniature schooner, when it foundered in a sudden afternoon storm in the Gulf of Spezia. His description of the landscape – or waterscape, rather – of death itself sounds uncannily like the Pacific Northwest.

In December 1815, six and a half years before his own death by water, Shelley finished his first major poem, *Alastor*, in which the hero, named the Poet, '. . . left / His cold fireside and alienated home / To seek strange truths in undiscovered lands'. The Poet is the archetype of the Romantic solitary wanderer. He journeys, in an introspective reverie, through Arabia, Persia, and Kashmir (where he enjoys a wet dream involving a veiled Oriental muse), until, lonely, lovelorn, and in the throes of a sublime despair, he reaches the ocean, where he spies a 'little shallop floating near the shore'. The boat is abandoned and unseaworthy ('its sides / Gaped wide with many a rift'), but its deplorable condition is an added attraction for the Poet, because

> *A restless impulse urged him to embark*
> *And meet lone Death on the drear ocean's waste;*
> *For well he knew that mighty Shadow loves*
> *The slimy caverns of the populous deep.*

At this point – for me, at least – the narrative of *Alastor* springs to sudden life, as the Poet gets under way on his deliberate voyage of death. The prolonged storm scene, in which the little boat flies over the night sea, propelled by a hurricane-force wind, is a little too much under the influence of what Richard Holmes calls 'Milton's epic drone', but it is full of interest and incident.

> *Along the dark and ruffled waters fled*
> *The straining boat. – A whirlwind swept it on,*
> *With fierce gusts and precipitating force,*
> *Through the wide ridges of the chaféd sea.*
> *The waves rose. Higher and higher still*
> *Their fierce necks writhed beneath the tempest's scourge*
> *Like serpents struggling in a vulture's grasp.*
> *Calm and rejoicing in the fearful war*

Of wave ruling on wave, and blast on blast
Descending, and black flood on whirlpool driven
With dark obliterating course, he sate:
As if their genii were the ministers
Appointed to conduct him to the light
Of those beloved eyes, the Poet sate
Holding the steady helm . . .

. . . .

      . . . At midnight
the moon arose: and lo! the etherial cliffs
Of Caucasus, whose icy summits shone
Among the stars like sunlight, and around
Whose cavern'd base the whirlpools and the waves
Bursting and eddying irresistibly
Rage and resound for ever. – Who shall save? –
The boat fled on, – the boiling torrent drove, –
The crags closed round with black and jagged arms,
The shattered mountain overhung the sea,
And faster still, beyond all human speed,
Suspended on the sweep of the smooth wave,
The little boat was driven. A cavern there
Yawned, and amid its slant and winding depths
Ingulfed the rushing sea. The boat fled on
With unrelaxing speed. 'Vision and Love!'
The Poet cried aloud, 'I have beheld
The path of thy departure. Sleep and death
Shall not divide us long!'

I knew the icy summits, the whirlpools, the crags with black and jagged arms, the shattered mountain, the slant and winding depths. As the boat fled farther on, I found more scenery to recognize: the 'steep cataract'; the 'ample chasm . . . filled with one whirlpool'; the 'knarléd roots of mighty trees'; the 'battling tides'; the 'dizzy swiftness' of 'the ascending stream'; the 'pyramids / Of the tall cedar, overarching'; the 'grey precipices' and 'barren pinnacles'; the 'pine, rock-rooted'; those 'knotty roots and fallen rocks'. As Shelley constructed a suitable imaginary landscape for his hero to die in, he built British Columbia, in iambic pentameters.

That elements of the real Pacific Northwest may have crept into *Alastor* shouldn't be surprising. The voyages of Cook, La Pérouse, Vancouver, and the fur-trade captains had brought the wilderness of that coast, with copious illustrations, into the libraries of Shelley's generation. By the 1810s, when the Alps and the Lake District were beginning to swarm with hikers, there was a hunger for some landscape more unvisited, wild, and sublime than Europe could supply. Extreme experience – the peaks and chasms of love and death, which were at the heart of the Romantic movement in writing and painting – required a corresponding extremity, and loneliness, in nature. The voyage writers brought back tidings of a land impossibly inaccessible to the tourist, replete with alpine heights, unfathomable seas, primitive men in their natural state, cascades, Stygian gloom, watery labyrinths, and impenetrable forests, where a man like Shelley's Poet could wander for ever in uninterrupted solitude.

That was the trouble with Market Harborough. For the first time in my life, I felt in need of a cathedral: a great, dark, vaulted space; somewhere old, musty, and enormous, where I could sit for a while in a carved pew, among pillars and cloisters, in a building constructed on the model of a forest; and if not pray, exactly, then meditate, alone, on what was happening to my father. It was space and solemnity I wanted, not the God-stuff.

Market Harborough, invincibly sunny, was neither spacious nor solemn. People went whizzing past on bikes. They shopped at Tesco's. They overflowed, babbling, from the pubs. Sneaking out to buy cigarettes at the scruffy Pakistani newsagent's, I found myself bewildered by the huge, silly headlines in the tabloids. I was too long out of the loop. Everyone in public life had nicknames, nearly all of them new to me. I knew who Paddy Pantsdown was, but beyond that,

I was in the dark. The tabloids' tone – wink-wink, nudge-nudge, ha-ha – seemed to have spread into the streets. At any other time, I might have warmed to the genial mateyness of middle England, the joshing and the new infusion of high spirits, now that the economy was, at last, on the up-and-up again. In the premature summer heat was an atmosphere of carnival. But I wasn't here for a carnival.

So I tramped up the High Street, thinking of Desolation Sound.

The boundary between sleep and death appeared to grow narrower by the day. My mother would sometimes say, with nervy brightness, 'Just pop in and see how Peter's doing, would you, dear?' In the bedroom, I'd stare at the yellow, immobile, tufty-bearded face and think *he's dead*, then search in my head for the word or gesture I should employ to break the news to my mother. Then I'd see the flutter of life in his so slightly moving chest, and report, 'He's fine. He's sleeping.'

'Oh, good. He needs a lot of sleep now.'

He was lucky to die as he was doing; at home, in the bed he still shared with my mother. He was feeling little or no pain, thanks to the drugs – a wall of vials and bottles whose labels I didn't want to read. I studied his face but could see no sign of terrifying dreams.

I stopped by the shop in Jermyn Street, and hung my altered suit in the closet of my room at the pub. It was a perfect fit.

I read eagerly about Shelley's death at sea, gate-crashing the London Library (my membership long lapsed) to fill in details absent from Richard Holmes's splendid life of the poet.

Though Shelley had sailed since he was a schoolboy at Eton, his experience was mostly on rivers, from the Thames to the Arno. Amateur sailing, like mountaineering, was itself a product of the Romantic revolution; in overcivilized Europe, the sea and the mountains were the last true wildernesses, and poets in search of wild nature inevitably gravitated to boats. The boy Wordsworth (according to *The Prelude*) stole a 'little boat' on Lake Windermere, and one of his first experiences of the Sublime was to be pursued by 'a huge cliff' striding after him as he rowed across the lake at nightfall. Byron owned a big boat, *Bolivar* (named after the South American liberator), equipped with cannons on whose barrels were engraved the Byron coat of arms and the motto *Crede Byron*. When Shelley moved his large and unconventional family to Lerici, on the Gulf of Spezia, in the spring of 1822, he spent £80 on a scaled-down model of an American-style schooner; sleek, fast, with little sheer and low freeboard, and only twenty-four feet long, or so the books say. (My own guess is, that was the waterline measurement; overall, at least according to Daniel Roberts's sketch of the boat, it appears to have been something over thirty feet. Roberts, who supervised its building, was surely in a position to know.)

Whatever its length, Shelley loved the boat he wanted to name *Ariel* but which ended up, at Byron's lordly and egotistical insistence, *Don Juan*. In May it arrived in Lerici from Genoa, and Shelley was delighted. He wrote to Daniel Roberts:

> *She is a most beautiful boat and so surpasses [our] expectations that it was with some difficulty that we could persuade ourselves that you had not sent us the Bolivar by mistake.*

To John Gisborne he wrote:

> *It is swift and beautiful, and appears quite a vessel. Williams [Edward Williams, Shelley's friend, retired from the Indian Army, and married to the 'Jane' of the next sentence] is captain, and, we drive along this delightful bay in the evening wind under the summer moon until earth appears another world. Jane brings her guitar, and if the past and future could be obliterated, the present would content me so well that I could say with Faust to the passing moment, 'Remain thou, thou art so beautiful.'*

'It serves me at once as a study and a carriage', wrote Shelley, who filled the boat with books and began his last important poem, 'The

Triumph of Life', while seated aboard, his back resting against *Don Juan*'s mainmast.

The boat was fast from the start, but Shelley, wanting even greater speed, added topmasts, staysails, and a false stern. To balance the enormous square-footage of canvas that *Don Juan* now carried, he had to line the bilges with twenty-nine pigs of cast-iron ballast. William St Clair, in his biography of Trelawny (who had a major hand in *Don Juan*'s design and building), describes it as 'one of the most unseaworthy vessels ever constructed'.

On 1 July, Shelley sailed for Leghorn, thirty-eight nautical miles south of Lerici, with Williams and a sixteen-year-old 'boat boy', Charles Vivian. He was escaping a household full of sorrow. Late in April, Allegra – Claire Clairmont's daughter, supposedly by Byron, though Shelley had reason to believe that he might himself be the father – had died of typhus in a convent near Ravenna, aged barely five. Claire was nearly out of her mind with grief. On 16 June, Mary Shelley had suffered a miscarriage, and was in a hardly happier state. Shelley, off to Pisa to consort with Byron and Leigh Hunt, was taking a vacation from this death-ridden summer.

Don Juan reached Leghorn seven hours later, making a steady five-knots-plus. Shelley disembarked, leaving Williams and Vivian to take care of the boat. In Pisa, he stayed at Byron's palazzo, roistering with his literary friends and making plans for their new magazine, *The Liberal*. On 7 July he returned to Leghorn, where a south wind was blowing fair for the Gulf of Spezia, and next afternoon Shelley, Williams, and Vivian put to sea. They were twenty miles north of Leghorn, and ten miles offshore, when, about six o'clock, storm clouds showed on the south-western horizon and all the local fishing boats made for harbour. At 6:30 p.m. the storm broke. The sea off that coast is shallow; the waves inevitably steep.

The Irish poetaster Count John Taaffe, known as the Laureate of Pisa, is everyone's source for what happened next. Taaffe talked to the captain of an Italian fishing boat that had passed *Don Juan* and offered help.

Seeing that they could not long contend with such tremendous waves, [he] bore down upon them and offered to take them on board. A shrill voice, which is supposed to have been Shelley's, was distinctly heard to say 'No' . . . The waves were running mountains high – a tremendous surf dashed over the boat which to his astonishment was still crowded with sail. 'If you will not come on board for God's sake reef your sails or you are lost,' cried a sailor through the speaking trumpet. One of the gentlemen (Williams it is believed) was seen to make an effort to lower the sails – his companion seized him by the arm as if in anger.

Don Juan foundered ten miles west of Viareggio. Days later, the bodies of Shelley, Williams, and Vivian were washed ashore. The fish had eaten their faces away. Shelley was identified by his reefer jacket, white nankeen trousers, and black leather boots. A copy of Keats's *Poems* was in the pocket of the jacket.

With the assistance of an Italian fishing boat, Daniel Roberts salvaged *Don Juan* with its tangle of broken spars (the water in which it sank must have been very shallow indeed). The boat was full of bluish mud. Roberts got out of her the twenty-nine pigs of ballast; two trunks full of books and clothes; a case of Marsala wine, the corks forced halfway out the bottles by the pressure of submersion and the wine impregnated with salt water; and seven teaspoons.

Was Shelley determined to recreate the suicidal voyage of the Poet in *Alastor*? I phoned Richard Holmes to quiz him about the sinking of *Don Juan*.

'Was it just foolhardiness, or a Romantic death wish?'

'I don't think there was any death wish at all. It was a very difficult summer for Shelley, and he had to battle on through long depressive episodes – like most writers do. But sailing was a wonderful release for him. It was a death trap of a boat, but it was the place where he was happiest. I think, when they were off Viareggio, it was reckless, and enjoyable, and he was giving the boat a go—'

'Let's see what this baby will do?'

'Yes. That sort of thing. Fast! Speed! Racing! Hot! He was enjoying himself. He'd sailed a lot, but had very little experience at sea, and he didn't realize how dangerous the boat was.'

The person to feel sorry for was the boy, Charles Vivian. Shelley and Williams were responsible for their own bad seamanship, of which Vivian was the powerless victim. I wondered who he was. Holmes had been able to find out little about him.

'I think they probably picked him up on the dock at Lerici. By the time Shelley took his house there, the place was already a sailing centre for English expats. It was the beginnings of marina culture . . .'

Suddenly, I knew exactly who Charles Vivian was. The sun-bleached teenager, head full of boats, wandering the pontoons in search of a berth on anything with furled sails. Falling in with Shelley and Williams must have seemed to him a brilliant stroke of luck.

Writing to Mary Shelley, after the salvage of *Don Juan*, Daniel Roberts reported: 'all the boys things safe in the forepeak'.

Poor Charles Vivian. Prior to sailing with Shelley, anyone should have studied the seagoing passages in *Alastor* in close detail, and worried about whether their author was likely to be a safe captain of a real boat in a real sea.

On 14 June (my birthday, as it happened) I was reading *The Debt to Pleasure* in my room at the pub when, just before eleven o'clock at night, the telephone rang. It was my brother Dominic, asking if I could lend a hand at the bungalow: my father's sheet needed to be changed, a three-person job.

I drove fast through the dark, the chimerical firs and cypresses crowding in around the narrow road. Every night now, I found England dissolving into the landscape I had left behind; its fields and meadows reverting to thick forest. On the long-haul drives between

Leicestershire and London, it was a pleasant illusion; I enjoyed depopulating the countryside and restoring it to wilderness.

At the bungalow, both my mother and my brother looked like haggard sleepwalkers, their faces chalky with exhaustion and anxiety. We muttered at one another and trudged, single file, into the bedroom where my father lay. He was close to coma now. My mother lifted the bedclothes. He was wearing only a diaper. The loincloth, the beard, the wasted body: he had become a deposition scene, a *pietà*, fresh from the cross.

Ravaged though he was, he was astonishingly hard to shift. We tried to tug the soiled sheet from underneath him; it wouldn't budge. My brother and I held on to a leg apiece and hauled him sideways across the bed while my mother cradled his head in her lap, saying, 'It's all right, darling, it's all right! We're just giving you a clean sheet—' To me it seemed that moving him limb by limb with such inexpert roughness, we were in danger of breaking him apart. My brother and I were a pair of amateur removal men, gasping for breath as we lugged my father about. Just as our job was almost done, my father rolled suddenly, face forward, and said, 'I'm going!'

'No, you're not, my darling! You are not!'

I had never before heard my mother speak with such fierce authority.

Five minutes later, as I was leaving the bungalow to go back to my pub, my brother came with me to the door. 'That was terrible,' he said in a dry, creaky whisper.

'We did OK,' I said.

In bed in my room, I found my place in *The Debt to Pleasure*, but the words skedaddled all over the page like a flock of impish bats. The book fell out of my hand. Seconds later, I was roused by the imperious British double-jangle of the phone. The red numbers on the clock radio said 7:01 a.m.

My mother's voice. 'Peter's – gone.'

Of course he'd known. He always had been a realist – and never more so than in his last spoken words. No more indignities now. I was glad for him. Driving to Harborough in the rising sunshine, I wound the windows down and heard the blackbirds singing.

In the bedroom at the bungalow, he looked strangely less dead than when he'd been alive – his face relaxed in sleep so deep that I might almost have envied it, as I envied Julia's total surrender to unconsciousness. My mother sat beside him. For her sake, I bent down and brushed his cheek with my lips. It was less than a kiss. We'd never kissed. The cheek was only a little cooler than it should have been.

My mother said, in a small voice, 'We've been so happy together. I love him so much.'

Now began the surreal administrative business of death, 'the arrangements'. I put a kettle on to boil for coffee, left a message on the undertaker's answering machine (whose greeting sounded as if recorded by Vincent Price), asking him to call me as soon as he got in. A nurse came, and quickly went away. The doctor arrived – a kindly, soft-spoken man, whose first gesture was to take my mother in his arms. The two absent brothers were on the road; Colin coming down the M1 from Sheffield, William coming up it from London.

I found the doctor on his knees in front of the toilet, and thought for a moment that he was throwing up. But he was flushing my father's drugs down the sewer-line one by one.

'Coffee?'

'That would be very nice,' he said over the rumbling cataract in the lavatory bowl.

My father, in full control of the morning, was in an amiable, even facetious mood. He had left behind a closely typed, ten-page document, headed IN THE EVENT OF A DEATH. He'd thought of everything, and clearly had enjoyed himself at the typewriter as he disposed of his own forthcoming remains.

The immediate information required by the funeral director from the Will is the manner of disposal of the body . . . burial or cremation. We both wish to be cremated, – simple, no grave to keep up and visit and a decent way of disposal . . . NO Ilkley Moor processes for us! Disposal of ashes: uncertain but NOT for keeping on a mantelpiece! ??Scatter – tho' frowned on by church authorities – on e.g. British Camp, Malvern Hills or somewhere in Worcs . . . Oddingley [his father's parish] in or near the churchyard . . . or in the New Forest? . . . or?? (Have a weekend of it, expenses paid for hotel rooms etc) More formally, St Nicholas' churchyard has a garden or rest. See the Vicar, of course.

'Funerals do not come cheaply!' he warned, advising us to instruct the undertaker that 'Simplicity is the order of the day.' He discussed car-parking arrangements for the reception at the bungalow after his funeral and cremation were finished:

The Police should be informed so that overflow parking on the cycle track, and preferably between that track and the roadway, is agreed. With the added parking space in front of the bungalow, it may be possible to let a few cars park further onto the grass if necessary, and if the ground is not too wet . . .

For the church service itself, he recommended that 'the general tone should be positive joy/thanksgiving/humorous etc etc rather than glum speculations or insurance policies!'

With my father affably chatting away in my ear, I uncorked a bottle of cognac and brought it out on a tray, with glasses, to the lawn, where the family was now building to full strength. The oddity of drinking brandy at nine in the morning seemed proper, and might easily have been specified by my father. My brothers and I, all pale and pouchy-eyed, clinked glasses. The undertaker arrived at a scene of genteel debauchery, like the hungover remnants of a party from the night before.

He said, *sotto voce*, 'My men are outside. For whenever you're ready.'

His round, rubicund face, full of laughter lines, was at odds with the death suit that was the obligatory uniform of his trade. He looked as if he'd been a bad boy at school. In his Harborough retirement, my father had been a freelance taker of funerals and often had worked with Mr Stamp, who seemed unaffectedly sorry about my father's death. 'He had a sense of humour,' he said. 'He used to make me laugh, sometimes. I tell you, I'm going to miss him.'

He declined a glass of brandy, though I sensed a pang of regret. 'A bit on the early side for me,' he said, excusing himself to go and 'have a quick word' with his men.

My mother sat in a garden chair, facing away from the house. Mr Stamp sat on her right, Dominic on her left. The rest of us completed an untidy circle. We passed our father's instructions from hand to hand, then settled into discussing coffins and their prices.

In the gloom of the house, behind my mother's cast-down head, I saw Mr Stamp's men, half a dozen of them, going silently about their morning's work. Six black cormorants, shuffling through the hall. I didn't want to see exactly what it was they were doing.

I said, 'Let's go for the plain deal—'

'With brass fitments?' suggested Mr Stamp hopefully.

That afternoon, having moved on from cognac to hock, my brother Colin and I sat on the little rockery at the far end of the lawn, mingling the scent of flowering lavender with the smell of red-pack Marlboros. Colin – sensitive to giving my mother further, wanton reminders of cancer – was carefully hiding his butts deep in the crevices between the stones. I was grinding mine into the gravel path with my heel.

Colin had always looked the most like my father. There were streaks of silver now in his neatly trimmed black beard. We talked about the ritual of changing my father's sheets, which had been his duty a couple of evenings before.

'The weird thing was,' he said, 'that even though his body was so wasted, I saw it was my body – you know? My arms, my legs, my torso . . .'

I realized that I'd felt that, too, but mine was a shadowy, inarticulate sensation. I was grateful to Colin for putting it into words.

'I'm worried about our carrying the coffin,' I said.

During the morning, perhaps elevated by brandy, we had agreed that the four brothers should carry the coffin from the hearse into the Kettering crematorium, after the funeral service in a Market Harborough church. Mr Stamp had nixed our plan to carry the coffin into the church; that was a job for pros. 'There are steps at St Nicholas's,' he said darkly, 'and a bit of tricky turn to make as you go in.'

'When you see them doing it on television,' I said, 'it's always six hulking marines, and they're always marching in step. If you fall out of step, what do you think happens to the coffin?'

'Oh, God.'

'Do you think William and Dominic *know* how to march in step?'

Colin and I had both been compulsorily enlisted into the Corps at our respective schools; our younger brothers had attended schools that didn't go in for Saturday mornings of khaki, blanco, Bren gun stripping, and parade-ground drill.

'Perhaps we could arrange for a practice—'

'With an empty coffin? *Left, left, left, right, left?*'

'Have you got another cigarette?'

'Hey . . .' I reached for my wallet and fished out a snapshot of Potts Lagoon, taken from the floatplane six weeks before. As if I were telling a bedtime story to Julia, I described to my brother the world inside the picture: the bears in the woods, the still-water pool, the neighbours paying visits in their boats, the irrelevance of the telephone, the fish and the game, the lilting house on its raft. I pointed out my own boat, tied to the Walderses' cabin with a cat's cradle of ropes. As a graduate student, Colin had read the standard texts on the Kwakiutl. I rattled on about how their art was a brilliant, stylized exploration of flux and chaos.

Colin sucked on his Marlboro. 'I wish I had a Potts Lagoon.'

Shelley's body, hastily buried in the sand and sprinkled with quick-lime, had turned indigo when Trelawny dug it up a month later in order to cremate it in a formal ceremony on the beach near Viareggio. Driftwood logs were burning in an iron furnace, specially constructed to Trelawny's specifications; and when 'the fire was well kindled', Shelley's corpse, disfigured and partially decomposed, was heaped into it. Byron stood by, with *Bolivar* anchored just offshore. Leigh Hunt sat in his carriage nearby, while Trelawny, a couple of local fishermen, and some members of the Tuscan militia got on with the business of the cremation.

In Trelawny's account:

More wine was poured over Shelley's dead body than he had consumed during his life. This with the oil and salt made the yellow flames glisten and quiver. The heat from the sun and the fire was so intense that the atmosphere was tremulous and wavy. The corpse fell open and the heart was laid bare. The frontal bone of the skull where it had been struck with the mattock, fell off; and, as the bottom of the head rested on the red-hot bottom bars of the furnace, the brains literally seethed, bubbled, and boiled as in a cauldron, for a very long time.

Byron could not face this scene, he withdrew to the beach and swam off to the 'Bolivar'. Leigh Hunt remained in the carriage. The fire was so fierce as to produce a white heat on the iron, and to reduce its contents to grey ashes. The only portions that were not consumed were some fragments of bones, the jaw, and the skull, but what surprised us all, was that the heart remained entire. In snatching this relic from the fiery furnace, my hand was severely burned. . . .

Byron wanted Shelley's skull, 'but remembering that he has formerly used one as a drinking cup, I was determined that Shelley's should not be so profaned'. Trelawny handed the heart to Leigh Hunt, who later presented it to Mary Shelley.

William St Clair writes:

Shelley the great pagan had a great pagan funeral. No priest was near. No prayers were said. Trelawny turned what might have been a tiresome and perhaps sordid administrative ordeal into an unforgettable drama.

Shelley's young death by drowning, and his beach funeral, ensured his apotheosis as a Romantic hero.

I could not now hear the word 'cremation' without thinking of the scene at Viareggio.

Two days after my father's death, his body was ready to be viewed in Mr Stamp's chapel of rest. I drove my mother there.

The room was lightly refrigerated, decorated with urns of white lilies. Muzak, of the kind probably known as 'light classical', and probably circulated exclusively within the undertaking trade, was playing at a volume so subdued that all one could hear was a faint mournful susurrus of woodwind and strings. The open coffin was placed on a trestle, on which had been spread a starched white tablecloth.

I stood back. My mother walked shakily forward, and I heard her racking intake of breath as she saw the waxwork figure in its wooden box.

He'd been dressed in clothes selected by my mother from his wardrobe: polished brown shoes ('Must have leather soles, can't be rubber; the crematorium won't allow it,' Mr Stamp had said); grey flannels; a salmon-pink shirt, open at the neck; a greenish-grey tweed sports jacket. His outfit suggested a picnic, or a round of golf. His unruly beard had been trimmed as neatly as Colin's, his swept-back hair combed into place with brilliantine. They had put colour in his cheeks and rouged his lips, which had been moulded into a strange smile. They'd robbed him of his character: it was as though he'd never lived.

My mother leaned over and kissed him – kissed *it* – on the mouth.

With my arm around her shoulder, we stood gazing at the unlikely piece of art that once had been my father. A minute passed – or was it ten, or just ten seconds? It wasn't a measurable time.

'I think I'm ready to go now,' my mother said.

I helped her back to the car. Inside, she said, 'It was quite like Peter, but it wasn't really Peter . . .' and began to cry, helplessly, inconsolably, as if the concrete dam of grief had burst inside her.

St Nicholas's was a tawny stone parish church, as old as England. My brother William, a film-maker, was crouched among the ancient tombstones, videoing the event, as the cormorant-crew carried the coffin into the church, followed by the family, then by a full-house congregation of relatives, friends, clerical colleagues, and ex-parishioners. The distended violet pupil of the camera lens tracked us as we came through the lych-gate, and I wouldn't have been much surprised to hear my brother call 'Lights! . . . Rolling! . . . Cut! . . . Wrap!' while we went through our parts in this classic piece of costume drama.

I took my place on the outside of the pew reserved for family, and nestled in the sombre comforts offered by the church: old stained glass, sturdy pillars, brass memorials, marble entablatures, flagstones worn smooth and engraved, faintly, with names of the people buried beneath them. Though the church was full, the dead far outnumbered the living. One could smell them in the ripe churchy odour of hassocks, hymnals, polish, and bone dust. The latest addition to their company lay just beyond my feet, at the head of the aisle, beside the corkscrew steps leading to the pulpit. My father was a freshman here, on his first day at a college whose traditions reached back into the Middle Ages.

The holy end was top-heavy with clergy robed like druids. We had a brace apiece of vicars and rectors, a dean, an archdeacon (or was he a suffragan bishop?), a canon or two . . . I lost count. The choir sat in their stalls. The organist was making heavy weather of a solemn piece by Bach.

The clergy did their thing, in the variety of Estuary English now favoured by the Church of England. I would have liked to have heard the old words:

> *Man that is born of a woman hath but a short time to live, and is full of misery. He cometh up, and is cut down, like a flower; he fleeth as it were a shadow, and never continueth in one stay.*
> *In the midst of life we are in death . . .*

But all that had gone by the board in the 1960s, when the Church tried to endear itself to the people by translating the language of the prayer book into a strained modern lingo whose tone was pitched midway between that of a kindergarten teacher and a tax accountant. But the dignified age of the church redeemed its new form of service.

As we sang a hymn, I dug into the inside pocket of my funeral suit for my page of typed notes.

All through my teens, my father and I had been at war. At twelve going on thirteen, I turned on his faith and secretly proclaimed myself an atheist. At fourteen I refused, on conscientious grounds, to take communion. At sixteen I skipped church more or less entirely. The pulpit I was about to ascend – symbol of my father's moral authority in the village – meant a lot to me, most of it bad. Watching him preach his Sunday sermon, white surplice billowing from his shoulders, I was suffused with envy and resentment when he confidently took the stage. His sermons were good; my indifference to them was more pretended than felt. But his command of the pulpit stood for me as the rigid, unreasonable, intolerant power of father over son. I had many times thought that if ever I got up there, I'd preach a sermon that would make him shiver in his shoes.

Now I had to step cautiously around his coffin to climb into my father's ordained place. Following his remembered example, I braced my arms against the pulpit's curving sides – it was like being up in the crow's nest of a square-rigger – and gained the parson's condescending view of his flock.

It was a good turnout – various in age and type, and just the sort of crowd one might expect at a well-attended reading in an American bookstore. I raked the faces with my eyes, looking for a focus point, and found three Catholic nuns, huddled together in their black habits; aliens in this overwhelmingly Protestant setting, though the church, dating back to before the Reformation, must once have been theirs. My task, I decided, was to make the nuns laugh.

I quickly raised a smile from Sister no. 1; a couple of sentences later, Sister no. 2 distinctly giggled, and I was away on home turf.

In my own fashion, I had followed in my father's footsteps, as he had followed in his father's. I had inherited the voice of an old-fashioned curate. I saw my independent living as a writer in much the same light as my father viewed his precious 'parson's freehold' (which has nothing to do with real estate, but is about intellectual liberty). In the matter of the dusty chaos of the study, where he puffed his pipe and wrote his sermons, I had managed to comfortably outshine him. Most of all, I had learned from him the flexible and eclectic form of the sermon itself, with its exposition of old texts, its stories, its drawing of morals and inferences from everyday anecdotes. 'A few days ago, I was walking down Pound Lane . . .' he might begin, and that incident would lead to the unravelling of some complicated theological point, or to the obligations of the individual in a Christian society. Over the last twenty-five years, I'd often used this tactic on my own account – though I wasn't a moralist, or a theologian, or a Christian. Sailing to Alaska, I was really walking down Pound Lane.

Now I hoped to sketch him as I remembered him most fondly – after I'd left home, after our war was over, when he and I and Colin would sit up in the drawing room of the vicarage, drinking and talking and talking and drinking, often until dawn. 'Argufying' was what he called these sessions, when we rambled about politics, sociology, and the problems of his parish – by then a vast, cheerless, council-housing estate on the outskirts of Southampton. He had been promoted to the position of Rural Dean – an ironic title for someone whose daily business lay in vandalized, graffiti-covered, urine-smelling, forty-storey tower blocks to which the most indigent of the industrial population had been consigned. Perhaps some curious streak of Episcopal humour had led the bishop to transfer him from a traditional Hampshire village to this unhappy and impoverished edge-city, but it turned my father into a reader and a thinker.

Surrounded by toppling piles of books, on social work, psychiatry, the new theology, urban history, economics; by novels bringing news of working-class life by writers like Alan Sillitoe and Stan Barstow; by government White Papers; by dozens of titles featuring the word 'Crisis' – my father, in the late 1960s, argufied himself into becoming a new man. Throughout my childhood he was a reflexive Conservative. In Southampton, he joined the Labour Party and was to be seen near the head of protest marches. He sported the badge of the Campaign for Nuclear Disarmament – the same badge that, ten years before, he had ordered me out of the house for wearing.

Turning fifty, he was suddenly more intellectually avid, quicker to rise to argument, and far more ironically self-aware than the clever university students whom I was teaching at the time. We pitched and dodged and parried through the night in front of the popping gas fire, while the dog at my father's feet slept and farted, and the supply of Spanish red ran out, and the clink of milk bottles on the front doorstep reminded him that he had an eight o'clock service to conduct in three hours' time and he'd better get some sleep.

Stepping down from the pulpit I forgot the coffin, and grazed it with my knee as I went back to my seat. After another hymn one of his younger colleagues in Southampton, an industrial chaplain, climbed the steps to talk engagingly of my father as the diocesan gadfly, the subversive joker in the Anglican pack.

The service ran longer than planned. Once the church emptied and the coffin was back inside the hearse, my mother was lost to view in a tight throng of people dressed in black. The cremation in Kettering, twelve miles away, was scheduled for 12:15, and it was already three minutes short of noon. Mr Stamp was twirling his top hat impatiently between his hands.

I said to him: 'Do you think I ought to try and get my mother out of there and into a car now?'

'Well, speaking frankly, sir, if we don't get a bloomin' move on now, we're going to lose our bloomin' slot.'

I winkled my mother out of the crowd, hustled her aboard Colin's Land Rover, and at last the funeral procession got underway, at walking speed, with Mr Stamp marching ahead of the hearse and the villagers of Little Bowden removing their hats as the coffin went by. This seemed a peculiar way of getting a move on; but as the hearse turned the bend past the last cottage on the street, I saw Mr Stamp jam his topper on his head and take a flying leap into the already open passenger door while the driver gave it the gas.

Varrooom!

My father had always been a fast driver and a nervous passenger. He was now being driven by someone who might have been moonlighting from a regular career in Formula One Grand Prix. The hearse was taking the bends in the country road like chicanes at Indianapolis. Colin, no slowcoach, was fast losing ground to the flying coffin. I drove with my foot hard on the floor, into the fog of brown dust raised by the Land Rover.

'Someone light me a cigarette, *please?*'

Someone – a brother, I think – did. Sucking on smoke, I dared a glance at the rear-view and saw a face, much as mine must have looked, contorted over the wheel; and behind that car, a trail of others, battling to keep their places in the race.

We reached a ring road, hurtled past a roundabout and, at the arrowed sign saying CREMATORIUM, the hearse braked at last, and we were transformed back into a stately funeral procession. After the ritual quarter-mile crawl in low gear, we entered the gates of a hygienic modern death factory, with its grimly marshalled gardens and walls of white concrete pretending to be marble. The crem. 'Simple, no grave to keep up and visit, and a decent way of disposal,' my father had written. His army days had given him a soldierly relish for the spartan, and a crematorium perfectly suited his impatience with anything that smacked of stuff-and-nonsense.

Under the supervision of Mr Stamp and his men in black, my brothers and I shouldered the coffin. I took, as it were, the starboard bow, with William to port, and Dominic and Colin at the stern. The weight astonished me. There had seemed so little of my father left when he died, yet now my knees were barely capable of holding up under the pressure of his gross tonnage.

'Ready?' said Mr Stamp. 'Off you go, then.'

I couldn't march, could only stumble, splay-footed, trying to keep upright as the coffin bore down on my shoulder. If I'd worried earlier that William and Dominic wouldn't know how to keep in step, I had my come-uppance now, with a body that had gone geriatric on me. Why *was* he so heavy? Or was it, perhaps, the weight of fatherhood itself that we were trying to bear?

Colin had come up with the perfect piece of music for the coffin's entry to the crem: a recording of a choral setting by Elgar, at once tender and grand, sung by the Worcester Cathedral Choir. Elgar was Worcestershire's own composer. As a boy, my father had gone to King's, the cathedral school from whose lower forms the choir was drawn. (In my turn, I'd gone to King's, too, though nothing in my time there gave me any cause for nostalgia.)

Played earlier on my nephew James's boom box, the music had made me weep: the voices of the boy trebles, coming in long slow waves like swell breaking on a beach.

> *Ecce sacerdos magnus, qui in diebus*
> *suis placuit Deo, et inventus est justus.*

Behold a great priest, who in his days pleased God, and whose coming is justice. On the crem's lousy sound system, the music was a thin drizzle of noise in the background, the splendid words inaudible.

The coffin lurched awkwardly from brother to brother, its intolerable weight giving new life to the phrase about carrying the burden of the world on one's shoulders. The aisle of the chapel stretched a very long way ahead. Our remote destination: a miniature version of the rollers at the loading bay of a department store. We trudged step by dangerously uncertain step to the faint Latin mutter of the cathedral choir. The cormorant-men, standing to attention on both sides of the rollers, grew slowly nearer, until, at last, they took my father into their professional care and helped to lay him on the conveyor that would take him to the furnace.

I tottered to a chair next to my mother and, as the prayers began, surreptitiously massaged my bruised shoulder. I didn't move my gaze off the coffin except once, to turn the page in the order of the service; and when I looked back it had vanished – gone clean through the red plush curtains from which the rollers protruded. *Abracadabra!* and my father had dematerialized, like a knotted handkerchief or a white dove.

Back at the bungalow, relatives and friends were all over the lawn, talking with their mouths full, balancing canapés and glasses; it was like a vicarage summer fayre, with everyone dressed in the wrong clothes. I had seen very few of the relatives since I was in my early teens, and I moved warily among them with a bottle in each hand, trying to pass myself off as a waiter.

'And what are you up to now? Apart from the scribbling?' said an auntly lady in her fifties. It came to me, slowly and uncomfortably, that I'd last seen her on a tennis court, in arousing frilly knickers.

How old we all were – the children of the 1950s – with our crow's feet, bifocals, paunches, jowls, bald heads, grey hair, varicose veins, turkey-wattles, back problems, cancer scares, hearing defects, and all the ills that came with second homes, stock portfolios, Volvos, time-shares in Tuscany, modest gongs and titles, and, already, a liberal sprinkling of grandchildren.

I sought out my godfather, Uncle Peter, hale and bluff at eighty. 'Well,' he said, 'you've had an interesting-sounding life.'

So I was past it, even to him.

Uncle Peter had been a naval officer during the war, and a yachts-man in peacetime. He was the real sailor in the family. We talked boats for a while, but his heart wasn't in the conversation. He'd had to sell the sloop he kept at Lymington. 'The old eyes weren't up to it. Every time I went out, I was sailing round in a dense fog, and your Aunt Connie had to put a stop to it.'

I passed Colin, who had also taken to waitering as the safest bet. 'Potts Lagoon!' he said.

By three o'clock, the cars – parked according to my father's instructions – had begun to leave for all points on the English com-pass, and the talk was of routes and shortcuts; as obsessive a topic of conversation in this country as the weather.

'Well, if you take the M45 turnoff for Coventry, you can nip down the A426 until it joins up with the A423, and then you just keep going down to Banbury. But don't go into Banbury. You need to take the road that just cuts to the side of it, and find the A361 for Chipping Norton.'

'You must look us up whenever you're in Cambridge.'

'Do drop in if you ever go to Bristol. We're only a lick and a spit off the motorway.'

The only journey not discussed, it seemed, was the one taken by my father. We'd get to making that one in our own time, on B-roads yet to be discovered.

'So you'll be going back to America?'

'Tomorrow.'

'Well, jolly nice to see you. Let's keep in touch.'

Few of us, I thought, would show up for one another's funerals.

Dominic and Ruth, his girlfriend, were staying with my mother overnight. Colin was heading back to Sheffield, William to London.

The caterers had taken care of the ruined plates of canapés and the half-empty glasses parked on every available rock and ledge in the garden. I drove to the pub at Great Oxenden, packed my bag, and sped south, thinking of my father – a little pile of ashes now, in a jar on a shelf, with a plastic tag on it, waiting for pickup.

At the outpost of Harrods at Heathrow, I bought a teddy bear and ran to catch my plane. Sitting in club class, I forswore the free drinks and sank bottle after bottle of mineral water. I made vows of abstinence from almost everything. Nicking the Arctic Circle, we flew over the north of Hudson Bay – a world of empty ice, soothing to contemplate from the snug of the cabin, 39,000 feet up. In the middle of the afternoon – nearly midnight, Harborough time – we crossed the raw and splintered peaks of the Cascades.

'Look, the Rockies!' said an assured English voice from the seat behind me.

Beyond the customs hall, Jean was waiting with Julia asleep in her stroller. A few hours earlier, it would have been a pushchair; and I was happy to be back in the American language.

'God, you look awful,' Jean said.

'It was like a long string of *Lost Weekends*,' I said.

Jean drove. I sat in the back with Julia as, now awake, she made friends with her new bear.

Julia said, 'Is my Grandad Peter really dead now?'

'Yes, Jaybird. He's really dead.'

'I'm sad.' She toyed with her bear for a moment. Then: 'Can we go to Coe Park now?'

For the next few days, I plunged back into family life – into cooking dinner, Disney movies on video, Lego, swings and slides, A. A. Milne at bedtime, singsongs.

Oh, they built the ship Titanic, to sail the ocean blue.
They thought they had a ship that the water could never get through.
So they had a big surprise when the water came inside –
It was sad when the great ship went down.

It was sad, it was sad, it was sad, it was sad;
It was sad when the great ship went down.

Oh, uncles and aunts,
Little children lost their pants.
It was sad when the great ship went down . . .

I dug a hole leading down to the bottom of the world in the sand of Golden Gardens beach, and visited the Malayan sun bears at the Woodland Park Zoo.

The salmon season was in full swing, and there were now scheduled flights from Seattle to the fishing camps of British Columbia. Early on a Monday morning, the three of us drove to the floatplane terminal at the head of Lake Washington.

'Just four more weeks, Jaybird. Then you and Mommy will fly up to Alaska, and we'll all have a vacation together. We'll catch fish from the boat and have them for supper. We'll see real bears in the wild. We'll see whales. We'll sail to a magical island and dig for treasure. We'll find families with kids for you to play with . . .'

But the futures market is not one in which three-and-a-half-year-olds can be persuaded to invest with any confidence.

'You're always going away, Daddy.'

'Look, Julia! See the floatplanes?'

Unfaithful to my daughter for the third time in three months, I rode off into the sky again, feeling like the Wicked Witch of the West.

Flying low through gin-clear morning air, the plane followed the route of the Inside Passage. It was mid-ebb on a big tide, and the water surface was creased and pleated by the drag of the tidal streams as they ran out to the Pacific. In narrow passes the current was braided, like heavy rope, and breaking white. In the open Strait of Georgia, one could see the serpentine outlines of eddies, miles in diameter, containing strings of smaller eddies; faint pencil doodles on the skin of the sea. The general drift of things was clear enough: the whole body of water was travelling south and west. But for every current there was a countercurrent, and the view through the plexiglas window of the plane was of a map of confusion, all scrolls and curlicues. I was reminded of the famous remark (made in 1932) by the physicist Horace Lamb, speaking to the British Association for the Advancement of Science: 'I am an old man now, and when I die and go to Heaven there are two matters on which I hope for enlightenment. One is quantum electrodynamics, and the other is the turbulent motion of fluids. And about the former I am really rather optimistic.'

At Nanaimo, we dipped into the sea to refuel and clear Canadian customs. Then we were up to 4,500 feet, flying at 128 knots, with the shadows of isolated clouds looking like Rorschach inkblots on the green water below. The clouds began to thicken underneath us as we neared Desolation Sound, where the mountaintops came crowding in from the east: splintered pinnacles of bare black rock, ledges and rifts of blinding snow. *Alastor* territory. The plane bounced and slewed on the boils and whirlpools of unstable air. The pilot, sitting next to me, called, 'Hang on to your hats!' over the din of the engine, and I watched the altimeter needle jiggering up and down on the dial.

The pilot found a convenient cloud-window over Knight Inlet, and dove neatly through it. When we splashed down off Minstrel Island, the water felt thick as glue under the floats and the plane came to a stop within a second or two. I was the only passenger to disembark at the dock.

I watched the plane wheel jauntily away and make its roaring, skiddering take-off from the wave tops. Then I sat on the stern of an upturned dinghy, seabag at my feet, and tried to get my bearings. After only nine weeks – I counted them off on my fingers – I felt like the returning Rip Van Winkle. I wanted the landscape to somehow confirm my absence from it, but in this country of evergreens an overcast July 1st looked no later in the year than a sunny April 20th, and nothing about Minstrel Island marked the passage in the voyage that had led to England and back. I stared at the tarred pilings, the rotting cabins, the sheltering hulks. They looked like last night's view – no further away in time than that.

I found one of the men who'd been at dinner – a son of the resort – tinkering with a skiff, and gave him $20 to run me down to Potts

Lagoon. He gave me a look of offhand recognition, as if he, too, remembered me from last night, and we set off at speed down the Blow Hole and into Clio Channel.

I sat up in the bow, with the boat slamming from wave to wave in the brisk easterly – the same wind that had been blowing back in April. The seventy-five-horse outboard limited our conversation to a few hoarse yells.

'That your sailboat down at Potts?'

'Yeah!'

'Thought it were!'

Trailing a great rooster-tail of wake, we roared through the outer islands and into the narrow entrance to the lagoon.

The boat was exactly as I had left it, tied up in front of the Walderses' floathouse. No one was home. I hoisted myself aboard, found the keys in their usual place, and removed the hatchboards. The air in the saloon was fresh – not a whiff of the pickled smell I'd expected. The bilges were dry, the batteries fully charged. Apart from a few splashes of dried gullshit on the coachroof, I could find only one sign of my having been away.

While my father had been dying, the boat had been growing a green hula-skirt of weed that descended from its waterline and cloaked its nether parts from sight. In the still, unruffled lagoon, algae ran as wild as in a neglected aquarium. On the exposed port side, where photosynthesis had gone on unimpeded, the tendrils of weed hung down six or seven feet deep. Metastasis again.

It came off easily enough when attacked with a deck-scrubber, and I spent half an hour hauling myself around the boat in the dinghy, getting myself covered in chlorophyll-green slime. I was glad of the work, for the reassurance it provided that my spell in England had not been a mere eyeblink back here in British Columbia.

I was up in the cockpit drinking coffee when John Walders and his dog arrived by skiff, towing two good $150 logs. He cut the motor and drifted in to the raft.

'Hi! We were just beginning to wonder what had happened to you.'

VI. THE CHARRED REMAINS

Awake at first light, I had two thoughts. The first was that the aching soreness of my left shoulder, imprinted by the weight of my father's coffin, wasn't going to go away and that I'd probably carry it for the rest of my life, an honourable stigma. The second was that the interior of the boat itself was constructed on the model of a top-of-the-line coffin. Before, I'd always thought that the Swedish passion for dark varnished carpentry, grain matched to grain, in teak and mahogany, made the inside of the boat look like an old-fashioned London club. Now it made me think of Mr Stamp, canoe burials, and the nineteenth-century habit of calling a ship a coffin if it was crank or leaky.

Or was it, rather, that coffins were deliberately designed to look like boats? In most societies, from Anglican England to animist Kwakiutl or Haida villages, death was seen as a solo voyage to a new world, and the coffin was the ultimate single-hander's vessel, solidly built for the long and stormy passage to the hereafter. All the early voyagers to the Northwest found canoes, hung in the trees, containing human remains and supplies for a voyage. Peter Puget, in Discovery Bay, saw 'a Canoe suspended to a Tree with a perfect Skeleton in the Inside & others in a forward State of Decay – There were likewise Square Boxes, Bows & Arrows Fishing Implements and a stick or two of Clams laid by them'.

I thought of my father in his open boat, dressed for the outdoors, artfully chilled, the waxwork mariner, as I dressed myself for the clammy cold of dawn on Potts Lagoon. The kettle came to the boil. I made a thermos of coffee and, moving quietly so as not to wake the Walderses, undid the bowlines I'd tied nine weeks before, and pushed the boat out from the raft, letting it drift a good distance before I started the engine. Not a leaf was moving on the madrona trees. The water was black and mirror-smooth. Even at tick-over speed, the noise of the engine was an affront to the deep silence of the forest and the sea. I crept out of the lagoon at a bare three knots, getting used to the feel of the boat again and trying not to fracture the eerie, suspenseful calm of a day yet to be born.

The tide ran earlier here than in Georgia Strait, and the ebb was already nearly at an end. The wet rocks, from which the water was shrinking, looked lacquered. The iodine smell of seaweed gave a bitter tang to the air. The boat slid down Baronet Passage, between Harbledown and West Cracroft islands, under a luminous overcast through which the sun was just beginning to cast long shadows.

Passing a broad half-moon of stony beach on West Cracroft, I saw a shifting shadow in the stillness and turned to look more closely. A black bear was foraging along the water's edge, then another shadow shifted: the bear's mate, following at a fifty-yard distance. I stealthily turned the boat around and drifted inshore.

No stealth was needed. The bears were intent on their breakfast; hindquarters up, heads down low, they disdained to notice the boat, even as I brought it right alongside the first bear, in six feet of water. I could see the individual hairs of its fur, the ripple of muscle beneath the coat, its big, watery brown eyes. It lifted its head briefly, only to gaze straight through me, then resumed its search for shellfish.

The myopia of bears gave them their gullible character in Indian stories, where they were always being conned by smarter creatures like the raven. At thirty-something feet, I apparently was invisible to the bear. Maybe it had registered the blurred boat as a drifting log. Maybe the stench of seaweed masked my human smell. There was, after all, some truth in the schoolboy rephrasing of the Easter hymn

'Gladly my Cross I'd bear' into 'Gladly, my cross-eyed bear', sung in Worcester Cathedral with heathen gusto.

Small stones crunched underfoot as the bear extended its investigations. With one paw, it tipped over a boulder the size of a domestic gas stove with a shocking, hollow clonk: the bear didn't grunt or sigh; the motion as effortless as a man turning over a pebble. It wedged its long muzzle into the shallow pool left by the boulder and chomped down some small but evidently satisfying morsel of seafood.

Moving slowly, I reached for the camera on the shelf in the saloon and ran through the dozen remaining exposures. When the film came back from the processors in Juneau, weeks later, I found some fine pictures of two boulders. The larger was black, the smaller grey. Showing them to Julia, I had to point out which one was the bear.

'True-life?' she said, the scepticism and disappointment large in her eyes.

'True-life,' I said. 'Look, there's its nose, and you see the eye here?'

I watched the bears for twenty minutes; then, as the tide turned, they came together and shambled back to the woods. Though black bears don't often attack people, except to defend their cubs, I thought a lot about the power of that enormous stone-rolling paw and vowed never to knowingly share a beach, however big, with a bear of any colour.

By mid-morning I was in Port McNeill, on Vancouver Island, lugging sacks of groceries down to the boat and filling the tanks with diesel and fresh water. The next proper town would be Prince Rupert, about two hundred and seventy-five miles to the north-west; I had to stock up for a week or ten days of isolation, with anchorages in remote inlets. As soon as my goods were stowed, I was away again under headsail and engine, moving west along Queen Charlotte Strait.

On the radio, a vessel named *Trianna* reported finding a body floating in the sea. The caller, a man, sounded like a pleasure-boater, his voice breathless and squeaky as he described his gruesome discovery. On the other end of the line, the Coast Guard officer at Comox was languidly matter-of-fact.

'You got the lat–long coordinates on that?'

The man on *Trianna* kept the Transmit button pressed down as he and someone else aboard – his wife, I guessed – scrambled to read the numbers off the GPS. He reported the latitude as longitude, and was duly corrected.

'Is that a male or a female? Any name on the clothing?'

I'd been shown more sympathetic interest by the same station when back in April I reported a large deadhead in Johnstone Strait. But a human body couldn't be considered a hazard to navigation; just a tedious pile of paperwork on some poor sap's desk. I wondered if the couple would continue their vacation, or if the sight of the corpse would turn them, shaken, back toward home.

In the spring of 1980, while idling an afternoon away in the newly purchased motorboat I kept at Hammersmith, I found a body spreadeagled on a mud bank in the tidal Thames near Chiswick. As I reported to the police over the phone, twenty minutes later, the body was that of a very plump teenage girl. She was wearing a pair of brand-new knee-length leather boots. When the police launch arrived, I led them to where she lay, beached by the falling tide; once the police had her in view, I ran for Hammersmith, and didn't take the boat out again for a month.

The body did not belong to a teenage girl. At the coroner's inquest, where I was called to give evidence, I found out she was a woman in her sixties, slenderly built. Several days' immersion in brackish water had blown her up like a balloon, removing every wrinkle and restoring her to a grotesque, tubby youthfulness. She had been treated, repeatedly, for depression. Leaving a long, incoherent letter on her dressing table, she walked to the river and threw herself in. The pathologist who examined the body recited a grim list of cuts and contusions on her hands and arms.

The coroner said: 'All these are consistent with drowning, in your experience?'

The pathologist agreed; most people who drowned in shallow water injured themselves in just this way.

So death by drowning was not a peaceful leave-taking, in which one's life passed before one's eyes, a sepia-tinted period movie. Even determined suicides clutched and scrabbled for survival, tearing their hands on sharp rocks, the outraged body fighting to repudiate the desperate reasoning of the mind.

When Shelley was washed ashore at Viareggio, after ten days in the sea, he must have resembled an obese child.

'*Trianna*, maintain your present position, please. A patrol vessel will be on its way there shortly.'

After the reliable deeps of the labyrinth, Queen Charlotte Strait was a tricky piece of water on which to be afloat. Twelve to fourteen miles wide, it was dotted about with shallows, reefs, drying rocks, and islets no bigger than the average four-bedroom house. The depth-sounder was all over the place, three hundred feet suddenly giving way to thirty or less. The chart was a tangled bird's nest of blue contour lines, as the cartographers sketched the holes, trenches, plateaus, and pinnacles beneath the surface.

Six miles to the north of where I was sailing, the Vancouver expedition nearly came to an early end when *Discovery* grounded on a submerged reef. All through the foggy morning of 7 August 1792, *Discovery* and *Chatham* had drifted on the tidal currents, barely able to make steerageway. When the sun burned through the fog, soon after noon, they found themselves in Queen Charlotte Strait, in hazy visibility, with the shore to the south-west still lost behind white cliffs of fog, and the steep, unfriendly mainland coast bending widely away to the north-west. For the first time since April, they had a misty glimpse of open ocean ahead.

A light offshore breeze from the north-north-west blew up soon after the fog lifted, and the two ships began to make slowly to windward, *Discovery* in the lead. Soundings were tried for – first with the fifty-fathom, then with the deep-sea line – but no bottom was found. Under full sail, *Discovery* was making three knots through the water when, at four thirty, as Vancouver wrote, 'we suddenly grounded on a bed of sunken rocks. . . . A signal indicating our situation was immediately made to the *Chatham*, she instantly anchored in fifty fathoms water, about a cable and a half [three hundred yards] distant from us, and we immediately received all her boats to our assistance.'

In Thomas Manby's account:

The Ship struck on a reef of rocks, every effort was made to disengage her, unfortunately the Ebb tide was running strong, which soon left her immoveable. The yards and Top Masts were struck and got over, in hopes of preventing her tumbling over. Our fears were too well founded: after laying upright for half an hour, a terrible crash ensued, that brought the Ship on her broadside. Fortunately the Breeze died away, and a Calm following, cheered our spirits up with the enlivening hope [that] the flowing tide might again float her, if the Rocks had not pierced her bottom. Seven long and tedious hours we sat on the Ship's side, without the ability of giving her any assistance, but that of carrying out an anchor and three cables, ready to heave upon at high Water.

In fact, more was done to help the ship than Manby suggests. Vancouver took as much weight off *Discovery* as possible, jettisoning the supplies of fuel and fresh water, along with much of the ballast from the bilges; he then ordered his men to shore up the ship's fallen side with spars and topmasts.

During this time, Zachary Mudge and Joseph Baker – neither of them a very competent artist – repaired in one of the small boats to sketch the wreck in their logbooks. Both drawings show *Discovery* careened hard over on her starboard side, the bow of the ship rearing skyward, the windows of Captain Van's private stateroom grazing the sea. In the foreground, two canoes full of rubbernecking Indians stand off at a safe distance from this scene of white men's folly. In the engraver's improved version of Mudge's sketch, the Indians are shown tactlessly holding up sea otter pelts for sale.

'A very irksome and perilous situation', in Captain Van's words. By nine o'clock, at low water, 'the ship's forefoot was only in about three and a half foot water, whilst her stern was in four fathoms'. According to Manby, 'the fate of the Ship appeared to be inevitable for three hours, and had she gone to pieces, we had the pleasing satisfaction of being rescued from the Wreck by our Consort the *Chatham*'. Manby's phrasing here suggests that the loss of *Discovery* would not have made him too unhappy. To save the ship is every seaman's instinct, but among the young gentlemen on Vancouver's quarterdeck there ensued some mixed feelings when, at 2:00 a.m., *Discovery* at last came upright on the flood tide and was hauled off the reef by the stern, without much apparent damage, leaving the expedition to continue, as Vancouver wrote, 'the adventurous service in which we were engaged'.

After such a close shave, Captain Van had the 'inexpressible satisfaction' at having been saved from the humiliation of losing his ship – a humiliation over which the juvenile Honourables Pitt and Stuart would have crowed unmercifully, and which would certainly have put an end to Vancouver's naval career.

Between the top of Vancouver Island and the bottom of Calvert Island lay a forty-mile stretch of ocean coast, a lee shore, swept by a continuous and sometimes very high westerly swell. Waves begun in storms off Japan would fetch up here as glassy rollers, steepening sharply as they felt the drag of the shallowing sea floor. The usual jumping-off point for the hop across this nasty corner of the North Pacific was Hurst Island, one of a string of small islands off the northeast tip of Vancouver Island – a lump of rock and forest barely a square mile in size.

The yachtsmen's pilot-book for the area warned one to stay clear of the perfect shelter of Harlequin Bay on the east side of the island – partly because of its rock-strewn entrance, and partly because of its unfriendly inhabitants.

One is advised against hiking to the east side of the island. Former residents have sighted a 'hairy man,' and strong evidence points to the existence of a Sasquatch family on the island, perhaps centred on Meeson Cone above Harlequin Bay. Indian residents of nearby Balaklava Island have had similar experiences, and now refuse to go ashore at either place.

The book, John Chappell's *Cruising Beyond Desolation Sound*, was otherwise drily informative; useful but dull. The sasquatch paragraph was by far its liveliest moment. Chappell might as well have described the perils of getting too close to Komogwa, with appropriate lat–long coordinates.

He recommended a U-shaped crevice in the island's west side, and a good three-quarters of a mile from the sasquatch lair on Meeson Cone. When I entered God's Pocket at five that afternoon, none of the fishing boats and yachts I'd expected were waiting to make the early-morning crossing to Calvert. I tied up at the empty float belonging to the little resort at the head of the inlet. The owners' extended family were the only guests in the handful of cabins overlooking the water. They'd come here for their annual reunion over the long Canada Day weekend, and at supper I found myself sandwiched between hearty great-grandparents – all older than my father – and a quartet of quarrelling heat-struck toddlers. The presence of the children stopped me from asking the grown-ups about the hairy neighbours on the hill: I could too easily imagine Julia's nightmares if she believed that a sasquatch tribe lived a few blocks up our street.

The pilot-book nicely reinforced the point made in the essay 'On the Cultural Track of the Sasquatch' by Wayne Suttles. 'I do not think we can assume that Indian categories are the same as Western ones. I see no evidence of a dichotomy of "real" vs. "mythical" or "natural" vs. "supernatural" in Coast Salish thought.' Between familiar creatures like the bear and the mink, and fantastic ones like the thunder-eagle and the double-headed flying sisiutl, there stretched a smooth continuum of increasing rarity, ranging from seen-most-days-by-ordinary-people to seen-very-infrequently-and-only-by-persons-with-special-gifts. The sasquatch lay somewhere mid-continuum, and quite often was glimpsed by lay observers. Beyond it lay the pantheon of even stranger beings; animals capable of instant self-transformation, and likely to wreak havoc in human affairs.

Suttles wrote: 'A description of Coast Salish culture that is truly "emic" – that is, organized by native categories – should describe whales and bears, sasquatches and two-headed serpents, all under the same heading as part of the "real" world of the Coast Salish.' It's a modest, commonsensical statement, yet no anthropologist of the Boas generation recognized its obvious truth. Even Claude Lévi-Strauss, the great cultural relativist, leaps for the word 'supernatural' whenever he meets a creature in an Indian story that doesn't fit with his rationalist, Linnaean version of nature.

That sasquatches and two-headed serpents should coexist on equal terms with other more common animals – in a white pilot-book as in Indian tales – was endemic to this landscape of fogs and mists, long twilights, dense forests, thick soupy water, and mysterious, utterly inaccessible mountains and deeps. Identifying creatures on slight and fragmentary evidence, by imaginative guesswork, was always an everyday activity here. You had to act on a sudden displacement of the shadows in the trees, seen from the corner of your eye, or on the large, vague gleam of something moving in the water below your canoe.

An eight-hundred-pound brown bear, seen standing on its hind legs as it craned to reach a bunch of high berries, would be a manlike hairy giant in anybody's book. The moment you assign a separate verbal category, 'giant', as distinct from the category 'bear', you are well up the road that leads to two-headed serpents and thunder-eagles. The art and stories of the Northwest Coast, with their marvellous beasts and beings, reflect the inevitable mind-set of a people who spent a great deal of their time peering apprehensively into the dark wood and the hidden depths of the sea – and saw their fears take monstrous shapes, in that region lying just beyond the limit of normal twenty-twenty vision.

Outside the shelter of the island, the water was like a bolt of grey silk, lightly undulating in the first intimations of the ocean swell ahead. Soon the swell was regular and well defined; rhythmical pulses of energy, like rippling muscles, moving at speed through the windless calm. The boat was pitching easily as it rode the low hills. I switched on the VHF to catch the 6:45 a.m. forecast and the weather reports from coastal stations.

There was disquieting news from Egg Island – the halfway mark between Vancouver and Calvert – where the lighthouse-keeper was estimating the offshore wind at twenty knots, a high figure for so early in the morning. Such a wind might easily build to thirty or forty knots by 11:00, which would put me in serious trouble. I called the lighthouse on channel 9 to make sure that the keeper wasn't being misquoted.

He wasn't. 'It looks to be getting a little blowy out there,' he said.

'That's funny. Where I am, there's no wind at all.'

That was typical, he said. Sometimes he'd have a flat calm at Egg Island, in Queen Charlotte Sound, while a regular gale was tearing up the strait just a few miles away.

I got the pilot-book from downstairs. Miles Inlet, on the mainland shore, promised 'shelter from all winds', and there was no mention of mythical beasts. I charted a zigzag course to get through the clutter of islands, rocks, and shoals, and set out for the inlet. During the ninety-minute passage, the wind began to fill in strongly from the north-west; by the time I had McEwan Rock abeam, running blind on a heading of 042° for an entrance that was perfectly invisible, I was jittery with relief at having aborted the crossing of Queen Charlotte Sound. The swell, sharpened by the wind, had begun to break, and surf was growling round the stern of the boat as I clung, trustfully, to my magnetic line.

A troop of Dall's porpoises elected to escort me into the harbour. They came up, chuffing explosively, on both sides of the cockpit, then dived ahead of the bow in strict scissor-formation. This had happened to me before: a difficult entrance made unexpectedly companionable and easy by porpoises who appeared to present themselves as local pilots. Coincidence, of course; it had to be. If I believed that of the porpoises, I'd soon find myself believing in sasquatches and sisiutls.

Too many submerged rocks bordered the compass course for me to make the necessary experiment, of deviating from the heading to see if the porpoises tried to correct my mistake. As soon as the dark cleft in the woods declared itself, a cable away, they went back to sea, leaving me with the spooked sensation that I was turning into an inadvertent animist. When you're alone out here, I thought, it's hard to resist the temptation to put two and two together to make five. Yesterday, I'd laughed at John Chappell for his family of sasquatches; now I had to laugh at myself for my porpoise-pilots.

The entrance channel was a long straight aisle of water, no more than two boat lengths wide, flanked by massive inky cedars. A doe and fawn scarpered at the sight of me: I listened to the snapping of twigs and the metallic clatter of hooves on rock. The channel dead-ended in a narrow pool as still as syrup, despite the wind in the tree canopy. The only disturbance was a tidal waterfall, at the pool's north end, which wheezed and chuckled amiably in my ear as I let the anchor go.

At nine o'clock, the day still yawned ahead of me, its hours like dusty miles. I hadn't faced such leisure in weeks, and was afraid of what it might bring. I scrubbed a bit of deck, drained a fuel filter in the engine, splashed around the pool in the dinghy, tried to read, tried to write, ate an early lunch, and watched the rising tide drown the waterfall and climb the sheer earthen bank; the exposed rocks and roots, welded to their reflections, formed another fine totem pole of grimacing faces. I lost ten minutes to photography. Five hours gone. Too many still to go. I would have liked to move to another anchorage, just for the moving's sake, but I could see the cedars' topmost branches thrashing in the wind and didn't dare to budge.

There was no avoiding my father now.

In the last two weeks he'd somehow broken free of the constraints of time. Before, he had inhabited each period in his life so fully and with such conviction that it was difficult, at any given moment, to imagine him ever having been otherwise. He'd brought to dying the same conscientious regard for form and performance that he'd given to being a soldier or a priest. Now, suddenly, all the people whom my father had been were with me, all at once. One could view him, simultaneously, from every angle and in every guise, like a dismembered killer whale on a painted chest – argufying from the left, preaching from the right; in his forties, twenties, fifties, thirties; bearded and clean-shaven; in battle dress, and cassock; swaddled in blankets in a wheelchair, and playing cricket on a windswept Cornish beach. For a returning ghost, if that is what he was, my father was disconcertingly lively and paradoxical.

Not for the first or the last time, I feared his arrival on the scene.

An interminable morning, in the autumn of 1945. I was three – a few months younger than Julia was now – and each minute was taking hours to pass. I'd played in the sandpit, digging holes. I'd visited my guinea pig in his cage in the potting shed. He was a creature of disappointingly low emotional wattage, and no use as a confidant. For elevenses, I'd had one of the last of the season's tomatoes, skinned by my mother, with a few grains of rationed sugar to sweeten its soft and bloody pulp.

Trains came and went on the line that ran within half a mile of the house, but none was *his* train. I kept on hearing their whistles, the heavy breathing of the locomotives, and the percussive rumble of the wagons on the rails.

'Only goods,' my mother said through the open kitchen window. She was a stranger to me that morning: her friendly jumper and slacks were gone, replaced by an ironed cotton frock and high heels. She was wearing scent. Her lips were rouged a dark scarlet.

I could remember meeting my father once, as a visitor on a brief leave: he had made no great impression on me. Now he was coming to live with us 'for ever and ever', as my mother said. I found her joy perturbing. I thought that she and I were happy as we were, and needed no third party in our life together; though I was much excited by the idea of meeting the train.

Our village, Hempton, had its own railway halt on the far side of the green, where the slow trains from Norwich made their last stop before Fakenham, a mile farther up the line. More hamlet than village, Hempton was a crossroads of farm workers' cottages with a scattering of 1930s bungalows. Just up the road from us lay Mr Banham's flour mill; beyond that, the camp for German POWs. A few miles to the south was an American airforce base. Convoys of military trucks, laden with gypsies and 'DPs', American airmen and German prisoners, gave wartime Hempton the illusion of busyness and importance. In the dead of night, long before the clopping hooves of the milkman's blinkered horse, I'd hear trucks crawling past our windows in low gear and the songs of drunken soldiers.

In 1942, my parents had paid a few hundred pounds for a white-washed, flint-fronted house on the village street. With three bed-rooms, it had at least one more than most houses in Hempton, and was grandly named The White House, Hempton Green. This out-of-the-way corner of rural Norfolk had been chosen by my father because it was far from any target city but conveniently close to the European theatre of war in which he expected to serve: from Hempton to Nazi-occupied Holland was barely two hundred miles along the flight path taken by the American bombers. In the event, after the Dunkirk evacuation of 1940 and a period of training in Scotland, my father had been posted to North Africa, Italy, and Palestine; places from which there was no nipping home to Hempton at weekends, as he'd ingeniously planned.

At last, my mother announced that it was time to go, and we set off across the green – a hillocky wasteland, overgrown with gorse, and veined with narrow forking paths. A wooded enclosure at the centre of the green held a plain Victorian chapel. Nearby, the idiot was tethered to his stake. In fine weather, he was put out to grass like a goat; a boy-man, dressed in hand-me-downs, with an oversize tweed cap on his head, who yelled and pointed, dancing up and down on the end of his rope.

'You mustn't say "idiot",' my mother said. 'That's rude. He's simple.'

But everyone called him 'the idiot'. He had no other name. I thought him more monkey than human, but was captivated by his clumsily waved hand and his big grin, which exposed irregular teeth, yellow as cheese.

'Come on, J. – don't stare.'

'Yah! Yah! Yah!' The idiot gibbered encouragingly at me, trying to make friends.

'We'll miss Daddy's train.'

I had forgotten my father and his train. I had to be carried across the rest of the common to the halt, where we stood on the platform for another age of waiting. Wind sifted through the tall grasses by the side of the empty track. Then came a faint muttering in the rails, which grew steadily and more urgent, until the clock-faced engine showed, trailing long dishevelled tresses of steam. As it approached, it took over the world with its commanding heat and stink and noise. The brakes hissed. Carriage-couplings clanked and shuddered. Out of the din and swirling smoke, my father was born, like Jupiter manifesting himself in a thundercloud.

He was an angular giant, tanned to the colour of a horse chestnut by the Middle Eastern sun. As he and my mother embraced on the platform, and my eyes stung with smuts, I knew that a phase of life had suddenly ended. Till now, I'd been the star of the show; hence-forth I'd be a supernumerary, the family spear carrier.

His belongings were packed in a khaki army kitbag with his name painted in black letters on the side: MAJ. J.P.C.P. RABAN R.A. For months, my mother had been teaching me to read, and I pored over the inscription. My father's army rank was an intriguing palimpsest: beneath the MAJ. lay the scrubbed-out remains of the word CAPT. I couldn't begin to guess at the meaning of this puzzle, but the old and new letters, on the nubby canvas weave of the bag, suggested to my mind (or so it now seems to me) some dawning notion of doubleness, ambiguity, danger.

As if in an afterthought, my father unbent himself – in sections, like a crane – to lift me up level with his face. The ascent was dizzying for me, the ground plummeting away beneath my feet. He was all bristles; his chin blue from the journey, his uniform as rough as cornstalks. I dimly recognized the fruity smell of his pipe tobacco. Riding insecurely on this giant's shoulders, I was seized with panic.

I had no physical substance worth speaking of, thanks to a chronic disorder of the intestines known as coeliac. In snapshots from the forties, I look made of sticks and string. But what I lacked in weight, I made up for in ego. I knew I was an object of unusual interest and concern. My diet was monitored meal-to-meal, and I spent much time throwing up into the toilet bowl, my forehead cradled in my mother's hands. By the time my father came home from the war, I considered being cosseted my right, and realized, as soon as I set eyes on my father, that he wasn't the cosseting type.

My father at twenty-seven had little experience of dealing with children, sick or well. His idea of play was rough-housing of the sort he'd enjoyed at boarding school and in the officers' mess. So he set out to get acquainted with his son by introducing him to games that subalterns might have played, after the silver was cleared from the mess table and the loyal toast drunk.

On the afternoon he came home, it was still warm enough to have tea in the garden. My mother laid out places on the lawn. My father had changed from his uniform into his old school cricket flannels, with a white jersey and open-necked shirt. There were scones straight from the oven – my mother must've had a private arrangement with Mr Banham's flour mill – and pats of rare butter. My parents couldn't stop touching each other. I sat, scowling and excluded, munching scones.

My mother cleared away the tea things. My father scooped me up and looked around the garden, searching for a suitable celebratory game.

A water cask stood at the back of the house, where brick and flint gave way to ancient creosoted wood. I couldn't see over the top of it, but had sometimes been held up to peer into its black depths. Wriggly mosquito larvae bred there – pollywogs, we called them. Full of ugly life at its surface, the dark and dusty water promised much bigger, nastier things living farther down.

Hoisted by the heels into the air, I found myself staring, in terror, at my father's laughing, inverted face. His mouth was opening and shutting as he talked nonsense, some kind of man-to-man language for which I had no dictionary or primer. He was dangling me over the brimming barrel and all its grey, squirming creatures.

I tried to scream, but it turned to a retch as I threw up, profusely, into the water.

We got off on the wrong foot, my father and I.

I could hear the links of anchor chain redisposing themselves, one by one, along the mud bottom, the boat swinging slowly around to face the new flood tide. It was nearly dark. The wind overhead had died, and the only sound in the inlet was the fiery crackle of the waterfall, a hundred and fifty yards at my back.

I hardly knew whether I was in Norfolk in 1945, or British Columbia in 1996; in a double exposure, one landscape was superimposed on the other. I opened a can of leek soup and chopped mushrooms for an omelette. I was now exactly twice my father's age then – and as a father to a three-year-old myself, I saw myself standing in his shoes, and felt the pang of appalled helplessness that must have seized him at that moment. The war had robbed him of the chance to learn to be a parent. Confronted with that strange, sickly, resentful child, he summoned up his courage and, like a shy man making an inept pass, lunged.

I sat in my mother's lap, sobbing and swallowing the taste of vomit, while my father, crouched on his knees in his cricket clothes, tried to make amends.

How keenly he must have looked forward to his homecoming; he cannot possibly have anticipated this miserable domestic scene, in which his only child's most fervent wish was that he'd go back to The War, where he belonged.

Memories of early childhood are never trustworthy. Memory always has its own dark purpose, often hidden from the rememberer; and it is a ruthless editor, with a facile knack for supplying corroborative detail. It's impossible to draw hard-and-fast distinctions between deep-dredge memory, retrieving material directly from the silt in which it has lain for many years, and the shallow-dredge variety, in which one remembers only an earlier act of remembering. Freud warned: 'Our childhood memories show us our earliest years not as they were but as they appeared at the later periods when the memories were aroused.' In fifty years, I'd had ample time to revisit the day when my father came home – going there on each occasion with a different agenda.

Now that my father was dead, I wondered if the scene might not be a work of self-serving fiction. Yet the horrible depths of the cask, the kitbag, the arriving train, the gesticulating idiot, the taste of sugary, overripe tomato – these were as real to me as the blackening cedars of Miles Inlet. Approaching the memory for the nth time, with a new agenda, I wanted to fault it, but could find no flaw except, perhaps, those pollywogs. Do mosquitoes in Norfolk really breed in November?

The boat rolled like a barrel in the swell. Leaving Miles Inlet at oh-dark-thirty, I'd winched up the mainsail to help steady the boat on the crossing, but the sail flapped and banged in the lifeless air as I stumbled toward Egg Island, rolling 35° one way, then 35° the other, as measured by the pendulum swing of the clinometer's little black ball. Down below, everything was on the slide, led by a heavy toolbox, a bottle of olive oil, and a dozen fugitive books. I had no appetite for breakfast.

To the west, the nearest land was Kamchatka, 2,700 miles away; the exhausted Pacific wave-trains were slopping up against the BC mainland and bouncing back, raising a steep, confused, but syrup-smooth sea. Behind me, a tug towing a bargeful of containers was exposing its rust-coloured bottom paint to the sun, and I feared for the health of its cargo: the oceans are littered with twenty-ton containers, floating awash like uncharted aluminium reefs and plenty big enough to sink a boat the size of mine.

Drawing level with Egg Island, I was overtaken by a purse-seiner, and struggled to focus it in the binoculars while it climbed briefly into view on the swells. Each time I found it, a fresh wall of water rose to curtain it from sight. *Chirikof . . . Seattle.* This was late in the season for a salmon boat to be making the run north; and from the look of its spanking cherry-red and sky-blue paintwork, it had been detained at Fishermen's Terminal for artistic reasons. It fell into a hole in the ocean, then soared high above the mountaintops on the eastern horizon. At the back of the deckhouse, arms stretched wide, as if gripping a horizontal girder for balance, stood a beanpole man, too skinny for his clothes, with a curly grizzled beard and abundant grey hair swept back across his skull. The sea blotted him out. When it covered him again, I saw that a pipe was lodged in the left side of his mouth.

The resemblance was dizzying. Weeks would pass before I got used to the fact that my father had shipped himself aboard half the boats in the Alaskan fishing fleet. He was the elderly hand, probably the cook, called Pop by the younger crew; they would bear with his stories of old times on the fishing grounds, and make fun of him behind his back.

It was a strange career move for my father, whose passion for maritime history went hand in hand with a deep mistrust of the sea. When he was made vicar of a parish outside Lymington, on the Solent, he bought an ancient wooden dinghy and named it *Sheltie*, in honour of my mother's seafaring Shetland ancestors. I remember three or four outings under sail, in gentle weather, each of them fraught with crises and alarms, before the boat was retired to a permanent berth in the shrubbery outside my father's study window. So it was doubly surprising to find him resurrected as a hoary shellback on the fringes of the North Pacific.

I watched *Chirikof* gain the shelter of Calvert Island, five miles or so ahead of me, while I stood braced at the wheel, contemplating a further hour at least of rocking and rolling through the swell. The motion was tiring, but not nauseating. Since childhood, I could hear much better through my left ear than my right, so that even on land my inner-ear system was busy balancing a life that appeared to be led continuously on the slant. My defective hearing made me too insensitive to be seasick – a happy discovery made at fifteen, in a North Sea gale, aboard the Aberdeen-to-Shetland packet. The ship's dark corridors were slippery with passengers' vomit, and I skated my way to the crew's quarters, where, at midnight, I was fed bacon sandwiches until, to general disappointment, I was pronounced immune. When we docked at Lerwick, we were a company of sheeted ghosts, everyone pronouncing this the worst crossing in memory. For me, it was the best, most vivid part of my three-week holiday. Knowing nothing then of the causes of seasickness, I put my cheerful bacon-sandwich feast down to the salt in my veins and, gloating over the miseries of the landlubbers, swanked all over the ship.

Discovery and *Chatham* made the crossing to Calvert Island on 10 August 1792, on a stiff easterly wind, with Vancouver in a low and irritable mood. He was a latecomer here. Between 1786 and 1788, three English fur traders – Captain Guise, of *Experiment*; Captain Duncan, of *Princess Royal*; and Captain Hanna, of *Sea Otter* – had named and charted the major islands and inlets to the north and west of Vancouver Island. Checking his own course against their notes and sketch maps, Captain Van had cause to feel the essential futility of his expedition. An explorer of land already discovered, he could do little more than make marginal corrections to the work of his predecessors.

There is a world of difference between being commissioned to find the needle in the haystack and being told to fork through the haystack to make sure that no needle is there. Vancouver did not believe in the existence of the Northwest Passage; nor did the Admiralty, nor the fur traders who'd sailed here before. The sorry task of the *Discovery* expedition was to ensure that there was no discovery to be made. Captain Van had been chosen as commander because of the very qualities his juniors found so oppressive: literal-minded and punctilious, he could be counted on to carry out his brief without cutting corners, as a more imaginative man would almost certainly do. Yet even the worm turns – as Captain Van was beginning to when he came into Fitz Hugh Sound. Before long, he would write frankly to his friend, James Sykes, in London, of being 'entrap'd in this infernal Ocean'.

The two ships anchored in Safety Cove on the east side of Calvert Island. That night, an intense depression came ashore on the Queen Charlotte Islands, bringing heavy rain and fierce south-westerly winds. Five small boats were equipped with a week's provisions. Captain Van took command of one; Puget, Whidbey, Johnstone, and Humphrys captained the other four. This bedraggled flotilla set out on the morning of the 11th, in horizontal rain and a short, steep, breaking sea, to explore a new maze of dead ends.

The depression barely moved. The rain kept coming, and the wind remained close to gale force. The crews were soaked to the skin, the shoreline was a grey blur at fifty yards, there wasn't a glimpse to be had of sun or stars. Sailing north by the compass in his yawl, Captain Van reached:

> *as desolate inhospitable a country as the most melancholy creature could be desirous of inhabiting. The eagle, crow, and raven, that occasionally had borne us company in our lonely researches, visited not these dreary shores. The common shell-fish, such as muscles, clams, and cockles, and the nettle samphire, and other coarse vegetables, that had been so highly essential to our health and maintenance in all our former excursions, were scarcely found to exist here; and the ruins of one miserable hut . . . was*

the only indication we saw that human beings ever resorted to the country before us.

In the afternoon of 14 August, the sun showed itself just long enough for Vancouver to capture it with his quadrant, establishing his latitude at 51°52′N. He rendezvoused with Johnstone, in *Chatham's* cutter, and turned south to return to Safety Cove. The wind was blowing hard up Fisher Channel, the men hungry and exhausted; for thirty-seven miles they rowed like galley slaves, reaching the parent ships a little after midnight.

Puget, Whidbey, and Humphrys were still away, somewhere to the south-east, where the coast was most exposed and the wind and sea at their worst. For two days Captain Van fretted helplessly over the safety of his missing crews. On the 17th a strange brig, flying English colours, appeared at the entrance to the cove. Lieutenant Baker went off in the yawl to meet the visitor: *Venus* out of Bengal, a 110-ton fur trader.

Captain Henry Shepherd must have been studiously taciturn, for Baker returned to *Discovery* with only the good news – that the expedition's supply ship, *Daedalus*, had arrived in Nootka Sound, bringing stores from London, mail, and the newly appointed astronomer, William Gooch. From the beginning, Vancouver had begged the Admiralty for an astronomer; Cook, after all, had William Wales, his own revered instructor in celestial navigation. Now, with Gooch on his quarterdeck, he'd have the company of a kindred mathematical spirit, and the problem of exact longitude (a continuing disparity of up to ten miles between the chronometer and lunar-distance measurements) might finally be settled.

By the hand of Captain Shepherd came a sealed letter, addressed to Captain Van, from *Daedalus's* master, Thomas New. According to Edward Bell's journal, not until late in the letter did New come to the point: the ship's commander, Richard Hergest, the astronomer Gooch, and an unnamed seaman had been murdered by Hawaiian natives at Waimea Bay, on the north shore of Oahu, where *Daedalus* had anchored to take on water. Their bodies had been dismembered by the mob. This had happened on 11 May, when Vancouver, in a dizzy upswing of mood, was discovering a new England on the banks of Puget Sound.

Anxious for his missing lieutenants, sick of the desolate and inhospitable wilderness and its vile weather, Captain Van had no reserve of emotional capital on which to draw. Though he'd never met Gooch, he claimed Hergest as 'my most intimate friend'. The news of the murders poleaxed him.

Next morning, Puget, Whidbey, and Humphrys sailed into the cove in consort, to find the ships strangely quiet, their colleagues nervous and on edge. Vancouver's graveyard cough had worsened greatly with the weather: when he breathed, loud gulls cried in his chest. He was white-faced, withdrawn, monosyllabic, and thought likely to explode at any moment. He received the lieutenants' reports – of inlets that went nowhere, of a large village of Indians who in Puget's words 'behaved in a most daring and insolent way' – then tersely announced that the coastal survey was finished for the year. The expedition would return here in the spring of '93, and continue its explorations northward.

On 19 August, a Sunday, came 'a pleasant breeze from the S.E. with serene and cheerful weather'. *Discovery* and *Chatham* got their anchors and set sail for Nootka.

Once Cape Calvert was safely rounded, Vancouver retired to his quarters. To the sounds of the ship, on a beam-reach to Cape Scott, was added the rumbling thunder of his cough.

Menzies, who doubled as the expedition's doctor and naturalist, had come to so dislike the captain as to find it hard to wish him well. Professionally, though, he was seriously worried about Vancouver's coughing fits, his increasingly bloated appearance, and his extreme shortness of breath. Menzies couldn't put a name to the disease, but he was now sure that Captain Van was dying of it.

I had pencilled a circle round Namu, twenty-seven miles up Fitz Hugh Sound, and the only marked settlement in the 1,500 square miles of land and water covered by the chart. *Cannery, store, P.O., tel.,* read the chart; and *Sailing Directions* added the promising word *cafe.*

Off Safety Cove, where *Discovery* and *Chatham* had sheltered in an anchorage too large and deep for me, I crossed paths with a sleek white cruise ship flying the red ensign, Cunard's *Sea Goddess II.* It was followed closely by an ugly giant, the parrot-beaked P&O *Regal Princess,* 70,000 tons and honeycombed with a thousand windows. Both ships inched through the water, leaving barely a ripple of wake, turning the Inside Passage into a slowly unspooling diorama.

John Muir might have been writing advertising copy for Cunard and P&O when he described how he and his fellow passengers (most of them Methodist missionaries bent on converting the Chilkat Indians) stood on the deck of their chartered steamer, *Cassiar,* in 1879:

> *Cares of every kind were quickly forgotten, and though the Cassiar engines soon began to wheeze and sigh with doleful solemnity, suggesting coming trouble, we were too happy to mind them. Every face glowed with natural love of wild beauty. The islands were seen in long perspective, their forests dark green in the foreground, with varying tones of blue growing more and more tender in the distance; bays full of hazy shadows, graduating into open, silvery fields of light, and lofty headlands with fine arching insteps dipping their feet in the shining water. But every eye was turned to the mountains. Forgotten now were the Chilcats and missions while the word of God was being read in these majestic hieroglyphics blazoned along the sky. . . .*

With binoculars, I raked the decks of *Goddess* and *Princess* for signs of the 'earnest, childish wonderment' that Muir commended as the fitting response to this landscape, but apparently it was nap-time on board.

The wilderness that led Vancouver to desolation and prompted Muir to flights of histrionic rapture had become, in the late twentieth century, a soothing, therapeutic wallpaper for cruise ship passengers. Compared to the tropical excitements of the Caribbean or the Mexican coast, the Inside Passage worked like a course of Prozac with its calm seas, muted colours, and diffuse, angled lighting. What it chiefly offered was emptiness on a luxurious scale – mile after indistinguishable mile of grey rock, grey water, and sludge-green forest, not a house or road in sight. In an overcrowded world, simple absence of population was enough to render this a compelling tourist attraction; and the cruise ships, floating cities with their own shopping malls, lingered greedily over these long empty reaches, inviting passengers to feast their eyes on an epic sweep of tenantless waterfront property.

Aboard each ship, a resident naturalist kept up a running commentary over the PA system, fragments of which came to me over the water: 'red cedar . . . spruce . . . bear . . . wolf . . . mountain lion . . .' You wouldn't see much wildlife from a state-room window; but the near proximity of mammals capable of killing and eating humans was a cruise-feature that figured importantly in the brochures. The ship's naturalist was employed to fill the forest with creatures red in tooth and claw, so that passengers could invest the passing undergrowth with action sequences worthy of the Discovery Channel. Deep in the brush, bears lunged; wolves ganged up on mountain goats; cougars sank their fangs into squealing mule deer; moose bellowed; and the long-eared lynx stalked the unknowing snowshoe hare. On B Deck, within a sand wedge of the dangerous wild, gentlemen obedient to the cruise-line dress code tightened their cummerbunds and eased themselves into white tuxedos, preparing to sink their own fangs into the five-star dinner.

Namu was tucked into a sheltered corner of Whirlwind Bay, named for the williwaws that fell into it from the surrounding mountains in autumn and winter, when *Sailing Directions* warned that the bay should be avoided. On a July afternoon, light airs gently teased the water in a shallow, protected basin, perfectly suited to my needs, but Namu itself was in ruins.

Trees grew through the collapsed roofs of bunkhouses. The raised boardwalks had sprung apart in a tangle of flailing black linguine. A stump-field of rotting pilings was all that was left of Namu's docks. A single tipsy float, missing half its boards, led to a blackberry jungle. There was no store, no tel., no P.O., no cafe. In another year or two, the whole settlement would be swallowed by the woods.

The first whites came here in 1893, in the boom years when sawmills and canneries dotted the shores of every inlet. During salmon season, the anchorages and docks were crammed with boats rafted together hull to hull: disreputable floating villages, loud with whiskey and concertinas. Now all these sprawling centres of industry and population were going the way of Indian shell-middens and fish-weirs, and the Inside Passage was even emptier of people than it was when Vancouver and the fur traders first showed up. The seeming wilderness was full of Namus; the forest carpeted with rusty bits of logging machinery, fallen joists and window frames, tar paper, tractor tyres, tin cans. The bears had the run of the place, making their dens in the overgrown ruins of enterprises that had thrived only ten and fifteen years before.

I could safely have put an anchor down in Whirlwind Bay, but had no appetite for watching night fall over the dismal remains of Namu, a memento mori disquieting enough even in full daylight. So I swung the boat around and headed for Bella Bella, an Indian village twenty-five miles farther north-west. That Bella Bella would still exist seemed fairly certain: the 1991 edition of *Sailing Directions* listed a grocery store, post office, bank, laundromat, marine hard-ware store, hotel, liquor store, school, churches, and a hospital oper-ated by the United Church of Canada. I doubted the hungry forest could've consumed quite that amount of civilization in five years flat.

Leaving Whirlwind Bay, I passed the entrance to Burke Channel, snaking its way north-eastward from the wooded promontory of Edmund Point. Here, Captain Van had spent a miserable two days in the wind and rain of August 1792, pitching his tent in an area so dreary that even the Indians appeared to have deserted it. Eight months later, when his expedition returned to the Northwest coast, he named it Burke's Channel.

Was this a unique sample of Vancouver's black humour? He probably meant only to honour Edmund Burke as the elder statesman of English Conservatism – and perhaps to pay homage to the memory of his father, Little Van, the dapper party-worker for the King's Lynn Tories. That he knew Burke's *Philosophical Enquiry into the Origins of Our Ideas of the Sublime and the Beautiful* seems unlikely, though Menzies and some of the younger officers and midshipmen were certainly on nodding terms with it. I think it was more by happy accident than deliberate wit that Captain Van christened one of the most gloomy and forbidding channels in British Columbia after the aesthetic champion of terror, privation, darkness, depth, and vastness. Burke Channel – narrow, tortuous, flanked by precipices, sun-starved – perfectly embodied Burke's theory of the Sublime.

I had, it seemed, arrived just in time. Though Bella Bella still existed, some kind of major exodus was going on. Sunset darkened the village on the west bank of Lama Passage, and gilded the broad pool of water at its doorstep. A convoy of small boats was disappearing around the headland to the east. Curious, I attached myself to the tail end to see where everyone was going.

Each boat was packed with people perching on one another's knees. Radios were playing at full blast, all tuned to the same soft-rock station, with bass and drums bouncing back – *thump-thump-thump-thump-thump* – from the surrounding cliffs. The passengers matched the music in period flavour – the young men in shaggy Beatle cuts, the young women dressed to kill with flouncing skirts, plunging necklines, and bangles that flashed wickedly in the last of the sun. All sported the tribal uniform of a silver nylon windbreaker, emblazoned on the back with a scarlet killer whale. Fully provisioned with cigarettes and six-packs, the boats gave off an air of reckless Saturday-night hedonism. They charged across their rivals' wakes like bumper cars, trading loud insults over the darkening water.

The procession wound past Bella Bella Island, Spirit Island, Whiskey Cove, its hullabaloo scaring the birds out of the trees, and made landfall at Shearwater, a fishing resort on Kliktsoatli Harbour. Soon girls with handbags, in all their finery, were taking flying leaps off the boats onto the pontoon. I found a vacant space at the end of the dock, between a coaster and a fish boat, and wormed gingerly alongside. My lines were immediately taken by a stocky young man wearing a loosely knotted, canary-yellow necktie; a surprising accessory, even on a Saturday night, in these parts. In seconds he had me tied to the dock, bow and stern, plus springlines.

I thanked him and offered him a drink.

He shook his head. 'You don't want to miss the free beer and food they got up there.'

The previous year, the resort had burned down. It had been rebuilt with labour from Bella Bella; tonight the white owners were laying on a party for the Indians.

'You can come,' my helper said. 'Anyone can.'

So I went along, feeling underdressed in sweater and jeans. I told him I'd meant to stop at Namu, but had gotten spooked by the ruined cannery.

'That was a big thing for us when they closed it – lot of jobs, whole lot of jobs. Everybody worked there in the summer, Indians from bands all over . . . Bella Coola, Heiltsuq, Haisla . . . Lot of white people, too.' He laughed. 'Most of us were conceived at Namu. It's why so many people have birthdays in April and May. We're the Namu babies.'

The remark made perfect sense when we stepped inside the barnlike resort building, where a buffet supper and kegs of beer stood on trestle tables. I saw Namu babies everywhere. Some of the party-goers looked as if they'd come across the land bridge from Asia just a year or two ago; squarely built, with dark skins, flat faces, and broad noses, they resembled Genghis Khan's tribesmen. Others, tall, with white-skinned knobbly features and weak chins, would've been comfortably at home in an English soccer crowd. Namu, the local melting pot, was the clue to the impressive variety of features – a range only emphasized by the identical black Beatle mop that framed most of the male faces.

Some of the party-goers were probably descendants of men aboard *Discovery* and *Chatham*. The expedition stopped at Bella Bella in 1793, when the village's painted stilt-houses covered tiny Bella Bella Island so completely that not a patch of bare rock could be seen. Edward Bell wrote in his journal that the vernacular architecture 'had more the appearance of one large House than many different ones, they were most curiously painted in all Colours, with the most extravagant grotesque figures of Men, Beasts, and Fishes'.

My escort with the necktie was named Owen, though he didn't know of any Welsh connection in his family. His voice was full of Scottish vowels, thanks to the missionaries who'd swarmed across this coast in the 1870s and 80s, setting up schools on the Indian reserves. He wanted, he said, to visit England.

'Why England?'

'For a rest,' he said.

A rock band, imported from Prince Rupert, was getting under way in the bar area – pitch-dark except for two fierce spotlights on the musicians – and couples were taking to the floor.

Shouting to make myself heard over the din, I said to Owen: 'Last time I was at an Indian dance, it was in Washington State – Tulalip. It was "spirit dancing", and there was only Kool-Aid to drink. This is more fun.'

'How long did the dancing last?'

'For ever. All night. On Kool-Aid.'

'OK, that was a real Indian dance. Tourist dances, they stop after an hour.'

'This is a more real Indian dance, I think.'

He laughed. 'Yes, this is real Indian dancing.'

At the table next to us, a lout with white skin reddened by drink was talking to his dark-skinned, Mongolian-looking wife. 'You fock! Get some food on your fockin' plate!'

I watched the wife's face collapse like a wet soufflé.

'You're a fockin' *embarrassment*!' The husband jerked his thumb at a table far down the line. 'Go sit with fockin' Wendy!'

She rose, mute and crying, while he smirked complacently at his friends. Moments later, he was laughing loudly and patting the knee of the woman sitting next to him; his insolent, contemptuous face full of beer and unbridled testosterone.

Since Bella Bella first came into view, I had been put in mind of the 1960s, and never more so than now. I hadn't heard a marital exchange like that since the Hull cod-fishing fleet was in port, and I was driving a taxi, carrying revelling fishermen and their wives and girlfriends from pub to pub along the Hessle Road. While male manners had not greatly improved since 1964, in my experience no wife nowadays behaved as this Indian woman had done, weepily accepting her subservience and going obediently to sit with fockin' Wendy.

'You see a lot of that, do you?' I asked Owen.

'What?' he said. He hadn't noticed, though the husband had been spitting out his lines straight into our faces.

In Bella Bella's sorry economy, there were a lot of men whose only bankable asset was their testosterone. The cannery was finished. The fishery, according to Owen, a fisherman himself, was dying fast. In recent memory, two good things had happened: the village dock had been strengthened and extended so that cruise ships could call there; and the Shearwater Resort's fire had brought a windfall of unexpected winter work.

'What do cruise-ship tourists do in Bella Bella?'

'They go to the dump and take pictures of the garbage-bears.'

I had to fight my way through the dancers to get to the bar, where I stood in the crush trying to signal for two whiskeys. While waiting, I saw the band's name on the face of the bass drum: the Charred Remains.

North of Bella Bella, the sea had drowned the land. Long spurs of fir and alder reached out across the water. The trees, in ragged single file, appeared to be afloat. The chart abandoned contour lines in favour of the words 'low featureless country'. Judged by the lie of the land, this should have been a swamp, with the boat's keel scraping bottom a few feet down. But the sea was two hundred fathoms deep, and the floating trees marked the ridge-tops of submerged mountains. A chilly Scotch mist softened every outline and enlarged every distance. Genesis 7 time: *And the waters prevailed exceedingly upon the earth; and all the high hills, that were under the whole heaven, were covered.*

A few other arks were riding the Flood: the lighted windows of a white cruise ship blazed in the grey, and a pair of trollers, like bugs with erect antennae, were moving slowly seaward, keeping close company. All in whose nostrils was the breath of life, of all that was in the dry land, died.

Such waterscapes gave rise to Indian stories of a great deluge – stories later confirmed by the facts of geological history. Within the last 9,000 to 12,000 years, when people were present to witness such events, they would have seen the sea close over islands as earthquakes rearranged the topography. You couldn't look at the delicate compromise made here between land and sea without imagining the Flood; and you couldn't imagine the Flood without inventing a Noah to escape it. The coastal tribes all saw themselves as survivors of a historic cataclysm, in which boats had been their instruments of salvation. In the folk history of Bella Bella, the tribe drowned in the flood, except for a few chosen ones who were carried in canoes to the mountaintop at the head of Rivers Inlet, where they camped out until the waters were dried up from off the earth. This land was dotted with Mt Ararats, on whose peaks fortunate Indians had risen above the flood-waters: Mt Benson, on Vancouver Island; Mt McNeil, north of Prince Rupert; Mt Cheam, east of Vancouver. In the Raven stories, Raven clings by his beak to a cloud during the deluge, and when the huge tide sinks he falls out of the sky into a soft bed of kelp.

Less than half a mile from shore, I was afloat on more than 1,300 feet of water; the numbers on the chart gave me a touch of vertigo. 'I am apt to imagine,' Burke wrote, 'that height is less grand than depth . . . a perpendicular has more force in forming the sublime than an inclined plane.' He would have been excited to sail high over these profound chasms, so deep that no leadline could find their bottom – and nor could my depth-sounder's electronic pulse. Confronted by real depth, the instrument registered the alarming figure of 0.9 feet as it searched vainly for something solid to bounce off, and kept on going, and going, throbbing feebly down there in the perpetual darkness, the haunt of octopuses with hubcap-sized eyes.

Narrow Seaforth Channel led to the mouth of Milbanke Sound, wide open to the ocean – and to a big south-westerly swell. At last there was enough wind for me to get the sails up and the engine switched off, with the boat riding the crest of the swell for minutes at a time before it was eventually outpaced by the wave, and sank back into the trough astern.

The swell quickly subsided. It's a law of nature that the sea must break in parallel with the coast. Whatever the wind direction, you never see a wave break sideways on a beach. So when a wave-train enters a constricted channel, it refracts, peeling away on both sides to align itself with the shores. The enormous accumulated energy of even the biggest wave-trains is rapidly exhausted by this process of bending and breaking, and a powerful twelve-foot swell loses all heart in a few miles of forced refraction.

After twenty minutes of roller-coaster sailing, there was no more than a brisk one-foot chop on a flat sea. Running before the wind, under the clearing sky, I sat back and listened to the twiggy sibilance of the bow-wave as it broke from the hull – air and water getting mashed up together like egg whites in a blender. By noon, in fitful sunshine, I was in the riverine steep-sided corridor between Cone and Swindler islands, looking out for the Indian village of Klemtu on its hook-shaped bay.

The yachting guides warned against staying in Klemtu because the natives were unfriendly. I was about to turn back from the fully occupied government dock when I saw two fishermen waving to me, and creating forty feet of extra space where before there had been none. A skiff was hauled forward and tied up to a gill-netter; then the gill-netter was unhitched and moved farther forward on the float, leaving me ample room to drift in alongside. The fishermen took care of my lines and plugged my electric cable into the socket on the dock. I'd never been met with such a show of smiles and 'No problem! No problem!'

I'd pulled in early in order to make a call before Market Harborough's bedtime. From the payphone at the dockhead I dialled my parents' number. At the bungalow it was nine o'clock. Waiting for the ringing tone, I pictured the long shadows of the saplings on the lawn, falling toward the house. The phone was picked up on the third ring.

'Hullo?' My mother's voice was very small.

One of the fishermen tramped up the cleated walkway from the float; passing me, he nodded and smiled again. I waved back, distractedly. What were these smiles about?

'Well,' my mother said, 'I have my good days and my bad days.'

Beamed down by satellite to Klemtu, her grief had a knife-blade sharpness that made the village drift out of focus. She was standing in the gloom of the hall. As in so many English houses, the telephone was sitting on its own high table, in a draughty hall; you were supposed to stand, not sit, when talking into it, as a further discouragement to idle and expensive chatter. I could hear the emptiness of the bungalow around her, with the TV tuned loudly to the evening news – not a broadcast my mother had followed with any avidity before now.

Her own news was all of my father. His ashes were to be buried in Oddingley, my grandfather's old parish. A stonemason in Worcester was carving his headstone. 'Just "James Peter Caplin Priaulx Raban". We don't think he needs "Canon" or "The Reverend", do you?' Trying for a level tone, she swooped from word to word in anxious hiccups. 'Then "Teacher, Soldier, Priest, Scholar" . . . '

'I think that sounds perfect.'

'Do you really, dear?'

Her voice, across 4,000-plus miles of empty blue, was as high and thin as a chaffinch's.

'St James the Great,' she said.

'Who?'

'The church. At Oddingley.'

When our call was finished, I took the winding boardwalk that led to the ferry dock and general store at the deep north end of the bay, munching on blackberries en route. There was a lot of foot traffic on the boardwalk, since the residential section of the village lay at the shallow south end of the bay, where single-storey shacks and houses clustered around the commanding bulk of the wooden church. Everyone I passed said hello. Even a surly-looking teenage boy managed to crack a wan smile in my direction. Something was definitely up.

I had to squeeze myself flat into the brambles to let a party of tourists go by – twelve or fifteen of them, in slickers and hiking shoes, chaperoned by a young woman from the village, who was in the middle of a story with killer whales in it.

The store was bare. Under fly-specked bulbs, its shelves displayed dusty cans of beans, some elderly potatoes, a couple of sad cauliflowers. I fossicked about, filling a basket with things I didn't need or want. The woman at the till, after another large smile, refused to charge me for a carton of freeze-dried chicken-à-la-king (*simply add water and heat*) because it had 'been around here a long time'. Since everything in the store looked as if it had been there for a year or more, I thought she was showing undue prejudice to my chicken; but she solved the mystery of Klemtu's baffling friendliness.

The guided tour was an experiment, the first of its kind. BC Ferries – which in summer operated as a cut-rate cruise line, advertising its scheduled passages as wilderness excursions – had arranged, as of today, to stop at Klemtu long enough for the village to sample the tourist business. Primed to be nice to strangers, everyone this afternoon was wearing a compulsory smile.

One had only to glance into the store to see that tourism was Klemtu's best chance. Before long, the villagers would be mounting ceremonial salmon barbecues-with-tribal-dancing, and selling miniature totem poles for souvenirs. If Klemtu wanted to turn itself into a tourist trap, it had fine material to work with – the picturesque sweep of the bay, the half-mile-long boardwalk, the church and village, which required no more than a coat of whitewash and a few tradition-ally painted housefronts to make it alluringly quaint. There were garbage-bears at the dump; the deep woods held the rare albino black bear, known as the kermode, or spirit bear, and usually described as 'legendary'. All the villagers had to do was to turn their society inside out and become actors in a folk pageant. With a Blackfish Hotel, native crafts shop, war-canoe races across the bay, and First Salmon ceremonies, this community of mostly unemployed loggers and fishermen could tap into the mounting flow of summer money that was running past its door. Today, with the BC Ferry's lengthened stop, was the first day of Klemtu's new life.

One fisherman was still working on his sick engine when I got back to the boat. I asked him about the Kitasoo nation, of which Klemtu was the tiny capital city.

'People here came from all over,' he said. 'The government moved them out here. Not just Tsimshian people, like the ones who were here before. Some of them came from other tribes, way inland. They'd never seen the sea. Spoke different languages. That's why everyone had to talk in English – it was the only way they could understand each other.'

As any tourist would, I had taken Klemtu for an ancient, local, organic society; it turned out to be another swirling North American melting pot. That part of its history would have to be glossed over in the pageant.

Late in the day, I had a visitor, a tall, loose-limbed marine biologist in his thirties who lived aboard the white sloop moored nearby and was director of the Klemtu fisheries programme. The native fishery was dying: though most families still went fishing for subsistence, only two commercial boats now worked out of the harbour. 'It doesn't pay for the licence.' His job was to teach villagers to monitor the diminished populations of abalone, shrimp, herring, salmon, clams. 'It's counting critters. Hardly rocking science.'

So the government employed ex-fishermen as naturalists, paying them to observe their former catch. A fully trained technician with five years' experience could earn $11 an hour, Canadian; $7.50 in US dollars, say, or about half the going rate for casual domestic help in Seattle. In Klemtu, it was big money, and people competed eagerly for this prospect of a settled career.

'It's not rocking science,' the biologist said again. 'But they're such good people. They're used to hard work. I'm here because I love the village. I love to come back . . . '

Each fall he returned to his base on Vancouver Island, then sailed up to Klemtu in the spring. Living in the village, his one anxiety, he said, was that he was invited everywhere by people who couldn't afford to entertain him. 'I sometimes feel I'm taking the food out of their mouths.'

'You've read the cruising guides on Klemtu?'

'They have attitude, the guys who write those things. It offends people here. It offends me. Klemtu's always been the nicest reserve on the whole BC coast.'

I told him about the hellos and the smiles.

'That's how people are. Any time. Any year. They're not putting it on for the tourists.'

I asked him to dinner, but he had a prior invitation in the village. So I sat down to eat alone, with my father's ghost.

Four days after the Allied landings in Anzio in 1944, a group of war correspondents was taken to see my father's unit in action. Weeks later, in an Italian farmhouse recently occupied by American troops, my father came across a scuffed copy of *Newsweek* (14 February 1944), which included John Lardner's 'Vignettes from the Italian Front'.

> *. . . The British were drawing a bead with 25-pounder guns on the Germans across a stream called Fosso della Moletta when we arrived at one coastal farm hamlet.*
>
> *They had an observation post upstairs in a bakehouse. A battalion commander was staring out of a window at the Germans in a farm building 2,000 meters ahead. Genially he needled his*

observer, a young captain called Peter who needed a haircut and smoked a pipe, as he studied the Germans through field-glasses and called signals.

'Drop three-oh minutes and add one hundred,' said Peter without taking the pipe from his mouth.

'Drop three-oh minutes and add one hundred,' said a sergeant through the telephone.

A gun spoke behind us and a few instants later we saw black puffs near the objective.

'You're slicing your drive, Peter,' said the colonel. 'A bottle of beer you don't hit the house where the Jerries are having lunch.'

Peter chewed his pipe and said, 'More one-oh minutes, repeat.'

The gun talked again. Looking along the level, brown and green sea-marshes, we saw one shell drop against the right wall of the house and nestle along the left wall. The house shimmered queerly and changed shape.

'You won't need your putter,' the colonel said.

Beside 'Drop three-oh minutes and add one hundred' my father had written, 'Makes no gunnery sense at all.' *Come off it, Lardner.*

I had never thought of my father as a character in a Hemingway story, and I cherished this snapshot of him, taken when I was nineteen months old and he was twenty-five. He had been rescued by the war and the officer's uniform that came with it. Rejected as a candidate for university, he left school to go to a teacher training college in Winchester. His probationary teaching year, from 1938 to 1939, was a trial and a misery. He couldn't keep order in the classroom. Yet as a one-pip second lieutenant in the Territorial Army he was an immediate success. The army's clear divisions of rank and authority provided him with a world in which he felt securely positioned, as he never had in his unruly secondary school, where the boys baited him for his accent and rioted through his over-prepared lessons. Maths had always been his best subject, and he loved the sheer orderliness of calculating a shell's trajectory. This was his version of longitude by lunar distance.

A second snapshot shows him in the uniform he wore while I was growing up. In *Will This Do?*, Auberon Waugh's autobiography, my very distant cousin Bron worries about whether his Raban ancestors were Jewish, then credits them with passing on their powers of 'imagination' to his father, Evelyn Waugh.

> *The Rabans undoubtedly had a touch of fantasy. Great-Uncle George, another clergyman, would desert his pulpit to chase imaginary mice round his church with a golf club. The Reverend Peter Raban . . . I met only once, at George's funeral, when he was wearing a cloak like Count Dracula.*

This was the cassock inherited by my father from his Uncle Cyril, who must have inherited it from an earlier clergyman forebear. Appearing to date back to the Church of England's formation under Henry VIII, it had a greasy antique patina like the sheen on a blowfly, and seemed to be made of some compound of black wool and lead. Sliding from a chairback onto the floor, it made something close to a house-shaking crash. When my father encased himself in this forbidding garment, it fell to his feet in heavy undulating folds like the plush stage curtains in a theatre.

Winter and summer, this was his usual weekday wear, and it turned him into a conspicuous landmark in the district. In my teens, I could spot him from a mile and more away – a black African vulture descended on the Hampshire lanes. His cassock separated him from the rest of humankind, lending him the gaunt authority of priesthood. Even Roman Catholic clergy, in their sparse black serge outfits, were inclined to defer to my father's super-cassock.

It wasn't a taste for fantasy that led my father to his strange costume; more the fear that, out of uniform, he might not pass muster in the world. He was acutely conscious of his lack of a university degree. Though he made canon, a shot at an archdeaconry, let alone a bishopric, would have been out of the question. At theological college in Chichester, in his mid-thirties, he was old beside his pink boy-graduate classmates; a blue-chinned avuncular type, still known as Major, with a youthful student scarf, his trio of sons, and his ancient sit-up-and-beg bicycle.

After he was ordained, Great-Uncle Cyril's cassock enveloped him like a destiny. It covered all the anomalies in his résumé. Robed in black, he was pure priest: ageless, serious, 'a man of the cloth'. I can still smell that cloth, ripe – especially on wet days – with the odour of the several generations of priests who had lived inside it. At boarding school, my housemaster, Major MacTurk, would single me out as 'Raban, Son of the Cloth', as if the dreadful cassock itself had fathered me – a notion that sometimes struck me as not at all unlikely.

Late in the 1960s, my father took to wearing the cassock only for funerals, and let his beard grow wild in a fleece of tight black and ginger, silver and grey curls. The badge of my father's new calling as a radical, for a while it coexisted with a black stock and low clerical collar; but before long the dog collar followed the cassock into exile, and the beard's reign was unchallenged. Flashing his unruly whiskers, my father became a thorn in the side of the episcopal hierarchy, and began to speak up on behalf of (as people on the Left were starting to call them) the unwaged. It was as if his suddenly piratical appearance emboldened him to think and talk along lines that would have been inconceivable just a few years before.

The beard belonged to the strange new world my father now inhabited, of multi-storey blocks of council flats, where the Church of England, if it ranked at all, was filed somewhere alongside morris dancers, and Robin Hood and his Merrie Men. But he was not about to concede its irrelevance. His intransigent beard, striking out in every hue and direction, bespoke his determination to establish a place for his church in the alien landscape to which he'd been posted by his bishop.

My father would have been happiest in a small community with a common cause, where he could put to good use his soldierly appetite for battle. Somewhere like Klemtu would have suited him perfectly. He would have turned himself into an expert on treaty rights, trained his guns on Ottawa and the provincial parliament in

Victoria, been the first to volunteer for a fishing-boat blockade. I saw him striding the boardwalk in his beard and plastic parka – the vicar, at last, of a parish he could thoroughly comprehend.

I awoke to voices. The VHF radio on a neighbouring boat was turned up loud, and two fishermen were gossiping over the airwaves. I couldn't quite make out what they were saying in this exchange of laconic growls, punctuated by bursts of gruff laughter. Pulling my right wrist from under the bedclothes, I looked at my watch: 5:40. Magnified voices trading incomprehensible punchlines tortured me out of bed. Groggy with lost sleep, resentful of my inconsiderate neighbour, I dressed and slid the hatch cover open.

The village was blanketed in mist, the water as still and grey as sludge. No one appeared to be up on any of the boats nearby. The radio voices belonged to two ravens, perched on adjacent pilings, who continued to natter to each other, oblivious to my movements ten feet below.

Exactly as Roger Tory Peterson described, the ravens had goitre throats and Roman noses: it was impossible not to see such human-sounding birds in anthropomorphic terms. Even after realizing my mistake, I couldn't stop trying to decode their conversation. Maybe they were talking in some lost Tsimshian dialect, but they were definitely talking; and if I couldn't make sense of their vocabulary, I could clearly hear their grammar, as in Noam Chomsky's famous demonstration piece, the sentence 'Colourless green ideas sleep furiously.' Peterson, so vivid on the raven's appearance, hardly did justice to its voice: 'A croaking *cr-r-ruck* or *prruk*; also a metallic *tok*.' Had he listened to the Klemtu ravens, he would have heard the mordant chuckle; the tone of sly, disdainful irony; the taste for talking, like William F. Buckley, in sentences extended by multiple dependent clauses; the habit of raising rhetorical questions and immediately answering them; the Bertie Woosterish *what? what?*; the old-womanish *tut! tut!*; the chronic grumbler's repertoire of nagging complaints and self-justifications.

In the stories, the raven is cleverest of all the animals: a master of disguise, a brilliant conman and thief, a gourmand and lecher, an inveterate survivor. Among his many adventures, Raven steals the box containing daylight from an old man, gets control of the tides from the tide-woman by sticking porcupine needles in her bottom, makes the waves, has sex with a princess by pretending to be a shaman. In Swanton's version of the Tlingit Raven cycle, a great deal of what Raven does has to be printed in Latin. In some stories, Raven creates the world.

The character of the guileful Raven was grounded in the everyday habits and behaviour of the ravens that were to be seen in any village. Anecdotes about real ravens needed only a little tweaking to be transformed into the happy extravaganzas of the Raven cycle. There is a perfect continuity of theme and character between the Indian stories and those told by Lawrence Kilham, the great popular expert on Corvidae and author of *The American Crow and the Common Raven*. Kilham's first experience of ravens was in Iceland in 1933, when he fired at one with his 20-gauge shotgun. A single feather drifted down from the sky while the raven, 'seemingly undisturbed', continued to circle.

> *The raven was back sooner than I expected. Just as I looked up he took a shot at me. A large, purplish splotch (the raven had been eating crowberries) landed on the front of my hat. I took it off and gazed in astonishment. One can say that it was all fortuitous. But that is not the way it seemed to me. The experience left me with a feeling that ravens, in addition to being sharp mentally, may have a sense of humour.*

In Kilham's book, a raven distracts some young wolves from their kill by pretending it has a broken wing, so its mate can steal food from behind their backs. A mute swan is similarly distracted, and three ravens rob its nest. Ravens dive-bomb gorillas, for 'deviltry', and reduce them to paralysed terror. Ravens take turns tobogganing down a snowbank on their fronts. Tame ravens attempt to court and mate with their human masters.

Painting the raven as a devious trickster, comfortably able to outwit grizzly bears, killer whales, and men, the coastal Indians had to invent very little. Most of what Raven does – short of actual fornication with an actual princess – is found in Kilham, not as legend but as natural history. Like the stories of the Flood, the Raven chronicles were essentially true to the observed facts of life on the Northwest coast, even as they nudged their material into the domain of the mythical and the marvellous.

Watched, without interest, by the gossiping birds, I undid the boat from the dock and pushed off.

It was a fine morning to be out early. Shafts of weak sunlight lit the breathlike spirals of mist on the water. The tide ran in lazy swirls and fingerling whirlpools. I drove through a tide-meet of flotsam – a sinuous, unbroken line of stray logs, green branches, yellowed chunks of polystyrene packing, soft-drink cans, condoms, fish crates, frayed rope-ends, old boots, half-eaten apples, a broken cane-back chair, a rubber ball. Wherever two tidal currents come into collision, they form a long thin floating junkyard, to which all superfluous items in the neighbourhood eventually gravitate. These trailing windrows suggest to the eye the natural affinity of the unwanted: all the local orphans collect here, jostling together in a buoyant democracy of abuse and neglect. I passed through every tide-meet with care, always hoping to rescue an abandoned fender, a Japanese glass float, or any of the other useful and decorative things that sometimes showed up in these anfractuous garbage dumps. Nothing this morning. The gulls were having a good time of it, though, picking over such delicacies as the triple-decker club sandwich that most likely had been tossed by a sated cruise-ship passenger.

I worked my way north up the Finlayson Channel, following Vancouver's track in June 1793, on his second surveying season. By now, even the dedicated Romantics on board had seen enough cascades, precipices, snowcapped peaks, and witchy fir forests to last them their lifetimes. The weather was monotonously wet and windy. This stretch of coast had already been explored and partially mapped by English captains; both Charles Duncan, in *Princess Royal*, and John Meares, in *Felice*, had sailed through five years before. Vancouver had copies of their charts: his dispiriting job was to verify their accuracy and fill in the blanks.

The ships pushed on, under Admiralty orders, in a fog of boredom and discomfort. The journals of the young gentlemen on the quarterdeck report none of the explosions and confrontations that had punctuated the 1792 season. Little happened. Each new dead-end inlet looked very much like the one before. Small incidents loomed large. Near Restoration Cove, James Johnstone, recently promoted to lieutenant, treed two bear cubs and dispatched them with a rifle-shot apiece. Their meat was greeted as a delicious change from the regular diet of oily Pacific salmon. On 4 June, the King's birthday, the officers on *Discovery* enjoyed a 'sumptuous feast' of bear steaks, stewed eagle, and roasted mussels, washed down with 'flowing bowls of Grog'. Brass buttons and copper kettles were traded for sea otter pelts. These were rare high spots, at a time when the coastline seemed interminable, and the voyage a forced march through a landscape grown so familiar that the men had come to see it as a vast evergreen prison.

Finlayson Channel ended at a T-junction: to the right, a broad inlet led eastward between two 3,000-foot mountain ridges; to the left, a crooked and much narrower channel ran out to the north-east. Vancouver took the left turn, but sent two boats to follow the large inlet to its inevitable ending. On the morning of 15 June, the boat party stopped at a cove at the head of the inlet, gathered mussels from the beach, and roasted them for breakfast. Thomas Manby's journal has the best description of what happened:

The last week had given the Blue Devils to everybody on board. The sun during the whole time had not once beam'd on us his Cheering ray. No view offer'd, to gratifie the imagination, a dull insipid Green colours the lofty Mountains that everywhere surround us, Whose presumptuous heads arrest the progress of the journeying Clouds, creating a weighty atmosphere and perpetual Rain. The same inconveniences attended our Boats, during their excursion and a scene of horror took place on the 15th, which threw a gloom on every countenance when they returned on board. The party stopt to breakfast in a small Cove, that produced an abundance of Muscles, in these they made their repast, without perceiving any difference, either in appearance or taste, to those we had always been in the habit of eating, since our arrival in America. In a few minutes, the whole were seized with convulsive pains, unusual swellings, and every other symptom produced by poison. A Kettle of Water being on the fire, fortunately gave relief to many, but dreadful to relate, one seaman died in an hour and three others are brought to the Ship, with scarce a hope of recovery. The Rocky inhospitable shore not affording sufficient Earth to receive the remains of our departed Countryman, the Body was consign'd to a watery Grave, and to commemorate the name of the deceased, this inland Navigation was call'd after him Carter's passage.

In Manby's telling of the story, the poison mussels are deeply embedded in the larger description – of a rocky, sunless, rainswept landscape of insufficient earth, burdensome air, and presumptuous mountains. The outbreak of paralytic shellfish poisoning is seen as yet another malign and inhospitable aspect of nature on the Northwest coast. Here nature kills, wantonly and on the instant, by tempting the innocent stranger with a dish of seafood. Manby, afflicted by the Blue Devils, puts the blame for Carter's death on the dripping, dark, hostile character of a country he was coming to hate.

If there was a reddish tinge to the water, caused by a bloom of the toxic dinoflagellate plankton, *Alexandrium*, it would have been hard to see in such rough and lightless weather; and the boat party probably would not have read a warning in it anyway. The first sign of trouble would have been a sense of numbness in the lips, followed by a swelling of the tongue, making it hard to pronounce words clearly. According to my on-board medical book, *The Waterlover's Guide to Marine Medicine*, 'you become dizzy, lightheaded, and nauseated, your teeth feel loose, and you have a devil of a time speaking and swallowing as paralysis sets in. You may become totally paralyzed and die of asphyxia, remaining awake and alert to the bitter end.'

The sick men rowed back with Carter's body to the junction with Finlayson Channel, where a bay on the north shore promised a decent burial site. (For the eighteenth-century seaman, Marcus Rediker observes in *Between the Devil and the Deep Blue Sea*, 'a marked grave was considered essential to peace and eternal rest'.) But wherever the men tried, their shovels rang on hard rock. The corpse, sewn into a sail-canvas parcel and weighted with stones from the beach, was tumbled over the gunwale of the launch into thirty fathoms of water. Lieutenant Johnstone, the senior officer present, bareheaded in the rain, recited the words of committal from the seamen's prayer book.

'We therefore commit his body to the Deep, to be turned into corruption, looking for the resurrection of the Body, (when the Sea shall give up her Dead,) and the life of the World to come, through our Lord Jesus Christ . . .'

I swung to port, as *Discovery* had done, just short of Carter Bay. Every few miles I sailed past the relics of great projects that had come to grief. A tall brick chimney stack, deep in the trees, was all that remained of Swanson Bay, once a mill town with a crowded wharf. The bricks of the chimney were coming apart; in a year or two the trees would topple it and it would go to dust. There was hardly an indentation in the shoreline without half a dozen tarred stumps, leaning any old how, to show where the docks had stood – and, beyond them, the houses, sawmill, or canning factory. Had I been here ninety years ago, the whole landscape would have hummed with industry, the channels thick with tugs, barges, fishing boats, and steamers. The forest had made a fine job of burying the lot.

Of the Indian villages seen by Vancouver, nearly all were gone, leaving an overgrown shell-midden, like the tumuli that dot the farmlands of southern England, and a few oddly placed boulders on the beach – the remains of the fish-weir, where migrating salmon were trapped by the receding tide. Because the Indians lived closer to the water than the whites, their deserted villages were generally easier to spot. But whites and Indians alike had built in wood; and in the rainforest wood rots as soon as people turn their backs on it. Totem poles, housefronts, mill owners' balustraded villas, docks, and warehouses all blackened, went soft, and crumbled away, leaving little more trace than the wake of a canoe, as it frays to nothing in the water. The surface tension of the forest closed very quickly over the disturbances made in it by mankind. Things turned into corruption much faster here than in drier climates, which gave the landscape, even at its sunniest and most beautiful, a sinister cast; *et in Arcadia ego . . .*

The most stubborn of the ruins was Butedale, at the southern end of Fraser Reach. Tucked into a deep bay, it slid importantly into view, building by building, by far the biggest settlement I'd seen since Port Hardy. One bunkhouse alone, on the hill above the cannery, might have done service as a medium-sized federal prison. The wharves, meant for a fishing fleet, were occupied by a single small motorboat. Though a glance suggested that a plague had struck Butedale, its dereliction didn't show until I was within two or three cables of the waterfront and could see the gaping windows, the crescents of sky in the bulging walls, the rope-lashings that held doors and tottering walkways just in place. If you found the right spot, and put your shoulder to Butedale, the biggest cannery on the coast would collapse into the waiting sea in a slurry of rotten wood and corrugated iron.

What Butedale lacked in its manifold desolation was silence. Right by the cannery, a big waterfall came down the cliff in a zigzag staircase of unbroken white. The noise it made – recommended by the pilot-book as an excellent navigation aid in fog – was of a freeway overrun by trucks with broken mufflers. This sound transferred itself to the ruins, giving them the misleading air of harbouring some very loud and repetitive industrial activity.

In Seattle I'd heard about the Butedale lights, which appeared now to have been finally switched off. Long after the cannery was abandoned, the waterfall powered a turbine which generated so much electricity that a caretaker had to be employed to replace the thousands of high-wattage bulbs that blazed, night and day, their only purpose to ease the surging power-current. Fishermen spoke of Butedale as the eerie Manhattan of the Western wilderness, at night the finest landmark on the Inside Passage.

Through binoculars, I searched for the owner of the lone motorboat, and found a man digging what appeared to be a cleared vegetable patch on the hill. He was resting on his fork, shielding his eyes with his hand, and gazing back at me in, I thought, a not unfriendly way. If he had a family or colleagues, I could see no trace of them, though Butedale could easily have held several thousand invisible squatters in its ramshackle honeycomb.

I wanted to visit, but the word DANGER was spray-painted all over the wharves in badly formed red letters. I waved to the man, and he waved slowly back, yet did not point out a landing place.

The abandoned settlements were magnets for rainbow-chasers of every kind. The canning and timber companies were glad to be rid of them, and communes of sixties hippies, New Age spiritual centres, or neophytes to the vacation-resort business would move in with high hopes, in promising spring weather. They'd patch up a building, start a garden, build a float, establish a Website on the Internet. The idea of creating utopia in the wild is programmed into the far-Western imagination, and the Northwest coast was littered with such projects, started by Hutterites, vegans, Indian spirit channellers, survivalists, Christian sects so fundamentalist that even fundamentalists thought them eccentric. To anyone wanting to found a New Jerusalem, Butedale would have looked like a dream waiting to come true.

These utopias usually had a life of a year or two. Loneliness, rain, and the unwinnable battle against the intrepid brambles and salal soon drove most of the idealists back to civilization. Others went quietly bankrupt. In a decade, each Butedale would sprout ruins within ruins within ruins, as successive bands of hopefuls tried and failed to make a go of it.

I waved again at the optimistic gardener. Sooner him than me. Even as he leaned on his fork and looked out over the water, the forest was extending its tentacles behind him.

In the flooded ravine of Grenville Channel, half a mile wide and 1,000 feet deep, I saw a surprising patch of orange in the mess of flotsam that had collected in the eddy just downtide of a blunt rock promontory. I recognized it, with a surge of adrenalin and nausea, as a twin to the Henri Lloyd foul-weather jacket I'd put on twenty minutes ago, as the afternoon began to cool into evening. The humped back and shoulders rode well clear of the surface; the crumpled hood floated a few inches ahead, like a large blowsy tea rose.

With the engine in neutral, I tied a running bowline to the end of the port-side stern line and prepared a noose. I got the boat-hook ready and crept toward the eddy at tick-over speed, watching the depth-sounder every foot of the way. The eddy was moving faster than I'd thought, and it was hard to steer; I found myself dancing a macabre pas de deux; the body and the boat circling each other, twenty feet apart, at a speed of one knot. At last I got the thing lodged squarely amidships on the port side, then went forward to secure it with the boathook and the noose.

For this to happen twice in one lifetime seemed a bit much, but my previous experience had toughened me, and my chief concern was to avoid slicing into him/her/it with the propeller blades. I had decided that the best strategy was to tow the corpse alongside, which meant somehow getting the noose over the head and shoulders, tightening it, and making the free end fast to the shrouds. If I kept on running, I could make Prince Rupert soon after midnight. Spending the night at anchor in some cove, the body knocking up against the hull all through the small hours, was more than I could bear. There was an automatic VHF relay station on the summit of Gil Island, a few miles back; with luck, I should be able to raise the Coast Guard in Prince Rupert, and maybe meet them – body in hand, as it were – midway.

These tactical considerations helped to steady my hands as I leaned over the lifelines and spread the noose wide on the surface of the water. ('Drop three-oh minutes and add one hundred.') The flotsam was moving in slow gyrations, like stirred porridge. With the boathook, I tried to push the body a little way clear of the hull, so as to slide the noose past it, but met a wholly unexpected, hugely liberating absence of resistance. I snagged the hood and lifted the empty jacket out of the sea. The raised back and shoulders, so lifelike, or deathlike, even at the closest quarters, were a balloon of trapped air. The fabric was torn and soiled; by the look of the knife-slashes on the inside, it had been used for cleaning fish. It was a garment that anyone would have been glad to see the last of.

Since first sighting it, I hadn't doubted for a moment that it was a body. Spread out on the coachroof, a harmless piece of garbage, the jacket made me feel foolish and hysterical. No one in his right mind would've been taken in as I had been. My trouble was bodies on the brain.

Breasting a sluggish ebb tide, I pushed on up the channel, the shaggy forest of both walls darkening fast. The skirmish with the orange jacket only confirmed what I already knew: that gallivanting around the world in a small boat is a continuing education in one's limitless capacity for self-delusion. You mistake deep water for shallow. You confidently identify that headland over there as being this one right here on the chart – and for the next few minutes, you busily assemble every visible landform into the shape of what ought to be, and everything appears to fit. You will soon be in for a big surprise.

The term 'Indian', applied to the aboriginal inhabitants of the Inside Passage, went back to a heroic navigational delusion, when

Columbus stepped ashore on the island of San Salvador with an Arabic interpreter, hoping to be shown the way to the stone city of the Grand Khan. Captain Van, putting too much faith in John Harrison's chronometers, put most of this coast dangerously far inland. Shipwrecks are usually caused by someone knowing exactly where he is.

All first-person narratives are like this. I thought it was a body. You thought it was a body. We were wrong.

Halfway up Grenville Channel, roughly at the point where I had planned to deliver the corpse to the Coast Guard, a long, deep double bay filled the crevice on the north-east wall of the ravine, between the Countess of Dufferin and the Bare Top ranges. The recommended yacht anchorage was in the second bay, behind the low headland of Pike Point. So at dusk I let myself into this perfectly secluded pool, and found it full of pleasure boats.

Since leaving Potts Lagoon, I had seemed to be so alone in these waters that I had taken to waving at captains of cruise ships – man saluting man in the wilderness. Occasionally, perhaps once or twice a day, I saw another pleasure craft in the distance, usually a white trawler-yacht or a red-and-green miniature tug. The current fashion was for faux workboats, motor yachts disguised as fishing vessels or kitted out with merely decorative, banded steam funnels that made them close kin to *Theodore the Little Tugboat* on children's TV. The trawlers couldn't trawl, the tugs couldn't tug, but their owners, on vacation from their usual perches high in the office towers of Seattle and Vancouver, wore braided captains' caps and liked to play at being hard-bitten old salts. For three weeks, they exchanged 'scuttlebutt', 'spliced the mainbrace' when 'the sun was over the yardarm', and went 'gunkholing'.

Nettle Basin was clearly a famous gunkhole. The boats were anchored in line before a pretty tidal waterfall. Salmon steaks were being charcoal-grilled on every stern-rail barbecue. Across the water came the voices of Neil Diamond, Joni Mitchell, and Elvis

Costello from rival stereo systems. One motor-yacht contributed to the racket by running its generator at full blast.

Ridiculously affronted by the scene, I sought out a spot as far from the waterfall as possible, let my anchor down, hid in the saloon, and got my own stereo system going (Henry Purcell, *Music for the Death of Queen Mary*).

'Lice!' my father used to groan when our Bradford Jowett van rounded the last bend in a Cornish lane, only to find more than two cars already parked in the dunes. He would throw the van into reverse and drive off in search of somewhere more consonant with his idea of gentlemanly solitude. This meant that the beaches on which we actually decamped were usually so small, rocky, dangerous, and inaccessible that every sensible holidaymaker spurned them. It was years before it dawned on me that 'Lice!' was a surprising epithet for a clergyman to apply to his fellow men. Tasting his word on my tongue, I parted the curtains above the stove and spat it at the happy rally of Bayliners, Tollycraft, and Nordic Tugs. *Lice!* My fist clenching the handle of a serving spoon, I swirled the spaghetti around in the pan and splashed the back of my hand with boiling water. The pain was intense, if brief. Salutary, too.

One of the bad legacies of Romanticism was this greedy prizing of one's own solitude in an increasingly crowded nature. The central conceit of the 'traveller', as distinct from the mere 'tourist', was that he was alone in the landscape; its sole, original discoverer. To this end, the travellers' books became engines of mass destruction. They exterminated parties of hikers in the Hindu Kush, wiped out convoys of tour buses, disappeared the cheerful caravan of motorhomes, assassinated park rangers, and left a world ethnically cleansed of everyone except the writer and his dusky native friends. The Inside Passage had more wild and empty stretches than anywhere I'd ever been, but Nettle Basin was a sharp reminder that I was a tourist among tourists. When the time came to go home, we'd each extol the cavernous solitudes we'd discovered and keep mum about tangling anchor chains with other sole discoverers in silly boats loud with silly music.

I could at least claim to be up earlier than the rest. They slept, wreathed in mist, lulled by the babble of the waterfall, while I sweated on the foredeck, recovering a hundred and twenty feet of muddy chain. My getting dressed in the dark was compensated for by the sight of Nettle Basin's primary featured attraction. On the stony beach at the south end of the bay, two bears, hindquarters up and heads low down, were nosing methodically along the tideline. The larger bear looked up, and knowingly sniffed the air. *Lice!*

At its far northern end, Grenville Channel opened onto an archipelago of big and little islands at the mouth of the Skeena River, where, for the first time on the trip, I ran into a fleet of gill-netters at work. Each regulation net, sixteen feet deep and up to 1,200 feet long, ran out from the stern winch of the boat in a drifting parabolic curve; it was kept aloft by a line of cigar-shaped white floats, and its end was marked by a coloured buoy the size of a soccer ball. With the sun on the water, the floats were painfully hard to pick out of the dazzle. Wearing Polaroid sunglasses helped, but I still found myself swerving away at the last moment from the quarter-mile string of pearls that popped suddenly into view, dead ahead. I nipped and tucked between boats, close enough to say 'Sorry!' to one and 'Morning!' to the next.

The hydraulic winch had made this industrial kind of fishing dangerously easy. In the old days, the length of the net was limited by the pulling power of a two- or three-person crew. Now you just put your foot on the button and the net reeled effortlessly home on the drum, while with gloved hands you picked the salmon out of the mesh and tossed each wriggle of silver into the hold. The mouth of the Skeena was blocked solid with trailing curtains of invisible web. Any fish unwise enough to swim within sixteen feet of the surface was likely to find itself thrashing, entangled in gossamer-thin nylon, and headed for the supermarket, not the spawning grounds.

Away to the west, a long white bolster of low cloud lay north-to-south down Hecate Strait, but in my neck of the woods the morning was full of dewy brilliance in perfect visibility. I could see Alaska ahead, fifty or sixty miles off, a line of squat purple blisters on the horizon – a sight that made my spirits leap. I got out the chart for Prince Rupert Harbour and began threading my way through the maze of sunlit rockpiles that dotted the suddenly shallow sea. The depth-sounder, confident now, was bouncing around the hundred-foot mark – deep by the standards of the North Sea or the English Channel, but very thin water for this coast.

I passed the Lawyer Islands, with Bribery Islet and Client Reefs close by. Looking back, puzzling over their names, I saw that the cloud I'd noticed before was fog, and the fog was making large strides toward me. A great cliff, as sharply chiselled in the sun as the cliffs of Dover, it filled the western horizon end to end; lemon-coloured shadows gave it spurs, buttresses, chimneys, and overhanging crags.

I could see the buoyed channel leading to Prince Rupert, but it was thick with gill-netters and hedged with sunken rocks. I saw the cliff of fog, now towering right above me, swallow the Lawyer Islands in one gulp. At 2,200 revs, I ploughed through the water at 7.5 knots, as fast as the boat could go, pursued by monstrous cotton-candy pillars of advection. I weaved and dodged past the floating nets. A deadhead, five feet across, surfaced just in front of the bow, like a fat trout smashing at a fly. I missed it by inches. The fog marched hard behind me, taking the Kinahan Islands, West and East, then half the fishing fleet. It stalled – miraculously – over Digby Island, and stood as a massive alabaster precipice along the western edge of the channel that led into the city.

Each time I snaked a glance behind me, I saw the fog closing over my wake. Another sixty seconds and the boat would've been engorged. I've rarely been so grateful to make port as when motoring past the long and busy wharves of Prince Rupert, with its hotels, stores, restaurants, still in sunshine, on the bluff above. 'Back in the fleshpots!' I scribbled in my log. 'Rupert's a metrop!'

Yet fresh from the ruins of Namu, Butedale, Swanson Bay, it was hard to view even a settlement as big and self-important as Prince Rupert without a tinge of Tiresias-like scepticism. I felt as if I, too, had sat by Thebes below the wall, traipsing along this coast of falling cities. Prince Rupert, with its large, ice-free, deep-water harbour, its trans-Canadian rail and road links, had every expectation of a long and happy life. Its port authority claimed it as 'Canada's closest marine gateway to Asia, thirty hours nearer than its nearest North American rival'. Fog permitting, you might peer beyond the western horizon and almost see Tokyo. What the port authority refrained from noticing was that Prince Rupert was so very far from anywhere else of real importance in Canada, or the United States, that its handy proximity to Tokyo might not be quite the godsend it seemed. But for now, given all the talk of the coming Asian Century, Prince Rupert could preen itself on its geographical good luck.

With Tiresias's eyes, I squinted up at the shopping mall, Philpott Evitts, the Highliner, the Coast Hotel, and saw fir trees poking through their roofs as over the horizon the yen went into free fall. All the wooden cities of the Northwest had this provisional, gimcrack quality, as if they might easily topple into sudden desuetude. Most of them had started life as a logging, fishing, mining, or army camp; a hundred years later, they still had the lingering air of camps that could be struck immediately on impulse, upon the receipt of a bad-news telegram. It wouldn't take much for Prince Rupert to go back to forest.

For a pleasant moment, though, the city could yield a table overlooking the ships and fishing boats manoeuvring down in the harbour, salmon cooked *en croûte*, and a bottle of lightly chilled Pinot Gris – metropolitan fleshpot luxuries. (Though when I returned, only weeks later, the restaurant was gone.)

I liked Prince Rupert. The city laundromat, full of fishermen and yacht-tourists, was like a big rowdy bar on Saturday night; the liquor store sold Laphroaig whisky, though at a fearful price. In the Safeway, I kept seeing Julia and her mother, always at the far end of an aisle, and always gone when I arrived.

The posted attractions were mercifully undemanding. The most interesting and significant exhibit was in the Pacific Mariner Memorial Park, a small green play-space on the bluff. Here, beside the

swings and slides, the Hecate Strait Rotary Club had restored a bat-
tered, barnacle-encrusted boat that had drifted on its own from Japan
to the Queen Charlotte Islands. A funny-looking craft, it was twenty-
seven feet long, flat-bottomed, and as narrow in the beam as a
Cambridge punt; I would have feared for its stability, even on the
Cam. On 26 September 1985 a retired civil servant named Kazukio
Sakamoto had gone out fishing in it from his hometown of Owase,
Prince Rupert's twin city. The wind got up, and he never came back.
Eighteen months later, *Kazu Maru*, his 'beloved boat', as the plaque
put it, was found knocking up against the rocks of Skidegate Inlet.

The westerly drift of winds and currents in the North Pacific
meant that bits and pieces from Asia were constantly fetching up on
the beaches of this coast. Long before Europeans arrived, Indians were
kept regularly supplied with evidence of alien civilizations. A glass
float . . . a piece of wreckage with iron and copper fittings . . . sometimes, as with *Kazu Maru*, a whole boat. These strange intimations of
another world, laid at the feet of the Indians by the ocean, gave them
tantalizing glimpses of a superior technology. The first white explorers
were surprised by the natives' knowledge of the uses of iron and copper: had they looked more carefully at the tidewrack, the mystery
would have been explained.

Copper, particularly, was very highly valued, and many stories
accounted for the origin of this precious metal. In a Tlingit version,
copper is discovered by the outcast child of the sons of the sun. He
lives alone with his mother in poverty, beyond the pale of the village.
When he is old enough to go hunting, his mother makes him a bow
and arrow, and he meets with a creature – not to be found in zoology
– with feet, fins, and wings. His mother instructs him:

> *'When it opens its mouth for you and puts its forefeet up on land
> run down to it. It is your father's canoe.' So he went there and it
> opened its mouth for him. His mother had said, 'Shoot it in the
> mouth,' and when he had shot it, it was heard to say, 'Ga,' like a
> raven. It was as if all its seats had been cut off. It was a copper
> canoe in which were wide seats. The canoe was nothing but*

*copper and broke entirely up. Throughout the night he carried it
into his house to his mother. No person knew of it.*

The boy becomes the copper tycoon and marries the daughter of a
great chief. That copper comes from the sea in the form of a canoe
puts the story squarely alongside the story of *Kazu Maru* as another
tale of marvellous flotsam, delivered here by the Kuroshio Current
and the North Pacific Drift.

Across the street from Mr Sakamoto's boat was a modest museum
largely given over to Tsimshian relics. To illustrate Tsimshian mythology, the story of Nagunakas, the whirlpool-being and canoe-
swallower, was printed up in large letters on a display board. One
detail of this variant was new to me: when Nagunakas returned the
fishermen he'd captured, he sent them home in a copper canoe, which
flew through the air when struck with a copper paddle. Copper,
mysterious in its origins, had magical properties, and the arrival of
Nagunakas's canoe would have seemed to the village like a visitation
from extraterrestrials.

Apart from a magnificent carved frog, which once stood guard
over a coffin in an open burial house, the museum had the usual
assortment of halibut hooks, cedar-bark vests, and repro ceremonial
masks. As in most public collections of Indian culture up and down
the coast, one's trip began with a little printed lesson informing the
visitor that the First Nations practised 'a philosophy based on respect
for nature and concern for the environment'. Indians – in the new
mythology – were the original designers of the eco-friendly life, the
first passionate recyclers.

Yet this sort of statement could be made only because the system-
atic extermination of Indian languages, customs, and beliefs, carried
out by zealous Christian ministers and government agents, had been
so shockingly successful that no present-day Indian could possibly
know what his great-great-great-grandparents had really believed.
So it was now easy to attribute to the ancestors almost any belief that
was thought desirable for them to have possessed. Most popular
books about the Northwest Indians claimed that they had been

monotheists, believers in the Great Spirit, a kissing-cousin to God the Father and Jehovah. There was no serious evidence for this at all – though the early missionaries certainly peddled the Great Spirit notion in an attempt to bridge white-Christian and Indian concepts. Likewise, the 'respect for nature and concern for the environment' line is hardly confirmed by the oral literature and surviving art of the Indians. That little or no trace remains of a belief in the supremacy of man over the natural world (the stories tend to suggest the reverse), that no Indian text parallels Genesis 1:26 ('And God said, Let us make man in our image, after our likeness: and let them have dominion over the fish of the sea, and over the fowl of the air, and over the cattle, and over all the earth, and over every creeping thing that creepeth upon the earth') doesn't – or shouldn't – imply that the Northwest tribes were protoecologists, dedicated to the postmodern cause of environmental conservation.

Like John Muir Indians and Fenimore Cooper Indians, these museum Indians were unreal in their milk-and-water nobility. Their art and stories were so full of complex life, so shot through with grim humour, so of-their-own-kind, that it was insulting to the Indians to cast them, in their current starring role, as people who apologized to salmon before killing them, who hugged the trees before turning them into war canoes, like good children of the 1990s, following Mother Nature's rule book.

Far better to turn away from the preschool digest of Tsimshian 'philosophy' and gaze instead at the inscrutable depths of jovial malignity gouged into the features of the great wooden frog.

Next morning, people were dematerializing at forty feet on the Prince Rupert Yacht Club dock, and the harbour sounded like a stockyard of distressed cattle. I watched the show on radar – twenty or so white blips, moving in every direction across the screen but never, quite, colliding. According to the pilot-book, Prince Rupert was socked in by fog 17 per cent of the time in July and 20.6 per cent in August. In high summer, the offshore waters were warmer than those inshore, so air moving inland from the west quickly cooled as it hit the frigid inlets and, as it chilled, thickened into woolly fog. The pilot had depressing news: 'The fog persists through day and night even with moderate winds . . . visibilities at or near zero persist over several days.' I steeled myself to face some long afternoons in Charley's Lounge and Dillon's Country Bar.

After mailing a batch of story-postcards to Julia, I monopolized the dockhead phone for an hour. Jean, fighting a deadline on a dance review, was fogbound in her own fashion.

I was, I said, within ten days of reaching Juneau. 'When you come, I thought we'd go up to Glacier Bay, then down and around to Sitka, at least. You could get a flight out from there. There'll be icebergs, whales, and bears for Julia – I can promise her that.'

'Great,' Jean said. 'I really have to go now.'

'I miss you.'

'I miss you too,' she said, and left me listening to the dial tone.

I was saved from Charley's Lounge by a sudden, spectacular, barred sunbeam that might have disclosed an annunciation in an Italian painting, but instead had lit on a raft of disreputable-looking fishing boats clustered around a single anchor in mid-harbour. The fog disintegrated in minutes, leaving ragged cottonballs snagged in the trees. I left Prince Rupert by the back door, worming my way past the rocks of Venn Passage and into the lagoon of Metlakatla, an Indian reserve whose fishermen's sheds and floathouses were sprinkled over the looking-glass water.

Too little daylight now remained for me to cross the open bight of Dixon Entrance and find shelter in Alaska before nightfall, but another Indian settlement, about twenty-five miles north of Prince Rupert, looked interesting. On one chart it was named Port Simpson; on another, Lax Kw' Alaams. Boxed in by reefs, with an approach too shallow for cruise ships, it was given short shrift by the yachting guides, though the pilot-book made it sound a place of substance. A muddy panoramic photograph showed a large village spreading out from the high spire of its central church. To me it looked like the

Cornish seaside villages my father used to seek out on our summer holidays. Abhorring such tourist favourites as Mevagissey and Polperro, he considered himself the Columbus of Portloe. Each year he'd groan that Portloe was being 'discovered', and eventually moved us all deep inland. Our tents would be put up in the lee of hills of powdery china clay, and our faces would go as dusty-white as any miller's. The landscape was memorably ugly, but to my father's eye it had the enormous merit of being as yet undiscovered by the holiday Vespuccis and Magellans in Morris Oxford estate cars.

My father would've enjoyed coming into Lax Kw' Alaams. In fine visibility on a rippled sea, it was a nice exercise in careful coastal navigation. I ran from buoy to buoy, skirting rocks and outlying sandbars, making close turns round islets, watching my wake for signs of tidal drift. The entire coast north of Prince Rupert was marked as Indian land, and appeared quite uninhabited. Not a louse to be seen.

Nor, when I made the last turn, past the FUCK YOU spray-painted for visitors by village delinquents in large red letters, was there a pleasure boat in sight. Along with three purse-seiners and a big crabber, the local gill-netting and trolling fleet had the place to themselves. My father greatly approved.

I pulled up alongside two men who were repairing a gill net on the dock. While I was fastening my lines, one of them lifted the net to show a hole that a Morris Oxford could comfortably have driven through.

'Fish!' he said.

'That's a serious project,' I said.

A gill net, fully loaded, with corks and a weighted leadline, cost about $5,000 to put together, plus several days of tedious dockside labour. The web alone cost $3,000. Sunlight, salmon, and the strain of being winched out of the water every sixty minutes or so quickly weakened the nylon mesh. Prosperous fishermen renewed their nets each season. The others made do by patching half-rotten nets, at the end of every outing, with a spool of green nylon and a mending-needle. The old, darned nets were said to fish much less efficiently than new ones, so the poorer fishermen caught fewer salmon, made less money . . . the usual story.

The men talked as they worked, but turned down my offer of Laphroaig. 'Half my friends now are on skid row,' one said.

'How do you pronounce the name of this place?'

'Port Simpson.'

'No – I mean *that* one,' I said, pointing to a sign saying LAX KW' ALAAMS MARINE INDUSTRIES INC. on the grey hangar-like building above the docks.

The man made gargling and spitting noises. 'Like that. Kind of.'

The village had changed its name ten years before. Lax Kw' Alaams was Tsimshian for 'place of roses', but it hadn't caught on except in official circles, for there were few people still alive, outside anthropology departments, for whom the words meant anything.

'My father, he knew some of the old language. His mother used to talk Indian to him when he was a kid, and his grandparents, they spoke it all the time.'

'What about the old stories? Does anyone still tell them now?'

'All the people have passed away. I should've made a tape. The young ones now, they don't give a damn.'

Something of the original Tsimshian survived in the talk of both men. Their vowels were pure Scottish-missionary, but their voices popped and clicked with the glottal stops of the ancestral language, like the Cockney *bo!-l* for 'bottle' or *pi!-ta bi!-er* for 'pint of bitter'.

The younger of the two, Curtis, told me he had four daughters, aged between five months and nine years old. All his ambitions were invested in these girls. 'I don't want them to live here. I don't want them working at the cannery. I want them to be doctors and engineers – like white people. I tell 'em, "You got to learn four languages. You got to speak Japanese. You got to speak Spanish. You got to go to school till you're *sick* of it!" Right now, I'm educating 'em up at home with flash cards and computers.'

Compoo!-ers.

I said I had a daughter, too.

'What you want her to be?'

This was a question I'd never been asked, and never addressed. I reached for the nearest available word on the shelf and said, firmly, 'A scientist.'

'You have to push 'em, John. Push 'em hard. It's pushing does it.'

I saw Curtis, like an Olympic shot-putter, trying to lob his daughters, one by one, out of the reserve and over the mountains to Heaven knew where: Vancouver, maybe, or Toronto; somewhere far enough, at any rate, for improbable dreams to come true.

Soon after seven, Curtis's wife brought the men's supper down to the dock. As darkness fell, the two were still at it, weaving away at the rotten web with their mending-needles. They must have spent more time repairing their net than they did fishing it.

Port Simpson wasn't quite off the beaten track. A ferry called there twice a week; the new school had a helipad in its yard; floatplanes regularly put down into the bay and taxied over to the cannery wharf. There was a plan to eventually cut a road south to Metlakatla and Prince Rupert. By boat, in gentle weather, the run to Prince Rupert took four hours, so it was possible – just – to shop in town and get back on the same day. Eleventh- and twelfth-graders went to the high school in Prince Rupert, boarding with Indian families there, which kept Port Simpson in continuous close touch with big-city life. The gang slogans on the wharf (for the Toyas) came up from Rupert along with the groceries and portable CD players.

Yet it felt remote. The grid of dirt streets at the foot of Town Hill, sunbaked and dusty, turned to gluey mud in the autumn rains. The two stores were wooden shacks, indistinguishable from the village houses. The main current of tourist money passed by about ten sea-miles to the west, and there appeared to be no way of diverting it – though a local artisan had become the object of envious amazement when he carved a thirteen-foot totem pole and sold it for $3,500.

Fishing was still Port Simpson's biggest business. A hundred boats worked out of the harbour, taking their chances on capricious salmon runs, yo-yo fish prices, and the arcane pattern of closings (long, and getting longer) and openings (short, and getting shorter) imposed by the Department of Fisheries and Oceans. Just now, the mood on the docks was one of dazed high spirits, for the Skeena River fishery was having its best season in years. The early prediction was for a strong run of sockeye salmon, at least three million; but the run had started early, the fish were crowding thickly off the estuary, and the marine biologists had upped their estimate to seven million or more. Boats were coming back to Port Simpson low in the water. I'd watched a small troller off-loading at the cannery, where a crane let down a white plastic tub the size of a bath. The tub came up, time after time, brimming with fish – an act of legerdemain, the little boat serving as the magician's bottomless hat.

I had passed so many ruined canneries that it was a surprise to find Port Simpson, of all places, in possession of a brand-new one; a massive prefabricated aluminium shed, painted pale grey on three sides to match the prevailing colour of the sky. Though everyone called it 'the cannery' out of habit, no fish were canned there. The Tsimshians were aiming at a narrower, more expensive, niche of the market, by producing frozen fillets, boxes of high-grade roe for the Japanese trade, and jars of low-grade roe for anglers' bait. In a nice match of tribal tradition and commercial opportunism, the next planned move was to build a smokery and make gourmet-quality smoked salmon.

The interior resembled the kind of hospital in which you'd hope never to find yourself a patient – a maze of conveyor belts, white operating tables, and concrete drains running with small rivulets of blood. It smelled more strongly of disinfectant than of fish, and its midwinter temperature made me eager to leave almost as soon as I'd set foot inside.

Yet this cold grey government-financed project was a cherished experiment. The Northwest Coast Indians had been producers of raw materials; they chopped wood and caught fish. Or they made souvenirs – from exquisite carvings in argillite in the nineteenth century to miniature totems, usually crudely done, today. But big profit always resides in the value-added component of the product, and all the canneries and pulp mills were owned and managed by whites, who employed Indians only as menial labour. At the Port Simpson cannery, Indians were adding their own value to the fish, and the profits – if and when they came – would flow back into the reserve. Much hope and anxiety was focused on whether the shed on the wharf could become self-supporting, and so light the way ahead for other villages on the coast.

On the seaward side, its long metal wall was painted with a giant *trompe l'œil* mural showing the landscape immediately ahead. The bay was bright blue, and the mountain range rose from the far shore in a swath of emerald-green. The clear sky was lightly streaked with mare's tails of high cirrus.

Some days the colours of the painting must have coincided with those of reality, but when I was there, the cannery wall stood in violent contrast to its surroundings. The real clouds were low nimbus, the mountains purple verging on black, and the water of the bay like ribbed grey fish glue.

At present – at the height of a startlingly good season – the cannery had ninety people on the day shift, and seventy on nights. Pay was $10 an hour; less than at the cannery in Prince Rupert, but here on the reserve the money was tax free. People like the tribal administrator, whose tinted specs and clipped moustache brought an unexpected touch of business-school fashion to Port Simpson, were crossing their fingers and touching wood that this near-miracle would hold. For now, at least, what was going on inside the shed was living up to the sunny optimism of the painting on its wall.

This experiment, if it worked, would demonstrate a realistic alternative to the usual Indian expedients of mounting folk dances and selling dream-catchers or fireworks, cheap cigarettes or tribal bingo, to the waterborne carriage trade. It would set Port Simpson apart as a modern fishing village with its own industrial plant; a place rooted to its traditional occupation while prospering from its export-order ledgers.

Everybody wanted this to happen, but no one really seemed to believe that it would. Even the chief evangelist for the cannery, the band's administrator, Don Reynierse, couldn't help hedging his bets. For the scheme to take off, all the grim variables of the fishing industry had to come into precise conjunction, like favourable stars. The examples of Butedale, Namu, and most other canneries on the coast haunted Lax Kw'Alaams Marine Industries from the moment of its conception. In the harbour was a shabby gill-netter named *Native Dream*. That plucky but wistful and ironic title seemed to naturally attach itself to Port Simpson's great painted shed.

A small-craft warning had been issued for Dixon Entrance; the morning forecast promised thirty-knot winds from the north-west, and I was glad of the excuse to stay. Only a few stray puffs of wind were reaching the harbour, but charcoal-grey clouds sped low overhead and the mountain range was lost behind a thick curtain of rain.

Climbing the walkway at the head of the dock, I was challenged by the man standing at the top. 'Would you like to fight?' His question sounded so entirely amiable that I presumed I'd misheard him.

'What did you say?'

'Fight. Eff, eye . . .' He paused. 'Gee . . . tee. Fight!'

'It's a bit early in the morning for me.'

The man pointed to a friend sitting on the step of the harbour master's sentry-box office. 'He wants to fight – he's just waiting for *you* to get in the mood.' The friend was seventyish, plump, rubicund, and quite toothless. He gave me a gummy grin and chuckled. 'Heh, heh, heh.' I sniggered feebly back. I saw the point of this joke rather too clearly, and resented its implications. The author of the joke, a cheerful pillar of brawn in a plaid shirt, who couldn't have been more than ten years younger than me, beamed complacently, the cock of the roost.

Between the dock and the village was a curious memorial park. Though no larger than twenty yards square, it had been laid out carefully, with concrete paths set in dandelion patches that had once been grass. At its centre, a rusty oil drum sat half full of garbage. To its far left was a weathered totem, carved in grey stone, supported by the well-sculpted figure of a beaver gnawing on a log. Behind the drum, a conventional marble plinth commemorated Abraham Lincoln: CHIEF OF KITSHEESE TRIBE, DIED AT PORT SIMPSON JULY 1, 1890, AGED 85 YEARS. This was flanked by two ancient brass bells, from a church or a ship. A few yards away, the barrel of a small naval cannon, the date 1833 stamped below its embossed crown, was pointed straight at Chief Lincoln. There was clearly some conscious artistic intent in the arrangement of these objects; and you couldn't look at them without seeing the beaver-clan totem, the cannon, the bells, Lincoln, and the trash can resolve into a rueful thumbnail history of Port Simpson.

I walked to the store along the beach, watching the sand at my feet for the glint of trade-beads. The Vancouver expedition hadn't put into the bay, deterred by the chain of exposed rocks lying across its entrance. Five miles to the north, Captain Van had named Maskelyne Point, on Maskelyne Island, for Nevil Maskelyne, the Astronomer Royal and chief advocate of the lunar distance over the Harrison clock as a means of fixing longitude. Maskelyne now was remembered, if at all, as the pompous establishment figure who stood in the way of the plain-spoken Yorkshire inventor, and tried to deny Harrison the Board of Longitude's £20,000 prize. Yet Vancouver's naming of the point in Maskelyne's honour reflected his own experience of the con-tinuing longitude problem: two years out of England, and 230° of longitude east of Greenwich, Captain Van was regularly having more success with his lunar distances than with his clocks. The 1907 edition of Lecky's *Wrinkles* notes that the problem of longitude was finally solved only by wireless and submarine telegraphy, when ships' clocks could be synchronized exactly from continent to continent. Maskelyne had a serious point – in the dispute about long-distance navigation, as on the northern tip of his eponymous island, where the sea was now breaking in a ragged skirt of white.

The store was bare. 'There'll be a lot more stuff later on, when the boat comes in – if they can make it in this wind.'

I trudged back to the harbour, where, through the morning, a dozen boats swung in looking the worse for weather. A Fisheries and Oceans patrol vessel – not one of Port Simpson's favourite callers – tied up just ahead of me. Its captain stood on the dock in the bowlegged half-crouch of the seaman who feels solid ground rearing dangerously under his feet. 'It's blowing like hell off Dundas,' he said, and whistled. Seeing him climb cautiously back aboard, I remembered how I'd fallen flat on my face in a Howth car park at the end of a rolly crossing from Port St Mary in the Isle of Man: grown used to the motion of the Irish Sea, I was felled by the billows of asphalt that raged between the moored boat and the pub.

A troller came alongside. 'We shouldn't have gone out. It broke my coffee pot and scared the shit out of the wife. Scared the shit out of me. It was all right till the tide turned. It's the tide that does the damage.'

We were at springs, and the ebb was running hard out of Portland Inlet and into Dixon Entrance, where it met a wind of forty knots and gusting higher. The collision of tide, wind, and ocean swell was raising unnaturally steep, close-packed, hollow seas, in which any fishing boat was liable to founder.

The owner of the troller showed me the local test for a bad sea. From the cannery wharf, you looked for a spot on the north-western horizon midway between Finlayson and Birnie islands, where the Pointer Rocks broke the surface in mid-channel four and a half miles off. If you could see nothing, Dixon Entrance was OK; if you saw white there, you should stay in harbour. First I saw nothing. Then a sudden pale exclamation mark appeared in the sky – an exploding gout of surf that must have been as tall as Port Simpson's church spire. The danger signal hung motionless in the air for two or three seconds, then collapsed. There was a surprisingly long interval before the next exclamation mark rocketed up from the sea. !...............!....................!............!...............! was as graphic a navigation-warning as any I'd ever seen.

During the afternoon the front passed, the wind slackened, the tide changed, Pointer Rocks ceased transmission, and the harbour emptied. Every hour counted when the fishery was legally open, and people lived in a communal high fever, forcing aside seasickness and lack of sleep in order to get their nets out, or trail their plastic-squid lures, in any conditions short of the plainly suicidal.

As afternoon turned to evening, and the low sun at last lit up the painted west wall of the cannery, the supply launch trundled into harbour. With its cargo piled in lumpy mounds under sea-splashed tarps, the boat looked like a bulging Christmas stocking, and a crowd of people quickly assembled on the dock to meet it. First out from under the tarps was a king-size mattress, shrink-wrapped in plastic. Next came a new gas range. A child's shiny red bike. Two boxed TV sets. A Yamaha home organ. Once it was copper kettles and brass buttons for sea otter skins; now it was home entertainment for sockeye salmon.

For the stores came crates of soft drinks, boxes of vegetables, and canned foods. A long line of helpers balanced these goods on their heads up the walkway to a waiting pick-up truck, Indians walking in Indian file. It was nearly dark when the truck drew away, climbing the hill in a swirl of dust, with four happy children riding on the tailgate.

Back at my boat, I found a gift on the chart table – a sockeye, about seven pounds, already cleaned, in a plastic shopping bag. The giver hadn't left his name.

I dined on poached salmon and a complex British Columbia Chardonnay, whose long finish left a powerful taste of kerosene on the back of the tongue. Checking the tide tables for the morning, I realized that today was 15 July, that my father had died a month ago, and that I'd missed his birthday on the 4th, when he would've turned seventy-eight. 'Only seventy-eight,' people said, as if septuagenarians now weren't properly qualified to ride in coffins.

He had become my Genie of the Lamp. I could summon him at will. As the level in the bottle of vile wine sank – plenty fast enough for two – I was argufying with my father about Port Simpson as if it were a troubled parish. The night was loud with voices, footsteps, engines, the squishing of fenders against the dock, the road-drill sound of the generator on a big purse-seiner (no bedtime for fishermen during an opening). Sprawled on the settee, evading unwashed dishes in the sink, I became aware that my lips were moving as I phrased my thoughts. I was talking to a ghost. I supposed that I'd go on argufying with him until my own time came to die, and that this was as close as people ever really came to enjoying a life after death. Sometime Julia would find herself talking to my ghost as I was talking to my father's. I hoped so, anyway.

VII. ON THE BEACH

In Dixon Entrance at first light, I had white fingers and a hangover.
The sea was tarnished silver, the swell flaccid and sleepy. Out to
the west, off the port bow, was an unobstructed view of windless,
empty ocean. After so many islands, so much contained water, it was
exciting to come face to face with the sheer absoluteness of the
open Pacific: seemingly the end of the world, with nothing beyond
the interminable horizon except sea, and more sea, and more sea
after that.

When Indians found strange things washed ashore by the currents, they cannot have easily imagined that the piece of wood with
metal fastenings, or the glass float, had come from another landmass.
Every instinct would tell one that such objects came from the depths
of the sea. Their stories of Komogwa and Nagunakas told of a techno-
logically advanced submarine civilization; both were associated with
the possession of copper (an alternative name for Komogwa meant
'copper-maker'), and their wealth and power derived from skills and
materials beyond the Indians' reach. The usual museum label for
these beings is 'sea monster' – a misleading term, given their enviable
human attributes and interests. What they do closely resemble is a
pair of fat undersea emperors. In effect, the Indians had dreamed
Japan into being, but located it, like Atlantis, somewhere at the
bottom of the ocean.

With the nearest available shelter twenty-five miles away, I searched the sky for signs of coming weather, but it was a uniform wash-grey, not a blotch in sight. If the sea had an unpleasant surprise in store for me, it was playing its cards close to its chest. That was the style of Nagunakas and Komogwa. Their mercurial temperaments, quickness to take offence, and taste for brutal jokes were aspects of the ocean itself. In Port Simpson, Curtis – the ambitious father of daughters – had told me that his father used to say of the sea, 'He don't have no pity for nobody'; and the personification of the sea as masculine was probably a relic of an earlier Indian way of thinking about nature. This morning, though, he seemed to be dozing, breathing evenly in his sleep, a sated shogun.

Just south of the Lord Islands, at 54°42′N, the boat crossed the pecked line on the chart and entered Alaska. In the far distance, I could see the daunting armada of the American gill-netting fleet. The entrance to Revillagigedo Channel, nearly ten miles across, was blocked solid with small boats. From where I was, it looked as if a swarm of bugs had settled on the water, like blowflies on a carcass.

As I came closer, the sea frosted over with a light breeze out of the south; more drifting air than wind, but just enough to give me steerageway under sail. To work slowly through the fleet with the engine off would be safer, since I wouldn't become inextricably wedded to a floating net if I blundered into one. With the genoa out and the water rustling softly past the hull, I began to thread the boat through the gaps between the serpentine lines of white dots.

The nets were laid across the grain of the new flood tide, and each boat was making constant small manoeuvres to keep itself squarely aligned with its own pearl string of floats. These American nets were longer than Canadian ones – three hundred fathoms, more than a third of a mile – and they bulged and kinked in the turbulence of the current. I was playing a game with shifting goalposts: one promising gap abruptly closed while another line of corks swung open like a door. Biting hard on my lower lip, I veered this way and that, sliding past the coloured marker-buoys at walking pace.

The boats were all Seattle-registered. I spotted some familiar names from Fishermen's Terminal, the fleet's winter quarters. Tree Point, as people called this place, to save themselves the tongue-gymnastics of 'Revillagigedo', was Ballard in summer exile. The boats were family concerns, crewed by brothers, husbands and wives, fathers and sons. On this calm morning, in the middle of an unexpectedly good season, the gill-netters might have been out on a happy floating picnic.

'When did you leave Seattle?' a woman called as I ghosted past her elbow.

'First of April,' I said. 'April Fools' Day. But stuff happened.'

'Where you headed?'

'Juneau.'

'For Christmas?'

I heard her retelling the joke to her husband as I drew out of earshot.

Two or three larger boats, with hand-painted signs saying CASH hung in their rigging, cruised the edges of the fleet. A gill-netter could spend the day fishing and selling, fishing and selling, without moving from its chosen pitch. Gasping salmon, picked from the mesh as the net came inboard, were being translated into dollar bills even before they died of asphyxia.

This was a landscape of spoliation. The surrounding hills were tonsured like monks: though their lower slopes were thickly furred with second-growth timber, above about 1,000 feet they displayed great bald skulls of grey rock, where the new pines had yet to find a footing. Since 1867, when the United States bought the territory from Russia for two cents an acre, Alaska had been continuously beset by transient hunter-gatherers equipped with harpoons, dynamite, shovels, axes, backhoes, gold pans, oil drills, chainsaws, and fishing nets. Few of these people had any intention of settling the land they came to plunder. Home was far elsewhere. They had no interest in farming the Alaskan soil: in 1958, when statehood was granted, only 20,000 acres were under cultivation. All their supplies came by sea, from Seattle: even in the temperate zone of south-east Alaska, people lived as if they were on an offshore oil rig or a research station in Antarctica; feckless clients dependent on the Lower 48 for their simplest needs.

Alaska was regarded as an inexhaustible treasury of natural assets, to be looted for the nation's benefit. One of its great attractions was its remoteness; and things could be done there that would not have been tolerated in Washington or Oregon. Young men could run profitably wild in Alaska without damaging the social fabric of their staid home-towns. In the dog days of peacetime, Alaska held out the promise of all the noise and excitement of a major foreign war.

It had been ransacked and abused. Anywhere else in the world, such punishment would have left a permanently wrecked ground zero. But the climate here was astonishingly forgiving; 160 inches of rainfall a year is a great healer of wounded landscapes. In Alaska, the wilderness quickly grew back to cover mankind's ugly depredations. It wouldn't be long now before these bald-pated hills were green again. Salmon still ran – amazingly – in sufficient numbers to support the greedy fleet on Revillagigedo Channel. In 1886, when Hubert Howe Bancroft published his epic *History of Alaska*, he wrote that '[Alaska's] resources, though some of them are not yet available, are abundant, and of such a nature that, if properly economized, they will never be seriously impaired'. The wonder was that Bancroft's claim had not yet been rendered laughable, after more than a hundred years of heedless logging, mining, hunting, and fishing.

I had on board the 1933 edition of the *United States Coast Pilot* for Alaska. Even then, half the sawmills and canneries on this stretch of water were described as 'not functioning', 'abandoned', or 'in ruins'. In this country of easy pickings, people were quick to give up and move on. There was always another bit of Alaska's 7,000-mile coast-line where ravaging would take less effort. The scale of the wilderness encouraged even its most predatory attackers to snack, nibble, and look elsewhere. To put down roots, clinging to the land until it was exhausted, had never been part of the footloose Alaskan ethic.

Revillagigedo Channel led to the tight bottleneck of Tongass Narrows, where the long, thin jerry-built city of Ketchikan stretched out on a ledge dynamited out of the north shore. The first sign of civilization was an old red double-decker London bus, parked on an apron of rock along with half a dozen trucks and parts of trucks. The exiled bus, with its patina of rust and grime, looked like a good idea whose time had come and gone. According to the chart, Ketchikan at its fattest had three streets: the prospect of riding around them on a London bus had evidently not been the irresistible tourist-draw that some hopeful entrepreneur must have envisioned.

Big canneries overhung the water on tarred stilts, and the Narrows were crowded with the gill-netters, trollers, purse-seiners, and buyers' tenders that jostled for position around the cannery wharves. I pulled into Thomas Basin among the fishing boats and called US Customs from the payphone at the dockhead. The duty officer took down my details, gave me a clearance number, and asked me how I was enjoying my trip.

'How far you going?'

'Juneau, Glacier Bay, Sitka – then back to Seattle.'

'Wish I was going with you.'

Across the boardwalk was the Potlatch Bar, a raucous cave into which I unwisely stepped for a beer. Apart from the light over the pool table in the far distance, the place was pitch dark. The wooden floor throbbed to the bass and drums of a rock group hyperventilating on the jukebox. Superimposed on the deafening music were fifty separate conversations conducted in shouts and yells. After quiet British Columbia, the Potlatch Bar had all the noise, violence, and energy of America trapped inside a single room. Groping tentatively toward the counter, I told myself I was glad to be back.

Perched on a razor-slashed barstool, waiting for a lull in which to holler my order, I listened to a man at my left shoulder telling a friend about his recent purchase of a pick-up truck. Swapping the word 'truck' for 'fuck', and vice versa, the story went roughly as follows: He'd got the trucking fuck from a truck way the truck up a trucking mountain; but the trucking transmission was trucked – he'd put the trucker in trucking third trucking gear, and *truck*! . . . he'd trucking gone back to trucking kill that mothertrucker for trucking with him. Et cetera.

'Shit,' said the friend.

There was no attempt at elegant variation in the scatological stream: 'truck' was used, impartially, to connote people and things, and to qualify every noun and every verb. When I tuned out of one conversation and into another, it was the same. From end to end, the Potlatch Bar was filled with trucks and trucking.

The bartender at last chose to notice me: I got a trucking beer out of her, drank the trucker, and got the truck out of the trucking place. This was, after all, trucking Alaska.

Back on the boardwalk, a drunk was trying to nap on a picnic-table bench. Each time he got himself more or less horizontal, he rolled off; a sack of insensate flesh. To me it seemed a vain ambition – he should've settled for the ground long ago. But he seemed determined to achieve the dignity of the bench, and I watched him clamber groggily upon it for the third time, find momentary equilibrium, then collapse back onto the boardwalk, where he lay spreadeagled, face down, and, for a minute or two, quite motionless.

There then appeared a cyclist, on an early-evening workout, in black Spandex shorts, green Spandex top, and a white banana-style helmet – a figure common in Seattle but looking strangely displaced in Ketchikan. The gender of this gleaming creature was indeterminate, though the white socks were distinctly girlish. At the sight of the body on the boardwalk, the cyclist dismounted and, from a posture of conscientious social concern, bent toward the drunk and said something I couldn't hear.

The drunk's head lifted an inch or two from the ground. 'Truck you!' he said, with surprising force and volume.

I could see his point. To be awakened from a sodden coma by a giant pale-green grasshopper would be just the kind of thing a drunk most fears.

The cyclist shot me an *And what do you think you're staring at?* glare, then pedalled off. I crossed the road to where an elevator, gouged into the cliff-face, promised instant transportation to a world of elegant fine dining and panoramic views. The glass cage took a long time to climb above the unruly city of tin roofs and cluttered masts. At the end of the ride, I stepped out into a hotel lobby empty but for light-orchestral Muzak and potted palms. After the boardwalk and the Potlatch Bar, this seemed as close to an ascension into heaven as Ketchikan was likely to offer.

I took a seat in the largely empty dining room, whose enormous windows looked out over Tongass Narrows to the blackened mountain ridge of Gravina Island. Ketchikan was beneath the picture frame, though two white beaked cruise ships, moored at the town centre, just scraped in. I smoothed open my notebook, asked for a glass of Hogue Cellars Merlot from Washington State, and settled down to write.

I hadn't enjoyed such height and space in weeks, and the dining room seemed a good perch from which to survey the voyage so far, and to try to see if anything resembling a pattern or a story was discernible in its tumble of places and events. Not much, not yet. While a number of wispy narrative strands had begun to emerge, I knew that journeys hardly ever disclose their true meaning until after – and sometimes years after – they are over.

I had just finished specifying to the waitress exactly how I wanted my steak cooked – 'on the rare side of medium-rare, please' – when a man at a neighbouring table raised his right hand in a ridiculous stiff-armed military salute.

'Hail, fellow Brit,' he said.

An Englishman, as Mr Yorick said, does not travel abroad to meet other Englishmen. I gave the man a crooked and, I hoped, deterrent smile, then made a show of scribbling intently in my notebook.

He was not deterred.

'I think I've heard you on the BBC.'

'Possibly.'

'Radio 4. The Valium of the middle classes.'

I wrote: 'Everyone in Ketchikan is drunk.' This one was in the early, uninhibited, loquacious stage. In a matter of seconds, he and

his girlfriend had established themselves at my table. Both smelled
of fish. He was full of aggressive bounce; she was pale, stringy, and
moved like a sleepwalker, making vague swimming strokes as she
came toward me. They were nearing the bottom of their second bottle
of wine, though her glass looked untouched.

They worked in the cannery at the foot of the cliff, and this meal
was their treat for having survived the first month.

'Know what my last job was?' the man said. 'The House of
Commons. I was — —'s assistant. Know him?'

I did, at least by reputation: a veteran Labour MP, and parliamen-
tary spokesman for Israeli interests in Britain.

'House of Commons to the fish cannery,' said the man complacently. 'What do you make of that?'

He'd gone to school at Dulwich College in South London, and
taken a degree in political science at Southampton University. Now
he was sorting salmon species on the wharf; shovelling the cohos,
sockeyes, pinks, kings, and chums onto their separate conveyor belts.
He, at least, was in the open air all day; his girlfriend was employed
doing something nasty in the bowels of the cannery.

'Where are you from?' I asked her.

'You won't have heard of it. Park City, Utah?'

He earned $12.50 an hour; she earned $10. They lived in the
cannery bunkhouse, and usually spent nothing. Working nineteen-
hour days, they hoped to come away with around $10,000 apiece at
the end of two months – enough to travel for a year, so Simon said.
'We'll be rich tourists.'

'Where will you go?'

'Ladakh.'

As he talked numbers, I saw that money was the least part of the
story. The pay was lousy. If one wanted to explain this couple's presence in Ketchikan, you'd have to look elsewhere – to winter mornings
on the Tube between Westminster and a shared flat in Stockwell;
to the stringencies of life in Park City, pop. 4,468; but most of all, to
Alaska's mythic reputation as the land of swaggering freebooters.
Trying to freeboot on $12.50 an hour would be damned hard going,

but they saw themselves as having arrived in the right state, at least, to kick over the traces, go on the lam, and scare their families sick with their postcards home. In Surrey, as in Park City, the Alaskan postmark on the stamp would be enough to raise a flutter of parental disquiet.

The cannery, Simon said, was a Babel of languages. There were Russians, Romanians, Hispanics, Chinese . . .

'Monique – she's French,' said the girlfriend, in a rare burst of articulacy. Her head was beginning to sink toward her plate.

My steak arrived. Not so much grilled as cured and tanned, it would have made a fine sole for a prospector's boot.

Glazed with drink and exhaustion, Simon began to rant, turning the heads of the handful of elderly couples who were our fellow diners. With a glance at his fading girlfriend, he took on the American educational system.

'A university degree in this country – it's fucking meaningless. It's like 'O'-Levels in England. Everybody's got one. *She's* got one—'

'What did you major in?' I asked her.

'Education,' she said sleepily.

'It's fucking laughable,' Simon said. But he wasn't laughing. He was challenging me to a fight. When I ducked this issue, he produced another.

'I hate English.'

'Oh, yeah?'

'It's a wanker's language. It's like the English are – polite and refined, and dishonest.'

He means me, I thought.

'If I want to express myself, I can't do it in English. There's only one language I can really say what I feel in.'

'Really? What's that?' I said, politely living up to his definition of Englishness.

'Hebrew. I can express myself in Hebrew.' He paused, swallowed half a glassful of wine, scrunched up his face, sawed the air with his hands, and began to shout at me in what might well have been Hebrew. His performance reminded me strongly of someone giving witness in a Pentecostal mission. He was speaking in tongues.

He now had the full attention of the dining room. The waitress was backed into a corner. The expressions of the elderly couples were frozen, as in a game of statues. Someone was having a coughing fit. And I was, too obviously, being held responsible for the behaviour of my dreadful charges.

The girlfriend, who'd been dozing with her head on her side plate, came briefly awake. She didn't appear to understand Simon's Hebrew any better than I did, but the noise of it was clearly familiar to her.

'You see?' Simon said, in a voice suddenly mild and enquiring.

'"Can you please show me the way to the railway station?"' I said.

'What?'

'What you were saying, in Hebrew.'

'You wouldn't understand.'

I thought for a moment he was going to cry.

'I want to go back to the bunkhouse.' The girlfriend's voice was a groan. 'I think I'm going to throw up.'

Abruptly, surprisingly, Simon was restored to sober solicitude. 'She's not strong,' he said. 'She's tired.' He helped her to the bathroom, giving me my chance to settle my bill and escape to the elevator.

Descending the bluff, watching the constellation of lights on Tongass Narrows, I thought that as long as the world had people like Simon in it, Alaska would never be short of migrant labour. He was made for the place: the prototype of that legion of young men whose rootless discontent made Alaska a transforming idea. Simon should have been here for the Gold Rush. I was sorry – almost, but not quite, to the point of paying for his dinner – that he earned only $12.50 an hour.

On the boardwalk, I was stopped by a young woman dressed from another age: fishnet tights, stiletto heels, black leather microskirt, fluffy pink sweater, and a lacquered bouffant hairdo. My own teenage years came back to me in a melancholy rush.

'Yawannadate?'

'No thanks.' But I was glad to have been asked. The streetlamps were dim, and she cannot have seen the crows' feet around my eyes.

She resumed her patrol, heels clicking on the boardwalk. There was rain in the air.

I woke to the bedside radio, which had been left on all night. On the local NPR station, someone was talking about the problem of garbage-bears. Ketchikan, she said, was afflicted more than any other Alaskan city by bears roaming through backyards, upending trash cans, diving in Dumpsters, and harassing old people on their way to the post office. Authorities were trying to chase them away with noisemakers and rubber bullets. Repeat offenders were being shot with anaesthetic darts and transported by barge to remote islands, from where they quickly found their way back to the Ketchikan honeypot. One bear, fitted out with a radio collar, had been exiled to Foggy Bay, forty-five swimming miles away; three weeks later, it was back in the city eating leftover pizzas and French fries. 'People create garbage-bears' was the slogan, and locals were being urged to inciner-ate their garbage and help drive the junk-food addicts back to the wild.

'It's a typical summer day in Ketchikan this morning,' said the announcer. 'Chance of precipitation – one hundred per cent. The weather's lousy. Now back to *Morning Edition*—'

I raised the forehatch and looked out. A cruise ship, moving slowly past the breakwater, was a faint shadow on a screen of dirty gauze. Visibility was down to about a hundred yards. I was glad of the excuse to stay on. I liked what I'd seen of Ketchikan, and wanted more.

One had to watch one's feet on the dock, dangerously slippery in places where puddles of yellow vomit had been spilled by revellers the night before. On this dank morning, Ketchikan revealed itself as a town adapted to the needs of men far from home, blessed with an unlikely abundance of pawnshops, tattoo parlours, and payphones. The payphones, in every available nook and corner, were of a design new to me, incorporating fold-up plastic seats and generous plexiglas umbrellas to deflect the rain. Even this early in the day, most were occupied by wrinkle-browed husbands calling distant wives. Walking past a half-dozen phones, I kept hearing the same half of the same conversation – that muttering, serious tone, those anxious enquiries, that halting recitation of dates and times, interpolated with *if*s and *but*s. My turn at the conversation would come later in the day.

In the Pioneer Cafe, sitting at the counter for breakfast, mine was the only pair of forearms bereft of tattoos, and the trucks were out in force again; trucking-this, truck-that, *I told the truck* . . . It seemed that in this town rigorous profanity was an official male duty, like taking out the trash or raking the fall leaves. You failed at manhood if you neglected to insert at least five trucks into an average sentence. In a lifetime as an occasional barfly, I'd never heard such a flood of casual, routine obscenities as drifted past my ears in Ketchikan.

By the time breakfast was over, the cruise ships had let their passengers go off to play and a bee-swarm of couples was out in the streets, everyone clad in the same pale grey diaphanous plastic mac, of the kind you could squinch into a fist-sized ball and stow in a pocket or a handbag. The macs must have come with the compliments of the cruise line. They made the crowd rustle as it moved – if movement was the word for its lethargic shuffling from storefront to storefront.

By non-Alaskan standards, Ketchikan was village-sized. If the streets were empty, it would take three or four minutes to walk the city centre end to end. In summer, it suffered thousands more strangers than it could reasonably bear: logging crews, cruise passengers, seasonal cannery workers, commercial fishermen, sport fishermen here for the charter fleet, boat tourists like me. The little town was bursting with us, and we were all in a bad temper with one another, crushed, haunch to haunch, like cows in a corral. We squeezed into an alleyway of gift shops, pushing and shoving, saying, 'Ex*cuse* me!' in voices that threatened rather than begged pardon.

Standing guard on either side of a gift-shop doorway were two teenage boys with acne-inflamed faces and golfball Adam's apples. Dressed in fake-fur busbies, red tunics, and black pants, they shouldered wooden dummy rifles. Both looked painfully embarrassed when the video cameras came out from under the plastic macs and the ratchety purring of the motor-drives began. The idea of dressing the boys up as Buckingham Palace Guardsmen had presumably sprung from the same brain that had brought the London bus to Tongass Narrows. What next? Pearly Kings and Queens? A mock-up of Big Ben? The gift shops sold the usual assortment of Indian souvenirs, from knitwear to dream-catchers, pint-sized totem poles, and 'trade-beads' of doubtful provenance.

A woman in the crowd said to her husband, 'We really need another day. There's so much to *see*!'

Excuse me!

I wriggled through.

It was no-go at the little one-storey Tongass Museum. That had been stormed long ago, and a line of couples trailed far down the sidewalk, queuing for admission. My view of Ketchikan was quickly changing: I found myself beginning to think fondly of the Potlatch Bar as a civilized haven from the slow-crawling mob.

I reached Creek Street, the southernmost point of tourist Ketchikan before the cannery workers and fishermen got the town more or less to themselves. The creek was a walled-in tidal drain overhung by a row of nondescript wooden cottages, once bars and whorehouses but now reclaimed for the picturesque by several coats of white, pale-blue, and coral-pink paint. Most were gift shops; one, Dolly's House, had become a museum of quaint, old-time prostitution.

All the videocams were trained on Dolly's House, which was meant to conjure rambunctious times in Historic Alaska, when whores weren't whores but ladies of the night. Its modern occupants, making come-hither gestures from the windows, were waxwork dummies, decorously swathed in crinoline, taffeta, and lace. Though Creek Street had in fact been a full-service combat zone well within living memory, the proprietors of Dolly's House managed to suggest that its heyday had been a century or two ago, when the tricks were probably cross-gartered and wearing powdered wigs, so you could show your video to the grandchildren without a blush. Dolly's House belonged to the colourful tapestry of 'heritage' – history wiped fastidiously clean of the last speck of grubby meaning.

Had the cameras swivelled through 135°, they would have found that Creek Street, far from being dead and gone, had merely relocated its businesses a few yards to the south. Instead of filming waxworks, the cruise-ship passengers could easily have shot the real thing, in unalluring close-up. For $50 or so, they could've got laid. That would be a worthwhile story. 'When your grandpa went to Ketchikan . . .'

I wondered how long it would take – ten years? twenty? – before the Potlatch Bar went the way of Creek Street and was refurbished as a tourist site, charmingly evoking the lost world of *fin de siècle* alcoholism and prostitution.

I missed the exact moment in the afternoon when the whistle blew or the clock chimed; but suddenly Ketchikan was empty. The performance finished for the day, with the mac-people back in their state-rooms and the ships sliding crabwise across the ebb tide, leaving behind a ransacked city. Tomorrow, another 4,000 middle-class invaders would be let loose on the town, but overnight we low-life visitors would be in the ascendancy, fighting and drinking and trucking.

I found a vacant payphone on the city wharf and called home. Julia was still at preschool, but Jean was in. She'd booked their flight; they'd be arriving in Juneau at 8:25 a.m. on the 1st of August. She was coping with single parenthood, she said, and with the dance season winding down had to write only one or two reviews a week. She and Julia were off to a party this evening. She sounded happy, and in confident control of things.

A roll of low cumulus grazed the water in the channel and hid Gravina Island from view. Nearby, the grey water was moving seaward in looping arabesques. I watched it stream out from a piling like a long braid of thick hemp rope, ravelling and twisting in the current.

'I can't wait,' I said.

'Me neither,' Jean said. 'When I put Julia to bed last night, she suddenly sat bolt upright and shouted, "I – need – my – daddy!" She really misses you.'

'She's getting my cards?'

'They're in every mail. Sometimes two at once.'

Though it was long before sunset, lights were on all over Ketchikan. With the smell of woodsmoke and the premature encroaching darkness, it felt like a late November evening.

Buoyed by Jean's news, I went to a supermarket north of the town centre and filled my cart. Since almost everything came up from Seattle by plane or ship, the bill at the checkout was arrestingly large; never before had I managed to spend $231 in a supermarket in one visit. That was another measure of Alaska's condition as a client-state of the Lower 48: a box of cornflakes, or a stick of butter, was a luxury import. Almost the only locally manufactured goods I could find were six-packs of beer at the neighbouring liquor store.

In the cab back to the boat, Gloria, the driver, told me that she'd first come to Alaska with her husband.

'He was a jerk. He was a good provider, but a real jerk. The grass was always greener . . . Know that type?'

'Don't I just?' I said.

After her divorce she'd taken her two children back to Los Angeles. But California city life was 'too scary'. Gloria got her licence as a nurse, then worked her way back to Alaska via Seattle.

'You ought to come to Ketchikan in winter. You can't see it now, but this is a real nice, safe, small town. It's a backyard place – we all talk over our fences – and just great for kids. I'll die here, I guess. It's just in summer that it looks bad. In winter it's real cosy – you should see.'

I could imagine. In the dark and cold and rain, Ketchikan would be a warm and neighbourly huddle on its rocky ledge, squeezed tight between the forest and the water. Down south, small towns had lost their self-containedness to the web of interstate highways, but here there'd be nowhere at all to go except Ketchikan. For months on end, it would be like living aboard a ship at sea.

The winter would bring auditions for *The Sound of Music* with the First City Players, performances by Ketchikan's amateur ballet company, classes in pottery and printmaking, ice fishing, the Build-a-Snowman Competition, fish art by Ray Troll at the SoHo Coho Gallery, quilting bees, meetings of the Writers' Guild at the Parnassus Bookstore at the far end of Creek Street . . .

An outgoing sort would not find it hard to be cosy in Ketchikan.

After breakfast at the Pioneer Cafe, where a fight broke out between two women ('That was my trucking husband, bitch!'), I pushed off under a leaky sky, draped between the tops of Ketchikan's tallest buildings and the trees on the far side of the narrows. Sweatered, gloved, and creaking uncomfortably in foul-weather jacket and trousers, I zigzagged through the traffic of cruise ships, tugs, and fishing boats. Columns of steam at the pulp mill – now threatened with imminent closure – appeared as the stalks from which the overspreading grey sky was blooming.

'Thick and rainey weather' had been the rule when the Vancouver expedition called here in August 1793. *Discovery* and *Chatham* had anchored in sixteen fathoms in Port Stewart, a deep bay just around the corner from the north end of Tongass Narrows. According to Archibald Menzies's journal, something happened that gave an abrupt new twist to the relationship between Indians and whites. His entry is short and matter-of-fact:

> *28th. One of [the] Natives was during this time very anxious in his solicitations to go with us to England & Capt Vancouver seemed inclined to indulge him as it was his own voluntary request, but on the 28th punishments were inflicted on board the Discovery of a very unpleasant nature, on seeing which all of the Natives left the Bay, & he that was before so solicitous to go*

*with us now went away without taking leave of us & never after-
wards returned to the Vessels.*

There are many white accounts of the barbarous customs of the Indians; but none of them are matched in grotesquerie by the English
tribal ritual that routinely took place aboard *Discovery* – the man
strapped to a grating, the boatswain's mate with the cat in the bag,
the flesh ripped open to the bone, the full-dress ceremonial of the
occasion, all the ship's company standing at attention while the victim
screamed. What can the Indians have thought they were witnessing?
How was the story told as it travelled up and down the coast? No
wonder the natives fled the bay in panic after the show.

Winston Churchill epitomized the eighteenth-century navy with
the phrase 'rum, sodomy, and the lash'. Captain Van was addicted to
the lash. The official logbooks for *Discovery* are lost, but Peter Puget
happened to copy out ten days of entries into his own journal, and
they suggest that Vancouver ordered a flogging every three or four
days. Between 30 May and 8 June 1792 (the happy period in which
Captain Van explored the promising and fertile landscape around
Puget Sound), three men were punished.

> *Wednesday 30th . . . Punished Willm. Wooderson Seaman with
> 24 Lashes for Insolence . . .*

> *Saturday 2d . . . Punished Jos. Murgatroyd Seaman with 12
> Lashes for disobedience of orders . . .*

> *Wednesday 6th . . . Punished John Thomas with 36 Lashes for
> Neglect of Duty . . .*

Even for the 1790s, these punishments were extreme. It looks as if at
six bells in the forenoonwatch, eleven o'clock, on Wednesdays and
Saturdays, Vancouver would single out some cheeky seaman and have
him flayed to within an inch of his life.

Menzies's distaste for these violent assertions of authority rings through his journal. The naturalist and the captain were now utterly at loggerheads.

> *Sir*
>
> *It is really become so unpleasant to me to represent to you verbally any thing relative to the Plant-frame on the Quarter-Deck that I have now adopted this method to mention to you all the alterations or rather additions which I wish to be made to its original plan, for the security of the plants within it, together with the occasional aid that may be required to look after it, in my absence; that my solicitation for its success may not subject me to such treatment . . .*

His letter's frigid tone says much about the atmosphere aboard *Discovery*. Menzies, a civilian, was alone among the gentlemen of the quarterdeck in being able to stand up for himself against Vancouver, whom he had come to regard as an irascible self-exalted madman. Writing to Sir Joseph Banks, Menzies would represent his captain as a pompous figure of fun.

> *I forgot to tell you that our Commander has already perpetuated his name on this Coast, for the great Island we circumnavigated last summer of which Nootka is a part, is modestly named Quadra & Vancouver's Island. . . .*

Captain Van retaliated by denying Menzies the use of a small boat for his botanical expeditions. Humoured to his face, abused behind his back, the friendless commander could take comfort only in his rank and the displays of arbitrary power to which it entitled him.

Indian chiefs demonstrated their power by embarrassing their neighbours and rivals with gifts so lavish that they couldn't be reciprocated. Captain Van resorted to the horrible ceremony in the waist of the ship. It was a much less subtle form of public humiliation than the potlatch, but both rituals served the same end, and trumpeted the status of the man who laid them on for the edification of the crowd. Vancouver was short, fat, sickly; and the more his body deteriorated over the course of the voyage, the greater his need to remind his audience that he was still the chief, the holder of a royal commission from King George.

For several generations, at least until the 1850s, when Judge Swan came to the Washington coast, white visitors were called by the Indians 'King George men'. So it seems that Captain Van made the impression he desired.

Following *Discovery*, I ran up Clarence Strait, close to the mountainous and rock-strewn shore of the Cleveland Peninsula. The names on the chart reflected Captain Van's drift of thought that August, as he claimed the wilderness for the House of Hanover. He named the Continental Shore New Hanover, though the title failed to stick. The water on which I was motoring was

> *the most spacious of [various channels], which . . . in honour of His Royal Highness Prince William Henry, I have called THE DUKE OF CLARENCE'S STRAIT; it is bounded on the eastern side by the Duke of York's islands, part of the continent about Cape Caamano, and the isles de Gravina. Its western shore is an extensive tract of land, which (though not visibly so to us) I have reason to believe is much broken, and divided by water, forming as it were a distinct body in the great archipelago. This I have honoured with the name of THE PRINCE OF WALES'S ARCHIPELAGO.*

Cloistered in his private quarters, in unhappy exile from the social life of the main cabin, Vancouver kept lordly company in the pages of *The Royal Kalendar*. By the end of the voyage, he had bespattered the coast with viscounts, earls, and dukes. The great families of eighteenth-century England – the Spencers, Portlands, Binghams,

Cokes, Lucans, and many others – still grace the windy capes and ice-cluttered inlets of Alaska with their names.

The grey sea was stippled, the cat's-paws of wind playing across it too fluky to justify the hoisting of a sail. The sodden air threw the world into pearly soft focus. I got my camera and photographed a flock of sandpipers flying north, wing to wing in close formation. Trying to catch the moody iridescence of the light, I took more pictures of a passing troller, *Peggie Ann*, out of Ketchikan – a cobweb of wet rigging, its four reined-in trolling poles scraping against the bank of cloud overhead. In the viewfinder it looked a strange creature, bred to the Inside Passage by some Darwinian process of selective adaptation: part insect, with long, probing antennae; part bird; part fish; and part snug family homestead.

I called *Peggie Ann* over the radio and got Mrs Nic Nebl, very pleased to hear that I'd been taking snapshots of her boat.

'We're so proud of her. We've always wanted a picture of her at sea.'

Weeks later, I sent the Nebls an enlargement of *Peggie Ann*, white with grey trim, afloat in what appeared to be a troubled sky, like a descending thunder-eagle or a double-headed flying sisiutl. At Christmas, a large parcel came from Ketchikan; a reciprocal gift of smoked sockeye salmon.

An escort of chuffing porpoises saw me through the entrance to Meyers Chuck, tricky with submerged offlying rocks. Despite all indications to the contrary, this wasn't really the flipper of friendship, extended by mammals to humankind: our divergent interests merely happened to coincide at the entrance channel, used by salmon and boats alike. So, with no fish to chase, the porpoises were keeping themselves in shape by chasing me. But the tight-muscled swoop of them, as they torpedoed past the cockpit and went scissoring ahead of the bow, gave a shine to my arrival; when tying up to the float, I realized that the weight of the journey was suddenly gone. Four days short of Juneau, I now could see beyond it to our floating family holiday . . . Julia and the porpoises . . . Julia and the icebergs . . . Julia and the bears. We'd need a fishing rod – buy it in Juneau. We'd need more kids' books for bedtime reading. We'd need a ton of macaroni, and the hideous yellow Cheddar considered by Julia to be the only cheese worthy of the name.

Before Meyers Chuck, I hadn't dared think like this. Now I indulged myself in a happy mental shopping list. Better get sun-block – tangerine soda – Kleenex – matzohs – candied ginger for the seasick – Beanie Babies – peanut butter – tuna fish in water – Travel Scrabble – crayons – M&Ms and herbal tea. Just framing the words in my head made me smile, and my elation spread to include every-thing in the little settlement.

Chauk was a Nootka Indian word for 'body of water'. Whites had borrowed it as a jocular term. West Coast Canadians – especially those who wrote for the yachting magazines – liked to call the sea 'the saltchuck', a usage I found irritating in its whiskery old-fangledness. But I liked the way the word worked here. Meyers Chuck, walled off from Clarence Strait by a wooded island and a reef, was like a glassy monastic pond, with herons wading in its shallows and a belted king-fisher dive-bombing out in the middle.

The twisted tracks of an old marine railway and a few rotted stumps in the ground were all that remained of the machine shop and blacksmith's mentioned in the 1933 pilot-book. Meyers Chuck's thirty-seven present residents lived in secluded gingerbread houses set a little way back from the water and linked by a winding muddy path, riddled with tree roots and curtained by trailing vines. Nothing was chichi or self-conscious in the place's prettiness: it seemed in con-tented retirement from the world, its only intruders a trickle of summer pleasure boats like mine. There was a small fishing lodge on the east bank, a tiny Catholic elementary school, a couple of commer-cial fishing boats; its post office was a padlocked shed, whose rare and eccentric opening hours were tied to the arrival of the weekly mailplane, where I disbelievingly slid a bear-postcard into the box.

I saw no one on my walk, though I heard my passage being telegraphed from barking dog to barking dog.

The only signs – hand-lettered shingles, nailed at odd angles to the firs – pointed the way to the Art Gallery, which turned out to be in a tree house at the end of the path. The strange quiet of Meyers Chuck was explained by the exhibits inside. The villagers evidently kept busy indoors stringing jewellery, bottling preserves, doing poker-work, throwing pots, stuffing felt birds-of-paradise, carving drift-wood, painting watercolours (and some of them weren't bad), grinding and polishing lumps of purple and green rock; crocheting, embroidering, whittling, varnishing, glazing, and creating whimsies out of seashells, silver foil, twigs, and glue.

The air was ripe with the smell of incense sticks and lavender bags. Whenever I moved, I set another bunch of wind chimes tink-ling. Looking forward to domestic life on the boat after Juneau, I bought, at metropolitan prices, a quilted pot holder and a jar of home-made jam.

During the afternoon, two families in motor cruisers came in, tied up, and took the posted trail to the gallery, from which everyone came back with something. So the cogs of the Meyers Chuck tourist economy turned at a pace that could inflict no serious injury to the life of the village. That evening, I sat out in the cockpit watching over the family high-jinks on the dock. The two parties were amalgamat-ing: barefoot children scalped each other with shrimp nets; husbands traded wisecracks over the barbecue grill, as wives emerged wrapped in towels, fresh from the shower, holding bottles and glasses. Every-one was deep in the temporary gypsy bohemia of a summer vacation on the remote fringe of the real world. I was the uninvited ghost at their feast.

Never mind. Not long to go now. My turn next.

In the morning, just as the sun scraped clear of the snow-caps to the east, and in a breeze that had sprung up from nowhere, the flat water was as yellow and coarsely granulated as a sweep of raked gravel. Clarence Strait was empty. Huddled under the doghouse roof, warm-ing my hands on a mug of coffee, I had nothing to do but monitor the course and listen to the monotonous donkey *hee-haw*, *hee-haw* of the autopilot as it sent corrections to the wheel. I'd woken at five, thinking of my father and me; his lifelong caution, my reactionary impulsiveness. Strangely, considering his profession, it seemed to me that he was the born sceptic, I the rash believer.

I turned the compass rose on the autopilot's control box to clear Misery Island. The previous day I'd passed Bittersweet Rock. A feature of the American West, at sea as on land, was that much of it had been named at a period when *Pilgrim's Progress*, in the umpteenth small-print edition, was on every family's short bookshelf, between the Bible, the Sears, Roebuck catalogue, and – here, at least – the tide tables. There was a Bunyanesque ring to many of Captain Van's names, like Desolation Sound and Deception Pass. The settlers had continued that tradition, signposting the sea with names of moral and emotional states. One could write a pilgrim's, or a rake's, progress from the chart. The infant hero would be born at Incarnation Point, with Hardscrabble Point the first milestone in his babyhood. His course would take him past Sunshine Island, Luck Point, and an early trial at Liar Rock. Trouble Island would lead to Seduction Point and a rough passage through Peril Strait, past Grief Islet and Ford's Terror, braving Point False Retreat and coming through the Eye Opener, where Cape Decision loomed through the mist, Point Escape hard by. For the shriven pilgrim there'd be Port Conclusion, with Harmony Islands, Happy Cove, and Paradise Flats. Given names like these, the wilderness became a three-dimensional allegory whose plot (depending on your route through it) changed continuously. Today I was bound from Misery Island to Cemetery Point.

As a child, I'd been in awe of my father's Sunday lunchtime performances with the carving knife. First there was the ritual swordplay with the sharpener, then the deep hush in which the meat was carved – shaved, rather, as each slice had the mottled transparency of a photographic negative. The knife was ancient. Like most things in our house, it had come down through the family, and a hundred or so years of weekly sharpening had reduced its blade to the narrowness of a rapier point. With this my father could make the smallest joint last until the next Saturday.

Growing up in the Depression had prepared my parents for a lifetime of saving, skimping, making do. My father wore his clothes to shadows. Great Uncle Cyril's cassock conveniently hid turned cuffs and collars, and grey flannel trousers worn to the shiny thinness of silk.

His one great luxury, in the austere 1950s, was his faith. Like his father and uncle, he was a High-Churchman, an Anglo-Catholic ritualist. For the communion service he would robe himself with white and gold, in chasuble and stole. Only the Low Church leanings of his churchwardens and parishioners stopped him from using incense. Up at the altar, his back to the congregation, he presided over the holy mystery of God making Himself manifest in wafers of bread and the silver goblet of Vino Sacro wine.

When he lifted the chalice for consecration and pronounced Christ's words, 'Drink ye all of this, for this is my Blood of the New Testament, which is shed for you and for many for the remission of sins,' the cheap, sweet, Burgundy-style wine changed into the very blood of the Redeemer.

'Theology,' my father would say in the early days of his ordination, 'is the queen of the sciences.' At the altar, with the priest dressed like an Egyptian magician, the laws of physics were miraculously suspended. My father could change bread into flesh and comprehend the divine secret of the three-in-one-and-one-in-three.

In every other department of life, his instinctive response was to doubt. He never saw a sky in which he couldn't find a cloud. He was at his happiest when exposing a fly in the ointment, a flaw in the argument. Only in his religious practice was he extravagant. To the council estate where he was a curate, then to the long, straggling village that was his first full parish, he brought a strangely de luxe version of English Protestantism, replete with genuflections, fine vestments, and the mystical paradoxes of such early Church of England apologists as Donne and Hooker.

In the otherwise indulgent 1960s, he started to apply the carving knife to his own beliefs, shaving them, sliver by sliver, to fit the new England of ring-roads, high-rise blocks, and windblown shopping plazas, where his ministry lay. He read 'existential theology' – Tillich, Bonhoeffer – while lamenting that he was a dunce at getting his head around philosophical ideas. In 1963 he read *Honest to God* by John Robinson, the Bishop of Woolwich, a book that raised a storm in the Church and deeply interested my father. I once picked up *Honest to God* from its permanent place by my father's chair on the drawing-room floor and saw that the inked annotations in my father's small, neat hand, with a touch of dandyism in its loops and flourishes, so thickly crowded Robinson's text that it was nearly illegible. For months on end my father argufied with the rogue bishop, before he came to side with him.

This was his passage through Peril Strait, in a nimbus of pipe smoke, amidst toppling piles of books, a farting dog at his feet. By the early 1980s he had pared down his creed to its ethical and symbolic bones.

In our late-night vinous conversations in front of the gas fire, I used to twig him on the subject. 'Where do you stand now on things like the Resurrection and the idea of personal eternal life, Peter?'

'Are we talking literally?'

The bushy eyebrow, cocked high; the lopsided, toothy smile. That pipe. He squinted at the level of the wine in his glass, as if taking aim along a gunsight.

'I'd say they were powerful symbols in anybody's book, wouldn't you, old boy?'

'But can you believe in Christianity without believing in a super-natural god?'

'Well . . .' He got a great deal into the word 'well'; head thrown back, face squinched, a long expulsion of breath. 'Of course, I'm sus-picious of the supernatural . . .'

He wouldn't be caught, but made it quite clear that between his belief and my disbelief was a fissure so narrow that one would need a micrometer to measure it. Not that he had lost his faith. At least my father certainly didn't see it that way. Rather, he had refined it, by the same process of rational economy with which he could make a joint last for a week, a pair of trousers for twenty years.

I did not know what he believed – or didn't believe – when he was dying, or what death meant to him then. I was reasonably certain that he didn't view it as the gateway to a bright hereafter. In forty years in the priesthood, most of his time had been spent trying to give consolation to other people; but I doubted if he had found much left in his religion with which to console himself.

Thinking of my father's voyage made me forget my own. I was at his bedside in Market Harborough, with shadows of the traffic outside moving in the room where he was lying still, when the boat collided with a log. The crash stopped it dead. The bow climbed high out of the water. There was the same sound that a house makes in an earthquake – the crackling, grinding noise of big trouble in the foundations down below. The log, black with age, two feet in diameter and about thirty feet long, slid past the beam, almost totally submerged. A pencil-line of light where it grazed the surface was its only give-away. Waiting to catch someone napping, it had caught me fair and square.

I got the floorboards up in the forecabin and saloon, but saw no alarming trickle in the bilges. The boat wasn't an oversensitive type; powerfully built, it was designed to take life on the chin. When I bought it, the marine surveyor said, 'She'll put up with more punishment than you can,' and the boat's toughness had several times saved me from the consequences of my own negligence, as an ark should.

Back in the here and now, I kept a careful lookout. I got the sails up, thereby killing the wind. The boat ghosted for a mile or so on the diminishing air, then its sails fell limp, and it began to turn in sluggish circles on the current. Reluctant to break the windless silence, listening for animals in the brush along the shore, I let the sky revolve overhead and watched an eagle soaring on a thermal like a scrap of charred paper against the blue.

The channels here were crevices between bare-skulled mountains. They appeared entirely landlocked until, at the last moment, a granite cliff would slide aside to disclose the next reach. In the narrowest crevice of all, where Zimovia Strait shrank to an islet-studded tidal river not much more than half a mile wide, was a deserted Tlingit village. Even in 1933 the place had been long abandoned. But one could still see where the Indians had rolled boulders away on the beach to make a sandy canoe-launching ramp; and though the houses had rotted back into the forest, an obstinately human, domestic atmosphere clung to the site.

It was tucked deep out of harm's way, this pretty small-scale refuge from the big, wild country that surrounded it. The water was shallow – only five and six fathoms in the buoyed channel – and perfectly sheltered. A full gale would do no more than ripple it. Willows and alders grew on the gently sloping banks, and the sunlight filtering through the leaves made speckled, pleasantly Augustan glades. Captain Van, who saw the entrance to Zimovia Strait but did not investigate it, would have approved of this sequestered pool, with its half-dozen miniature islands and level, curving lawns.

The early explorers had viewed the Indians as creatures of whatever landscape they happened to inhabit. The natives were as much a part of the flora and fauna as bears and wolves. The farther north the Vancouver expedition sailed, the more the Indians appeared to grow darker, dourer, more granitic and hostile, borrowing their character from the terrain in which they were encountered. The 'treacherous', 'jabbering' Tlingits (Menzies's words) were the fiercest and most alien tribe that the whites had met so far. They incorporated in their persons all the bad weather of the summer of '93, the frustrating, many-branched nature of what is now the Alexander Archipelago, the forbidding cliffs and impenetrable black forest of the wilderness. Had the travellers found them in settings like Zimovia Strait, the Indians would surely have been seen in a more favourable light.

In fact, Vancouver's men were in far greater danger from the natives of Tahiti and Hawaii. But the English tourists, then as now, had fixed ideas about the character of people from the warm south and attributed to the Pacific islanders an essentially sunny disposition, a love of pleasure, an un-English appetite for sex in the afternoons. Even when murder was in the air, the English sailors clung to the notion that Tahiti and Hawaii were run on the lines of an eighteenth-century Club Med.

The Tlingits were northerners, living on the same latitude as the citizens of Aberdeen. Parsimony and joylessness were what the English always expected of people of the north, and they were quick to nail the Tlingits as surly, mean, and rowdy. It was as if *Discovery* had made a three-quarter-circumnavigation of the world only to discover a race of grim, half-naked Scotsmen with lip-ornaments and bows and arrows.

Past the last islet, the strait opened out into a U-shaped valley whose mountainsides exhibited massive, angular clearcuts and the vertical mud-chutes down which logs were tumbled to the sea. The water here was a milky soapstone green – glacier-melt from the Stikine River, or so I guessed. Flecks of dust and pollen were riding on the surface, which was as smooth and thick-looking as paint.

Labouring hard against the tide, the boat seemed stuck fast in this unlovely stretch. I could see Cemetery Point across the miles of eerie green water and slash-littered hills, a smudge on the starboard bow that grew no closer, though the engine was running at full tilt. An hour passed. Two. Then, at close to four o'clock, Wrangell slid into view from behind the point: a big fleet of fishing boats tied hull to hull in the harbour and, behind them, a low, shambling wooden town under a mile-long pall of industrious steam.

Wrangell was in trouble, and full of afternoon-men. Moon-faced, hands deep in pockets, they scuffed their heels around the docks; sat in the cabs of stationary pick-ups, playing the radio with the windows down; pushed infants in strollers up and down a main street on which half the businesses were closed and up for sale. In the smoky fug of the Diamond C. Cafe, I read a ten-day-old *Wrangell Sentinel* and got the story. A sawmill had recently shut down, putting two hundred and fifty people out of work. More closures were on the way. The curbs on logging in national forests, imposed by the Clinton administration, were seen in Wrangell as a vindictive attempt by the federal government to destroy the town, now a fortress of militant Republicanism. Four months before the election, the VOTE DOLE placards were out, planted in every front yard like so many saplings. In the Diamond C. Cafe, the President was known to all as Trucking Bill.

Wrangellites were not mollified by the $32 million of federal money, payable over four years – a grant from the Economic Disaster Relief Fund – but the city manager was pleased. The *Sentinel* quoted him as saying, 'We have to spend $7.5 million a year – it's a good problem to have.' It seemed a lot to me: $3,000 per annum for every man, woman, and child. But the Diamond C. patrons, in bush hats and seaboots, were complaining that 'the Money', as they called it, had already been woefully misspent, even before a cent of it had been seen in town. The mood in the cafe was gnarly and corrosive; I thought it smart to keep my head down and ask no questions while the diners derided the stupid trucking projects of trucking City Hall.

A poster was stuck to the window: WE SUPPORT RESOURCE DEVELOPMENT JOBS. The words 'logging' and 'fishing' had largely disappeared from the political discourse – a measure of the conservationists' victory in the rhetorical war. Now the fishing and timber industries had to take cover behind a smokescreen of tortured euphemisms. Netting a salmon run or denuding a mountain of its trees was called 'wise use' or 'resource development'. When the *Sentinel* referred to the ban on logging in national forests, it did so in the slyest terms, calling it 'Congress's failure to open more land for timber production'.

Licence plates proclaimed Alaska the Last Frontier; and given the state's long history of cheerful rapine, the new restrictions were construed as an affront to liberty itself. Wrangell, harder hit than most towns on the coast, was enraged. Every house enjoyed a view of great stands of timber that Washington, DC, had put out of bounds, for reasons considered vengeful and capricious.

Class had much to do with it. The wilderness – which by rights ought to be used as a tree farm – was being artificially preserved for merely aesthetic reasons, to provide a scenic backdrop for the enjoyment of *tourists*, a word pronounced with venom. People in Wrangell were losing their traditional livelihoods because liberal politicians in Washington were playing to a gallery of kayakers, hikers, cruise-ship passengers, birdwatchers, and other know-nothing urban intruders like the putty-faced Englishman in baseball cap and Docksiders reading the paper in the corner.

For a picture of Wrangell daily life, I turned to the *Sentinel*'s police blotter:

> 3:09 p.m. *Bear Complaint. Citizen reported a Mama bear and two cubs in the back of the Forest Service parking lot.*
> 3:40 p.m. *Bear Complaint. A citizen reported a bear in their garbage at Bloom's Trailer Court.*
> 10:33 p.m. *Disturbance/Disorderly Conduct. Three people yelling on Grief Street.*
> 11:38 p.m. *Disturbance/Fight. Two men fighting between First Bank, Benjamin's, and Parking Lot. A misunderstanding over who was the owner of a vehicle.*

That evening, *Compass Rose*, a sloop registered in Victoria, tied up alongside me. Beside my boat, *Compass Rose*, with its coiled lines and scrubbed decks, looked as if it were slumming. Its owner was kitted out to match, in yachting cap, guernsey sweater, and yellow oilskin trousers. His pepper-and-salt beard appeared to be a summer experiment, not a permanent fixture. Though beefily built, he was quick on his feet and danced adeptly from bow to stern, flicking lines onto cleats as he lashed our boats together. His travelling companion, a slight, elfin woman, hung back in the cockpit, deferring to his expertise. I saw the muscular effort that her determined smile was costing her.

They introduced themselves. Derek's voice had the sonorous deliberation of someone used to being listened to. Linda's had the hasty, apologetic note of someone expecting to be cut off in the middle of her next sentence. As a couple, they had evidently spent a few days too many inside the emotional pressure-cooker of a 34-foot boat. I knew the feeling.

I uncorked a bottle of wine, glad to have company, and intuiting that Linda and Derek would welcome the distraction of a stranger. But Derek took charge, giving a lecture-demonstration of the electronic wizardry aboard *Compass Rose*: the laptop computer on the chart table, with all the charts for Alaska encoded in a CD-ROM, the autopilot and GPS interfacing the chart display, so that the boat could sail itself around the world while Derek kept an eye on the computer screen. He pressed buttons, talked chips and bytes. Linda confessed to seasickness and fright.

'This is all very new for me.'

'Click on that icon,' Derek said. 'See?'

'Derek likes gadgets,' Linda said.

Derek gave her a puzzled stare, then said, 'Is there a Federal Express box here?'

I said that I doubted it. Wrangell didn't strike me as that sort of town.

'I have to Fed-Ex some papers.' Derek nodded significantly as he said this. He turned to Linda. 'If we can't do it here, we'll have to do it in Petersburg. Tomorrow afternoon. At the latest.'

Take that down, Miss Pennyfeather.

'I shall talk to the harbour master,' Derek said.

I couldn't fathom him. Linda had let drop the fact that in her other life she was a schoolteacher, but Derek and I were being careful to play our cards close to our chests. Meeting as sea captains, we were reluctant to own up to any other occupation. After the interesting topic of the Fed-Exed papers had come and gone, we talked weather and tides; and not lightly, for Derek had the gift of imparting gravity to his every passing fancy. When he said, 'I was thinking of going to Sitka,' it came out sounding as if he meant to send a task force there to take the place by storm.

Close to my age, he came from Victoria; his beard was a temporary disguise; he was accustomed to being taken very seriously. By the time we said goodnight, I had settled with reasonable certainty on the notion that he was a member of the provincial parliament in Victoria, if not of the federal one in Ottawa. Did the Canadians have a Minister of War?

I slept late, for once. The tide in Wrangell Narrows, where both *Compass Rose* and I were bound, wouldn't begin to run in our favour until the afternoon, and Derek and I had agreed to leave together around 12:30. Over breakfast I listened to the local radio news. The human remains found by a roadside were, in the opinion of the police, a bear-kill. An armed loner was still on the loose in the wilderness area of Dundas Bay; he had threatened to kill a charter-boat captain with a .44 Magnum, asking him, 'Do you know what a .44 can do?' Icicle Seafoods was branching out into sophisticated value-added products including microwaveable chum salmon in teriyaki sauce. The University of Alaska was offering new extension courses in 'The Visitor Industry' – another too-delicate phrase, which showed how tainted the word 'tourist' had become. As tourists had wrecked the economy of Wrangell, so visitors now promised to revive it.

There followed a slew of 'radiograms' – messages for telephoneless people on islands and up inlets. The Robertses, to Harold Bergman: 'We'll be over Thursday, on the morning high tide.' 'Sharon Evans – please contact the Wrangell Police Department.' 'Will the Crabtrees please get in touch with Denise at Cripple Creek?' The announcer made it sound as if he knew everyone concerned, and perhaps he did. It was true here, as elsewhere in the West, that the tightest, most intimate communities were also the most isolated and scattered; and the Wrangell radio station was the nerve centre of an extended watery village that stretched up the Stikine River and through the archipelago.

Derek tapped on my hatch. He had breakfasted, he said, and solved his Fed-Ex problem. His guidebook noted that there were Indian petroglyphs on a beach to the north of town; he had ordered a cab to take him there. Would I care to join him?'

'And Linda?' I said.

'Linda,' said Derek, sorting his words carefully, 'has things to do on the boat.'

Our driver was a wrinkled nut of a man, his face engulfed by a Santa Claus beard. He insisted on first taking us to see Wrangell's chief tourist attraction, the dump. Among the junked fridges, bikes, busted furniture, and old crab traps were dozens of mauled kitchen bags, with nasty-looking leftovers leaking through the gashes. But we saw no bears.

'There's always bears here,' the driver said in an affronted tone.

The watchman came over from his hut, carrying what looked like a .44 Magnum. 'Haven't seen one all morning,' he said.

The driver clearly felt that his honour was being impugned. To the watchman he said, 'Every time I come here there's bears.'

'Not now there isn't,' the watchman said.

'Up there.' The driver pointed to a vacant ledge of rock at the back of the dump. 'That's where they hang out.' He stared at the ledge, willing the bears to appear.

'We've seen bears,' Derek said. 'We want to see the petroglyphs.'

With aggrieved reluctance the driver turned the minivan around and crawled away from the dump, his eyes fixed on the rear-view mirror.

'That's the first time I ever took anybody to the dump and they didn't see bears.'

'I am not interested in bears. I am interested in petroglyphs,' Derek said, reducing the driver to silence.

At the beach, the driver sulked inside the van. The tide was far out, the beach stony and boulder-strewn. We searched for petroglyphs without success.

'Every time I come here there's petroglyphs,' I said.

Derek stared gravely at me, fearing lunacy or worse. I gestured toward the parked van, and said, limply, 'The driver . . . '

'Ah.'

Derek spotted a small Indian girl playing with her brother in a tide pool and interrogated her. She pointed to a boulder we'd already inspected; and as soon as we saw one petroglyph, we found them everywhere. They'd been chiselled into the rock with great skill, though the tide had worn them down to shadows as pale as the lost lettering on old tombstones. Some were human faces, but most were salmon – lifelike and life-sized, all pointing the same way, to the south-west. If you swam here at high water, you'd see a hazy shoal of carved fish.

They cannot have been very ancient, or the sea would've obliterated them by now. The traditional Northwest ovoid had been incorporated, as a decorative feature, into a realist style of drawing learned from whites. My guess was that they might date back as far as 1900, or thereabouts.

'Direction signs,' Derek said.

The mimic fish were headed away from the Stikine River, toward Zimovia Strait and the village site I'd passed the previous day. If they were direction signs, meant to encourage real salmon to take the right-fork at Wrangell, it was hard to understand why the Indians should have wasted so much artistic labour on making the inevitable happen. In the Alaskan past of huge salmon runs, with every inlet choked with fish, why had the petroglyphs been thought necessary? Or were the Indians simply doodling on the rocks for their own amusement?

Derek, a purposeful and efficient tourist, strode from petroglyph to petroglyph, pausing before each one just long enough to focus his camera and press the shutter. In ten minutes he'd covered the beach and was impatient to be back on his boat. When I dawdled, tracing with my forefinger the dimpled outline of a cadaverous dog-salmon, its head shrunken around its long hedge-clipper jaws, Derek made a show of consulting his watch and being concerned by what he saw there.

Our route back to the harbour took us past a small white hospital, in which Derek suddenly interested himself, quizzing the driver about its exact number of beds, staff, operating theatres, and other facilities. This wasn't the driver's day. His answers were garrulous and artfully vague. I saw that I'd been wrong about Derek's occupation: he must be in the medical business. Doctor? Hospital administrator? As we climbed aboard our boats, I thought I had him pegged. Urologist.

Twenty miles west of town lay Wrangell Narrows, a dredged and dynamited hairline crack between three islands, and the busiest waterway in Alaska. The zigzag channel was festooned with navigation aids, and it was easy – in daylight – to thread one's passage through the clutter of buoys, posts, wooden dolphins, and concrete pillars that marked the fairway, though a strong tide was doing its best to sweep the boat sideways into muddy shallows.

The concentration of traffic in Wrangell Narrows had led to much building along the low-lying eastern shore. Half the wharves and jetties had fallen to bits, but new structures were sprouting between the collapsed roofs and mouldering stumps of homes and businesses that had been left for dead. It was typical of the fever-chart rhythm of Alaskan life that one commodity would rocket in value just as another went into free fall. So gold, timber, fish, and blue fox (a big resource under development on this reach in 1933, according to the pilot) peaked and hit bottom in chaotic sequence, creating a distinctive architecture in which the ruins of the latest bust jostled for position with the rising timber frames and Sheetrock walls of the current boom. Nothing looked meant to last for long: the classic model appeared to be the prospector's tent, pitched one day and struck the next.

The richest state in America had a hobo mentality. Alaska travelled light (in expenditure on education, for instance, it ranked forty-eighth) and lived for the moment, sowing the wind, reaping the whirlwind. Watching the unlovely shoreline slide past on the beam, I felt a kinship with it. It answered to the thick streak of nomadism in my own makeup. It mirrored all my slovenliness, my taste for the temporary and the makeshift, my weakness for crazes, discarded almost as soon as embarked on. Were I ever called on to construct and populate an American state, it would look a lot like Alaska; and I wouldn't care to live there.

The straggle of sheds and houses along the bank at last thickened into the low, pale, floating city of Petersburg, whose canneries and bunkhouses, built out on stilts over the water, were doubled by their reflections in the oily calm. Boats greatly outnumbered buildings. In the half-mile narrows, Petersburg needed no sheltering harbour wall, so the boats were scattered piecemeal along a mile of pilings, moorings, piers, and floating docks, making the town look more like a fleet at anchor than a permanent settlement. The whole place rippled and shimmered. I felt faintly dizzy as I tied up among the reflections, then went to report to the harbour master's office.

As Wrangell was sunk in depression, Petersburg was on a high and suffering from a labour shortage. In the middle of the best sockeye run in years, fish were piling up on the wharves. Cannery managers were running around town, rousting drunks out of bars and pressing them into service. The glut was causing the price of salmon to fall by the hour, making fishermen race back to sea from the dock in an attempt to make up in bulk what they were losing in dollars-per-pound. So both canneries and fishermen were working flat out, and Petersburg was flush, loud, wired, and unsteady on its feet.

Petersburg was only forty miles away from Wrangell, but these were Alaskan miles of sea and mountain – sufficient distance to render the two towns as remote from each other as summer and winter. On the docks, where disappointed men were swapping numbers from boat to boat ('Seventy trucking cents a trucking pound!'), I found *Compass Rose*, just arrived, and went off in search of supper with Derek and Linda.

The dim and smoky Homestead Cafe was crammed with fishermen and cannery workers. Waiting in line for a table – 'Fast, Friendly, Efficient – *Self* Service', warned the notice – I caved in and asked what it was that Derek did for a living.

'I am a professor of molecular biology.'

'Ah. I was almost there. Not quite, though. I had you figured for a medical man.'

'I have delivered papers to international congresses on medicine,' Derek conceded.

By the time we managed to grab a table for ourselves, with Derek revealing a possible past as a rugby forward, both our occupations were out in the open, and we were talking more easily. We had both taken to boats in middle age, and both were inclined to approach the sea as earnest, late-coming undergraduates tackling a new academic discipline. On *Compass Rose* the night before, I'd noticed several books that were twin to my own, like Van Dorn's *Oceanography and Seamanship*, Willard Bascom's *Waves and Beaches*, and Rachel Carson's *The Sea Around Us*. Now we talked whirlpools, overfalls, tidal gyres, capillary waves – subjects I usually kept under my hat. I'd seen too many people glaze over whenever I worked the conversation around to the fascinating movements of water. But Derek did not glaze over; warming to the theme, he shed his ponderous demeanour. His trip north, like mine, had taken him past a succession of wonders in physical oceanography. When he spoke of the places he had visited, he meant rips, swirls, boils, chutes, slippery water.

I mentioned the great exclamation marks of surf that exploded from Pointer Rocks when a sea was running off Port Simpson.

'Port Simpson?' Linda asked. 'I spent ten months in Port Simpson.'

Her then-husband had taken a teaching job at the band school. They had arrived in Lax Kw' Alaams just two days after Linda discovered she was pregnant. Autumn turned to winter, the village streets to gluey mud, then rutted ice. Marooned there, unbearably far away from the city of friends with whom she might have shared the adventure of her pregnancy, Linda was lonely beyond measure.

'It was the worst time in my life.'

'How were the Indians?'

'Hostile.'

'It's an Alice Munro story,' I said. But I was thinking of Derek and Linda, and their eight summer weeks aboard *Compass Rose*. That was another Alice Munro story, one I could almost write myself.

'She's a great writer,' Linda said.

This talk of writing led Derek to describe a novel he'd read by Michael Crichton. He couldn't recall the title – was it *Eaters of the*

Dead? – but it was about primitive people, and had caught Derek's attention as a rare work of fiction that was faithful to scientific fact. I thought, *This is exactly what he'd say in the Munro story.*

It was dark when we left the Homestead Cafe. The walkway down to the dock was treacherously slick after a recent shower. We clambered apprehensively down it, while Derek talked of the present state of research on the flow of water through pipes.

'The results,' he said, 'aren't altogether what you might expect. The most nearly laminar flow occurs in pipes with a roughened surface. The most turbulent flow occurs in smooth pipes, where the surface does nothing to hinder the formation of eddies.'

'That's strange,' I said. For I instinctively thought of turbulence as something caused by an obstruction – a projecting headland, a rocky and uneven sea-bottom, an island in the stream. 'But I like it. It means that turbulence just happens. It needs no provocation.'

'Well, that would depend, wouldn't it,' Derek said, 'on whether confining the flow of water to a pipe counted as provocation?'

I saw it exactly: the confinement and the turmoil; the trapped water boiling in the pipe, spinning furiously off that smooth containing surface. Back inside the boat, I scribbled a note on the behaviour of water in pipes, thinking it an image that was bound to come in handy for something, sometime.

Next morning, the sky was blue – not the usual shallow, faded-denim of the Northwest but the blue of deep ocean. Above the snowy mountains to the north and east were a few chalk scratches of very high cirrus. With the clear sky came a dry easterly breeze, just enough to keep the boat jogging along quietly under sail at four to five knots: the saloon table was so perfectly level that an egg would barely have rolled to leeward on it. It was the best weather I'd seen since leaving Seattle.

Juneau was less than a hundred miles off, and Jean and Julia's arrival was still five days away. I had time to loaf and enjoy the landscape, with no pressing need to clock up mileage. With the sheets set and the wheel on autopilot, there was little to do but loll in the cockpit as a passenger while the boat made its own placid way up Frederick Sound.

Though the sky was blue, the water kept changing colour. First, it was a yellowish tan, from a dozen muddy rivers; then, as Thomas Bay and Beard Glacier came abeam, it turned a streaky jade green. Off Cape Fanshaw, from a distance, it appeared to go quite black, where a miniature tide race of close-packed ripples somehow robbed the sea of light. Beyond the cape it altered again, to the powder blue of a butterfly's wing.

On previous days, the visibility had been too thick for me to see the extent of the country I was passing through, all low cloud and dark forest, the setting for a Grimms' fairy tale. Now the curtain was lifted, disclosing a gigantic land in which ranked lines of ice-cream alps receded, range on range. I could see clear into the Yukon and beyond, with ribs and chimneys of bare rock rising from snowfields that turned from white to raspberry-pink in the far distance.

The forest was the least of it. Above and beyond the treeline, Alaska looked like the work of a megalomaniac confectioner. In any other light but this freakish sunshine, its snowy barrenness would have appeared intimidating and oppressive. These were the forbidden mountains of Indian stories – a chthonic region to which unfortunate humans were occasionally abducted by terrible powers. On days like today, the Indians of the Inside Passage were confronted by the extreme narrowness of the habitable world; a tortuous green threadline, with a wilderness of rock, ice, and snow on one side and empty, undifferentiated ocean on the other. These boundaries were absolute and clearly visible; you kept to the centre of the path, or risked falling victim to thunderbirds on the right, monsters on the left. Only inside the serpentine line of riddled islands could you count on being halfway safe. No wonder so many of the stories harped on the dreadful fate awaiting wanderers who did not stick to the beaten track.

I skirted a group of wooded islets that resembled upturned hearth brushes and came into Stephens Passage, a broad seventy-mile reach that ran north by west almost all the way to Juneau. Twenty yards off to starboard, a whale surfaced: I saw the scythelike blade of its dripping black dorsal, then a humungous swirl, then a hole in the water, as if a plug had been pulled from deep underneath.

The breeze dwindled. The boat made little headway against a south-going tide that kept on flowing more than two hours after it was predicted to turn in my favour, according to the tables. Searching for an explanation, I found a note in the pilot: when the moon was in quadrature, a continuous ebb sometimes ran in Stephens Passage. This was less arcane than it may sound. The sun and moon had to be in line (as they are at the new and full moons) and pulling in consort to raise a flood tide strong enough to overcome the mingled river currents as they ran south to the ocean. Useful to get that learned. More often than not, the Alaskan tide tables seemed to me the work of a bogus fortune-teller, so little did they correspond to the water's actual behaviour. They described an ideal world in which snowmelt and river outflows had no place, and at neaps (when the moon is in quadrature) they went haywire. With the boat making three knots through the water and the land barely shifting against the shrouds, I turned into Hobart Bay to look for somewhere quiet to spend the night.

I was hailed on the radio by an NOAA research vessel, *John A. Cobb*. Turning around to pick up the mike, I saw that the big trawler was right astern, and ploughing into my wake. I'd thought I had the whole sea to myself. The captain was making a courtesy call: planning to drop anchor in Hobart Bay himself, he wanted to know where I was thinking of putting down my hook. I told him to go ahead and pick his spot; the bay was big, roomy enough for a fleet. A few moments later, I called *Cobb* and asked if I could pay a visit, curious about its oceanographic research. Perhaps they were revising the tide tables.

When *Cobb* was comfortably settled on the ten-fathom shelf, I went alongside. My lines were taken, and I scrambled over the rail to meet the tanned and bearded gang of seamen and scientists. The captain, in his thirties, announced himself as a yachtsman, currently between boats, and flatteringly interested in mine. I mentioned my hope that they were doing something about the weird tides.

That, the captain said, was a job he would relish. 'But tides aren't sexy. Physical oceanography isn't sexy. There isn't the funding for it.'

Whirlpools not sexy? The quadrature of the moon not sexy? I felt aggrieved.

The project under way on *John A. Cobb* that summer was the investigation of historical salmon populations. The scientists, from the University of Alaska at Fairbanks and Juneau, were taking core samples of sediment from the bottom of inlets, going out in small boats and sinking six-foot plastic tubes into the sea floor. The tubes, filled with mud, were stacked on the trawler's afterdeck like banks of organ pipes. When they returned to their laboratories, the scientists would search the contents of each tube, millimetre by millimetre, looking for traces of the fish scales, bones, phosphorus, and nitrogen that dead salmon had left behind in the black glop. Sediment accumulated at the rate of about half a centimetre every five years, so each tube held about 1,820 years of mud history. The researchers were studying salmon runs from the European Dark Ages to the present day.

'Is there much variation?' I said, for the project did not yet strike me as sexy at all.

One of the scientists, Bruce Finney, from Fairbanks, gave me an informal digest of his own work so far, which included research on historic sockeye populations based on sedimentary traces in Alaskan lakes. The yearly fluctuations in the size of runs were of no great significance. But their 'decadal' variations, in clumps of twenty and thirty years, were enormous. Finney said that he was looking at a wavelike pattern, over several centuries, in which the salmon populations diminished, troughed, surged back, only to diminish again after a crest lasting five or ten years.

'Like in the early 1500s, there were big runs then. Then you see a steady fall to about 1550. Then they start coming back again.'

'What about the eighteenth century?'

'Low in the early 1700s, but very high close to the end of the century.'

'When Vancouver was here.'

'Right. It goes down again in the early 1800s – the time of the Little Ice Age. There's a high from about 1870 to 1900, which is about when commercial fishing got going. You get another low beginning in the 1950s. We seem to be coming out of that right now.'

'When you say "low" in the historic period, before the whites were here, how low do you mean?'

'As low as anything we've seen this century.'

The sexiness of the project was now dawning on me.

There was a sharp net decline in Alaskan salmon numbers since the mid-nineteenth century – the result of heavy commercial fishing and the pollution by the timber industry of so many inland spawning grounds – but the wave pattern was stronger in outline than the steady downward curve attributable to the 'anthropogenic' impact of white commercial interests.

So the cause of each wave clearly lay in what Finney called 'climatic and oceanographic factors', but precisely which factors these were was still a mystery. There was a loose fit between warm periods and large runs, and for a while Finney had assumed that this was the clue to each successive wave. Trees grow larger rings in warm years, so that a cross-section of an ancient tree was a reliable guide to changes in weather. But when Finney graphed his salmon runs against the tree records, the two lines frequently diverged. He was now looking at the intensity of the seasonal Aleutian Low, and at temperature changes in the sub-Arctic gyre and the Japan Current, to see if he could find a pattern that more accurately duplicated his undulating waves of fish.

Climbing back aboard my own boat, I was greatly excited by what I'd heard: it was like being casually tossed the key to a puzzle I had fretted over ever since arriving in the Northwest.

I had absorbed the standard dogma, that before white men interfered with the balance of nature in the Northwest, the Indians lived in a state of reliable natural abundance. The richness of their art and ritual was often ascribed to the fact that they never had to work very hard to fill their stomachs. Uniquely among Native Americans, Indians on this coast were people of leisure; with their subsistence taken care of, they dedicated themselves to the cultivated pursuit of status and wealth.

The notion had its critics. Wayne Suttles warned of the too-easy acceptance of the 'myth' of abundance, pointing out that bad weather and rough seas had led to stories of starving villages in pre-contact times. But Suttles agreed that abundance was the normal condition of Indian life, broken, on occasion, by exceptional climatic circumstances.

Here was the puzzle – at least for me. Almost every tribe along the coast had a First Salmon ceremony, in which the first catch of the season was ritually prepared and eaten, its remains then given back, reverentially, to the river or the sea. Salmon – fresh in spring and summer, smoked in winter – was the staple diet of the coastal tribes; and this ceremony was generally held to be the single most important piece of evidence about the special relationship between the Indians and the natural world in which they lived, and from which they got their food.

In 'The Fish God Gave Us', an article in *Arctic Anthropology*, Pamela T. Amoss summarized the details of the First Salmon ceremony as it was described by early observers of several different Northwest tribes.

When the run began, no one was allowed to fish until the first catch had been ceremonially welcomed. Freshly bathed, painted with red ochre, and sprinkled with bird down, the children or the oldest person assembled on the beach to receive the fish from *the fishermen. The fish was carried on outstretched arms up the bank to the fire pit. There, the fish was laid on a bed of ferns and daubed with red ochre. Women butchered it, carefully removing the flesh in one piece from the spinal column which was to be preserved intact. The flesh was then fastened to skewers and roasted over the coals. Often hogfennel seeds (*Lomatium nudicale*) were sprinkled on the fire while the fish cooked. Some groups at the south end of Puget Sound boiled the fish instead of roasting it.*

The person officiating, who might be a special ritualist or simply the leader of the people assembled at a fish camp, prayed that the fish would look kindly on the people and return in great numbers. Usually, the whole community partook of the cooked fish, although in some cases only the children, or only the very old, actually ate any. People in ritually contaminated states (e.g., menstruating women, widowers, and widows) ordinarily did not eat any of the salmon. In most cases, all of the fish had to be eaten. The bones and entrails were carefully collected in a basket or new mat and reverently deposited in the river or sea, so that the salmon would come to life again and lead their fellows to the fishing sites.

The red-carpet reception of the salmon-people was interpreted, in every commentary I had read, as a recognition of the spiritual kinship that existed between the Indians and the wild creatures with whom they shared their world. Year after year, the salmon came. Year after year, the Indians paid homage to them, greeting them by honorific names, like 'Noble One', 'Lightning Following One Another', 'Chief Spring Salmon', 'Two Gills on Back', 'Quartz Nose', 'Three Jumps'. In Erna Gunther's 'A Further Analysis of the First Salmon Ceremony' (1928), she wrote:

Honorific names are of great importance and significance. That the salmon should be addressed in this way while being cut up, shows very clearly that the ceremony is partly one of propitiation.

The use of honorific names is important in a culture where names are high social privileges.

So the salmon were treated as gentry of exalted status – the lords and ladies of the sea.

In the 1970s, First Salmon ceremonies, which had not been practised since the twenties, were widely revived, under the supervision of white anthropologists. By the time I arrived in the Northwest, they were an annual feature of local TV news magazines, where they were held to demonstrate that the Indians, in revering the environment, were dedicated ecologists from time immemorial. As the Indian never cut down a tree without first praying to it, so he had valued the salmon and sought to preserve it for future generations, long before the runs were endangered by the heedless and destructive activities of white men.

This was pretty stuff, but I found it hard to believe. Some other, more functionalist reason had to inform the ceremony, beyond the desire to mount an elaborate paean of thanksgiving and deference to Nature. Now Bruce Finney's salmon-population research cast a great shaft of new light on the matter.

In 1792, when every inlet thronged with splashing sockeye, there would have been elders who could remember when so few fish came to the traps that the drying-frames on the beach remained empty; and in times of dearth there would always be old men prattling about the great salmon runs of their youth. Like present-day whites, the Indians assumed responsibility for an apparent steady decline of salmon – who evidently had taken offence at their reception by the tribe, and swum elsewhere in search of people who would treat them better.

Finney's wave pattern made instant sense of the First Salmon ceremony: the fish were honoured because there was a real and proven likelihood that they might not come back again in sufficient numbers to feed the tribe. It also had a very familiar ring. The whole corpus of Northwest Indian oral literature added up, in my reading of it, to an epic parable about the capricious and untrustworthy nature of nature. The regnant powers in the stories – raven, Komogwa, thunder-eagle,

Tsonogwa – were all dangerous jokers, dispensing bounty one moment, doling out punishment or death the next.

Now the salmon – the creature nearest to the stable centre of Indian life – was being unmasked by Dr Finney and his team as an inconstant flirt. On the coast of perennial abundance, the steady diet of the Indians could be no more certainly relied on than the sweet temper of the grizzly or the benevolence of Raven. Only by obsequious flattery, with much expenditure of red ochre and hogfennel seeds, and by the exclusion of unclean people, could Lightning Following One Another be persuaded not to leave the tribe and condemn it to starvation.

At five o'clock the water was like glass, tinged with the rose-petal pink of dawn. Nearly half a mile away, *John A. Cobb* was deep asleep, the slack catenary of its anchor chain hanging from the motionless trawler's bow. I was up early, to work my way north against Stephens Passage's perpetual ebb.

West of Entrance Island, six smoky campfires were burning on the water. Still barely awake, I took an absurdly long time to realize that the fires were whales lazily exhaling into the morning air. The sun turned their gouts of steam to gold. One huge tail slapped the surface, sending out ripples that rocked the boat. I sniffed, but caught only the mulchy-piney smell of the forest, mixed with the salt and rotting kelp of low tide. It's said that human halitosis has nothing on the foul breath of whales, and I was disappointed that these ones – greys, I thought – were out of smelling range.

Two whale sightings in two days was a good omen: having promised Julia whales for certain, I hadn't spotted one all summer. Now I was in the land of whales galore. At 6:45 I saw another – or at least heard the crash, and turned round to see the great spreading bruise on the water that the whale had left behind.

The boat, quite unexpectedly, was eating up the miles, doing seven and eight knots over the ground on a wayward flood tide that had decided to run this morning, even though we were only two days past the moon's third quarter. There was no reasoning with this sea. It flouted every rule in the book.

At 8:10 I saw my first icebergs; half a dozen of them strung out across the passage near Tracy Arm, where a receding glacier was continuously calving. From a distance they appeared white, like flakes of snow; closer, they turned an unearthly, luminous pale turquoise – a colour much imitated by manufacturers of eau de toilette. The smaller bergs were no bigger than Volkswagen Beetles, the largest the size of eccentric, many-gabled two-storey houses. But since only one-eighth to one-ninth of an iceberg's mass shows above the surface, even the little ones were potentially deadly, and I steered to give them a berth of several hundred yards.

I had long admired R. H. Dana's eloquent and unmanly description of icebergs, in *Two Years Before the Mast*, as 'little floating fairy isles of sapphire', and I now saw exactly what he meant. Sluggishly drifting on the breeze, radiant in the fierce sunlight, they were surreal, illusory. They might vanish in a blink.

Over the last two days, I'd watched the light harden as forest gave way to glaciers on the mainland shore. Now the rivers of ice – Sumdum, Sawyer, Taku, Norris – were coming thick and fast, spilling from the mountains to the sea like chutes of rippled china clay. You could feel the dry chill of their presence on your skin from miles off. Their melted prehistoric water stained the whole sea a milky green.

Soon after noon, as I neared Gastineau Channel, the approach road to Juneau, the radio began to broadcast live coverage of rammings and sinkings, the Coast Guard fielding a succession of distress calls. An excursion jet-boat, *Seymour*, or *Sea Moor*, or *See More*, collided at speed with a chunk of floating ice in Tracy Arm; all eighteen passengers were being ferried to the hospital in Juneau. Next, a gillnetter, *Lady Helen*, went aground on rocks and was reported by her distraught skipper to be sinking fast.

'South of the lighthouse! North end of Entrance Island!' he shouted.

Another fisherman came on the line. 'He's not too bright. I think he's off the south end. There's a light there, not a lighthouse.'

A halibut boat chimed in with the offer of a portable pump. Someone else was standing by, ready to launch his skiff. The Coast Guard arranged for the rescue of the skipper and his mate, while their boat broke up on the rocks.

I wondered if it was always thus around Juneau, and as the traffic thickened at the channel's entrance I kept a careful lookout for mad captains – the radio was full of them, grumbling and cursing on channel 16. This was the height of the fishing and tourist seasons, when everyone was on No-Doz or something stronger; in the broadcast voices was the ring of mania. I clung to the extreme edge of the channel and watched my back.

Nine miles up the narrowing gorge, Juneau was hunkered down low at the foot of the mountains on the east bank; a huddle of buildings backed by a ragged precipice of tawny rock, like the face of a great cheese after the mice have been at it. The pilot-book told one to look out for the conspicuous governor's mansion, but that was a forlorn instruction. Juneau announced itself by an oil terminal, a concrete office block, and three cruise liners parked on the waterfront. The ships grandly belittled the town. None of Juneau's buildings could hold a candle to the many-storeyed, snow-white magnificence of the floating republics of Holland-America, Princess, Royal Caribbean.

Watching the radio antenna at the top of the mast, I squeezed under the bridge with inches to spare and turned into the fishermen's harbour, where I found a slot between a gill-netter and an elderly wooden motor cruiser. Stepping ashore with an armful of rope, I was followed from cleat to cleat by a fearless child of Julia's age, a grubby water-gypsy whose permanent home was the motor cruiser. After I finished tying up, I sat cross-legged on the dock and chatted with Rebecca. We discussed helicopters, her new yellow life jacket, and the interesting way in which her gobstopper darkened from pink to red the more she sucked it. Long starved of such conversation, I had to explain myself, with some embarrassment, to Rebecca's mother, who interrupted us when I had just embarked on the final stanza of 'The Owl and the Pussycat'.

'I have a daughter, just about her age . . .'

Scepticism was writ large in the mother's face, but she receded behind a villainous tarpaulin slung over the afterdeck.

'They dined on mince, and slices of quince, / Which they ate with a runcible spoon; / And hand in hand on the edge of the sand, / They danced by the light of the moon, / The moon, / The moon, / They danced by the light of the moon.'

Five more days.

The Juneau branch of Rent-a-Wreck took their name at face value. My wreck was an old tan Datsun with 97,000 miles on the clock, spongy brakes, vague steering, and an air conditioner that blew a rank simoom wind into the car when set to Cold. But the radio worked. Drifting boatlike down the highway on Saturday morning, I listened to Juneau's bad news.

Five people were dead, seventy-one injured, two of them critically. *Universe Explorer*, a cruise ship on a week-long tour of the Inside Passage, was trundling quietly along Lynn Canal, its passengers asleep, when fire broke out in the main laundry. The flames and smoke quickly filled the deck above, on which crew members had their sleeping quarters. Four of the dead were Filipinos, one was Puerto Rican. Their names were being withheld until relatives had been informed.

The ship was now at anchor in Auke Bay, a dozen miles northwest of Juneau. The injured were being cared for in the local hospital. The remaining passengers were being flown to Seattle on chartered planes. Reports, said the announcer, were still coming in – and were buzzing around the harbour when I returned. The fishermen, who lived on VHF radio, knew everything. *Universe Explorer* was American-built, American-owned, but registered under a flag of convenience in Panama. This was a sore point on the waterfront, where people remembered the days when only one cruise ship a week called at Juneau, usually flying a red ensign and registered in London. Since then, the cruise lines had 'reflagged', re-registering their vessels in Third World countries in order to evade inconvenient American regulations, taxes, and wages.

This was true of every cruise ship I'd seen. While they preferred to hoist a big stars-and-stripes on the jackstaff at the stern, a close look at the transom revealed, in the smallest possible print, that the ship's home port was Panama City, or Monrovia, or Manila. Under international maritime law, they were in effect chunks of Panama, Liberia, or the Philippines afloat in US territorial waters, and every bit as 'foreign', legally speaking, as any rust-bucket freighter from Vladivostok or Inchon.

There was nothing new in this. In the first pages of *Typhoon*, Conrad prefigures the disaster that will overtake Captain McWhirr's steamship by dwelling, with seamanlike distaste, on its 'queer flag'. The *Nan-Shan*, Scottish-built and British-owned, flies the flag of Siam, a white elephant on a red ground: 'Length twice the breadth and the elephant exactly in the middle,' as MacWhirr observes.

Universe Explorer sailed under another queer flag, and on the dock people were inclined to blame its misfortune on its Panamanian registry. Most of the ship's officers were Anglophone Americans, but many of the crew spoke little or no English and, not equipped with personal radios, had no way of communicating directly with the bridge. When a hamper caught fire in the laundry, a message had to be passed, voice to voice, from the bowels of the ship to the officer on watch, many storeys above, and way forward of the crew's quarters. The message began in Tagalog, switched to Spanish, was translated into English . . . and, by the time it reached the bridge was said to be in a state of terminal entropy, too garbled for comprehension. Time was lost, and lives. When the fire alarm was at last sounded, and the dazed crew and passengers struggled in their night-clothes to their muster-stations, five people had already died of smoke inhalation.

News of the accident hadn't dampened the spirits of the 2,000 or 3,000 cruise-ship passengers who were shopping in downtown Juneau, or perhaps it had not reached them. Taking a car into these narrow streets was a mistake; one couldn't move for Zimmer frames, wheelchairs, video cameras on slow pan, and people stopping in the middle of the road in order to point out the totem pole, the sculpted bear, the old gold assayer's office, the miners' dissolute saloon. One couldn't buy anything useful in downtown Juneau because the shops were now 'galleries' of gifts and souvenirs. There was a marine chandler's by the harbour, but for anything domestic one had to go nine miles 'out the road' (there being only one) to the Valley.

The Valley was Juneau in exile from its own triumph as a tourist attraction. Here, on the boggy debris left by the shrinking Mildenhall Glacier, people had established an amiable alternative city, whose functional cinderblock architecture and windblown parking lots were calculated to deter even the most resolute sightseer. With its malls, gas stations, nondescript housing developments, and low flying aircraft noise, the Valley was the sort of place that tourists came from, not the sort of place they went to visit.

The jewel in the Valley's crown was a vast and splendid Kmart, with more departments, including a fine liquor store, and more amply stocked, than any I had seen before. Beyond the Kmart, close to the airport, lay the grocery stores, bar-restaurants, law practices, and all the businesses, big and small, that had fled Juneau proper and its hectic cruise-ship trade. The state legislature remained in town, but the daily newspaper, the *Juneau Empire*, had gone out the road.

In town, I had to brave the rigid smiles and brush-off manners of people severely overdosed on strangers. In the Valley, I was met with help, advice, and small talk. At Kmart, where with Julia in mind I bought a rod, reel, lures, and fishing licence, the man in the tackle department told me how Juneau's last redoubt had fallen earlier in the year, when Lyle's Hardware, an institution as old as the city, moved out. No sooner had it gone than Little Switzerland moved in, with watches by Patek Philippe, leather by Gucci, perfume by Givenchy and Dior. The symbolic contrast between Lyle's honest penny-nails and these luxury baubles was held up as a sorry sign of the times.

The cruise-ship passengers were derided as unwelcome invaders, in the jocose, grumbling way of working locals the world over, from Stratford-on-Avon to Williamsburg, who have to deal with slow-moving crowds of holidaying visitors. They were labelled 'tourons' for their brains, and 'tourosauruses' for their great age. The *Capital City Weekly* was running a competition for 'The Silliest Question You've Been Asked by a Tourist All Summer', though the entries were lacklustre: 'How much does it cost to ship your fish back to America?' 'Will I have to pay duty on this when I get back to the States?' 'How far is Juneau above sea level?' A citizens' initiative was being placed on the ballot in the November election, proposing that a $7 head tax should be levied on every cruise-ship passenger who disembarked at Juneau.

For all this ritual bad-mouthing, few people really wanted to see the tourist industry decline. The cruise ships were a resource that Juneau was eagerly developing. In wholly Alaskan fashion, the workaday city was packing its bags and moving north and west, leaving its old haunts to be turned into a theatrical simulacrum of Juneau's gold-mining past, with a hundred gift shops centre stage.

For two days I worked hard on the boat, getting it ready for Jean and Julia. The aft cabin ceased to be a chartroom and was restored to a child's bedroom, with a new bear on the pillow and new storybooks on the shelf above the bed. I scrubbed the decks and polished the interior woodwork. I got the galley so clean that I didn't dare cook there. Two sacks of washing, fresh from the laundry, gave us ironed sheets, crisp tea towels, and cushion covers that smelled like fresh bread. A vase of welcoming flowers stood on the saloon table. A family-sized bottle of sunblock was added to the first-aid drawer.

I was in good company. The dock was full of men carrying fids, brooms, paintbrushes, buckets. The old term 'ship's husband', for the agent who supervised a marine refit, nicely suited these uxorious, house-proud fishermen as they tended to their nets and boats, showing an appetite for fastidious domesticity that must have baffled their wives. They sat on the dock, patiently sewing, or could be seen with yellow dusters, applying lemon-scented Pledge to their boats' wheels.

My neighbour on the gill-netter to starboard was a fretful Pole who appeared permanently attached to his broom. He had come to America, he told me, in the 1940s, but his English was still fractured. He always went out on his boat alone. He had much on his mind.

'In two weeks, I go to the hospital. For tests.'

Evading the question of what the tests were for, I asked him about the hospital.

'Fred Hutchinson.'

'The Fred Hutchinson in Seattle?'

'Seattle,' he said, pronouncing the name like a death sentence.

His fellow fishermen were doing their best to cheer him up, though their attempts sounded like rough comfort in my ears. A roaring, pale-bearded guy, half the Pole's age, came by one afternoon, to say, 'Hey, Joe! So you got syphilis at last! Too many tricks, man. Too many tricks!'

Joe's answering laugh was broken-backed. A few minutes later, he said to me, 'Is not for syphilis. The tests.'

'I know,' I said, and he and I went back to spiffing up our boats.

Though I had travelled 1,000 miles to reach Juneau, it sometimes seemed that I'd only come full circle. Almost every car on the road wore the plates of dealerships in the Seattle suburbs – Auburn, Bellevue, Redmond, Lake City. One evening, after the tourists had returned to their ships, Juneau went eerily silent for the duration of a Seattle Mariners' home game. I watched an inning in the Triangle Bar, an obstinately local dive that still survived downtown, perhaps because its shaggy clientele could pass for veterans of the Gold Rush, and any fights in the street outside as part of Juneau's historic *mise en scène*. Ken Griffey, Jr., and the Big Unit were the heroes here, and were barraged with advice as they swam like fish across the jumbo TV screen.

For groceries, for major-league games, for cancer tests, cars, ship repairs, clothing, Juneau was dependent on Seattle. Like the parent of a toddler still in diapers, Seattle took care of Juneau's copious waste products. I watched the fortnightly garbage scow being loaded with junked cars, bedsteads, fridges, washing machines, about to be towed down the Inside Passage to a scrapyard on the Duwamish Waterway. It seemed not unlikely that my Rent-a-Wreck Datsun would find its way back to Seattle before I did.

I dug an old Mariners cap out of my closet. Wearing it made me look – or so I hoped – as if I came from Juneau.

Even in cruise-ship hours – from ten to five – I liked to walk the fringes of old Juneau. A little above the gift shops, it became a steep town of alleyways, narrow contour-hugging lanes, long flights of steps, and banked wooden cottages with gardens in full bloom. A climb of fifty to a hundred feet was enough to put one well clear of the tourist trade, alone with the hummingbirds and honeysuckle. I took to dropping in on Mrs Longenbaugh's antiquarian bookshop on Second Street, which was just one block too high for most casual visitors. The shop, full of dusty corners and unsorted boxes, reminded me pleasantly of a second-hand bookseller's in an English cathedral town.

I bought an engraving, razored from the first edition of Vancouver's *Voyage*, of 'VILLAGE of the FRIENDLY INDIANS at the entrance of BUTE'S CANAL', based on a sketch made by Midshipman Thomas Heddington on a survey expedition when *Discovery* and *Chatham* were anchored in Desolation Sound. I would dearly have liked a copy of the *Voyage* in its original four-volume edition of 1796, but it had been so plundered for its charts and engravings that it was now a rare book, at a price of around $15,000. Mrs Longenbaugh hadn't seen a copy in a long while.

I paid $90 for the 1901 edition of Joshua Slocum's *Sailing Alone Around the World*, and counted it a bargain. Slocum in life was a cantankerous piece of work, a 'bucko' merchant captain hated by his men. He went on trial three times, for wrongful imprisonment, murder, and child molestation. He couldn't live in the same house (on Martha's Vineyard) as his wife – a powerful factor in his decision to take to the ocean alone in a small boat. He was not particular about baths or changes of underwear. But in the pages of his book, he was modest, funny, sweet-tempered; the best possible company. So it often is with writers.

From a cardboard box I fished out a tattered Penguin edition of the *Meditations* of Marcus Aurelius, because its identical twin lived on the shelves in my father's study and I was curious to find out what had drawn my father to the Stoic emperor.

But that could wait. For now I sat out in the cockpit of the boat with Rebecca and her six-year-old brother, reading *Clifford the Big Red Dog* and *Madeline and the Bad Hat*. Though my father was never far away. In Juneau, as in Petersburg and Ketchikan, he kept cropping up on the far edge of my field of vision: long-faced, gaunt, with tangled silver beard and a shock of home-barbered hair swept back from his widow's peak, he ambled down the dock holding a fid or paintbrush in his hand.

A quarter-mile from the harbour, Gold Creek emptied into Gastineau Channel. The silt of the creek had once made Juneau rich and famous, but recently the city had turned Gold Creek into an ugly open drain plunging straight from the hilltop to the tideflat below: a bare concrete duct, with a steep, unvarying gradient. Water dribbled down its corrugated face, barely an inch deep. At anything above half-tide the last thirty yards or so of this algae-infested spillway were the site of a desperate and pathetic enterprise.

Several thousand chum salmon milled around the foot of the duct, trying to make the impossible climb to their old spawning grounds. The water was packed solid with them, their humpbacks riding proud of the surface as they jostled for the chance to make the run. When their turn came, they hurled themselves out of the channel and onto the concrete, wriggling up it on their bellies like frenetic eels. From the outset, the fish were in bad shape. They were a sickly olive-green marked by large, irregular blotches of bubble-gum pink. Their scales were falling off in clumps, their tails and fins in rags, their jawbones protruding obscenely from their skulls. They were only just alive enough to spawn and die.

They thrashed, flopped, squirmed, and slithered on the concrete, catapulting themselves up into the air only to fall back with a smack on the same spot. Blind to everything except the need to multiply their kind, they threw themselves against the duct until they died. Bit by bit, over a period of many minutes, their contortions slowly weakened, until their inert hulks slid back over the algae into the channel. Eager newcomers flung themselves past the dead and dying, some walking on their tails as they gained the fresh water and scented the ancestral hills.

No salmon ever made it. The water wasn't nearly deep enough for them to breathe, and the slimy concrete offered no purchase. A heroic few somehow managed to cover the two hundred yards to the second bridge; most were washed back within the first twenty yards.

There must once have been dozens of holding-pools and rapids, allowing salmon to ascend Gold Creek on a gentle staircase. This horrible man-made, piscicidal drain astonished me. I asked my neighbours how it had come about, and was told that people used to complain about the smell of dead fish after spawning. Residents hated living with it, and it put off the tourists. So Gold Creek was regraded and lined with concrete.

On the flood tide, putrescent salmon corpses drifted north into the harbour, where they lodged between boats. Rebecca and her brother liked to poke at them with sticks until they fell to bits and sank in a gaseous pink cloud. In the bed in the forecabin, reading late at night, I could hear the soft thump of their bodies as they knocked against the hull, caught in the current that eddied through the floats.

These chum salmon were said to be the result of an accident in Gastineau Channel a couple of years before, when a container of hatchery-fry broke open and released the fish on Juneau's doorstep. I wasn't persuaded. This story represented the fish as alien visitors, mere salmon tourons. But the fish I saw knew exactly where they had to go – to their family gravel beds on the upper reaches of Gold Creek.

On Tuesday morning, after laying in the last of our provisions from the Valley, I drove over to Auke Bay, where *Universe Explorer* was being detained. Before the ship was allowed to sail to Vancouver for repairs, the Coast Guard required the crew to perform a satisfactory fire drill. Two drills had been held so far, both failures. The *Juneau Empire* reported on its front page:

> *Lt. j.g. Lindsay Dew of the Coast Guard Marine Safety Office said fatigue, communications problems and lack of crew knowledge probably led to the drills' failure.*
>
> *Dew said today the drills went 'very poorly,' explaining that during the first drill he notified a crewmember that a fire had broken out in the ship's pantry.*
>
> *The woman, who spoke good English, did not know how to contact the bridge to report the fire or where any fire alarm boxes were located, he said.*
>
> *Dew flagged down another crewmember, who reported the fire to the bridge, but because both the crewmember and the bridge crew had heavy accents and were from different European countries, the wrong location was reported.*

The ship was anchored well out in the neck of the bay, with a Coast Guard cutter a short distance off. The sun was up. The still water was frosted, here and there, with vagrant cat's-paws. I stood under the drooping boughs of a hemlock to take a picture. Down on the beach, a mink scarpered from rock to rock. I got the ship in focus and clicked the shutter on an advertisement for an idyll.

It took for ever for the ground staff to manoeuvre the swaying, accordion-pleated tunnel into position around the aircraft door. Julia, one of the first out of the chute, bulleted into my arms with a happy shriek. Jean was several passengers behind, lugging a pair of bags, her face tied in a knot of exhaustion.

'I was working till three. We had to get up at five to catch the plane.' She attempted a smile, but it was not a great success.

I laid my free arm across her shoulders. 'You can sleep on the boat. I'll take Julia off. There's no shopping to do. We have all we need.'

'I'll be OK.'

Passengers arriving in Juneau were met by a stuffed, somewhat moth-eaten grizzly bear. It reared up on its hind legs, eight feet tall, like a giant boxer, claws extended, jaws agape. The bear was a kissing cousin to Balloo in Disney's version of *The Jungle Book* – the psychotic cousin with unfocused glass eyes and tawny fangs, the one the other bears never mention.

Clinging tightly to me, Julia braved *Ursus horribilis* with an undeceived yet not quite certain grin. 'Are there real bears in our world?'

'Lots of real bears. We'll see real bears from the boat.'

'For true-life?'

'True-life. Alaska is the best place in the whole world for real wild bears.'

'Dad-*dy*,' she said, in her *come off it* voice. 'Are we in Alaska now?'

'Yes, Jaybird, you're in Alaska now. What do you think of that?'

'You're not joking me?' She searched my face. I was apt to spot pterodactyls perched in the trees around our house, so she had reason to treat all information got from me as suspect.

'No, truly. You're in Juneau, Alaska.'

'Mommy!' she called across the arrivals lounge. 'This is *Alaska*! We're in *Alaska*!'

On the drive to the harbour, Julia prefaced her every remark with 'Mommy-and-Daddy . . . ?' I watched her in the rear-view mirror: she couldn't keep the smile off her face, in her pleasure at regaining the correct number of parents.

'This is your *rental*?' Jean said as we weaved through the Valley.

'It was all I could get.'

'You should have gone to Hertz.'

'I did. All their cars were booked.'

'It's a wreck.'

At the boat, I buckled Julia into her new Kmart life jacket, then introduced her to Rebecca while Jean went down to the forecabin for a rest. Julia was quickly swallowed into family life aboard the motor cruiser.

'We'll take care of her,' Rebecca's mother said, and I went below to talk with Jean before she conked out. The interior of the boat was hot, and full of voices and footsteps from the dock.

'It's smelly in here.'

I'd stopped noticing the tang of dead chum salmon in the harbour air. I said, 'We'll be out of here tomorrow. We could leave this afternoon—'

'No,' Jean said with sudden sharpness. 'I haven't seen Juneau yet.'

'Are you all right?'

'I'll be fine. I'm just tired. I had four pieces to write. And then I had all the packing to do. I just need to lie down. Give me an hour, OK?'

I sat up in the cockpit, listening to Julia's voice carrying from behind the tarp next door. She was having too much fun for me to reclaim her. From under her bed in the aft cabin, I got out the chart that would take us to Glacier Bay and pencilled in our course, around the northern tip of Admiralty Island and into Icy Strait.

Jean came up after forty-five minutes, saying she felt better. Her face was still knotted, but the knot looked looser than before. With Julia, we joined the tourist procession through downtown, trailing past gift shops and eating an overpriced lunch in a waterfront restaurant, where Jean picked at a Caesar salad while I babbled about icebergs, bears, whales, and anchorages so isolated that we would seem to have all Alaska to ourselves. Julia, having found a friend, was already desolate at the prospect of leaving her behind, and suggested that we should take Rebecca too.

We drove to Sheep Creek, to watch salmon mobbing the entrance and leaping from pool to pool. We stood on the rocks, the fish at our feet oblivious to everything except their rage to climb upstream and drop their spawn.

Julia stared at their protuberant jaws and weird colours. 'I don't like them. They're scary.'

'They just need to lay their eggs and hatch their babies.'

'Will they die?'

'Yes. But they'll leave thousands and thousands of babies behind. Then the babies will swim down the river and out to the ocean, where they'll grow into big fish like this, before they come back to lay their eggs.'

'They make me sad. I don't want them to die.'

'You want to go to a playground?'

'Yes!'

I had spotted a good one during my prowls in the wreck. It lay across from Juneau on the Douglas side of Gastineau Channel, where the tailings of an abandoned gold mine formed a big sandy beach, with swings, slides, and a jungle-gym up at its top end.

'She ought to take a nap,' Jean said.

'After the beach. Let her get some exercise first.'

The pulverized rock of the tailings was grittier than real sand, but Julia sprinted through it, shedding socks and shoes as she went. I put them in my pockets and followed her to the swings.

'Higher! *Higher*, Daddy!'

The chains creaked and muttered in their ring-bolts. The sun shone. Feeling the live heft of my daughter in her seat was pure balm; though, not for the first time, I found Jean's mood hard to fathom. Pushing my daughter, I watched my wife.

She had lit a cigarette and was sitting on a low dune, forty yards down the beach, looking out over the channel. Lines of stakes and pilings ran out ahead of her toward a small tower that stood a little way out on the water, among the interlocking tongues of the receding tide. Coming into Juneau in the boat, I'd taken it for an abandoned lighthouse, but it was the last remaining building of the gold mine: a pumphouse, whose tin roof had rusted to the colour of Tuscan tiles, and whose concrete walls had weathered to the texture of old grey stone. Close up, as I'd found the previous day, it was a homely derelict; from this distance, an ancient, picturesque folly.

Julia tired of the swing and headed for a slide.

I walked down the beach to where Jean sat on her dune, picking my way past rusty lumps of mining machinery, encrusted with barn-acles and mussel-shells, and twisted rail-lines half-buried in sand.

She was smoking a brand of cigarette I hadn't seen before, low-tar-and-nicotine jobs called True. I fished one out of her pack and lit it; it tasted, faintly, of wet straw.

'Jean – are you all right?'

'Yeah, I'm OK.'

I told her about the mine in whose ruins we were squatting. The Treadwell Mine had been famous, once, in the 1880s and nineties. The steep hill behind Julia's playground was honeycombed with tunnels. Mr Treadwell, a handyman-builder from San Francisco, had become a multi-millionaire, then made some bad investments and died bankrupt in a New York flophouse – an American life in the classic mould.

Jean shrugged, answering the story with a plume of True smoke. 'What's up?'

'I wanted to talk about separating. Like, I wondered if you've thought of separating?'

'Separating?' My stomach went south.

'I always thought it would be harder to live without you, but since you've been away I've found it easier, with just me and Julia. We're happier when you're not there.'

'You don't mean *we*. You mean you. *You're* happier.'

'Mommy and Daddy! Mommy and Daddy! Look at me-ee-ee!' Julia was a monkey-figure in the climbing-frame. Jean and I each raised a hand and waved in unison. 'Great!' I called back across the sand. 'Great!'

'OK,' Jean said. 'I'm happier.'

'This is what you've come to Juneau for? To tell me this?'

'I wanted to be honest.' The cigarette pack in her lap read like a subtitle in a French movie: *True!*

The ebb tide was running hard, and a gill-netter, pushing up-channel to Juneau, was stuck fast in the space of water between the pumphouse and Jean's head. The boat was throwing up a roiling V of wake but making no visible progress over the ground at all.

'I have to take charge of my own life. I can't go on depending on you for handouts like I've been doing. I have to get my shit together. Like, get a real job. There's a job at Microsoft . . . '

Her voice was dry, curt, void of tone and colour. Jean had many voices. This was her Manhattan voice. A child of the Upper West Side, she was proud of her impatience with good manners. She could revert at will to the rapid, flat, nasal patois of the New York streets, and sounded now as if she were delivering a food order at a deli.

'I need to forge a new identity,' she said.

I was lost. This was all wrong. I wanted to put Jean on rewind, yet the words kept coming, as if memorized by rote, with no inflection at all. She must have rehearsed this speech for weeks – or months? Had she been preparing it back in May, when we were all in England? Somewhere behind the speech I heard a dialogue coach. I didn't want to know who the coach was.

'You can forge a new identity,' Jean said. 'You'll be free, too. You'll have more money to spend when you don't have to help me out all the time.'

A new family had arrived on the playground. I saw Julia attaching herself to it. 'My mom and dad are over there . . . ' She was effortlessly, ebulliently sociable, making instant friends with large dogs and older children.

'When you get used to the idea, you'll see it's all for the best.'

I couldn't speak. She had her script, I had none. There was nothing to discuss: that was plain from the rigid furrows in Jean's forehead, the jut of her nose, the tight clamp of her lips on the filter of her cigarette. Her eyes, tungsten hard, refused to meet mine, offered no way in. She had ended our marriage long before today, and now was only going through the wearisome motions of informing me that what was done was done.

My stupidity. I had thought we were secure. Though much divided us – the abyss of nearly twenty years; her America, my England – we looked at the world through the same dark glass. When misery descended on us, as it had done lately, I thought it circumstantial, capable of being lifted by a change in the weather, by a decent job for Jean, money, a reliable babysitter; a fortnight in Alaska. In our worst moments – and some had been dire – I still thought we were so much more like each other than we were like other people that we must be safe.

And we had Julia, the light of both our lives. Surely two lives lit by one light were meant to consort like moths fluttering in the same beam?

'Where do you think Julia fits into your big adventure?'

'Without the tension between you and me, I can be a better mother,' she said, burying her cigarette butt in the tailings.

'She needs two parents – she needs a family, Jean!'

'You'll have visitation rights.'

'I don't "visit" Julia. Never, ever.'

'We can discuss that. We can draw up a parenting agreement.'

She had become as remote as some government functionary shuffling papers behind a teller's window. I might have been dealing with Ms Lopez or Ms Takimoto at Social Security or Immigration. Yet even as she removed herself from me – the coach, surely, had rehearsed her in this frigid and official style of delivery – I was struck by how alike we were. 'Forging a new identity' wouldn't be my phrase for it, but America as the land of perpetual self-reinvention had always been my theme. Whenever there had been walking out to do, I was the one who walked. Now Jean had seen a new life and was going for it, exactly as I had done in the past. Her cruel, cold dismissal reminded me uncomfortably of me.

'She needs a *family*,' I repeated weakly.

'When she's, like, ten, half the kids in her class will have divorced parents.'

'She's not a fucking statistic!'

'Don't shout at me.'

The fishing boat hadn't budged. The world had changed, but the gill-netter was in exactly the same place as before, driving at full power into the current and getting nowhere.

'Where do you think you're going to live?'

'I'll start looking for a place when I get back. I'll need some money, and we'll have to divvy up the stuff in the house. You can have your share.'

'My *share*? Jean!'

But Jean was long gone. The face that turned to me was Ms Takimoto's.

'Mommy and Daddy! Mommy and Daddy!' She was running toward us now, kicking up the barren dust of the gold mine as she came.

Thirty-six unspeakable hours later, I drove Jean and Julia to the airport, left them outside the entrance, then returned the car to Rent-a-Wreck.

'Enjoy your vacation?'

'Yeah, fine,' I said.

At the harbour, I was ashamed of my conspicuous aloneness. Julia was known to half the people on the dock. I lacked the energy to invent even the feeblest death-in-the-family story, which would require more corroborative detail than I could manage. I ached to leave, to slake my heartbreak in motion for motion's sake; but a southerly wind of twenty-five knots and gusting higher was blowing up Gastineau Channel, and predicted to increase during the afternoon. Never had I left harbour in the teeth of a gale forecast, and to do so now would prove only that I was unfit to take the boat south and complete the trip.

Wearing a mask for a face, I hurried down the dock to the slip (the word 'our', suddenly, was no longer mine to use) and hid in the saloon, fitting the hatchboards in place, closing the hatch, and drawing the curtains on the ports. I could hear Rebecca bickering with her brother next door.

The bear I'd bought Julia in Juneau was lying on the floor under the saloon table. A half-empty juice carton, its straw bent, was parked beside the galley sink.

As if made of clockwork, I filled the kettle, lit the gas, chucked the old coffee filter into the garbage, replaced it with a fresh one, and spooned grounds into the basket. While the coffee was brewing, I got out a sheaf of paper, enough to pen an epic, and began writing to a friend on Cape Cod.

Dear Paul,

Every successful voyage ought to culminate in a major discovery, and at the end of this voyage I feel like Sir Walter Raleigh. Not far from Juneau, I found my own private Guiana, though I wish to God I hadn't. . . .

VIII. KOMOGWA

I lived by numbers. The days were shortening now, but from the first dull glimmer of dawn, soon after five, to the last of blue dusk, there were still fifteen or sixteen hours in which it was safe to be on the move. With the engine going at full tilt, I could do 6.5 knots – say ninety miles a day; at a stretch, a hundred. I didn't dare to travel at night for fear of ripping the boat open on a deadhead or a floating log.

I kept Hansen's *Handbook* in the shelter of the doghouse, ticking off the marks and running down the miles. My logbook, which had gone into a second volume, bloated as it was with fancy landscape descriptions, became a model of austerity: columns of scribbled figures – times, distances, wind speeds, courses, barometric pressures.

I avoided settlements. Provisioned with food and drink for three, the boat had more than enough for my needs. Steering clear of the pretty, enclosed anchorages recommended by yachting guides, I instead searched the channel for unpicturesque bights that offered minimal aprons of shallow water and partial shelter in the lee of headlands. I'd start looking close to sunset. There was always some-where, and a certain uneasiness at night (is the wind shifting? why is the chain rumbling on the bottom?) suited my mood.

I learned to read and keep watch at the same time. I had to keep my mind elsewhere, and found I could take in a paragraph –

sometimes only a sentence – and hold the words in my skull while studying the water for hazards, checking the course, and fiddling with the autopilot before going back to the book for the next chunk. Chapters advanced rather slowly, but it was a good way of reading: by the book's end, I could nearly recite it by heart. Alaska and British Columbia turned into a passing blur; on the neutral screen of sea and forest were printed moving pictures from another world.

I read Evelyn Waugh's *A Handful of Dust* like this. As soon as I finished the last page, I turned back to the beginning and read it over again. Watching Waugh transform the humiliating disaster of his first marriage into triumphant, grave comedy was a delight. I laughed, for the first time since the Treadwell Mine, over the sly opening's deadpan portrait of the useless piece of dining-room furniture named John Beaver. Waugh had been cuckolded (his word) by just such a man. While he was writing *Vile Bodies* in a country hotel, his childish wife, Evelyn Gardner, ran off with a devout London party-goer, John Heygate. At the time, Waugh wrote: 'I did not know it was possible to be so miserable and live.' Three years later, in the winter of 1932, he began *A Handful of Dust*, turning Heygate into Beaver, a dim savage in the jungle of fashionable London, with his precious collection of crested silver hunting flasks, tobacco jars, and hat brushes. There was revenge in the pages, but it was revenge accomplished with serene craftsmanship, in light, pitch-perfect prose.

Waugh and his wife were recast as Tony and Brenda Last. Brenda picks up John Beaver as a plaything, an amusing diversion from the boredom of life in the country, and the Lasts' marriage disintegrates. Their six-year-old son – John Andrew – is killed in a hunting accident. Presiding over the chaos, Waugh wrote better than he'd ever done before, or would do again, mingling mischief and pain in equal parts.

A friend breaks the news of young John's death to Brenda:

> '*What is it, Jock? Tell me quickly, I'm scared. It's nothing awful, is it?*'
> '*I'm afraid it is. There's been a very serious accident.*'

'John?'

'Yes.'

'Dead?'

He nodded.

She sat down on a hard little Empire chair against the wall, perfectly still with her hands folded in her lap, like a small well-brought-up child introduced into a room full of grown-ups. She said, 'Tell me what happened. Why do you know about it first?'

'I've been down at Hetton since the week-end.'

'Hetton?'

'Don't you remember? John was going out hunting today.'

She frowned, not at once taking in what he was saying. 'John . . . John Andrew . . . I . . . oh, thank God . . .' Then she burst into tears.

I read that passage aloud to the trees.

In his bravura ending, Waugh posts Tony Last from the chattering roosts of Mayfair and its feral inhabitants to the real jungle of the Amazon basin, where he joins Dr Messinger, an explorer in search of a mythical Inca city. Bratt's Club and the Old Hundredth give way to howler monkeys, tree frogs, bats, spiders, alligators, iguanas, and cabouri flies. The transition is imperceptible. The same law obtains in both worlds. Lost in unmapped territory, Tony falls into a delirious fever in which England and Amazonas are scrambled in his waking dreams, while Dr Messinger goes off, alone, to get help from the Indians. The river he travels by canoe is the turbulent essence of the jungle – muddy, swirling, full of rapids and cataracts. He is quickly drowned.

Looking up from the book to check the course, I saw my own jungle close at hand: swift, tidal water riddled with small whirlpools; mossy stumps; the creeping, many-tentacled salal; the hunchbacked eagle, perched on the dead limb of a lightning-struck fir.

I had breakfast in the dark: coffee and a bowl of Froot Loops.

My early rising was rewarded with many sightings of bears. Getting up the anchor, I'd see a black boulder suddenly ripple into motion as it went truffling for seafood on the beach. Every bear caused a pang. Sometimes I'd go below and fetch up my camera, but showing Julia the pictures would be a dismal substitute for what I'd daydreamed of showing her, true-life.

Five days out of Juneau and safely past Dixon Entrance, I ran into a spell of vile weather. A long trough of low pressure had raked the Queen Charlotte Islands, then stalled over the Inside Passage, bringing a wild and gusty southerly wind and slanting rain squalls that clattered like gravel on the doghouse windows. In Princess Royal Channel, the sea was ribbed with close-packed three-foot waves, the ragged clouds were at masthead height, and the mountainous shore to starboard was a streak of mottled darkness in the enveloping grey. The waves and wind had slowed the boat to less than three knots, though the tide was with me and I was making nearly five knots over the ground.

My reading (*The Ordeal of Gilbert Pinfold*) was interrupted by the snarling engine of a floatplane close behind me. The pilot was trying to fly below the clouds, but the clouds were pinning him nearer and nearer to the water, which was too rough, I figured, for him to make a touchdown without losing his plane. He had to climb a few feet to clear my mast, then thundered overhead in a panic of noise. Though I knew nothing about flying, he looked to be in dire straits, with the visibility closing down to zero and the twisting, precipitous walls of the channel only a mile or so apart. Hoping he knew what he was doing, I listened to his engine as it faded into the clatter of the rain; and for the rest of the day I kept half-expecting to come across his floating wreckage.

But I, beneath a rougher sea, / And whelm'd in deeper gulfs than he. The passing of the floatplane pilot had put into my head the final couplet of William Cowper's last and best poem. I got out *The Oxford Book of the Sea* to reread 'The Cast-Away' – the most despairing poem in the English language, though Cowper's four-beat line, ti-tum-ti-tum-ti-tum-ti-tum, gave it a subversive jauntiness; at least it did whenever I tried speaking it aloud.

Cowper was sixty-seven when he wrote 'The Cast-Away' in March 1798, and he was dying in exile from the Methodist faith to which he had become a passionate convert in his twenties. He believed he was 'damned', in the strict sense of being a stranger to the knowledge and love of God. Cowper, like many retiring, stay-at-home types, was an avid consumer of armchair adventures, and found an analogy to his own miserable situation in the pages of Lord Anson's *A Voyage Round the World*. Anson's ship, *Centurion*, had run into a violent storm off Cape Horn, where the order had been given to 'man the shrouds' – a terrifying business in which all sail was taken off the ship, and seamen climbed aloft to give the wind purchase and the ship steerageway. One seaman lost his footing and was thrown into the icy South Atlantic. Unable to turn the ship around, Anson and his crew watched impotently as the bobbing figure disappeared among the waves. Anson wrote, and Cowper read:

> *Notwithstanding the prodigious agitation of the waves, he swam very strong, and it was with the utmost concern that we found ourselves incapable of assisting him; indeed we were the more grieved at his unhappy fate, as we lost sight of him struggling with the waves, and conceived from the manner in which he swam that he might continue sensible, for a considerable time longer, of the horror attending his irretrievable situation.*

So it was with Cowper in old age. The ship had left him behind. He longed for his death, which showed no immediate sign of arrival.

In 'The Cast-Away', Cowper turned Anson's account into verse, then moved, in the last two stanzas, from the seaman's plight to his own.

I, therefore, purpose not or dream,
  Descanting on his fate,
To give the melancholy theme
  A more enduring date;
But mis'ry still delights to trace
Its semblance in another's case.

No voice divine the storm allay'd,
  No light propitious shone;
When, snatch'd from all effectual aid,
  We perish'd, each alone;
But I, beneath a rougher sea,
And whelm'd in deeper gulfs than he.

Poor Cowper, whose whole adult life was lived on a roller coaster, with short flights of religious mania punctuating long passages of suicidal depression, had always been inclined to see himself as a hapless seafarer. His actual experience of seagoing was confined to one trip on a small sailing boat on the Solent, not far from Southampton, but he plundered the great eighteenth-century voyages for metaphors for his own condition. Sometimes he saw himself as a sinking ship:

Me howling blasts drive tedious, tempest tost,
Sails ripped, seams opening wide, and compass lost,
And day by day some current's threatening force
Sets me more distant from a prosperous course.

When a friend safely returned from Ramsgate, after a trip from Calais in a Channel packet, Cowper wrote him:

Your sea of troubles you have passed
  And found the peaceful shore;
I, tempest-toss'd, and wreck'd at last,
  Come home to port no more.

To the same friend, he described his work on a verse translation of Homer as giving him 'some little measure of tranquillity' in 'the performance of the most *turbulent voyage* that ever Christian *mariner* made.'

A lifetime of sea-reading and sea-metaphors crowded behind the writing of 'The Cast-Away' – and surely Cowper must have felt a moment, at least, of jubilation as he found the words of the poem's last two lines. There was triumph in such a pure distillation of misery. Cowper lived for thirteen months longer and wrote nothing more. The final couplet passed into the language of popular quotation. In Virginia Woolf's *To the Lighthouse*, Mr Ramsey declaims it at every possible opportunity; it is his signature tune. And, for a day or two, I made it mine, chanting, with unseemly gusto:

> '*But* I, *be*-neath *a* rough-*er* sea,
> *And* whelm'd *in* dee-*per* gulfs *than* he.'

On the sixth day, I left Center Cone Island to starboard in Finlayson Channel – according to Hansen, the halfway point between Juneau and Seattle. The Cocoa Puffs I tried for breakfast were even worse than the Froot Loops. Then I sampled my father's book – the Penguin Marcus Aurelius – and before long my text for the day jumped out at me from page fifty-one:

> *In the life of a man, his time is but a moment, his being an incessant flux, his senses a dim rushlight, his body a prey of worms, his soul an unquiet eddy, his fortune dark, and his fame doubtful. In short, all that is of the body is as coursing waters, all that is of the soul as dreams and vapours; life a warfare, a brief sojourning in an alien land; and after repute, oblivion.*

Following Heraclitus, Marcus saw all of human life in terms of the turbulent motion of fluids. Time was a river, 'The resistless flow of all created things,' the Primal Cause 'like a river in flood; it bears everything along'. If you want a mirror for your own existence, you need look no further than tumbling rapids or the strings of dying whirlpools downtide of a piling.

For Marcus, unquiet eddies and coursing waters weren't merely a convenient figure of speech. In spring and autumn, the Tiber grew from a noxious trickle to a storming flood in just an hour or two. Containing the river was a major enterprise of Roman civilization, and it was hemmed in with stone levees by the time of Augustus. When Marcus Aurelius became emperor, in AD 161, the city had spread over to the west bank; so even as the great marble walls of imperial Rome closed around it, the turbulent and brimming Tiber remained as an ungovernable wilderness in the heart of the Eternal City.

I saw how congenial Marcus's *Meditations* must have been to my father, who was always a small-*s*, stiff-upper-lip stoic. His thrift, modesty, and increasingly ascetic style of religious practice were Aurelian virtues, and sometimes Marcus seemed to speak to me in my father's own voice.

> *You cannot hope to be a scholar. But what you can do is to curb arrogance; what you can do is to rise above pleasures and pains; you can be superior to the lure of popularity; you can keep your temper with the foolish and ungrateful, yes, and even care for them.*

Old boy . . . He would have knocked out his pipe dottle on the edge of the hearth, then drawn himself back into the folds of his cassock.

I realized he must have known the *Meditations'* translator – another rural dean, Maxwell Staniforth, whose bailiwick was Blandford in Dorset, just thirty-five miles west of my father's rural deanery of Southampton. It interested me that Anglican clergymen, labouring through the long decline of the established Church, should find spiritual comfort in the astringent philosophy of a pagan Roman emperor. Yet facing rows of empty pews, with no money in the kitty for repairs to the church roof, one might well find more of relevance in Marcus than in the epistles of St Paul.

I broke my new rule, copying two quotations into the logbook:

Loss is nothing else but change, and change is Nature's delight.

There is a doom inexorable and a law inviolable, or there is a providence that can be merciful, or else there is a chaos that is purposeless and ungoverned. If a resistless fate, why try to struggle against it? If a providence willing to show mercy, do your best to deserve its divine succour. If a chaos undirected, give thanks that amid such stormy seas you have within you a mind at the helm. If the waters overwhelm you, let them overwhelm flesh, breath, and all else, but they will never make shipwreck of the mind.

I read Swanton's *Tlingit Myths and Texts*. 'The Woman Who Was Killed by a Clam'. 'The Woman Taken Away by the Frog People'. 'The Man Who Was Abandoned'. 'The Monster Devil-Fish and the Cry-Baby'. Stories of serial misfortune, of minor transgressions and major punishments, of the whimsical and malevolent humour of Nature, most of them began with someone leaving the house – to go for a walk in the woods, or gather clams on the beach, or set off on a hunting or fishing expedition. Then more or less inexplicably, shit happened.

I had been familiar with these tales for six years now. So what did I expect – that a friendly godling would rubber-stamp my plans and wave me on my way? Running for shelter over the cold grey ocean swells of Queen Charlotte Strait, I distinctly heard the gurgling, undersea laughter of Komogwa.

The weather cleared on the morning I passed through the Yuculta and Dent rapids and made for Desolation Sound under a fathomlessly high blue sky. To the south, in vacationland, sailboats and motor cruisers zigzagged from inlet to inlet, trailing fishing lines; water-skiers towed by nippy white runabouts were making figure-eights around the slow-moving anglers. With only a few gallons of diesel left in the tank, I needed to put in at the seasonal marina in Refuge Cove. The floats were chock-a-block with pleasure craft, and the place reeked of suntan lotion. Kids in life jackets pelted up and down the dock. On decks and flybridges the bodies of young mothers were laid out under the sun on striped towels. I took on fifty gallons of diesel, then went below to drain the fuel filter.

The last time I'd filled the tank had been at Klemtu, and lately the engine had missed a beat or two whenever the boat rolled, a sign of water in the fuel. I unhooked the companionway steps and pulled them back to get at the mechanical guts of the boat.

The engine compartment was suffocatingly hot. With diesel fumes in my eyes and on my tongue, I unscrewed the drip-valve at the base of the inverted glass dome of the filter to let the accumulated water out. Droplets of polluted fuel trickled slowly into a paper cup, and it was several minutes before a thin stream of violet diesel followed the nasty, emulsifying gunk. Whatever the cause, I found myself sobbing and vomiting at the same time. Feeling foolish and displaced, I wiped up the mess and fled the marina.

The pleasure boats dwindled as I came into the open water of Georgia Strait, where a light north-westerly ruffled the sea's surface and, for the first time since leaving Juneau, I switched off the engine and pulled up the sails. For the next three hours, I forgot myself. I was on a leisurely summer vacation. No more reading. I sat at the wheel, playing the boat against the shifting angles of the wind, watching the knot-meter, trying to squeeze 4.3 knots up to 5.0, until the sun sank behind Vancouver Island and I turned into the strange, Irish-accented harbour of Vananda.

Thirteen and a half days out of Juneau, I was back in Ballard Locks.

A familiar-looking lock-keeper took my lines, scrutinizing the boat and its captain. For the first time in my life, I had a mahogany tan. I weighed less than I had done in years.

'You been away?' he said.

'Up in Alaska,' I said, aiming for a tone of proper nonchalance.

'Good trip?'

'Yeah, great.'

The lock-gates opened. Marine Seattle crowded in on the Ship Canal. Even in August sunshine, the welders' torches dazzled. The air was gritty with particles of rust as they drifted over the water from the shipyards. Most of the ships were turning into scrap – ancient freighters from Archangel, Vladivostok, Okhotsk, tugs and fish-processors from Anchorage, Juneau, Ketchikan. The city, large as London, took me in.

I tied up at the moorings on Ewing Street, flung a handful of essentials into a duffel bag, and went ashore, feeling the dry land roll unreliably underfoot. Above and beyond the brick buildings of the Bible college, I could just see the tree-shrouded, white-balconied top storey of our house on the hill. Crossing the tracks of the disused railroad, I took a deep breath before I climbed the last suburban quarter-mile and faced the rougher sea.